▦ Confucianism and Human Rights

Confucianism and Human Rights

Edited by Wm. Theodore de Bary and Tu Weiming

Columbia University Press   NEW YORK

Columbia University Press
Publishers Since 1893
New York   Chichester, West Sussex

Library of Congress Cataloging-in-Publication Data
Confucianism and human rights / edited by Wm. Theodore de Bary and
   Tu Weiming.
       p.   cm.
   Includes bibliographical references and index.
   ISBN 0-231-10936-9. — ISBN 0-231-10937-7 (pbk.)
   2. Human rights—China. 2. Confucianism. I. de Bary, William
Theodore, 1919–   . II. Tu, Wei-ming.
   JC599.C6C66   1997
   323'.0951—dc21

                                                              97-14687
                                                              CIP

Casebound editions of Columbia University Press books are printed on
permanent and durable acid-free paper.

Printed in the United States of America

c 10 9 8 7 6 5 4 3 2
p 10 9 8 7 6 5 4 3 2 1

Columbia University Press wishes to express its appreciation to the Chiang
Ching-kuo Foundation for International Scholarly Exchange for assistance in the
publication of this book.

The Press also acknowledges with thanks a Centennial gift from Hugh J. Kelly,
former Chairman of the Press Trustees.

To Louis Henkin

University Professor Emeritus at Columbia University and
Founding Director of its Center for the Study of Human Rights

Contents

CONTENTS

Preface

If one recalls how the Great Proletarian Cultural Revolution rent China in the late 1960s and early 1970s, with its bloody vendetta against any supposed remnants of Confucianism, or how youthful phalanxes of Red Guards, waving Little Red Books, waged lethal campaigns against intellectuals and state officials, targeted as covert agents of the ancient sage—or indeed if one's memories reach back to the early founders of the Chinese Communist party, a generation of young iconoclasts bent on smashing the old "Confucian Curiosity Shop"—one may observe with some irony today, and perhaps with more of a sense of relief than of shock, how the current regime in Beijing is retreating from its revolutionary past and claiming for itself the right to speak for China's Confucian heritage.

In October 1994, the month in which the annual celebration has been held of China's national day—marking the overthrow in 1911 of the Manchu dynasty—a major international congress was held to commemorate the 2,545th anniversary of the [putative] birth of Confucius. Scholarly conferences are no longer unusual occurrences, as they were in the days of Mao; what marked this one as more than routine or merely "academic" was the presence at the opening ceremonies of prominent figures in the leadership group identified with the policies of Deng Xiaoping: Gu Mu, widely credited as a prime architect of Deng's economic modernization program; Li Ruihuan, chairman of the Chinese Peoples Political Consultative Congress; Zhou Nan, tacitly understood to be Beijing's "man" in Hong Kong; and a host of dignitaries—public officials and heads of academic bodies and cultural organizations—from abroad.

Most striking of the opening speeches was that of Li Ruihuan, who frequently quoted Mencius, the most liberal of the early Confucian thinkers, in his repeated admonitions for rulers to "listen to the people," to which Li's packed audience responded with enthusiastic applause. Mencius's brand of humanitarianism and egalitarianism may not exactly equate with Western liberal democracy but it plainly appealed to populist sentiments among Li's hearers.

Best known, no doubt, among the featured participants in the opening ceremonies was Lee Kuan Yew, the former prime minister and founding father of Singapore. Lee's world reputation as a leading actor on the Southeast Asian stage—out of all proportion to the tiny size of his city-state—and now his prestige as an elder-statesman, has outgrown even the monumental success of Singapore's economic miracle and Lee's early role in rallying Southeast Asian resistance to Communism. At a time when many writers in the West still saw Confucianism as a drag on modernization, and well before the Confucian work ethic, social discipline and zeal for learning came belatedly to be recognized by others as a shared cultural resource among the Little Economic Dragons of East and Southeast Asia, Lee had seen these Confucian traits as key factors in Singapore's success, all the more significant in the absence of any substantial material resources or strong territorial stake among these island states. On this basis then Lee began the process of reviving, reinforcing and reinvigorating Confucian traditions among Singapore's largely Chinese population.

One cannot gainsay the fact that Confucianism's attraction for Lee is his perception of it as an essentially conservative teaching, which could be supportive of the increasingly authoritarian, law-and-order style of politics with which he is identified in Singapore. Nor can we overlook the touch of anti-Westernism in Lee's espousal of Confucian social discipline versus the decadent libertarianism and individualism he sees as undermining the moral fiber of the West and eating away at its social fabric. Thus, when Lee made a magisterial entrance on the stage of the great amphitheater wherein the Confucian anniversary was celebrated, he was greeted with a thunderous ovation, not so much because he embodied the wisdom of Confucius, as because, in large part, he stood before this admiring audience as the Oriental David who had repeatedly stood up to the Western Goliath and triumphed. Indeed on that occasion Lee had little to say about Confucianism as such, and much more, against the Western media critical of him, in defense of the policies his government has pursued in Singapore. Probably few in that audience of would-be Confucians noticed how much Lee's self-confidence and self-assertiveness, and even the kind of strong personal machismo he projected, was world's re-

moved in manner and spirit from the gentle charisma of Confucius—from the modest, questioning, self-deprecating picture of the Master as it is conveyed in the classic *Analects*. Confucius most often came to inquire, to learn, and share opinions with others. Lee declaimed from the pedestal of superior authority afforded him there in Beijing, and left without waiting to hear what anyone else had to say.

Still it would be a mistake to see no more at work here than a put-down of the West and liberal democracy. Lee himself and his Chinese colleagues have better things to do than twist the tails of Western leaders they consider only paper tigers—as they do, and did, liberal democrats like Bill Clinton after the Most-Favored-Nation/Human Rights showdown of 1994. Though not openly acknowledged, what these leaders probably sense, and correctly, is that their real problems arise from within the very modernization process with which they now so proudly identify. Moreover, there is reason to believe that the Confucian revival now being openly promoted in the Chinese press, shown in TV coverage of this event, and subsequently picked up as hot news by the Western media, is only the latest in a series of developments issuing from a considered policy, adopted not long after Deng's rehabilitation and ascent to power following the death of Mao and the overthrow of the Gang of Four.

In the 1980s Confucius came gradually to be rehabilitated through conferences on various aspects of Confucian philosophy and culture. One of the first of these, convened at Hangzhou in 1980, though held in the name of Chinese philosophy more broadly defined, saw discussion concentrated more on Confucianism than on any other philosophy. True the tentative, exploratory nature of this move toward recanonization, was shown in the circumspection with which anyone at that earlier gathering hazarded a good word for the Confucians—at least while hard-line veterans of the Long March stood by, monitoring the proceedings, and sometimes intervening as devil's advocates. Occasional long silences gave section meetings the atmosphere of a Quaker prayer meeting; the scholarly assembly waited quietly to see which way, or how far, a certain favorable or unfavorable thrust might carry. Overall, however, the clear message came through: Confucianism was no longer taboo.

The ice thus broken, supporters of a Confucian restoration began to organize themselves. In 1984 a China Confucius Foundation was formally established, with its main headquarters in Beijing and a branch office at the newly restored temple in Qufu, Confucius's birthplace in Shandong province. Officers of the Foundation were chosen from among personages then or formerly identified with the regime, including prominent Party men as well as academicians. Obviously no such undertaking could have gone far without official backing; the sizable international conferences subsequently sponsored by the Foundation could not have been held without state support on many levels.

These included a major meeting at Confucius's birthplace in 1987 and an even more important one in Beijing in October of 1989, to celebrate Confucius's 2,540th birthday.

The sponsors of this 1989 symposium were no less prestigious than the celebrants cited earlier. Among the prominent speakers at the opening ceremonies were Li Xiannian, a senior party and government figure (since deceased) formally listed as the chairman of the National Committee of the People's Consultative Conference. Present too was Goh Keng Swee, a close associate of Lee Kuan Yew. Goh was then president of the Board of Directors of Singapore's Institute of East Asian Philosophies, a cultural think-tank and research center entrusted with the promotion of Confucian studies and education. He had played a major economic planning role in Singapore prototypical to Gu Mu's in the Peoples Republic, and his presence suggested that in Beijing as in Singapore the Confucian program was inspired by political-economic considerations no less than cultural.

Especially significant was the keynote speech given by Gu Mu, the "noted economist" who was nominally honorary chairman but actually more than that, a vital presence at the whole meeting. Since Gu's speech forecast what has become increasingly evident as the government's long-term policy in these matters, the following excerpts from the official English text are worth noting.

> The Chinese nation has had a long history and brilliant ancient culture. For a long period of time in human history, the Chinese culture, with the Confucian school of thought as the main stream, glittered with colorful splendor. . . .
>
> Culture serves both as the emblem of the level of civilization of a nation or a country and the guidance for its political and economic life. To promote prosperity and peace for a nation and for mankind in general, it is necessary to develop a compatible culture. In this regard, a proper attitude toward the traditional national culture is very important. It is inadvisable either to be complacent about the past or to discard the past and the tradition. The correct attitude is to inherit the essence and discard the dross.
>
> The Chinese people are working hard to build socialist modernization and a prosperous and strong socialist country. In order to reach this goal, we must develop and improve our new culture, which, we believe, should be national, patriotic, scientific and democratic. This calls for inheriting and reforming the traditional culture of our nation and parallel efforts to courageously and yet selectively assimilate the advanced cultures of the outside world, merging the two into an integral whole.
>
> As for the attitude toward the traditional culture and foreign cultures, there is no doubt that the traditional culture should be kept as the mainstay. . . .
>
> As is known to all, the idea of harmony is an important component of the Chinese traditional culture. As early as in the last years of the West Zhou dynasty three thousand years ago, ancient scholars elucidated the brilliant idea of "harmony-making for

prosperity." Later Confucius and the Confucian school put forward the proposition of "harmony above all," and established theories on the coordination of interpersonal relations, the protection of the natural environment, and the maintenance of ecological balance. These thoughts not only made positive contributions to the prosperity of ancient Chinese society, but also have profound practical significance for the survival and development of mankind today.

As a keynote, the speech was meant to serve more than one purpose, and can be read several ways. First there is the point, as in the earlier prospectus, that culture should provide the guidelines for politics and economics (not the other way around as with Mao) and that Chinese culture (read "Confucianism") should thus set the criteria for judging what is acceptable or unacceptable among the foreign influences to which China is inevitably exposed in the modernization process. In the context of the 1980s this might sound new insofar as Confucianism was being reintroduced to a scene from which it long had been banned, but anyone familiar with historic Chinese debates on the issue would recognize it as a return to a nineteenth- and early twentieth-century reformism that sought to adopt Western methods while still holding to a Chinese "essence."

Another key point is the "ancient" and "brilliant" idea of "harmony making for prosperity." No doubt Confucius and the Confucians would have subscribed to this idea, though the Master himself chose to underscore rather the idea that peace and harmony depended on trust and confidence in the ruler, which could only be won by moral example, humane governance and reliance on consensual institutions (the rites). Nevertheless one can see the appeal here to peace and stability as the keys to economic progress (rather than class struggle à la Mao and the Cultural Revolution, or by contrast, the anarchy attributed by the government to the T'ien-an men demonstrators). Understood as a demand for compliance with or conformity to direction from above, such "harmony" today might yield the stability needed for economic progress, but hardly the fiduciary, consensual society Confucius characterized in terms of "Harmony without conformity" (*he er bu tong*), much less the Chinese-type civil society Mencius advocated, with a class of activist Confucian officials constantly pressing the ruler to listen to the people and enact humane policies of benefit to them.

For his part Gu Mu, while claiming the world-honored Confucius as China's own, and Chinese culture as quintessentially Confucian, presents Chinese tradition and the current regime as enlightened, progressive and open to the world. Yet, by retaining and relying on the Confucian values of harmony and social discipline, according to Gu, it has "traditional" criteria for excluding decadent libertarian influences from the West—screening out the "spiritual pollution" already diagnosed as the source of the alleged unbridled disorders of T'ien-an men.

What is new here, especially in contrast to the Cultural Revolution's earlier vicious attacks on Confucianism and bourgeois liberalism as the twin enemies of militant proletarian virtue, is that now Confucianism, not Marxist revolutionary morality, will guard the gates against Western decadence. Meanwhile, niftily appropriated to Confucianism are the Western liberal causes of environmentalism and ecology, which the Communists had long before dismissed as specious imperialist pretexts for denying to undeveloped nations the benefits of industrialization.

This is not at all to say that Confucianism has now replaced Marxism-Leninism as the ideology of the one-party state. For the present, Beijing's line still calls for the reaffirmation of Communist orthodoxy and discipline. But the prevailing pragmatism of the modernization campaign in so many aspects of economic and cultural policy continues steadily to erode doctrinal orthodoxy. Although the Party can still compel lip-service to time-worn slogans, it cannot, by fiat, command assent or genuine commitment.

In this unfavorable climate, with much of the erstwhile Communist world (including the homelands of Marx, Engels, Lenin, and Stalin) having repudiated the original doctrine of the Party, Beijing's pragmatic leaders are increasingly disposed to lean on a conservative version of Chinese tradition as the best guarantor of the status quo. Even at that, though, the status quo has its own real problems, caught in the obvious disparity between a failed Maoist morality of revolutionary class struggle and a new pragmatic emphasis on whatever gets results (which for the individual means: whatever enriches one). The leadership can hardly be unaware that this "new" morality (actually not so "new" to Chinese entrepreneurs of the past, but a view of self-enrichment traditionally contained within the larger Confucian concept of the common good)—and its new motivation have proved deleterious to any ethos of service to society. This in turn has had serious adverse consequences, especially in education, as technically qualified scholars and teachers have been drawn off into more profitable uses of their talents, outside of school.

Implicated in this crisis of public morality is the question of whether one can expect, as some prominent Western personages do, that liberalization and expansion of the economy will naturally bring in train a gradual political liberalization, with greater public involvement in and support for a constructive political program. Recently, in the West, especially during and after the confrontation between the United States and China over human rights and trade policy in the summer of 1994, many observers consoled themselves with the thought that expanded trade and economic development would itself lead to

such an improvement—that with growing affluence and a rising middle class, political liberalization would necessarily follow as a result of economic liberalization. There may be some truth in this as a general tendency over the long term, but it makes assumptions not warranted either by Chinese history or recent experience. At several stages of Chinese history commerce, industry, and a nascent middle class have grown to significant proportions, but the translation of these into a civil infrastructure has been handicapped by state-imposed limitations and stultified by bureaucratic complications. Again and again the Chinese have shown their entrepreneurial aptitude and skills whenever and wherever conditions were conducive to them (especially overseas and under the protection of Western law, beyond the reach of Chinese rule), but in the long run of Chinese history these capacities and tendencies have not prevailed in the homeland. In other words the continuing dominance of a centralized bureaucratic state in China has frustrated what Westerners tend to think of as a normal sequence of economic, social, and cultural development.

In the present situation, what this means is that if Western businessmen urge going slow on human rights and relying on economic development to do the job, an attitude similar to this on the part of Chinese businessmen may again, as repeatedly in the past, lead to an accommodation with the state, a modus vivendi between business and officialdom very similar to the limited bureaucratic capitalism of the later dynasties—a quite natural collusion based on shared self-interest: the state guaranteeing order and stability, if not interfered with politically by the entrepreneurial class, and the entrepreneurs profiting from the security and stability provided by the state. From this one gets an alliance of opportunism between businessmen and officialdom quite different from the liberal middle-class politics that is presumed to be the natural product of economic development in the West. There are already many signs of this collusion and rampant corruption between business enterprise and opportunistic officials in a position to profit for themselves. On the other hand one may ask, where is there any evidence of businessmen in China actively interesting themselves in liberal democratic politics or human rights? Moreover, since this pattern of collusion and corruption between new entrepreneurs and old apparatchiks has become so widespread in former Communist countries generally, one can hardly ignore it as a powerful factor complicating the prospects for liberal democracy.

Nevertheless, there has been a significant movement to extend and improve legal protection for property and investment, and in general to regularize the conditions of trade. It is also true that businessmen and others who suffer from official corruption and favoritism wish there could be greater legal and judicial protection against these. Whether this will have any significant effect on reducing corruption, which is endemic, remains to be seen, but at least the new and widespread emphasis on the rule of law is significant. It would be a natural extension of this that certain types of human rights might become more formally established.

But what of Confucianism itself—traditionally not much identified with law—as a force for anything but unquestioning support of the new dynastic establishment? Most young Chinese, if they have any yearnings at all for democracy, are unlikely to think of Confucianism as the vehicle to get them there. For most of this century educated Chinese have learned nothing about Confucianism except the Party's negative characterizations of it as "reactionary" and "feudal." Quite apart from the closing of schools for years during the Cultural Revolution, and the turning over of instruction to workers, peasants, soldiers, and Red Guards, only a few college majors in classical studies have read any of the Confucian texts, while all students have been compelled to read the "classics" of Marx, Lenin, Stalin, and Mao. Other, increasingly rare, exceptions would be the likes of Jiang Zemin, concurrently General Secretary of the Chinese Communist Party, President of the People's Republic, Chairman of its Military Commission—in other words Deng's designated heir apparent—who came to both of the Confucian symposia referred to above, gave them his blessing, concurred with what Gu Mu said, and reminisced fondly about how his old-fashioned father had taught him in the home, outside of school hours, the Four Books of Confucianism.

As Jiang Zemin's case suggests, certain Confucian traditions may have survived in the home, primarily in connection with family life. True too, these traditions are often characterized by a certain reciprocity, mutual support and give-and-take within the family, rarely taken into account by the stereotypical renderings of Confucianism as an authoritarian, "feudal" system. Nevertheless there is a question as to how much carryover there could be from such customary practices in the intimacy of the home, or even in family enterprises, into the larger world of political discourse and the framing of governmental policy. Only with the reinstatement of some genuine Confucian culture, and the reading of basic texts in the school and college curriculum—which would require the retraining of a whole generation of teachers as well—could Confucian learning be articulated to the level of literate discourse so that it could have any significant influence on educated Chinese today, as well as on those who might participate in higher level decision making or policy formulation. Short of this the New Confucianism in Beijing would amount to little more than spoon-feeding and mass indoctrination in official formulae, as mechanical and meaningless as the failed slogans of Maoism.

At issue here is the question of whether Confucianism is to be recognized as more than just a social discipline and work ethic. Properly speaking it is a form of liberal learning (in the classic sense of liberal as broadening and liberating, and not simply in the modern political sense). Today, mostly outside of the People's

Republic, educated persons are becoming aware of the long neglected but deeper and richer resources to be found in the learning tradition of Confucianism. It is precisely in recognition of the progress made in Confucian studies abroad that the leadership of the new movement wishes to establish links with scholars elsewhere, through its new International Confucian Association. What remains to be seen, however, is how serious and substantial these links will prove to be. Skeptics have a right to question whether the whole transaction is not merely an exercise in the co-opting of scholars by cultural commissars.

Having attended three such meetings and having felt no overt constraint myself on what could be said, I would testify to their relative openness. At October 1994's symposium in fact I raised the question of whether a conference of Confucians could ignore questions of pressing public concern. At the opening ceremonies, with the leadership present for keynote speeches, I pursued the implications of Li Ruihuan's invocation of Mencius as follows:

> Discussions among scholars at conferences like this one have tended to avoid difficult political issues. If, however, we are serious about the study of Confucianism, we must recognize that Confucius and his later followers like Mencius had a strong sense of public responsibility and public service. Mencius said he did not like to appear argumentative, but his moral concerns compelled him to speak to difficult pressing issues. Thus Mencius had much to say about education, human welfare, economic and social justice, the legitimacy or nonlegitimacy of profit seeking, political remonstrance, etc. So too in our own case, these pressing, shared concerns might warrant a series of conferences focussing on such current issues as human rights, in a spirit of mutual respect and on the basis of shared multicultural concerns. Let the new worldwide community of Confucian scholarship not just leave these issues to political figures who may not themselves be culturally well-informed. The latter have a right to expect from us scholars, on our own part, constructive advice in the spirit of mutual respect so impressively exemplified by Confucius himself. "Even in the company of just three persons, there must be someone from whom I can learn. Their good points I can take for emulation; their bad points I can take for self-correction" (*Lun-yü*, 7:21).
>
> How much more should this be true in our company of so many hundred scholars!

Gu Mu and Li Ruihuan seemed to take no offense at this. In fact they applauded it. Therefore, after the Symposium I prepared, in concert with other colleagues, a specific proposal for a dialogue on human rights and sent it to the sponsors in Beijing. It read:

> The members of the undersigned American committee, in cooperation with the American Council of Learned Societies, the East-West Center, the Heyman Center for the Humanities and the Human Rights Center of Columbia University, propose to hold one or more conferences on human rights in a comparative Confucian-

Western perspective, in order to promote nonconfrontational, multicultural dialogue on the basic value issues underlying human rights concepts and practices. Possible topics to be discussed include:

1. Confucian concepts of the self, person and individual in relation to state and society. Self-discipline as the key to governance.
2. "Rights" protected in Confucian ritual and Chinese law; the relation between rights, responsibilities, and duties.
3. Human rights in the perspective of Confucian concepts of social justice.
4. Religious and intellectual freedom in the Chinese and Western traditions.
5. Constitutionalism and the Rule of Law in China and the West.
6. A reappraisal, in historical perspective, of the earlier critiques of Confucianism (especially the May 4th movement).

In general it would be our intention to air all sides of these issues, pro and con, in a spirit of academic inquiry as well as of Confucian humane concern. We would hope to include scholars from China, East and South Asia, Europe, and America.

The initial response to this proposal by the leadership of the Confucius Foundation in Beijing was favorable, and with their assistance we have been able to hold two conferences at the East-West Center in Honolulu on "Confucianism and Human Rights." Papers from the first of these meetings, held in August 1995, are contained in this volume, and we anticipate further publications from subsequent meetings. A third conference is to be held in Beijing, May 1998, under the auspices of the International Confucian Association.

Considered in their larger dimensions, both Confucianism and human rights problems extend to other civilizations of East Asia than China. In our meetings Japan and Korea have been included in the discussions for comparative purposes and we expect to extend these comparisons in further conferences and publications. In the present volume however, our focus has been on the central reality of China and the People's Republic.

The progress made thus far in these discussions, though hardly spectacular, is reassuring if one recognizes the inherent difficulty of trying to conduct serious, nonconfrontational dialogue on a subject usually fraught with sharp political tensions. The vicissitudes of U.S.-China relations, such as the extreme tensions that arose over the Taiwan situation in 1995, did indeed have an effect on the ability of some scholars from the Peoples' Republic to attend our first conference; the second, however, was not subject to such political interventions, and at its conclusion the senior member of the Chinese delegation, who is also the academic director of the official International Confucian Association in Beijing, expressed the hope that the latter could sponsor a return conference (the third) in Beijing in 1998.

Though the discussion of important current issues like human rights can never be wholly nonpolitical, there is a need for discussions of these problems on the basis of a deeper cultural awareness than is commonly shown when human rights are linked directly to economic issues and pressures—as in trade negotiations—or in highly publicized diplomatic confrontations, spotlighted by the media, which may give the appearance of one country's interfering in the affairs of another. Our own approach is long-term. It acknowledges that historical conditions and cultural differences may affect both people's understanding of human rights and their practice of them, but it also affirms the possibility of working out some consensus on fundamental human values, in the light of which cultural differences may be—if not reconciled—at least recognized and respected.

Further we assume that human rights as presently formulated are neither fixed forever nor in all respects complete. They can be expanded, enriched, and deepened by reference to diverse historical and cultural traditions. What cannot be acquiesced in however is the idea that unbridgeable value differences separate East and West, wherefore human development in Asia must take a basically different course from Europe and America, ignoring or dismissing the "culture-bound" conceptions of the latter. Recently it has been reported that certain authoritarian African regimes have begun to identify themselves with a so-called "Asian model" of development, rather than follow the Western liberal democratic model. By further identifying this Asian model as "Confucian," these regimes' restriction of human rights seems to be given the sanction of some traditional Oriental wisdom. It is precisely such specious claims as these that our conferences aim to contest—that either Confucianism or human rights can be appropriated as they please by any regime, or Asian consortium, to suit their own political purposes. Today Confucianism and human rights are now fully in the public domain, open to discussion by anyone with relevant knowledge and experience. To promote such dialogues among those whose qualifications can pass the test of informed scrutiny in public debate is the aim of the present volume.

For their generous and timely support of the conferences held so far, the organizers wish to thank Henry Luce III and Terrill Lautz of the Luce Foundation; Stanley Katz and Jason Parker of the American Council of Learned Societies; Kenji Sumida, Bruce Koppel, and Larry Smith of the East-West Center, Honolulu; and in the preparing of this volume for publication the assistance of Marianna Stiles, Martin Amster, and Renee Kashuba. We are also much indebted to the Chiang Ching-kuo Foundation for its support of the conference through travel grants to attending scholars and the subvention of this publication.

Contributors

Irene Bloom is Class of 1941 Professor of Asian Humanities at Columbia University and Chair of the Department of Asian and Middle Eastern Cultures at Barnard College. She is the author of *Knowledge Painfully Acquired: The K'un-chih chi of Lo Ch'in-shun* (Columbia University Press, 1989; rev. ed. 1995); as well as coeditor of *Principle and Practicality* (CUP, 1987); and *Approaches to the Asian Classics* (CUP, 1990). With Joshua A. Fogel, she is editor of *Meeting of Minds: Intellectual and Religious Interaction in East Asian Traditions of Thought* (CUP, 1996) and, with J. Paul Martin and Wayne L. Proudfoot, of *Religious Diversity and Human Rights* (CUP, 1997).

Wejen Chang is a research fellow at the Institute of History and Philology of Academia Sinica in Taiwan and a member of the Global Law Faculty at the New York University School of Law. He has written extensively about the Qing legal system but now concentrates on traditional Chinese legal thought. He is currently writing a book entitled *Jurisprudential Wisdom of Ancient China*.

Chung-ying Cheng, authority on Chinese philosophy and East-West comparative philosophy, received his doctorate in Philosophy from Harvard University and teaches in the Department of Philosophy at the University of Hawaii. He has published many books in Chinese philosophy and edits the *Journal of Chinese Philosophy*. He also founded the *International Society for Chinese Philosophy* and the *International Society for the Yijing Studies*.

Julia Ching, University Professor at the University of Toronto and Fellow of the Royal Society of Canada, taught earlier at Columbia and Yale. Among other writings, her book, *Probing China's Soul: Religion, Politics and Protest in the PRC* (Harper & Row, 1990) also discusses human rights issues.

Ron Guey Chu has taught at St. Lawrence University, Bryn Mawr, and Columbia University. Currently he is assistant research fellow at the Institute of Chinese Literature and Philosophy, Academia Sinica. His primary research interest is Chinese intellectual history, with particular emphasis on Neo-Confucianism. He has done work on Neo-Confucian statecraft thought and on popular education and academies. His more recent research interest is in Confucian rituals and popular Confucianism.

Alison W. Conner is an Associate Professor at the University of Hawaii School of Law. She has written articles on modern Chinese and Hong Kong law as well as on Qing and Republican legal history.

Wm. Theodore de Bary is John Mitchell Mason Professor and Provost Emeritus of Columbia University, and was President of the Association of Asian Studies, 1969–1970. He is the author most recently of *Waiting for the Dawn: A Plan for the Prince* (Columbia University Press 1993) and *The Trouble With Confucianism* (Harvard University Press 1991).

Louis Henkin is University Professor Emeritus at Columbia University. Before his appointment as University Professor he held chairs in Constitutional Law and, earlier, in International Law and Diplomacy. Professor Henkin served as law clerk to Judge Learned Hand and to Justice Felix Frankfurter, and was an officer of the United States Department of State before turning to academic life. Among public and professional activities, he was Coeditor-in-Chief of the *American Journal of International Law* (1978–84) and from 1992 to 1994 served as President of the American Society of International Law. His many books include *The Rights of Man Today* and *The Age of Rights*.

Joan Judge, who teaches Chinese history at the University of Utah, received her Ph.D. from Columbia University in 1993. She has published in *Late Imperial China* and *Modern China*. Her book *Print and Politics: Shibao and the Culture of Reform in Late Qing China* was published in December 1996 by Stanford University Press.

Daniel W. Y. Kwok is Professor of History, University of Hawaii. Born and raised in China, Professor Kwok holds degrees from Brown University and Yale University. Among his publications are *Scientism in Chinese Thought, 1900–1950; Cosmology, Ontology, and Human Efficacy: Essays in Ch'ing Thought* (ed. with Richard Smith); and, as translator and editor, *Turbulent Decade: A History of the Cultural Revo-*

lution by Yan Jiawi and Gao Gao.

Jeremy Paltiel is Associate Professor of Political Science at Carleton University in Ottawa, Canada. He received his B.A. in East Asian Studies from the University of Toronto (1974), a diploma from the Philosophy Department of Beijing University in 1976, and his M.A. (1979) and Ph.D. (1984) in Political Science from the University of California, Berkeley. Recent publications have included "The Cultural and Political Determinants of the Chinese Approach to Human Rights" (Ottawa, Human Rights Research and Education Centre 1966).

Randall Peerenboom, Ph.D. in Chinese philosophy from the University of Hawaii, J.D. from Columbia University, is the author of *Law and Morality in Ancient China: The Silk Manuscripts of Huang-Lao*, as well as numerous articles on Chinese philosophy and law. He is currently practicing law in Beijing with the British law firm, Freshfields.

Henry Rosemont Jr. has written *A Chinese Mirror*, and edited and/or translated six other works, the most recent of which (with D. J. Cook) is *Leibniz: Writings on China*. He is George B. and Willma Reeves Distinguished Professor of Liberal Arts at St. Mary's College of Maryland, and Distinguished Consulting Professor at Fudan University in Shanghai.

Tu Weiming is Professor of Chinese History and Philosophy at Harvard University and Director of the Harvard-Yenching Institute. He is the author of *Centrality and Commonality: An Essay on Chung-yung, Neo-Confucian Thought in Action*, and *Confucian Ethics Today*.

Sumner B. Twiss, Ph.D., Yale 1974, is Professor of Religious Studies and Department Chair at Brown University. He is coeditor of *The Annual of the Society of Christian Ethics* and Book Discussion Editor of the *Journal of Religious Ethics*. He has coauthored or coedited five books, including *Comparative Religious Ethics: A New Method*, and *Religion and Human Rights*.

Yu Feng is a Professor at Peoples (Renmin) University of China, in Beijing, and research associate (1995–96) at the Fairbank Center of East Asian Research, Harvard University. He is the coauthor with Professor Leo S. Chang of Regis College of an English translation of the Four Texts published by the Yuelu Press, Changsha, 1993.

Peter Zarrow teaches modern Chinese history at the University of New South Wales in Sydney, Australia. He is the author of *Anarchism and Chinese Political Culture* (Columbia University Press, 1990) and *Twentieth Century China: An Interpretive History* (Boulder: Westview, forthcoming). Currently he is engaged in research on the cultural significance of the monarchy in the late Qing and early Republican periods.

▦ Confucianism and Human Rights

Introduction

Wm. Theodore de Bary

To many contemporary observers Confucianism and human rights would seem to be an unlikely combination, if not a completely incompatible couple. As far away as Africa, the *New York Times* reports, authoritarian regimes restrictive of human rights are looking to an Asian model of development based on Confucianism, rather than to a Western one.[1] The presumption is that Confucianism spells authority and discipline, limiting individual freedom, and strengthening the state. How then could it be reconciled to a view of human rights fundamentally premised on the dignity and autonomy of the individual? Moreover, anyone familiar with the Confucians' reservations about law as an inherently defective instrument for dealing with conflicting human interests, would wonder how they could make room for a Western conception of human rights so bound up with legal guarantees and dependent on constitutional protections.

The negative view of Confucianism on these scores owes much to critics of the Chinese tradition earlier in this century, as we can see from these words by one of the prime Chinese advocates of liberation from Confucianism:

> The pulse of modern life is economic and the fundamental principle of economic production is individual independence. Its effect has penetrated ethics. Consequently the independence of the individual in the ethical field and the independence of property in the economic field bear witness to each other, thus reaffirming the theory [of such interaction]. Because of this [interaction], social mores and material culture have taken a great step forward.

♪ In China, the Confucians have based their teachings on their ethical norms. Sons and wives possess neither personal individuality nor personal property. Fathers and elder brothers bring up their sons and younger brothers and are in turn supported by them. It is said in chapter thirty of the *Record of Rites* that "While parents are living, the son dares not regard his person or property as his own" [27:14]. This is absolutely not the way to personal independence. . . . In all modern constitutional states, whether monarchies or republics, there are political parties. Those who engage in party activities all express their spirit of independent conviction. They go their own way and need not agree with their fathers or husbands. When people are bound by the Confucian teachings of filial piety and obedience to the point of the son not deviating from the father's way even three years after his death[2] and the woman not only obeying her father and husband but also her son,[3] how can they form their own political party and make their own choice? . . .

Confucius lived in a feudal age. The ethics he promoted are the ethics of the feudal age. The social mores he taught and even his own mode of living were teachings and modes of a feudal age. The objectives, ethics, social norms, mode of living and political institutions did not go beyond the privilege and prestige of a few rulers and aristocrats and had nothing to do with the happiness of the great masses.[4]

These words were written in December 1916 by Chen Duxiu, who subsequently became a founder of the Chinese Communist Party—though he was later disowned by the party and thus, for all of his troubles on behalf of individualism, became a nonperson.

Now consider what was said even earlier by a leading feminist who championed a blend of anarchism and communism for the liberation of women:

• Almost all of the writings since the Chin and Han dynasties have followed Confucianism, and Confucian learning is marked by its devotion to honoring men and denigrating women. . . .

Later generations of Confucians respected what the founders had to say and followed their example in venerating men like gods while condemning women to the hells. They felt that as long as it was of benefit to men, then it was fine to twist the truth around in any way to gain advantage. . . .

The learning of Confucianism has tended to be oppressive and to promote male selfishness. Therefore, Confucianism marks the beginning of justifications for polygamy [for men] and chastity [for women]. Confucians, representing the ancestral learning of the Han dynasty, felt free to twist the meaning of the ancient writings as they pertained to women in order to extend their own views. . . .

Just as men loyal to a fallen dynasty went into hiding, women should die faithful to their deceased husbands like a loyalist giving his life to his country. . . . Thus are women driven to their deaths with this empty talk of virtue. We can see that the Confucian emphasis on propriety is nothing more than a tool for murdering women. . . .

This proves that women have duties but no rights. Household responsibilities cannot be assumed by men but all the tasks of managing the household are given to women. Out of fear that women might interfere with their concerns, men said women had no business outside of the home. This deprived women of their natural rights.[5]

Clearly these writers saw Confucianism as an obstacle to the adoption of Western standards of individual freedom, with which they had become acquainted through the new Western-style education in China and the so-called New Culture of the early decades of the twentieth century. But even a scholar like Kang Youwei, widely recognized in his time as a leading modern exponent of Confucianism, believed that China (and even Confucianism itself) had to be liberated from a Chinese family system intrinsically repressive of the individual. Hard though it is to conceive of Confucianism stripped of its family system, this is what K'ang had to say about it:

● We desire that men's natures shall all become perfect, that men's characters shall all become equal, that men's bodies shall all be nurtured. [That state in which] men's characters are all developed, men's bodies are all hale, men's dispositions are all pacific and tolerant, and customs and morals are all beautiful, is what is called Complete Peace-and-Equality. But there is no means by which to bring this about this way without abolishing the family. . . . To have the family and yet to wish to reach Complete Peace-and-Equality is to be afloat on a blocked-up stream, in a sealed-off harbor, and yet to wish to reach the open waterway. To wish to attain Complete Peace-and-Equality and yet keep the family is like carrying earth to dredge a stream or adding wood to put out a fire; the more done, the more the hindrance. Thus, if we wish to attain the beauty of complete equality, independence and the perfection of [human] nature, it can [be done] only by abolishing the state, only by abolishing the family.[6]

Kang Youwei envisaged a universal order, the Grand Commonality, in which the traditional Confucian value of public-mindedness would be fulfilled by the dissolution of virtually all traditional forms of particularistic loyalty and obligation. The state (if it existed at all) would have few functions, and in the absence of any significant social infrastructure regulating human activity, there would be almost no limit on individual freedom.

If however Kang was ready to go this far in modernizing Confucianism, it is hardly surprising that the authors of our first two quotations above should have gone further to promote violent revolution, aiming at total liberation, rather than to rely on a shaky parliamentary democracy as the vehicle for achieving individual rights. Nor, given this powerful liberationist impulse (later enshrined in the official declaration of the year 1949 as marking China's "Liberation"), is it surprising that Mao's Great Proletarian Cultural Revolution in the late sixties should have urged young Red Guards to press on to final "liberation"—only revolutionary zeal and one last campaign of unrelenting class struggle were needed to make it a complete reality.

As is well known the outcome of this new revolutionary struggle was not the anarchist utopia dreamed of earlier, but a kind of disorderly freedom that Deng Xiao-ping and his colleagues found necessary to suppress, first by putting down the Cultural Revolution, and later by cracking down at Tiananmen Square. Yet we can understand this as a not unexpected consequence of the revolutionary elan generated earlier and the violence it would work on China. Moreover if Confucianism, seen all along as essentially conservative, had been a main target of such attacks, early and late, we can understand too how the more moderate or conservative elements under Deng, having put a stop to these revolutionary excesses, would have taken a second look at Chinese tradition, and found a conservative version of Confucianism to their liking—not only a potential force for stability but also a work ethic that could be supportive of Deng's modernization program.

Although the views of Confucianism cited above have swung sharply from contra to pro in the protracted revolutionary process, a key line of continuity persists through it all: the promise of total liberation bore within it the need to accept total revolutionary mobilization, and in the end total political control by the revolutionary party has survived the demise of liberation and individual rights. Success in unifying the country itself now suffices to justify the party's long-term monopolization of power, and in this light even anarchy—or rather the threat of it—has become a pretext for withholding many of the human rights which the anarchist ideal had once been meant to foster and serve.

Which of the alternatives outlined above speaks for the Chinese people—the rejection of Confucianism in the name of human rights, or the denial of human rights in the name of a conservative Confucian tradition, remains an open question. Either view is open to challenge; both are still held and propagated. Among the poster writers of the Democracy Wall movement in the early eighties and the activists in the Tiananmen demonstrations, there were (and still are among the survivors) heirs to the May Fourth Movement and Cultural Revolution who, even though long cut off from any informed contact with Confucian teachings, distrust Confucianism as it is now associated in their minds with the repressions of the current regime. And among the current spokesmen for a Confucian revival there is enough involvement of officialdom to warrant the suspicion that the government as sponsor has its own vested interests and illiberal ends in mind.

Meanwhile we do well to note that the alternatives so characterized by no means exhaust the available approaches to human rights in China. Alongside the more extreme liberationists quoted above, there were more moderate advocates of liberal reforms, "peoples rights" and "human rights," who saw these as lacking in China but did not see Confucianism as necessarily, or in all ways, an obstacle to their adoption. Among these perhaps the most influential spokesmen were Liang Qichao (1873–1929) and Hu Shi (1891–1962). Others, including some who continued to identify themselves as determined defenders of Confucianism, supported liberal democratic reforms, most often in diaspora or exile. Indeed enough of these later spoke for China in concert with representatives of other Confucian-influenced cultures, so that when the Universal Declaration of Human Rights was adopted by the United Nations in 1948, Chinese delegates saw to it that Confucian sentiments found expression therein, in support of human rights). This makes it awkward now, if not actually specious, for opponents of human rights in Asia today to dismiss these as merely culture-bound "Western" concepts, incompatible with "Asian communitarian" values.

The purpose of the present symposium has been neither to endorse nor to discount any of the views characterized above, but to take them all into account, and especially to consider what has been said on the subject in China— not just in agonizing moments of extreme national travail and cultural disorientation, but in the larger perspectives of past, present and future.

For these purposes we take as our working definition of human rights the above-mentioned Universal Declaration of Human Rights adopted by the United Nations in 1948—which is not to adopt it as the final or definitive statement on the subject, but only to accept it as the going one—universal to the extent that it was ratified formally by representatives of many world regions and cultures, and not thereafter repudiated by any official body but only confirmed and added to in subsequent protocols. Thus it represents a growing consensus on an expanding body of human rights concepts.

Moreover, many of these "rights" have been incorporated in the constitutions of nations the world around. This suggests that there is less disagreement on the concepts themselves than one might suppose, which belies the notion that irreconcilable cultural values or cleavages are the basic issue. Rather the problem is, as it has been all along, what material and political resources are available for their implementation, how effective are the processes of enforcement, whether or not there is a supporting cultural environment, and whether there may not lie in Confucianism other resources, as yet not fully developed, for the further enhancement of human rights. Hence our symposium attempts to deal with both concepts and practices, seen in historical, institutional, and evolutionary perspectives.

It is obvious enough that Confucianism itself did not generate human rights concepts and practices equivalent to those now embodied in the Universal Declaration; it is not obvious that Confucianism was headed in an altogether different authoritarian or "communitarian" direction, incompatible with the rights affirmed in the Declaration. Our aim has not been to find twentieth-century human rights in Confucianism, but to recognize therein certain central human values—historically embedded in, but at the same time restive with, repressive institutions in China—that in the emerging modern world could be supportive of those rights. In this our concern is not so much to render judgment on the past record as to clarify the bases on which past judgments have been made—those which could inform our understanding of human rights as still in the process of formation.

In accepting as our working definition of human rights the Universal Declaration adopted by the United Nations in 1948 and amended in the mid-1970s by a covenant on Civil and Political Rights and another on Economic, Social, and Cultural Rights, we conform with the general practice in human rights studies today, i.e., we refer to a consensus statement ratified by an international body, and to a public document widely available.

Apart from this, definitions and understandings of human rights vary greatly, as is the case among the scholars represented in this volume. Indeed, such disagreement is immediately apparent in the papers of Sumner B. Twiss ("A Constructive Framework for Discussing Confucianism and Human Rights") and Henry Rosemont Jr. ("Human Rights: A Bill of Worries"). The latter considers that human rights, as commonly known, are based on a belief in the radical autonomy of the individual, which Rosemont takes to be a false and unrealistic premise. Thus in Rosemont's eyes the whole human rights project is misbegotten. Whether in fact the original signatories to the Universal Declaration, or human rights advocates championing it have made the same assumption regarding individual autonomy, is, for Twiss, questionable but not a crucial point. No matter how long debated, such philosophical issues are unlikely to be resolved. Meanwhile it is better to leave such questions open to diverse and even revisionist interpretations rather than predicate the human rights program on any one set of philosophical assumptions. Indeed for just such reasons, Twiss argues that a pragmatic approach is called for, starting with the initial consensus of the Universal Declaration and amending it as new understandings are arrived at.

Here we might note that if Rosemont believes liberal democratic notions of individual autonomy were unduly influential in the formulation of human rights concepts, in the history of Western liberalism itself one may observe an evolution from the early emphasis on individual liberty in the nineteenth century to a greater concern for social and communitarian values in twentieth-century liberal movements. It was precisely on this account—their socialist leanings—that liberals were often characterized as "leftist" or "pinko" in mid-century America.[7] Thus the evolution of liberal thought in the United States provides a parallel to that of the Universal Declaration and its protocols, with their increasing emphasis on social, economic and environmental rights.

Twiss believes that in this process it is possible for new understandings of human rights to develop out of different moral and cultural traditions, and for these to help in identifying both common grounds among these traditions and different appropriations of rights concepts among them. An early example of this is seen in the very process leading up to the formulation of the original Declaration itself. Since this occurred just after World War II, in what might be thought the heyday of Western liberalism and internationalism, it could easily be suspected that concepts of radical individual autonomy might have dominated the framing and terms of the Declaration, yet in fact Confucian and Mencian concepts of humanity and humaneness (*ren/jen*) were accepted, at the instance of the Chinese delegation, as keynotes to the Declaration, to be enshrined in its preamble in the family-centered language of the Confucian *Analects*, e.g., the saying "All men are brothers."[8] Curiously it was only after admission of the People's Republic of China, in place of the Nationalist delegation, that objection was raised to these Confucian sentiments by PRC spokesmen on Marx-Leninist grounds (i.e., arguing from doctrines of European provenance), that Confucian universalistic humanism, as expressed in the quotation from the *Analects*, was obsolete if not wholly reactionary. Having been superseded in Communist China by an ideology of continuing class struggle, which left no room for a classless humanism, the offending Confucian sentiments, it was argued, should be stricken from the document.

A further irony in the course of this continuing evolution is that a member of the earlier Chinese delegation, instrumental in the framing of the original preamble, later became head of the Institute which sponsored the Confucian revival in Singapore during the 1980s and subsequently promoted the same revival in Beijing after the eclipse of Mao's anti-Confucian movement in the People's Republic.

A central point of Twiss's argument is that a moral consensus was arrived at pragmatically in the original Declaration—"a common vision of central moral and social values compatible with a variety of cultural anthropologies." Even if the latter had not conceived of these rights in the same way, as living traditions they could find the internal moral resources to recognize the validity of these rights and generally abide by them, each culture interpreting them in ways most congenial to it, which others who do not necessarily share in them could still respect. Rights so recognized do not depend on any one epistemological position or philosophical theory, but can draw support from many.

Twiss offers a variety of evidence from Confucian tradition supportive of human rights, even if not couched in the current idiom of human rights. One such example is a passage from the text of Mencius which is often cited (as it is by several writers in this volume) as expressing "the people's right of revolution." The passage reads:

> King Xuan of Qi asked, "Is it true that Tang banished Jieh and King Wu marched against Zhou?"
>
> "It is so recorded," answered Mencius.
>
> "Is regicide permissible?"
>
> A man who mutilates benevolence is a mutilator, while one who cripples rightness is a crippler. He who is both a mutilator and a crippler is an "outcast." I have indeed heard of the punishment of the "outcast Zhou," but I have not heard of any regicide.[9]

When considered in its own terms, and in the larger context of Mencius, the passage does not support the popular modern interpretation of a "peoples right of revolution," but does, I believe, confirm Twiss's main line of argument. First one should note Mencius's central point: the proper exercise of kingly power and the likely consequence of its abuse—that a ruler forfeits his claim to kingship and exposes himself to being overthrown. Nothing at all is said about "the people" or "revolution," much less a people's "right" to revolt. As a matter of fact, elsewhere Mencius makes it clear that, while the people's welfare should be a prime concern of the ruler, he does not expect, in the normal course of things, that the people should take an active part in the political process. The common people, engaged in heavy labor are in no position to do so—lacking the education, training, or time necessary to become well-informed about governmental matters (*Mencius* 3A4). Instead Mencius lays this responsibility on scholar-officials who serve the ruler. If the ruler misbehaves, it is the duty of his ministers to remonstrate with him. Then, if repeated remonstrances fail, they are to leave his service in silent protest (4B4). Should enough of them leave, it is a signal that the king has lost legitimacy and is due to be removed.

Does this then, call for revolt? No, for Mencius the next move is to have the responsible members of the ruling house depose the errant ruler (5B9). Failing that, it is understandable that some other leader will overthrow him, punish his misuse of power and replace the defaulting dynasty. While recognizing that unchecked misrule may well provoke rebellion, Mencius recommends a process entirely consistent with his—and the general Confucian— view that violence is to be avoided at all reasonable costs. Revolt is only a last desperate recourse for an exasperated people, understandable but not to be commended. That violence often prevails, Mencius is well aware, but the point of his teachings is to replace the use of force with a well-considered civil process, and above all with due process (what is right, fitting and orderly in the circumstances). It is in this sense then—that the observance of human rights is dependent on civility and due process—that Mencius and the Confucians can be said to offer what Twiss calls informed moral resources in support of human rights.

Twiss's paper, characterizing the Human Rights movement as an evolving one that potentially draws on the resources of diverse cultural traditions, is followed by that of Henry Rosemont Jr., who presents a sweeping critique of the whole Western human rights concept. He argues that the purposes of the movement would be better served by disassociating it from a rights-based conceptual framework and from notions of individual autonomy; better, instead, to turn to a Confucian conceptual framework for the expression of moral sentiments, preferably one defining people in terms of kinship relations and community.

In Rosemont's view the rise of human rights concepts in the West, as well as of views of individual autonomy and liberal democracy with which it has been closely associated, was concomitant with the rise of industrial capitalism and a legal system protective above all of individual property rights. He believes further that a rights-based approach is incapable of dealing with the conflicting claims and contradictions generated within the liberal capitalist West. Thus his title, "Human Rights: A Bill of Worries."

One can share his concerns and most of his Bill of Worries, including the increasing inadequacy, if not bankruptcy, of policies based on individual autonomy and property rights, to deal with the social dilemmas and ecological challenges of the contemporary world (whether Western or Eastern, it makes no difference today), and yet still believe that human rights concerns are among the legitimate "worries" of us all.

As one who, from the 1940s was "worried" like Rosemont over the effects of industrialization in both America and East Asia, and convinced that Confucian personalism (with the self and society seen in an indivisible, balanced relation to one another) had much to recommend it over the "rugged individualism" of the American West, I can see the human rights movement as embodying humane concerns that would be shared even by great Confucian reformers like Fan Zhongyan (989–1052) in the Sung period, who said that the Confucian noble person (*junzi*) should be "first in worrying about the world's worries and last in enjoying its pleasures." Confucian personalism, family ideals, and social conscience do have much to offer the contemporary world, and in key respects may provide a better grounding for both human rights and environmental rights. Yet it is also true that Confucianism had its own problems adapting in later times to the complexities of a society and state that had grown beyond (but not necessarily "outgrown") the homely truths of Confucius and Mencius. Increasingly the concerns we refer to as "communitarian" were overshadowed by a dynastic state that proved far more intractable than the rulers of the relatively decentralized late Chou city-states. And, as I argue in my discussion of "constitutionalism" in *Waiting for the Dawn*,[10] Confucian noble men like Huang

9

Tsung-hsi were already "worrying" about the dynastic Leviathan, while others were worried about the state of the community, in an age when their counterparts in the West were just beginning to worry about laws and constitutions that would restrain despotic power.

I shall pursue this question of socially and culturally diverse, but in some respects convergent, evolutions later. Here, having made a case earlier for a Confucian "rites-based" approach as compared to a "rights-based" one,[11] I would like simply to register the increasing awareness among Confucians themselves that "rites" alone had proved insufficient to cope with the realities of power in late Imperial China, and when informed Confucians of the late nineteenth and twentieth century in China became aware of constitutional law and "peoples right's" in the West, some recognized it immediately as having relevance to the "worries" of earlier Confucians.

As do Twiss and Rosemont, other contributors to this volume, depending on how they define human rights or interpret Chinese tradition, come up with somewhat ambivalent responses to the question: "Are human rights concepts alien to China and Confucianism?" Julia Ching concedes immediately that human rights as expressed in the Universal Declaration are largely a modern Western creation, but she sees them as products of earlier developments in the West for which rough counterparts existed in traditional China ("Human Rights: A Valid Chinese Concept?"); hence it was not difficult for cultured Chinese to recognize, appreciate, and accept these values as they did when the Universal Declaration was ratified. Not only have several East Asian countries—Japan, South Korea, and Taiwan—claimed and made these their own, finding them not incompatible with their own Confucian values, but they have demonstrated by their economic success and rising standard of living that there is no necessary conflict between individual rights and economic/social/communitarian rights. Rather these are seen as in many respects complementary. To assert otherwise—that in underdeveloped countries individual rights must be subordinated or even sacrificed to so-called group rights—may well be specious—serving, not the advancement of society, but some one party's monopolization of power.

Daniel W. Y. Kwok ("On the Rites and Rights of Being Human") poses a similar question for himself—whether human rights existed in traditional China—and he comes up with a similarly qualified answer, but in rather different terms from Julia Ching. To him, individual rights of the modern type could not exist because there was no room for a free-standing, completely autonomous individual. Rather the self was always seen, and acted, within a network of socially differentiated human relations, governed by rites, wherein rights and duties were always interconnected and similarly differentiated. "Being human," which

was for Kwok the aim of Confucian self-cultivation through the rites, always subordinated personal rights to the duties and responsibilities of the person within the network of social relations.

In this context something like rights, as legitimate expectations, did exist but not for the isolated individual as an anonymous cipher but only in a form that subserved the interdependence and harmony of the social group. Too often, according to Kwok, this meant subordination to the interests of the stronger party in the relationship, especially parents, husbands, and rulers. Given the fact of unequal power relationships, even today, after almost a century of revolutionary change, one hears, as Kwok says, amidst protests against despotic rule, "Cries for laws and rights that safeguard human decency."

In contrast to Kwok's emphasis on the socially differentiated aspects of Confucian ethics, Irene Bloom ("Mencius and Human Rights") places herself squarely on the side of Mencius's belief in the moral equality of a common humanity (whether understood as the human species or the human potential). This common humanity, she argues vigorously and with impressive evidence from Mencius, is "the single most important connecting link between traditional philosophical and religious ideas and contemporary human rights documents." Indeed the thrust of Bloom's argument is to call into fundamental question whether, in Mencius or the influential Mencian tradition in East Asia, it is true, as Kwok avers, that human equality is always subordinated to the unequal relations embedded in the rites.

This view of natural equality by virtue of a common human nature, though rooted in shared human sentiments of sympathy, shame and respect, and less exclusively identified than in the Western Enlightenment with the human capacity for reason, bears marked resemblances to the views of seventeenth- and eighteenth-century thinkers whose natural law philosophies were influential in the rise of human rights thinking in the West. The principal difference between the West and China lay in the rapid assimilation of these sentiments into public declarations and legal enactments in Western Europe and America— especially in such formulations as "equality before the law" and "equal protection of the law."

Mencius's view of natural equality, Bloom argues, is closely allied to his view of the inherent natural dignity of all human beings, which for Mencius is primary as compared to all social distinctions including "aristocratic dignity." One can even affirm, she says, this natural equality as fundamental to all of the distinctions and differentiations associated with ritual relations and social roles. Whatever the status distinctions to be observed, all human beings are entitled to an irreducible measure of respect. Thus Bloom emphasizes, "there is a consistent sense in the *Mencius* that the claim to receive respect from others and the disposition to behave respectfully toward them, are both psychologically and morally correlative. This is as true of ordinary people, including wayfarers 11 and beggars, as it is of ministers and kings." The reference to "wayfarers" and "beggars" in the *Mencius* is especially pointed and poignant; even the most transient and least substantial of human lives manifest something of this dignity.

These two basic elements in Mencian thought, human moral equality and natural dignity, did not, for reasons having to do with other factors in the evolving Chinese tradition, directly generate democratic ideas or human rights thinking of the modern Western variety, as Bloom readily concedes, but they "are consistent with, and morally and spiritually supportive of, the consensus documents [on human rights] that figure importantly in our emerging modern civilization."

Wejen Chang's essay, entitled "The Confucian Theory of Norms and Human Rights," includes an extensive examination of many of the same Confucian moral relations, or norms, referred to by Daniel Kwok, analyzing in some detail the references to them in key Confucian texts such as the *Analects, Mencius, Xunzi,* and *Record of Rites (Liji).* He finds that most of those having a bearing on political matters, especially the ruler/people and ruler/minister relationships, emphasize reciprocal obligations, mutual respect, and the repayment of boons or benefits received. He stresses that if anything—if indeed there is any imbalance in these mutual obligations—the heavier burden lies on the side of the ruler's obligations to the people and his responsibilities for their welfare.

The closest thing to the Western notion of human rights according to Chang is the Chinese concept of *fen,* "share." Whereas "human rights" are grounded in the natural order and seen as innate (in the way that *Mencius* and the *Mean* see the moral nature as an innate endowment from Heaven), shares (*fen,* understood variously as "role," "function," or "duty") are defined in some proportion to the role or function performed—a connection of "shares" with "duties" that corresponds to some extent with Western views of rights as going together with duties and responsibilities.

Chang believes that these two different approaches to the problem, "rights" and "shares," each has its advantages and limitations. The particular virtue of "rights" is the confidence they give to the individual in claiming, and even struggling for, his own entitlements before state and society. On the other hand this can lead to contentiousness and conflict. The virtue of "shares" is precisely in the sense of sharing, based on mutual respect and reciprocity. Where the latter qualities are encouraged and developed, contentiousness can be reduced. Nevertheless, if genuine reciprocity does not prevail, the individual may lack the confidence to assert himself, or the people may be without the means to claim their legal rights; hence resentments deepen. For this reason Chang believes that the two approaches, rather than being mutually exclusive, may complement one another and offset each others' weaknesses.

In Chung-ying Cheng's paper on "Transforming Confucian Virtues Into Human Rights," he argues that in Confucianism virtue and duty go together, and that the duties of rulers carry the implication that they also possess the authority or right to perform these duties for the benefit of humankind. Further, in the other Confucian moral relations a similar power or right is implied for the carrying out of the duties appropriate to each. Since however it is only in the relationship of friend and friend that we find relations of equality, it is on this basis, and as an extension from it, that one could see the possibility for grounding the rights of the individual in a Confucian theory of correlative duties among members of a community. "The only thing lacking," he says, "is an explicit assertion of these rights as the basis for their political recognition."

Cheng recognizes that in the absence of such explicit recognition in the past, as well as in the modern period (especially in the May Fourth Movement of 1919), there has been a strong need for "rational liberation" to achieve a more open, more explicit, and more orderly procedure for public policy making. In his view such a process could well be grounded in the Confucian values of equality, self-respect, and mutual respect for personal dignity, predicated on the Confucian conception of the mutual co-inherence of self and society.

As a Confucian basis for the exercise of democratic political rights, Cheng cites a passage in *Mencius* wherein Mencius enjoins the ruler from taking any action to appoint or dismiss an official, or to execute an offender against public order, without fully consulting the people as a whole. This is a most significant claim on Mencius's part, but a real difficulty also attaches to it: though the passage in question clearly implies that there should be a careful and deliberate process of consultation—a sense of due process in governance—the agent throughout is the ruler, and nowhere does Mencius explain how the people themselves would become active in the process. One can easily conjecture that in a relatively simple agrarian society, processes of local consensus formation could be assumed to exist and thus be taken for granted. However the nature and extent of such participation in higher policy formulation becomes a serious question in the changed circumstances of the later imperial dynasties.

Cheng acknowledges this problem; given the failure historically to articulate individual rights and the people's political rights, ruling dynasties have dominated the situation, asserting their own interests as in effect representing the public interest. When this domination has become too oppressive, revolution has been the inevitable consequence. This too, Cheng says, is justified by Mencius in what has become known as Mencius's "right of revolution," as discussed above.

In this case Mencius, consistently with views of his expressed elsewhere in the text, favors due process and not the resort to force. At another point, he says one should not wish to take power if to do so meant committing even one   13 unrightful act, which has always been understood as avoiding the taking of life. Moreover, it is consistent with a long-standing, widely accepted, view among Confucians that force should be resorted to only after all other remedies have been exhausted, i.e., when it has been made clear that a ruler or criminal is incorrigible.

When, then, Cheng suggests in his conclusion that after almost eighty years of revolutionary and republican history in twentieth-century China, resistance to oppressive rulers may still have to take the form of revolution, it is doubtful whether he would have Mencius on his side. Revolutions may be understandable when all else fails, but they have come and gone in modern times without solving the problem. No one was more conscious of this than Mencius, i.e., that violence breeds violence and in the long run proves counterproductive. The power organized to lead revolutions, which mobilizes the force to prosecute them, remains thereafter to fill the power vacuum with its own, now entrenched and coercive, methods.

For the most part the papers in this volume address human rights questions as they relate to classical Confucian conceptions, based on evidence in the prime early Confucian texts. Yet most of our contributors acknowledge that the subsequent Chinese tradition hardly bespeaks, or well exemplifies, these classical values. Thus even while one might grant that these Confucian values are compatible with certain modern human rights ideas, there remains a question as to why Confucianism did not develop along these lines in later times. A common answer to this question is that China's subsequent historical development, especially in the political sphere so crucial to Confucian concerns, was dominated by an imperial dynastic system in many ways at odds with Confucianism. This does not, in itself, suffice to answer our question however, since, while other systemic and ideological factors could be held accountable for the actual result, Confucians too were involved in the process. Hence, in order to assess the respective roles and relative weights of these factors in the developing Chinese tradition, we must consider the contending elements and alternatives to Confucianism that may have affected the outcome.

Yu Feng does this for the so-called Yellow Emperor tradition ("The Yellow Emperor Tradition as Compared to Confucianism"), based on a recently discovered document known as *The Four Texts*, which represents a distinctive mix of Daoist and Legalist ideas known to have played a prominent role in the earlier period of Chinese dynastic history. Feng believes that this tradition known as the "Way of Might" (rather than "Right," as with the Confucians) upheld certain universalist conceptions of law and political practice that contrast with the particularism inherent in the Confucian rites. Hence if one considers that the rites may serve as a plausible Confucian ground for human rights, one must also consider those ways in which the Yellow Emperor tradition offered viable alternatives to, and pointed to certain limitations of, the Confucian approach.

Where Yellow Emperor theorists agreed with the Confucians was in the principle of providing for the people's livelihood as fundamental to rulership. They also shared the idea that the ruler's power should be limited, in the Yellow Emperor's case by subordination of the ruler to the law as truly universal and applicable to all. For this purpose the latter tradition advocated Daoist nonaction or "doing nothing" (*wuwei*), with the ruler restraining himself as much as possible from interfering in the people's conduct of their own affairs. In this view the people's pursuit of their own interests would eventually redound to the material advantage of the ruler himself. Feng goes further to assert that this laissez-faire political policy also implies that people, managing their own affairs, would be entitled to their own opinions, and even to express them as a way of informing the judgments made by the ruler who, holding to no preconceived opinion of his own, would be completely open to them.

This approach to rulership, characterized by Feng as "covert" because the ruler conceals his own inclinations, is nevertheless supposed to yield a more "public" process of policy formulation inasmuch as it would "objectively" reflect people's opinions. It remains unclear, however, as to just how these opinions are to find expression, and how influential they could be when, in the end, the ruler, as the unquestioned locus of all power and authority, makes the sole decision.

Feng believes the influence of this school of thought was beneficial in the early years of the Han, as manifested in its laissez-faire policies, and in the early T'ang, as embodied in a process whereby the Emperor instituted several stages of policy review before making his decisions. This Feng calls "mild autocracy" in contrast to the strong autocracy that prevailed in the Sung and after. Feng does not, however, speculate as to why, in the continuity of dynastic rule, the milder form, if so successful, should have given way to even stronger autocracies.

In the end Feng credits the Yellow Emperor tradition with promoting the idea of the people's right to subsistence and also the idea of universal law as, ideally, limiting the ruler's exercise of his power. He concedes, however, that it is deficient in respect to other human rights that would be better served by Confucianism.

Unfortunately, while this gives us a fuller picture of the conceptual resources available in Chinese tradition, it does not get us far in explaining an outcome, in the later dynasties, acknowledged by almost all to be deficient in political and legal rights of the Western variety. That outcome has to be considered however, in the perspective of the continuing contest between laws and rites, and the further development of Confucian thinking in regard to both.

The nearest equivalent to constitutional law in China is found in the great law codes of the Tang and Ming, widely emulated throughout East Asia. Parallel to this, however, was a continuing development of Confucian thinking about rites, which often at the Chinese court involved a serious contestation between imperial authority and Confucians at court who saw the rites as an important means of challenging that authority.

Ronguey Chu calls attention to four episodes, of which two are particularly dramatic, at the court of the Ming dynasty founder, Taizu (r. 1368–1398), which illustrate how Confucians contested imperial power by invoking the superior authority of the Confucian classics. In the first of the instances to be cited here, Taizu, overriding a centuries-old tradition, decreed that the performance of the sacrificial services to Confucius should be reserved only to the emperor himself and Confucius's own family in Qufu; they should not be allowed to Confucian officials and schools elsewhere in the empire. Ritually speaking, the implication was that the emperor stood above all others in speaking for Heaven and the Confucian Way. Despite the harshness with which Taizu was known to deal with his critics, prominent Confucian ministers remonstrated with the emperor against this, and eventually he rescinded the edict.

The second incident has to do with Taizu's expurgating of passages in *Mencius* he considered contumacious of rulers, and Taizu's banishing of Mencius from the Confucian temple. Again courageous ministers protested, and after Taizu threatened death to anyone who opposed these actions, one minister brought his coffin with him to court saying, "It would be an honor to die for Mencius." Again Taizu, as powerful and cruel a despot as any China has seen, backed off in the face of this heroic defense of Confucian tradition.

Incidents such as these demonstrate that there was indeed a moral culture in traditional China which could stand up in certain spectacular cases to abuses of power—a moral culture that served, in its own day, some of the same function as the moral culture, or "constitutional culture," spoken of earlier in our symposium by Louis Henkin, who attributed the fall of Richard Nixon to the moral pressure exerted on him by a constitutional culture that constrained even a supreme commander of the armed forces and head of law enforcement agencies.

Individually impressive as were these heroics of Confucian ministers, they were more the exception than the rule, and while they testify to a moral culture compatible with human rights sentiments, something more was needed. That "something more" as perceived by Huang Zongxi in the seventeenth

century was what might be called a civil society protective of political freedom and of public discussion at the Chinese court. Huang's father had died a martyr to the cause of outspoken criticism at the Ming court, and Huang believed that a truly humane government should not depend for its workings on such extreme self-sacrifice of honest, conscientious Confucian ministers. Whereas the keynote of the great Neo-Confucian Zhu Xi's political doctrine—widely accepted in Neo-Confucian East Asia—had been the self-disciplined, dedicated service of the Confucian noble man, totally at the service of the public good and defiant of all despots, Huang discounted the idea that the heroics of such noble men could accomplish much without strong constitutional supports of a structural, institutional character. The Confucians had the moral culture; what they lacked was a legal structure that would do more for the Confucian than the rituals of the imperial court. The systemic details of Huang's constitutional plan for a balancing of powers, so as to make the people (*min*) masters in their own house, are given in my *Waiting for the Dawn*. True, this was only one man's plan, but before one dismisses it as no more than that, one should recognize that other leading scholars in the seventeenth century (Ku Yanwu, Lü Liuliang, Tang Jian, and Wang Fuzhi) were thinking along the same lines, and although Huang's ideas could not circulate freely in the seventeenth and eighteenth centuries, they became an inspiration to reformers in the late nineteenth and early twentieth centuries, providing them with an indigenous resource to be invoked in support of the constitutional movement. Moreover, as further evidence that Confucian culture at large might be compatible with constitutionalism, we should note that at the founding of the Yi dynasty in Korea, a leading Neo-Confucian statesman, Chŏng To-chŏn (1342–1398), drew up a monumental constitutional plan including many features similar to Huang's, but almost three hundred years earlier!

By this point it should be obvious that the implementation of Confucian principles in Imperial China was greatly conditioned by the structure and processes of bureaucratic administration, and this was true both early and late, from the Han down to the Qing. It is also true that the administrative system, which combined both executive and judicial functions, for the most part recognized levels and areas of social activity in which the Confucian rites were respected by the state and thought to be the most effective means of maintaining social order in localities beyond the effective reach of the mandarinate. Likewise, on levels and in areas of governance where Legalist-type laws rather than Confucian rites were thought to be more applicable (i.e., beyond the normal reach of family or village control), it was still Confucian-educated officials who administered legal procedures. Thus Confucian values and Legalist systems were inseparably involved with one another, while, as we see with Huang Zongxi, they coexisted in some degree of tension with one another.   17

One consequence of this was a judicial system oriented more toward the upholding of administrative law and order than to defending the interests of the individual, as Alison W. Conner's article ("Confucianism and Due Process") confirms, but it was at the same time influenced both in its stated procedures and actual practice by Confucian humane concerns. Thus, in regard to the use of torture, which is universally condemned in theory (as in the Universal Declaration of Human Rights), though it was legally allowed down into the Qing period, its practice was clearly circumscribed by explicit due process, as Conner argues. Thus the Qing system of confession by the use of torture was one, as she says, "based on detailed rules, even if bureaucratic ones; it was neither arbitrary nor unregulated, and it embodied a clear conception of what constituted a "fair trial." The best of this system, she is inclined to think, reflects Confucian influences, and in the present situation it could well be in order to review and reappropriate "the best of that tradition."

Although by the seventeenth century important Confucian thinkers like Huang Zongxi, Gu Yanwu, Lu Liuliang, Tang Jian, and others had made progress in their critique of dynastic rule, the success of the Manchu conquest and the preoccupation of most scholars with relatively nonpolitical (e.g., philological, text-critical, and bibliographical) projects, directed attention away from ideological issues. Not until the later years of the dynasty, especially under pressure from the West and Japan, did both reformers and revolutionaries take renewed interest in broad constitutional issues of the kind that Huang, Gu, Lu, and others had addressed.

When they did it was in an atmosphere of increasing crisis and soul-searching. Radical alternatives were being considered, including some from the West transmitted through Japan (and these somewhat transmuted into Chinese terms). In both Japan and China there was a tendency to interpret the Western conception of natural rights in Neo-Confucian terms as "Heaven's endowment" (*tianfu*), which is Zhu Xi's explanation of "Heaven's imperative (*tianming*) in the first sentence of the *Mean* (*Zhongyong*): "Heaven's imperative" is called the moral nature (*xing*).[12] Here "Heaven's imperative" (commonly rendered politically as Heaven's Mandate) has the broader meaning of "what Heaven has ordained." "Heaven" had always had a sense of the "natural," but this included a moral aspect, i.e., not an amoral, "objective" view of nature, but one which included the subjective element revealed in the human moral sentiments associated with *xing*. "Natural law" so interpreted was thus, for Confucians, grounded in human moral sentiments more than in some abstract universal construct.

A related problem was the tendency for Confucians to think of human relations in terms of mutual obligations or duties, as has already been shown in our earlier discussions, especially in Chung-ying Cheng's article. In this conception rights and duties necessarily went together, but if "rights" were grounded in the inborn moral nature, and understood in this sense as an inalienable endowment from Heaven, they would achieve a certain dignity and priority over duties, i.e., not contingent on recognition by the state or the performance of duties incurred in society. This was a question of serious concern for those who believed, as a practical matter, that the most urgent priority of the day was the building of an effective, functional state, without which no individual rights could be guaranteed.

Joan Judge's "The Concept of People's Rights (*minquan*) in the Late Qing: Classical and Contemporary Sources of Authority" illustrates the process of adaptation by constitutional reformers in the late Qing who sought to incorporate "people's rights" in a movement that asserted the "people's powers" without directly challenging the monarchy. In these circumstances it was natural for Chinese writers to reformulate new political ideas in the vocabulary of earlier Chinese discourse—as the Japanese themselves had done and were continuing to do. And while evocations of the past sometimes led to revisionist misconstructions and to some misconstruing of Western ideas as well, one cannot discount the importance of this effort to deal with fundamental issues of the cultural encounter between East Asia and the West. Although sometimes dismissed by Western observers as sentimental effusions or nostalgic reveries of the past—essentially conservative, if not reactionary—this is to underestimate the depth and persistence of the issues at stake, to which subsequent discourse and debate have repeatedly recurred.

It should have been no surprise that after the high tide of the twentieth-century revolutionary movement had been reached in the Great Proletarian Cultural Revolution of the late 1960s and 1970s, in its backwash would reappear with renewed—and indeed heightened—significance several of the figures referred to in Peter Zarrow's discussion of "Citizenship and Human Rights in Early Twentieth-Century Chinese Thought." In this process there are notable elements of both continuity and discontinuity. Both reformers and revolutionaries, even those powerfully moved by new currents from the West, are affected in their selection and adaptation of new elements by both cultural predispositions and indispositions, both dissatisfactions with a present seen as seriously handicapped by its past, and by worries over the effects of too rapid and abrupt an intrusion of new ideas and practices from the West.

Zarrow focuses on two leading thinkers of the early twentieth century, Liu Shipei, the leader of a significant anarchist movement who anticipated many of the revolutionary changes to come, and Liang Qichao, probably the most influential intellectual figure of the first three decades. Both Liu and Liang represent a scholarly capability for bridging past and present that became increasingly rare after the major shift to Western-style education post-1905 rendered

19

it difficult for Chinese to acquire the command of the classical tradition that still stood Liu and Liang in good stead (and the virulent antitraditionalism that prevailed from the New Culture and May Fourth movements down through Mao's Cultural Revolution only added to this difficulty).

Liu's anarchist ideas were marked by a basic commitment to the value of equality—a prime value in Chinese tradition as well, but one historically held in some balance with the need for expertise and structured authority as the meritocratic bureaucracy attempted to reconcile them. In Liu, however equality was pushed to the limit, circumscribed only by a totalistic, cosmic/human holism that, paradoxically, gave little attention to the definition of individual human rights. It is understandable that this unstructured utopian idealism should lend itself eventually to communism, wherein the egalitarian ideal, governed only by emphatic political authority, would eventually prove inimical to individual rights.

Liang Qichao, by contrast, was far more concerned with both structure and due process. Initially, in the late Qing, an advocate of constitutional monarchy, after 1911 he accepted republicanism but held firmly to constitutionalism and to the promotion of "people's rights." The latter he conceived, however, not so much as "individual" rights but as rights necessary to the exercise of citizenship in a nation-state.

Liang's strong adherence to constitutionalism could be seen as consistent with his early admiration for Huang Zongxi as a kind of Confucian constitutionalist; moreover, his concern for developing the kind of civil infrastructure associated by him with the people's participation in citizenship, while it set a certain limit on the interpretation of people's rights as individual rights, was not inconsistent with a Confucian view akin to Huang's. Where Liang decidedly departed from tradition was in his acceptance, under Western and Japanese influence, of the nation-state (rather than the professedly universalist or cosmopolitan dynastic state) as the primary form of political organization, and in his reformulation of Confucian self-cultivation to serve the roles and duties of citizenship. In this respect he could be said to have advanced beyond both Zhu Xi's concept of the self-cultivation of the leadership elite and Huang Zongxi's conception of a constitutional infrastructure still largely in the hands of Confucian scholar-officials.

If several of our contributors believe it possible to ground the practice of human rights in the Confucian concept of rites, Randall Peerenboom, who both practices law in Beijing and has written on ancient Chinese legal philosophy, seriously questions this. For him Confucian rites may have a value in establishing a moral consensus and promoting beneficial customs within a community, but this does not protect the individual or the minority from the

tyranny of the dictator or the majority. Moreover since rites place a premium on the ideal of social and political harmonization, they, and rites-based views of sound order, lend themselves to authoritarian rule and to conformity, rather than freedom, of thought. Thus in his opinion, a revival of Confucianism in a conservative form emphasizing "harmony" as the supreme value (as currently is the case among its sponsors in the PRC), would be prejudicial to the protection of individual human rights and to the freedom of thought essential to political democracy.

Generally Peerenboom believes that the Confucian rites and Western conceptions of rights serve different purposes but may be, to some extent, complementary. "In most instances rites can complement rights, providing a moral dimension to interpersonal actions, suggesting possibilities above and beyond the legal relations defined by rights. . . . The rites may remind us of our moral obligations, our duties to others." Nevertheless he also sees a danger in it "to the extent that rites represent the moral consensus of the community, they exert pressure to conform one's thinking to others." (p. 26) Then too, according to him the emphasis in rites' thinking on social solidarity, has contributed to "the enduring appeal of the utopian myth of harmony, thereby blinding rulers and reformers alike to the realities of disharmony."

Peerenboom is on strong factual ground when he says that historically Confucianism did not produce liberal democracy, popular sovereignty, democratic elections, civil liberties and the like. Nonetheless his argument leans heavily on a theoretical model of Confucianism, and may not take into account the developing historical awareness of later Confucian thinkers that moral cultivation and ritual norms were insufficient, in themselves, to cope with the excesses of authoritarian rule, as for instance Huang Zongxi and Liang Qichao correctly perceived the matter, or even as an orthodox Neo-Confucian like Lü Liuliang (prime exponent of Zhu Xi in the seventeenth century) came up with a radical critique of Chinese despotism, in the context of the rites.[13]

No doubt Peerenboom is correct theoretically, and to some extent practically, when he sees the ruler as cast by Confucianism in a supreme leadership role, harmonizing divergent views and interests in the society; there are, indeed, abundant examples of courtly, if not utterly sycophantic, officials who credited emperors with such sage-like authority. This is not, however, the whole story. There is evidence also, as early as the *Mencius*, the *Zuo Commentary* (*Zuozhuan*), and *Discourses of the States* (*Kuoyu*) that contests the legitimacy of rulers who do not listen to criticism and remonstration. And if Peerenboom sees the ruler as the unique interpreter of, and authority on, the Way this was not undisputed; there was the alternative tradition, abundantly recorded in Neo-Confucian literature, that saw the custody of the Way as divided, from the Chou on down, between the ruler who held power, and wise Confucian mentors, without whose advice and the ruler's acceptance of it, the latter lost all authority and legitimacy.

Among prominent twentieth-century spokesmen for Confucianism, such as Tang Zhunyi, Mou Zongsan, Carsun Chang, and Xu Fuguan, one finds a readiness to acknowledge that this dissenting Confucian tradition, unable historically to prevail over the politically more dominant dynastic tradition, has welcomed Western constitutional democracy as a support for the more liberal Confucian tradition as they espouse it.[14]

Our final two papers present different views among Chinese intellectuals with regard to the continuing influence of Confucianism. Merle Goldman sees a considerable residue of that influence among leading intellectuals down into recent years, but it is a Confucianism having mostly to do with how intellectuals perceive their role in relation to the state, which bears many resemblances to the role of the traditional literati, especially in their sense of obligation to serve in government out of a responsible concern for the welfare of the people.

The efforts of Wu Han, a scholar and writer as well as vice mayor of Beijing under Mao, is illustrative of this idealistic strain of Confucian-inspired resistance to despotism. What aroused Mao's ire and resulted in Wu's martyrdom as a target of the Cultural Revolution, was Wu's play, *Hai-Jui Dismissed*, in which a sixteenth-century Confucian minister paid with his life for criticizing the emperor. It dramatized the Confucian concept of true loyalty consisting in honest remonstrance to the ruler, i.e., in true dedication to the public interest. Besides making thinly veiled reference to Peng Dehuai's criticism of Mao, it prefigured Wu's own martyrdom for challenging Mao.

The historical case and Wu's play illustrate some key features of how the Confucian legacy has operated in the post-Confucian setting. First of all, history has uses in serving as indirect political criticism when circumstances preclude more direct reference. This has not only been a traditional Confucian use of the past for very present purposes, but it also shows in what way Confucian values may live in popular art (here the drama) long after they have ceased to be taught in doctrinal form—which is as much as to say that, no longer being taught, Confucianism does not survive in its traditional form, as an articulated doctrine, but now lives on in forms more subtle yet still palpable in the popular imagination—in poetry, song and drama, as the moral grounding and tone of a whole culture rather than as the philosophy of the elite. In such circumstances, the influence of Confucianism may be inchoate and almost impossible to estimate, but it is there, exerting an immeasurable power of attraction.

It may indeed be true, as Jeremy T. Paltiel reiterates, that younger generations in post-Mao China know little about and think less of Confucianism. Rather they perceive it either as a "feudal" remnant being revived and reimposed

by an oppressive regime, or else as an idealistic, even romantic evocation of the past, mainly by foreigners, that is being adroitly manipulated by the current regime for its own conservative purposes. To some degree this view may hold for a supposedly "liberated" generation, long since cut off from any knowledge of Confucianism except for the vague, negative impressions they formed of it from repeated anti-Confucian campaigns of the twentieth century. It must be admitted too that recent advocates of human rights and liberal democracy see little relevance of Confucianism to their own cause. Meanwhile writers like Wu Han, rare in their own time, are still rarer today. Wu was the product of an education and scholarship under the Guomindang that was at least liberal enough for Wu Han, as a scholar, to learn something of Chinese history and become aware of its traditional moral and political resources. This has been far more difficult since 1949, and thus far less typical of the present generation—many of them unschooled Red Guards—whose political activism in the 1980s and 1990s is more informed by the libertarian May Fourth Movement and by China's belated opening to the West as part of Deng's modernization program, than it is by anything Confucian. The same is largely true of the developing Chinese legal community in recent years, as is evident from the debates over human rights in legal journals, of which Paltiel gives a most revealing account.

For all this, the exposure of the more recent generation to intellectual trends outside China will make them aware of the importance increasingly being attached to Confucianism abroad, both as a newly recognized—or at least imputed—factor in the successful modernization of other East Asian states, or as a serious object of scholarly study outside China. If the new generation expects to live in this larger world, it will have to reckon with these currents abroad, and with more of an understanding of them than May Fourth allowed for. Moreover, if Jeremy Paltiel is right that problems of "national identity" persist in all East Asian countries historically under Confucian influence, and there is ample evidence pointing in that direction, it is unlikely that these can be resolved without the Chinese becoming better informed than they are now of the contents, historical development and wide cultural extension of Confucianism. If no people can ignore its own past, or fail in some way to come to terms with it, it is no less true that Chinese, like other East Asians, will have to deal with such problems in a better educated and thoughtful way, lest this cultural battle be lost by default to those busily appropriating Confucianism for their own regressive—and sometimes repressive—purposes.

In arranging this symposium its initial sponsors wished to open up a dialogue, as wide-ranging as possible, between China and the West—a dialogue that would go beyond the immediate political confrontation over human rights demands and accusations, in order to get at some of the deeper cultural issues that underlie the claims and counterclaims now being made in the political arena. This dialogue was meant to be open and open-ended, exposing issues without necessarily settling them. In clarifying them however, one could, I believe, say that a rough consensus emerged on some points that may serve to advance future dialogue:

1. Confucian values and Confucian discourse over the centuries have been involved with many of the same issues that have concerned Western human rights thinkers, though in somewhat different language.

2. Thinking about human rights, in the form recognized by the Universal Declaration of 1948, is a relatively recent development in the West, which, however, emerges from a long historical development of humanitarian concerns expressed in different religious, ethical, social and legal traditions. Human rights as currently understood have deep and diverse roots in the West, are hybrid in cultural character, and are still evolving in practice.

3. The same is true with regard to Confucian values in China, and more broadly in East Asia as a whole, to the extent that East Asian countries otherwise culturally diverse have shared in certain common Confucian values, and in the modern period have faced a similar challenge from Western ideas and practices. It is significant however, that several East Asian countries (Japan, South Korea, Taiwan) have not found their Confucian past an obstacle to the acceptance of Western-style constitutions and guarantees of human rights. Cultural diversity did not prevent Chinese representatives from actively participating in the formulation of the 1948 Declaration of Human Rights, as they found no incompatibility between the essential humanistic values of Confucianism and these new human rights initiatives.

4. Although some contrast may be drawn between a greater emphasis on individual autonomy in modern Western conceptions of human rights and a greater emphasis on social and communitarian values in Confucianism, the contrast is often overdrawn at the expense of shared concerns and understandings. Social and communitarian values have by no means been lacking in traditions that have contributed to human rights thinking in the West, while respect for the dignity of the self and person have been central to Confucianism from its inception.

5. Key to these questions is the linking in Confucianism between the primacy of the morally responsible self and the social norms embodied in Confucian ritual decorum, as compared to the "Western" coupling of individual rights and legal protections. To some extent the Confucian reliance on ritual norms was at the expense of legal protections for the individual, but in the long-term evolution of Confucian thinking there was

an increasing consciousness of the need for law in a constitutional sense and in the sense of due process. This rendered it possible for at least some prominent Chinese thinkers in the early twentieth century to view the advent of Western constitutionalism and human rights legislation as quite congenial to their own sense of need in this respect. At the same time, some Westerners concerned with social and communitarian values have been ready to find in Confucianism a remedy to what they see as an excessive individualism and libertarianism in the West.

6. One could look, as some scholars do, for a reconciliation of the two in a complementary relationship, but the picture is complicated by the legacy of anti-Confucianism in the successive liberationist, revolutionary movements in China from the early twentieth century down to recent times. Thus there are cleavages today, cutting across China, East Asia and the West, as between divergent understandings of both Confucianism and human rights, and whether priority is to be given to individual rights, social duties or communitarian needs. Should these indeed be seen as anything but mutually implicated and equally necessary? Is it not specious to assert that subsistence needs and economic progress in underdeveloped countries should come before political freedoms? Can either be achieved without the other? What gauge could there be for a satisfactory level of subsistence as a precondition for the granting of civil rights, or for the level of economic progress to be achieved before human rights are recognized?

7. The foregoing are all questions that bear further investigation and discussion, but at least two others have a major bearing on the outcome of human rights issues. One is the question of civil society: Could any kind of human rights program, whether conceived in individual/social, or legal/ritual, terms, be effective in the absence of both a civil political infrastructure and a moral culture supportive of them? The other question is whether the urgent industrial, technological, environmental and ecological problems that confront us today—and China in some respects more urgently even than most others—do not demand new human rights conceptions and practices, with a humane concern extending beyond the human to the earth and all forms of life. These cannot but concern us all, East and West, in equal measure today. Thus the dialogue must go on.

Notes

1. Howard French, "Africa Looks East for a New Model," *New York Times*, Feb. 4, 1966, 4:1.

2. Referring to Analects 1:11.

3. *Record of Rites*, 9:24.

4. Wm. Theodore de Bary et al., eds., *Sources of Chinese Tradition* (New York: Columbia University Press, 1960), vol. 2, pp. 153–56.

5. By Ho Shen, wife of Liu Shipei, founder of the Anarchist movement in China. Ho Chen, "Nuzi fuchou lun," *Tianyi bao*, no. 3 (10), 7–13. Trans. by Peter Zarrow.

6. Lawrence G. Thompson, *Ta T'ung Shu: The One-World Philosophy of K'ang Yu-wei* (London: George Allen and Unwin, 1958), p. 183.

7. See the article by the prominent liberal philosopher, Morris Cohen, in the *Encyclopedia of Social Sciences*.

8. See Twiss article and Tu epilogue in this volume for elaboration of this point.

9. Mencius, trans. D. C. Lau (London: Penguin, 1970), IB:8, p. 68.

10. W. T. de Bary, *Waiting for the Dawn: A Plan for the Prince* (New York: Columbia University Press, 1993).

11. Papers of the General Education Seminar on Human Rights, Columbia University, New York. 1976; see also my "Human Rites: An Essay on Confucianism and Human Rights," delivered at the symposium in honor of Vitaly Rubin, Hebrew University of Jerusalem, 1983, published in Irene Eber, ed., *Confucianism, the Dynamics of a Tradition* (New York: Macmillan, 1986).

12. Zhu Xi, *Zhong yong zhang ju* 1, in *Sishu zhangju jizhu* (Beijing: Zhonghua shuju), 1983.

13. See my *Learning for One's Self* (New York: Columbia University Press, 1991), pp. 332–42.

14. See their manifesto in Carsun Chang, *The Development of Neo-Confucianism* (New York: Bookman Associates, 1962), vol. 2, pp. 471–72.

1

A Constructive Framework for Discussing Confucianism and Human Rights

Sumner B. Twiss

I write this paper from the perspective of one who works in the field of comparative ethics and who has been involved in recent intercultural dialogues on the relationship between international human rights and the ethics of religious and philosophical traditions.[1] In the latter context, I have focused especially on recent debates about whether human rights are relative only to particular cultural moral traditions, or whether they are properly conceived as universal and interculturally applicable. In these debates three issues have arisen as dominant concerns: (1) how international human rights and their justification ought to be construed within intercultural moral dialogues; (2) whether the perception of some scholars about an incompatibility between universal human rights and particular cultural traditions is sound; and (3) how one ought to respond to the difficult hermeneutical and moral issues likely to arise when quite different cultural moral visions and idioms confront each other in dialogue about human rights. These issues establish the parameters for the remarks that follow. My goal can be simply put: to develop a constructive framework for intercultural human rights dialogue and to illustrate its utility with respect to the Confucian tradition.[2]

For the purposes of this discussion, human rights are to be understood as the set of rights articulated in the 1948 Universal Declaration of Human Rights and in the two subsequent and related covenants that came into force in the mid-1970s (jointly known as *The International Bill of Human Rights*), as well as in subsequent treaties and conventions.[3] The Covenant on Civil and Political Rights guarantees rights such as freedom of thought and expression, freedom from arbitrary arrest and torture, and freedom of movement and peaceable assembly. The Covenant on Economic, Social, and Cultural Rights provides for such rights as the right to work and receive fair wages, to protection of the family, to adequate standards of living, to education, to health care, to people's self-determination regarding their political status and economic, social, and cultural development, and to ethnic and religious minorities' enjoyment of their own culture, language, and religion. International human rights have been further expanded and elaborated by treaties on prevention of genocide, elimination of racial discrimination, elimination of discrimination against women, protection of refugees, rights of children, elimination of discrimination based on religious identity, and the rights of indigenous peoples (the latter is pending action). Although many of the rights articulated in these conventions are uncontested and accepted as universally normative, others are contested in the international arena, a fact which partially accounts for intercultural human rights dialogues.

These conventions are often interpreted as projecting a characteristic understanding of the conceptual features of human rights, which are worth introducing at the outset.[4] Human rights are typically regarded as moral (and legal) claims with such high priority that they are construed as entitlements to certain conditions and goods which must be socially guaranteed. Moreover, these priority claims or entitlements are conceived as being held by all human beings, who, particularly under adverse circumstances, can legitimately assert them against specified others, usually states or state representatives, who have correlative duties to satisfy their claims. Adapting a well-turned phrase from Ronald Dworkin, human rights are internationally recognized "trumps" held by all persons against specified others. Furthermore, it is also typically asserted that human rights must be claimed, recognized, and responded to *as* rights if they are to be fully functional as priority claims.

I take some exception to this typical characterization of the conceptual features of human rights, for I do not think it is sufficiently nuanced to account for other features which I discern in the international practice of human rights. Let me offer a few examples. First, as we will see later, there is an entire generation of developmental-collective human rights, some of which are cited above, that address the priority claims of entire peoples and communities, and these appear to be excluded by the standard characterization. Second, this characterization clearly holds that the priority claims of human rights must be recognized *as* rights in order to be effective, but this seems to discount cases where the conditions and goods enjoined are guaranteed in a strong way by means other than explicit rights in certain traditions and societies—for example, as systemic requirements of a morally legitimate government or political system; as prerequisites for the appropriate fulfillment of people's sociomoral responsibilities in pursuit of the common good. It strikes me that the priorities identified by the subject matter of human rights can be normatively guaranteed by systems and traditions that lack or otherwise resist the explicit conceptuality of rights.[5] Third, although this is not a point that I discuss further in this paper, the typical characterization of human rights appears overly oriented to conceiving of human rights as priority claims against states or state representatives, but increasingly a large bulk of human rights problems—particularly those being addressed by social-economic human rights—stem from the practices of nonstate entities such as transnational corporations, which may be largely beyond the control of states. This is an important issue that is only now being recognized, and addressing it may well entail further nuances in a proper understanding of international human rights.[6]

Revised Understanding of Human Rights and Their Justification:
A Historical and Pragmatic Approach

In order to explore the aforementioned issues and to develop a heuristic framework, we need at the outset to attend closely to a concern that arises when representatives of certain cultural traditions and scholars of those traditions consider international human rights.[7] The concern is this: human rights appear to many to represent a Western moral ideology intended to supplant the moral perspectives of diverse cultural, religious, and philosophical traditions. This perception has become a serious obstacle to progress in both intercultural dialogue and comparative ethics when considering human rights. Addressing this concern head-on may have the salutary effect of not only removing an obstacle to intercultural and scholarly work but also permitting us to develop a revised understanding of human rights that may benefit such work in the future.

The fundamental question raised by this perception is: What is the relationship between the universal claims of human rights conceived as a kind of "minimal morality" and the more particular, usually richer and more extensive moralities advanced by cultural traditions?[8] In particular, many cultural representatives and comparative philosophers worry that a typical liberal understanding of human rights, conceived as a set of core principles that ground moral judgments about behavior in diverse cultural settings, means that human rights are implicitly imperialistic.[9] More precisely, they worry that a human rights based core morality oriented to the rights of individuals is designed to supplant those moral traditions oriented to (for example) more communitarian visions and categories, implying the end, or at least the irrelevance, of the particular moral traditions that have emerged in the context of various cultures. And, they ask in a pointed way, would such replacement really be a

29

moral advance for the peoples of the world, or rather (for example) a regression and entrenchment into a myopic social atomism?

In addition to this concern about hegemony over and replacement of rich and thick moralities by a thin morality, questions are raised about the metaphysical and epistemological assumptions seemingly associated with the promotion of human rights as a foundation for universal moral judgments. Here we encounter charges of an outmoded theory of moral knowledge (foundationalism), of narrow and myopic conceptions of human nature (e.g., as principally and narrowly self-interested), or truncated conceptions of persons and communities (e.g., as, respectively, isolated individual monads and market societies of unrelated strangers), and of loveless visions of the world stripped of interdependency, thick relationships, and compassion.[10] If, as many assert, claims about human rights are based on problematic conceptions of human nature, personhood and community, and moral knowledge, then cultural representatives at human rights dialogues may well wonder whether they are being asked to accept invalid ideas, notions that are no longer accepted even by many in the West.

These concerns and questions, however, betray a serious misunderstanding of the nature, source, and function of human rights, and it is crucially important to set the record straight in this regard. Despite the common perception that human rights are simply an outgrowth and entailment of Western assumptions about human nature and moral rationality, it is a fact that the Universal Declaration of Human Rights (1948) was reached through a pragmatic process of negotiation between representatives of different nations and cultural traditions.[11] While it may be true that Western representatives had the upper hand in this process, the simple fact remains that pragmatic negotiation between differing views about the subject-matter was the process of choice, not theorizing about matters of moral knowledge, political philosophy, or even jurisprudence. Moreover, this pragmatic approach has continued to characterize the drafting and adoption of subsequent human rights covenants, conventions and treaties. We need to ask, therefore, what this process signifies or suggests about the nature, status and justification of human rights, and the answer may be reassuring to those who worry about the hegemony of a particular ideology in human rights.

The framers of human rights declarations, conventions, and treaties explicitly take—for better or worse—a pragmatic approach to the relationship between human rights norms and particular cultural traditions. This approach starts with the facts of moral plurality and cultural particularity and finds that in situations of crisis people of quite different traditions are able to acknowledge their mutual respect for certain basic values. The Universal Declaration

was, for example, the historical product of a very particular crisis brought about by the genocide and brutalization of persons and communities during the Second World War. In the face of this crisis, representatives from a number of cultural traditions were able to recognize their mutual agreement in the judgment that such acts are antithetical to each and all of their traditions, and through a process of pragmatic negotiation, they were able to agree on incorporating this judgment in the language of specific human rights. The fact that rights-language was employed was doubtless due to the dominance of the Western legal tradition in the international arena, but the mutually agreed upon judgment about the proscription of certain acts was not exclusively a "Western" moral judgment.

Similarly, the subsequent human rights covenants of the 1970s were born from the mutual recognition that the oppression and material disadvantages suffered especially by peoples in developing countries were incompatible with moral sensibilities contained in a number of particular cultural moral traditions. Significantly, the influence of non-Western (or at least non-First World) cultural representatives was more prominent here, accounting in part for negotiated agreements to give greater emphasis to social and economic rights as well as collective rights of self-determination and development. A similar process led to the 1979 convention on the protection of women's human rights, and more recently, the 1993 UN Draft Declaration on the Rights of Indigenous Peoples. The point is that far from preempting or replacing the rich moral teachings of various cultural traditions, specific expressions of human rights concerns have arisen from the mutual recognition by adherents of these traditions that they have a shared interest in the protection of certain values. Brutality, tyranny, starvation, discrimination, displacement, and the like are recognized by adherents of all traditions as their common enemy. This recognition implies that despite cultural differences many, if not all, traditions do in fact share important substantive moral values. At least in certain critical moments, participants in otherwise diverse traditions find that they have a shared set of aspirations as well as a shared capacity to suffer at the hands of those who violate the dignity and well-being of human persons and communities.

On pragmatic moral grounds, then, participants in particular cultural traditions and in the community of those concerned for human rights might consider specific expressions of human rights as products of successive recognitions by diverse peoples of a set of values embraced by their own distinctive cultural moral traditions. No one cultural tradition is the sole source of human rights concerns. Human rights are, from this point of view, the expression of a set of important overlapping moral expectations to which different cultures hold themselves and others accountable.[12] Moreover, since there is as yet no end to the suffering that human beings impose on one another, we can expect to see additional moments of recognition, the addition of new human rights to those already recognized and the emergence of new types of human rights emphases.

One implication of this record of human rights negotiations and recognitions is that it is most appropriate to take a historical perspective on the emergence and formulation of human rights norms. The intercultural recognition of human rights has a history, and, as pointed out by Burns Weston (following Karel Vasak), this history marks at least three distinctive generations (types) of human rights, with each successive generation not supplanting the earlier one(s) but rather adding to, as well as nuancing, the earlier.[13] The first generation, emerging most definitively in the aftermath of World War II, is generally comprised of civil-political rights or liberties, although also touching on certain social and economic rights, as influenced by the background of Franklin D. Roosevelt's "Four Freedoms" speech and the identification of "freedom from want."[14] The second generation, emerging most definitively in the human rights covenants of the 1970s, adds a new emphasis on social and economic rights to crucial goods and services and their just allocation, though this generation is also clearly linked with the first and looks forward to the third (by identifying the rights of peoples to self-determination and their cultural rights). The third generation, which is now most definitively emerging amidst Third and Fourth World claims for global redistribution of power, wealth, and the common heritage of humankind (e.g., ecosystem, peace), adds yet another new emphasis on developmental-collective rights to peoples' self-determination and development (e.g., political, economic, cultural) as well as to a more just distribution of material and nonmaterial goods on a local and planetary scale. This generation also is linked with the preceding ones, inasmuch as it is concerned not only with the collective rights of peoples but also the liberties and material welfare of their individual members. The international human rights community recognizes all three generations or types of human rights as important and interrelated and needing to be pursued in a constructive balance or harmony. These three generations are, in a word, indivisible, though in a given situation or context, one or another generation may merit special emphasis.

Now, it is important to note that in some quarters there appears to be a tendency to correlate strongly these three generations with distinctive assumptions about human nature, persons, and community, in such a way as to seemingly undermine the contention that all three generations are interrelated and indivisible.[15] Weston associates civil-political human rights with the philosophy of liberal individualism, social-economic rights with the socialist tradition, and developmental-collective rights with the philosophy of holistic community.[16] Inasmuch as different cultures and traditions make their own distinctive

contributions to international human rights, there is something to this contention, but it could also be misleading as well, for, as argued by Weston, it deflects attention away from the fact that successive generations not only add new human rights emphases to the earlier generations but also modify our understanding of the nature and import of earlier generations. There is, in effect, a recursive and spiraling hermeneutical process at work here that needs to be taken into account—recursive in the sense of returning to and interpreting the earlier generations in light of the succeeding, and spiraling in the sense of interpreting the later generations in the light of the recursive move. International human rights constitute, in short, a dynamic tradition in their own right that may mitigate the effects of perceived internal incoherence.

For example, in baldly characterizing civil-political human rights as the "negative" liberties (or "freedoms from" oppressive political authority) advanced by liberal individualism, one might risk deflecting attention away from the fact that these liberties are also understood as "enablements" or "enpowerments" for persons to function as flourishing members of a polity or community where they try to convince others of their ideas about the best way to live together in their society.[17] That is to say, civil-political liberties are not simply the negative "freedoms-from" associated with a caricatured liberal individualism concerned with protecting the privacy of radically autonomous, isolated, self-interested, ahistorical and acultural selves, but rather are positive enpowerments to persons' involvement in a flourishing community that are compatible with, for example, communitarian traditions of moral and political thought. The subsequent generation of social-economic human rights, with its concerns about exploitation of certain classes and colonial peoples, helps to highlight this positive function of civil-political rights, by driving home the point that certain minimal social-economic conditions are necessary for people to flourish fully as politically involved members of their societies. By the same token, however, we can also see the wisdom behind the thesis that civil-political liberties may be crucially important to the enhancement of peoples' social and economic situation: for example, exercising civil-political rights may result in pressures for change in social and economic conditions.[18] Thus do these two generations change our understanding of both, beyond the traditional philosophies and assumptions often associated with them, enabling us to appreciate their interdependence and mutual effects.

A similar point can be made about the effects of the third generation of human rights (developmental-collective) on the other two. To associate these third-generation rights with the philosophy of holistic community on a planetary scale without further adumbration could run the risk of permitting these rights to be seen as in dramatic tension with, for example, the civil-political rights generally ascribed to individual persons. While it is certainly true that collective rights of self-determination and development of material and nonmaterial goods are primarily ascribable to communities and people, it is not true, as Weston indicates, that these need be construed as incompatible with the other generations.[19] With respect to social-economic rights, we can easily interpret collective human rights as an emphatic and more just generalization of social and economic benefits to the oppressed and suffering peoples of the world (conceived both collectively and individually). Indeed, the collective rights of, for example, the peoples of the Fourth World are in principle compatible with civil-political liberties—the Iroquois Six Nations Confederacy being a prime historical example, and the Draft Declaration of the Rights of Indigenous Peoples being another, more contemporary example.[20]

My point in this discussion should not be lost: all three generations of human rights in fact identify and forward a wide range of enpowerments, both individual and collective, that are crucial to individual and community flourishing on a local and wider scale. And, insofar as they do this, they are interdependent and mutually influential and compatible all the way down, so to speak. Furthermore, under this understanding, human rights in general are compatible in principle not only with cultural traditions that emphasize the importance of individuals within community (which is a more apt characterization of Western liberalism) but also with cultural traditions that may emphasize the primacy of community and the way that individuals contribute to it— that is, *both* more liberal individualist *and* more communitarian traditions. Rigid dichotomies as well as static understandings of the historical sources of human rights may be quite misleading with regard to the conceptual flexibility and development of international human rights.[21]

Now, some may think that I am glossing over necessarily large differences between liberal and communitarian interpretations of, for example, civil-political rights or liberties. In particular, they may contend that in liberal traditions these rights are held by individuals against the state, whereas in communitarian traditions they are granted by the state only so long as they are exercised in the interests of the state. While such a contention may be applicable in some cases, it is not true for all, and it may not be necessarily true for any, pending clarification of the social ideals of the traditions in question. Insisting on the supposed gap between liberal and communitarian traditions runs the risk of identifying traditions with states. It also overlooks those cases in which civil-political liberties are regarded as constitutive and defining elements of both liberal and communitarian ideals of a flourishing community that can be used to critique deviations of respective states from those ideals. There may indeed be a large difference between, on the one hand, liberal and communitarian social ideals incorporating civil-political liberties in their traditions of moral and political thought, and, on the other, the actual constitutions and practices of states in measuring up to those ideals. This is an unfortunate fact of our less-than-ideal world, but it does not undermine my claim that both liberal and communitarian traditions can recognize and value the importance of civil-political liberties in their respective ideals of community flourishing. The differences between liberal and communitarian traditions would then devolve on the differences in the content of their respective ideals of communal flourishing apart from their shared commitment to civil-political liberties. It is this understanding of a shared commitment to the role of civil-political liberties in diverse social ideals that is forwarded by international human rights.[22]

A second important consequence of this historical and pragmatic conception of human rights involves a revised understanding of their status and justification. Human rights identify and specify conditions that are crucially important for a life worthy of human persons and communities as negotiated and agreed upon by representatives from diverse traditions.[23] In effect, human rights represent a common vision of central moral and social values that are compatible with a variety of cultural moral anthropologies—a unity within moral diversity. At one level their justification depends on a practical moral consensus amongst diverse traditions which have acknowledged their mutual recognition of the human importance of these values. This recognition is grounded in shared historical experiences of what life can be like without these conditions, as well as in a negotiated agreement and commitment to see these conditions fulfilled. Moreover, this negotiation, consensus, and commitment are open and public: made by, to, and before the peoples of the world.

At a second level of justification, each of these traditions may justify its own participation in the consensus by appealing to its own set of moral categories as appropriate to its particular philosophical or religious vision of human nature, person and community, and moral epistemology. Thus, internal to a cultural moral tradition, the subject matter of particular human rights (what they are about or what they address) may be justified as, for example, divinely ordained precepts, implications of natural law or natural reason, self-evident moral truisms, systemic moral assumptions about appropriate relations between state and citizen, entailments of certain virtues, etc. (the list is open-ended precisely because of the rich variety of cultural moral traditions). This distinction between levels or arenas of human rights justification makes possible the recognition that a tradition may have the resources to justify its agreement to participate in and abide by international human rights without necessarily being compelled to forge its own internal human rights categories. Even if they lack the internal conceptuality of rights and human rights, most (if not all) traditions have the internal moral resources at least to recognize the importance of the subject matters being addressed by international human rights and to justify on internal cultural moral grounds, pertaining to their own visions of human nature and welfare, their agreement to abide by the pragmatic international

35

consensus on human rights. This may constitute a different, possibly more attainable, burden of justification for some traditions than that of having to develop their own internal human rights subtraditions. While these traditions would presumably develop internal understandings of how their moral visions and idioms relate to the subject matters addressed by international human rights (i.e., a "theory" of relationship), they are not compelled to adopt or develop an internal human rights subtradition in any stronger sense (e.g., the active internal deployment of the language and discourse of human rights).[24]

Recognition of a two-level approach to the source and justification of human rights has a number of advantages, not the least of which is that it appears to capture the actual state of affairs about how human rights are justified. Moreover, it permits us to acknowledge in a reasonably sophisticated manner both commonalities and differences among cultural moral traditions—they share a set of core values while at the same time articulating and living by the richer and more variegated moral visions appropriate to their historical circumstances and cultural settings. Furthermore, it allows us to acknowledge that while human rights may be justified on grounds of pragmatic agreement at the point where moral traditions may overlap in their shared insights and commitments, they may also be justified and even construed within different moral idioms as appropriate to cultural moral diversity. Additionally, this approach permits us to appreciate the historical specificity and development of human rights norms at the international level as the result of reciprocal interactions among diverse traditions, while still being able to respect internal variations among different conceptions of human nature and corresponding moral conceptualities, languages, and epistemologies. Moreover, inasmuch as this approach is founded on a historical and pragmatic vision of the source of human rights, it allows us to appreciate more thoroughly the specific contributions that different moral cultures might make to the recognition and formulation of human rights norms. Finally, the two-level approach permits us to handle some of the epistemological controversies about human rights by resisting the imposition of one culture's moral epistemology on all the rest. Human rights need not be justified monolithically by one particular epistemology, entailing the rejection of all other epistemic approaches, precisely because we can distinguish between levels of appeal—pragmatic and negotiated consensus for all at the international level, but tolerance for a variety of approaches at the cultural level.[25]

I admit that this two-level approach will not resolve all problems about the moral epistemology of human rights, much less all tensions between the universality of human rights and the particularity of cultural moral traditions. But it may mitigate these problems and tensions for the purposes of intercultural human rights dialogues. If, for example, cultural representatives, or scholars on their behalf, can see that they are not being asked to relinquish their epistemic appeals and moral idioms, but only to confine their use to the context or level where they would have the greatest effect, then they may be somewhat freer to operate pragmatically and consensually at the international level and in intercultural dialogues. Moreover, the two-level approach may assist cultural representatives and scholars in seeing and dealing with the big issues of crucial conditions for human well-being rather than getting bogged down in smaller issues of cultural nuance, in a context that calls for pragmatic negotiation between cultures rather than cultural proselytization aimed at the wholesale conversion of others. Furthermore, the two-level approach may well prompt cultural representatives and scholars to deal explicitly with issues of how to translate their internal cultural views into a language and idiom that is more broadly persuasive at the intercultural or international level: for example, Buddhist dependent co-origination or Confucian one-bodiedness with heaven, earth, and the myriad things may only have "moral bite" for other Buddhists or Confucians, respectively, but insofar as these notions can be translated into terms of shared responsibility for the ecosystem and possibly recognition of the claims of all sentient beings, they can in fact function to greater effect at the intercultural level.[26]

Issues will remain about how to adjudicate contestable human rights norms that fall outside the agreed-upon international consensus, especially when these norms may appear to conflict seriously with particular cultural visions of social relations. But, again, the two-level approach may assist the adjudication process by encouraging cultural representatives and scholars to consider whether there might not be correspondences between the positions of other cultures and more submerged voices within those traditions that have not been heard or taken seriously enough. Thus the level of pragmatic negotiation can direct attention to the question of internal cultural moral diversity and possibly bring new resources into human rights dialogues.

To summarize: The facts, as I have represented them, of an international pragmatic moral consensus regarding human rights and of the history of their three successive generations, inspired by the socio-moral visions of diverse cultural traditions, contradict the simplistic claim that human rights represent a hegemonic Western moral ideology. Furthermore, the fact of three generations of human rights, together with their recursive and spiraling hermeneutical interaction, contradicts also the myopic perception that human rights are exclusively civil-political liberties. Moreover, the two-level approach to human rights justification, together with the historical and pragmatic perspective I have provided on the background of international human rights, implies that these rights are not strongly associated with or grounded in problematic metaphysical and epistemological assumptions. On the contrary, they are in a significant sense "theory thin" at the international level, permitting wide diversity at the internal cultural level and mitigating the temptation to locate human rights within any one moral or political theory.[27] Finally, I might observe that while it is an open question as to whether certain cultural traditions may lack, either explicitly or even implicitly, their own internal human rights subtraditions, it seems more than likely that all cultural traditions have the resources necessary to justify on internal grounds and in their own moral idioms, their agreement to abide by the international human rights consensus, for this constitutes a lesser burden of justification that does not require cultural traditions to employ the conceptuality of human rights at the cultural level.

Applying This Revisionary Understanding to the Confucian Tradition's Role in Intercultural Human Rights Dialogue

To clear the way for this application, I need first to consider some contemporary scholarly debate about universality versus relativism in human rights. This debate appears to take place on two levels. The first level involves explicit debate between competing conceptions of human rights, one of which emphasizes their universality as legal norms and the other emphasizing their particularity as moral norms (with the suggestion of their ideological adventitiousness as legal norms in the world community).[28] This level of debate is conducted among scholars of human rights per se. The second level of debate is more implicit coming as it does from scholars of particular cultural traditions who take differing positions about whether human rights are or can be compatible, conceptually and morally, with these traditions. At this second level, one encounters scholars who tend toward an incompatibility thesis as well as scholars who are open to finding compatibilities between human rights norms and culturally particular moral norms and idioms.[29]

While it is not possible to discuss in detail the work of scholars engaged in these debates, I do want to discuss certain general traits of their work that will help us to identify significant shortcomings in our consideration of human rights vis-à-vis the Confucian tradition. For convenience, I will use the simple labels of "universalists" and "particularists" to refer to the two camps that predominate at both levels of scholarly debate. Universalists tend to emphasize the universality of human rights as legal and moral norms as well as some sort of foundationalist epistemology to ground their status as universal moral rights.[30] Particularists, by contrast, tend either to deemphasize the legal status of human rights norms or to stress their roots in Western moral ideology (e.g., liberal individualism) as well as resisting the supposed legitimacy and persuasiveness of moral epistemology traced to and linked with the seventeenth- and

eighteenth-century Enlightenment period in the West.[31] In the latter case, they see moral norms and modes of reasoning as more significantly conditioned by historical and cultural context than may be admitted by universalists. Particularists also tend (1) to emphasize, in order to resist, the ideological individualism supposedly associated with civil-political human rights, and (2) to contrast the communitarian moral visions of non-Western societies and cultures with this ideological individualism.

In my view there are problems with the positions of both camps. With respect to the universalist position, there are dangers implicit in trying to justify *tout court* human rights by appealing to a contestable moral epistemology (e.g., Western foundationalism) in the international arena. Such a move not only undercuts the benefits attained by a two-level approach, but it also deflects attention away from the power and function of justification through negotiated pragmatic consensus, and enmeshes human rights in what could be endless epistemic uncertainty and debate. Moreover, such a monolithic approach to human rights justification runs the serious risk of interfering with the processes of both pragmatic negotiation and human rights dialogue among diverse cultural moral traditions.

For their part, human rights particularists can be charged with significant myopia about the complexity and historical development of human rights. The myopia stems from the failure to recognize that there are three, not just one, generations of human rights—civil-political, social-economic, and developmental-collective—and that the latter two generations significantly modify the ideological individualism that particularists associate with civil-political rights. Thus particularist arguments about tensions and incompatibilities between non-Western communitarian traditions, on the one hand, and civil-political individualist human rights, on the other, overlook possible (and I believe likely) compatibilities between these same traditions and social-economic, collective, and even civil-political rights (under our revised understanding). Some particularist comparisons between supposedly radically individualistic human rights and communitarian traditions may suffer from a further problem: some of the materials employed in the comparisons tend to emphasize rather exclusively classical texts from very ancient periods of those traditions, without giving proper attention to later texts and periods which might provide relevant data about the diversity of views internal to the traditions in their more modern form.

An example of a particularist comparison that illustrates these problems is provided by Henry Rosemont's article critiquing the relevance of human rights to the Confucian tradition.[32] In this article Rosemont not only assumes that human rights are exclusively civil and political individual rights—overlooking social-economic and collective rights as well as the nuances I have suggested with regard to a more communitarian understanding of civil-political rights—   39 but also confines his comparison to ancient Confucianism, rather than including within his scope of comparison later neo-Confucian developments as well. Strongly contrasting with this tendency toward problematic comparison is Wm. Theodore de Bary's earlier article.[33] After taking an explicitly historical view of "human rights as an evolving conception," de Bary identifies a range of Neo-Confucian thinkers, principles, and recommended reforms that seem to be plausibly compatible with selected first- and second-generation human rights: e.g., humane governance (nontorture, penal reform), fairness in taxation and charitable granaries (reform of social-economic conditions and allocation of material goods), legal reform and recognition of "the inherent worth of the individual" as well as "the essential voluntarism of the political and social order" (tendency in the direction of civil-political liberties understood as enpowerments to community involvement). While I admire Rosemont's work in Chinese philosophy generally, I am inclined to regard de Bary's approach as the more valid and useful when it comes to examining the possible place of human rights in the Confucian tradition.

I now want to offer a sketch of how human rights under my revised understanding can fit within the Confucian tradition. I shall do this in five steps. First, especially since I am not a scholar of Confucian tradition, it seems appropriate for me to outline my general understanding of those parameters of the tradition that may have a particular bearing on human rights. Second, in order to provide some hope and relevant background for this project, I shall mention briefly a historical contribution of the Confucian tradition to the Universal Declaration of Human Rights that appears to be little known. Third, I shall propose that all three generations of human rights, with varying degrees of emphasis, can be compatible with Confucian moral and political thought; that is, I shall offer as hypotheses for other's consideration how I regard human rights as fitting within this tradition. Fourth, in conformity with my two-level approach to human rights justification, I shall further suggest that it is fully open to the Confucian tradition to justify on its own terms, to its own participants, its agreement to participate in human rights consensus at the international level. Finally, I shall conclude by proposing that the two-level approach permits us to chart interactions in the future between the Confucian tradition and the international human rights community.

My understanding of the parameters of the Confucian tradition relevant to human rights is as follows: Confucian moral and political thought is basically communitarian in outlook: (1) emphasizing the fact that the human person is essentially a social being; (2) giving primacy of place to the duties that persons have to the common good of the community and the virtues needed for the fulfillment of these duties; and (3) casting reciprocal social relationships and roles (especially the Five Relationships) as fundamental to communal flourishing and its shared vision of the good. At the same time, the tradition also emphasizes the importance for all its participants, ranging from rulers to ordinary people, of moral self-cultivation, predicated on an innate moral potential to develop virtues of benevolence, righteousness, propriety, and discernment, and guided by paradigmatic moral exemplars (sages) who are themselves guided by the tradition's basic texts and the moral and political compasses contained therein. This strong orientation to persons in community is grounded in a vision of the interdependence of all beings in the universe, which in turn sustains a basic sympathy for the whole and its constitutive parts, in the image of extending care from family relationships into ever larger concentric circles of care. When one reviews the range of Confucian thinkers, from Confucius himself, through Mencius, to the Neo-Confucians such as Zhu Xi, Wang Yang-ming, and Huang Zongxi, one gains the sense that the Confucian moral and political tradition is greatly concerned about all those conditions—for example, social, economic, educational—that have a bearing on people's cultivation of their moral potential to flourish as responsible members of an organic community in a harmoniously functioning universe.[34]

Pier Cesare Bori, referring to records of the debates surrounding the drafting of the Universal Declaration of Human Rights, reports that the Confucian tradition, as represented by the Chinese delegate P. Chang, influenced the formulation of Article 1.[35] As reported by Bori, the first version of this article stated: "All men are brothers. As human beings with the gift of reason and members of a single family, they are free and equal in dignity and rights." With respect to this article, Chang argued for the inclusion of "two-men-mindedness" (the basic Confucian idea of *ren*) in addition to the mention of "reason." At the forefront of Chang's mind, suggests Bori, was the idea of a fundamental sympathy, benevolence, or compassion (as represented by Mencius) as constitutive of human beings generally. The wording finally adopted included "conscience" in addition to "reason," with the understanding that "conscience" was not the voice of an internal moral court but rather the emotional and sympathetic basis of morality, "a 'germ' objectively present" in all persons, "which reason must cultivate." Thus was a basic Confucian concept inscribed in the opening article of the Universal Declaration, a fact that ought to suggest to us (1) international human rights are not, contrary to the common perception, simply an ethnocentric Western construction, and (2) the Confucian tradition may well be compatible with and have more to contribute to a proper understanding of these rights.

Given the Confucian tradition's historical emphasis on the responsibility of the ruler to ensure the subsistence, livelihood, and education of the people as a qualification of political legitimacy (stemming from the Mencian notion of righteous revolt against an emperor who, in oppressing the people, loses the   41 mandate of Heaven)—it seems a further short step to contend that the tradition supports the second generation of human rights.[36] And in fact we can see this at work in the background of a long-standing openness of twentieth-century Chinese regimes to social and economic human rights as well as their efforts to better the material conditions of the people. The influence of Marxism may be in the foreground here, but there is evidence of Confucian influence as well. Ann Kent, a particularly sensitive interpreter of human rights in the contemporary Chinese context, argues persuasively that both Confucianism and Marxism tend to emphasize an organic society oriented to the primacy of the collective good over the individual and the responsibility of the ruler or state to ensure social stability and the material welfare of the people, as well as informal social mechanisms for adjudicating conflict.[37] And she relates the first two of these parallels or elective affinities in part to the Chinese openness to second generation human rights. My first hypothesis, then, is that the Confucian tradition is quite properly open to the recognition of socioeconomic human rights. Whether or not it chooses to employ the language of human rights, the tradition's emphasis on the importance of this subject matter indicates that its representatives can sensibly participate in an international consensus on their formulation.

My second hypothesis is that the Confucian tradition, at least in some of its phases, is also compatible with first-generation civil-political human rights. In his *Liberal Tradition in China*, de Bary argues persuasively that a number of Neo-Confucian thinkers put forward ideas of, respectively, the moral nature of humankind and individual perfectibility (Zhu Xi), autonomy of the moral mind and individual conscience (Cheng-Zhu), generalized human potential for sagehood (Cheng Yi, Zhu Xi), personalism understood as the concept of the person's flourishing in community with others (Cheng Yi, Zhu Xi), self-governing community and voluntarism at the local level (Zhu Xi, Wang Yang-ming), and even a reformed conception of the law as a check on political abuse as well as a conception of public education for enhancing people's political participation (Huang Zongxi).[38] While these ideas do not support a radically individualistic interpretation of civil-political rights—since the true person is construed as a thoroughly social being—they are quite compatible with such rights conceived as positive enpowerments for persons' involvement in and contribution to social and political processes aimed at communal flourishing. Moreover, there is no gainsaying the judgment by de Bary that Huang's ideas in particular "could have provided a framework for what we call today 'human rights,' " which I interpret to refer primarily but not exclusively to civil-political liberties. In sum, the Confucian liberal tradition seems in principle compatible with first generation human rights under the communitarian-open interpretation of those rights that I advanced earlier.

It also seems relevant to point out that some Confucian-influenced human rights activists appear to agree with this second hypothesis. For example, Kim Dae Jung, a Korean human rights activist, has publicly rebutted the challenge by Lee Kuan Yew, former prime minister of Singapore, to the relevance of human rights to East Asian societies.[39] In so doing, Kim Dae Jung self-consciously represents Confucian political philosophy as a tradition that incorporates a heritage of ideas and practices compatible with and open to civil-political human rights. As Confucianism reemerges as an increasingly important factor in the Chinese context, one can envisage internal cultural dialogues about, for example, the relative balance of civil-political and social-economic human rights that might result in a more explicit commitment to the former as well as the latter.

As a third hypothesis, I want to suggest that the Confucian world view also seems compatible with the third generation of developmental-collective human rights. This hypothesis is supported in part by the aforementioned notion of righteous rebellion by the people and by the Neo-Confucian emphasis on the principle of voluntarism in self-government in community structures, which taken together appear but a short step from collective rights to self-determination and development. But an even deeper consideration stems from what Tu Weiming has called "the highest Confucian ideal"—namely, "the unity of Man and Heaven, which defines humanity not only in anthropological terms but also in cosmological terms," extending Confucian humanism and its sense of moral responsibility to a planetary or even universal scale.[40] I wager that combining these elements—self-governance and the unity of Man and Heaven—would support not only Third and Fourth World developmental claims to participate in the power, wealth and common heritage of humankind, but also their rightful claims to peace and harmony on a total world scale. The Confucian moral and metaphysical vision—its one-bodiedness with Heaven and Earth and myriad things—is clearly intended to advance the welfare of the entire holistic community of interdependent beings, covering the subject matters of human rights and even extending these to "green" rights as well.

I suggested earlier that a two-level approach to human rights justification permits particular moral cultures to justify on their own terms to their own constituencies their agreement to participate in human rights consensus at the international level, where that consensus is itself justified on pragmatic moral grounds. This means that the recognition of particular human rights may be justified at the internal level in terms of Confucian moral categories and idioms. Some scholars of the Confucian tradition have maintained that, internally, this would not be possible because the tradition lacks the conceptual resources to do so.[41] The reason given is that the Confucian tradition is a virtue-based communitarian morality that can have no room for the concept or recognition of

43

rights, human or otherwise. There are at least three lines of counter-response to such a contention. One is to show that communitarian traditions do not, simply by virtue of their community-orientation, lack the conceptual resources for handling human rights. A second is to show that the Confucian tradition in particular does not lack such resources. And a third is to show that even if the tradition lacked rights conceptuality per se, it could nonetheless use its resources to justify its agreement to participate in international human rights consensus.

The first line of counterresponse is demonstrable in light of a number of considerations. First, there are communitarian moral traditions which do in fact recognize the categories of rights and human rights (for example, varieties of Christian moral traditions, including most prominently Catholic social teachings, which simultaneously reject radical individualism, advance a thoroughly social understanding of the person and the importance of community as well as duties and virtues oriented to the common good, and yet accept human rights in their three generations) and varieties of indigenous cultural moral traditions, which are thoroughly communitarian in outlook and yet build in recognitions of all three types of human rights (otherwise the draft declaration of indigenous peoples' human rights would not be possible as it stands).[42] Second, there appears to be no logical reason for contending that rights-discourse is incompatible with communitarian traditions, so long as we resist asservations that such discourse must presuppose assumptions about the radical autonomy of persons abstracted from communal bonds, social roles and historical and cultural traditions.[43] As I have suggested, such assumptions seem manifestly inapplicable when considering the meaning and history of human rights. Moreover, as Seung Hwan Lee has pointedly argued, referring to the work of Joel Feinberg, it is difficult to conceive of any moral tradition which incorporates practices of property, promises, contracts, loans, marriages, partnerships, etc. as devoid of conceptual counterparts (to duties) that have the function of rights.[44] As he says, "in this sense, the concept of rights is indispensable for our moral life regardless of social ideals (whether communitarianism or liberalism) and regardless of the types of morality (whether virtue-based or rights-based) we adopt." Indeed, I know of no cultural moral tradition which lacks a sense of claims that can be made against others in the context of cooperative social practices relying upon interpersonal or intergroup expectancies produced by the behavior they regulate.[45]

In the particular case of the Confucian tradition, Lee also convincingly argues that there are "plentiful instances from Confucian literatures" of "the substantive content of rights," ranging from Mencius' examples of entrustments of the care of one's cattle or one's family to another (with implicit duties and rights) and his defense of a people's apparent "right to revolt against tyrannies,"

to Chung-ying Cheng's and Hyung I. Kim's interpretations of *yi* (though I concede that there may be interpretative issues with regard to these examples).[46] And I believe that de Bary's lectures on Neo-Confucian liberalism and its openness to human rights categories reinforce the persuasiveness of a compatibility between Confucian thought and human rights. This suggests to me that the Confucian tradition does have the conceptual and moral resources to recognize and even justify internally international human rights. Even if this were not the case, I think that de Bary's discussion makes it clear that, even without the conceptuality of rights per se, the tradition has the resources to recognize and justify the subject matters of human rights, that is, to support the importance of meeting people's social and economic needs and to support the civil and political enpowerments that people need for communal self-governance and personal self-cultivation. That is, even if the tradition itself preferred not to use the languages of rights or human rights, those resources seem more than adequate to support the tradition's agreement to participate in and abide by, on pragmatic moral grounds, an international human rights consensus.

On the matter of explicit procedures and appeals within the Confucian tradition for justifying internally its agreement to participate in international human rights consensus, I suspect that there are myriad possibilities, and I am content to let representatives of the tradition handle that matter. My own sense of those possibilities ranges across appeals to the moral compasses and standards contained within classical texts (e.g., *Analects*, *The Mencius*), to various sages, teachers, and advisers who exemplify the Way (i.e, appeals to the behavior and thought of paradigmatic characters), to the normative content of Confucian virtues as expressive of human moral destiny, to the *li* (principles, patterns) revealed by the innate heart/mind or its intuitive practical moral knowledge, etc.[47] With any of these appeals, it is important to be clear that the tradition need not derive and justify human rights per se from its own moral categories (though that may be possible as well, as I have suggested), but only use them to justify its agreement to participate in and abide by the pragmatic intentional consensus for reasons pertaining to its own vision of human moral nature and welfare.[48] This constitutes a different and possibly more attainable burden of justification than that of having to forge its own internal human rights tradition (though the resources seem to be present for this as well).

Let me now recapitulate the three theses proposed in this section of the paper: (1) that the Confucian tradition has moral content overlapping with international human rights in their three generations; (2) that this overlapping content can be plausibly framed internally in the idiom of human rights; and (3) that this overlapping content, even if not framed in human rights language, is sufficient for the tradition to justify internally its agreement to participate in an international human rights consensus.[49] Much of what I have argued supports all three theses. Confucian parallels to the three generations of human rights are intended to support at least thesis (1), though they have some bearing on theses (2) and (3) as well. The points about communitarian traditions in general and the Confucian tradition in particular being compatible with idioms of rights and human rights are intended to support thesis (2). And the point that even if thesis (2) were resisted for some reason, the Confucian tradition has resources sufficient for justifying its participation in an international human rights consensus is an articulation of thesis (3) that combines thesis (1) with my earlier discussion of a two-level approach to human rights justification.

Finally, I think it important to point out that the two-level approach to justifying human rights permits us in principle to chart past and future interactions or reciprocal influences between the Confucian tradition and the international human rights community.[50] The historical contribution of the Confucian tradition to the Universal Declaration of Human Rights illustrates one influence of the tradition on an international human rights negotiation. I see no reason why Confucian moral and political thought could not make further contributions—for example, strengthening a more communitarian-receptive understanding of civil-political liberties as enpowerments aimed at community involvement and flourishing; strengthening the thesis about the interdependence and indivisibility of the three generations of human rights; advancing the cause of those developmental-collective human rights particularly concerned with matters of peace, harmony and ecological responsibility. Moreover, I believe that the tradition's further involvement in human rights dialogues, at national and international levels, might result in its gaining clarity on its own commitment to the subject matters of human rights. Nascent and prescient resources of the tradition that bear on human rights may well be highlighted and brought into promising intercultural dialogue. With the ever-increasing awareness of global diversity, the recognition that a greater number of voices need to be heard at a higher degree of participation might lead to more subtle accounts of human rights at both of the levels that I have discussed here.

Acknowledgments

I wish to acknowledge my gratitude to a number of colleagues for their critical comments and support in preparing this paper. First and foremost, I am especially grateful to Wm. Theodore de Bary for organizing and inviting me to participate in the 1995 Conference on Confucianism and Human Rights on which the present volume is based. His vision for this dialogue was inspiring. Second, I am indebted to all the conference participants and authors for their provocative contributions and most especially to Irene Bloom, Louis Henkin, and Henry Rosemont for their critical responses to aspects of my paper. Third,

I thank my colleagues at Brown University for their critical feedback on this paper as well as earlier and concurrent ones, most especially John Reeder, Mark Unno, Hal Roth, Giles Milhaven, Wendell Dietrich, Aaron Stalnaker, Andrew Flescher and Jung Lee. Finally, I owe a debt of gratitude to my former collaborators, Bruce Grelle (California State University, Chico), John Kelsay (Florida State University) and Ann Mayer (University of Pennsylvania).

Notes

1. See, for example, John Kelsay and Sumner B. Twiss, eds., *Religion and Human Rights* (New York: The Project on Religion and Human Rights, 1994), and Sumner B. Twiss and Bruce Grelle, "Human Rights and Comparative Religious Ethics: A New Venue," *The Annual of the Society of Christian Ethics*, 1995, pp. 21–48.

2. This framework is more extensively elaborated in my concurrent essay, "Comparative Ethics and Intercultural Human Rights Dialogues: A Programmatic Inquiry," in Lisa S. Cahill and James F. Childress, eds., *Christian: Problems and Prospects* (Cleveland: Pilgrim Press, 1996), ch. 21, an essay which was inspired in part by my experience at the 1995 Conference on Confucianism and Human Rights on which the present volume is based. A few of my reflections in that essay are incorporated in the present paper.

3. See *The International Bill of Human Rights* (New York: United Nations, 1993), which is also reprinted in many volumes dealing with the subject matter of international human rights. This summary characterization is drawn in part from "Terms: 'Human Rights' and 'Religion,' " worked out in consultation with Kusumita Pedersen (former Executive Director of the Project on Religion and Human Rights), in Kelsay and Twiss, *Religion and Human Rights*, pp. iii–iv.

4. This characterization is articulated by many human rights scholars; see, for example, Henry Shue, *Basic Rights: Subsistence, Affluence, and U.S. Foreign Policy* (Princeton: Princeton University Press, 1980), ch. 1, and Jack Donnelly, *The Concept of Human Rights* (New York: St. Martin's Press, 1985), chs. 1–2. The source for the subsequent reference to Ronald Dworkin's notion of rights as trumps is his justly famous *Taking Rights Seriously* (Cambridge: Harvard University Press, 1977).

5. This point contrasts strongly with the approach of Henry Rosemont developed in his "Why Take Rights Seriously? A Confucian Critique," in Leroy S. Rouner, ed., *Human Rights and the World's Religions* (Notre Dame, Ind.: University of Notre Dame Press, 1988, pp. 167–82, and rearticulated in his contribution to the present volume.

6. For some recent illuminating and provocative discussions of this issue, see Neil Stammers, "Human Rights and Power," *Political Studies* 41 (1993): 70–82, and "A Critique of Social Approaches to Human Rights," *Human Rights Quarterly* 17 (1995): 488–508.

7. This section of the present paper is drawn in part from Twiss and Grelle, "Human Rights and Comparative Religious Ethics," pp. 30–35. The entire discussion is now

more extensively developed and refined in my "Comparative Ethics and Intercultural Human Rights Dialogues."

8. The following reflections were inspired in part by Michael Walzer, "Moral Minimalism," reprinted in his *Thick and Thin: Moral Argument at Home and Abroad* (South Bend, Ind.: University of Notre Dame Press, 1994), pp. 1–19. This issue was discussed in a preliminary way in "Concluding Reflections by the Editors," in Kelsay and Twiss, *Religion and Human Rights*, pp. 113–23; see especially pp. 118–20.

9. This worry was quite pointedly articulated by some participants at a Conference on Religion and Human Rights, sponsored by the Project on Religion and Human Rights and held in New York City, May 22–24, 1994, as well as some participants at the 1995 Conference on Confucianism and Human Rights.

10. Henry Rosemont makes such criticisms in his contribution to the present volume.

11. For a revealing discussion of this pragmatic process of negotiation by one of its participants, see John P. Humphrey, *Human Rights and the United Nations: A Great Adventure* (Dobbs Ferry, N.Y.: Transnational Publishers, 1984).

12. See Walzer, "Moral Minimalism," esp. pp. 17–18.

13. Burns H. Weston, "Human Rights," reprinted in Richard Pierre Claude and Burns H. Weston, eds., *Human Rights in the World Community: Issues and Action* (2d ed.; Philadelphia: University of Pennsylvania Press, 1992), pp. 14–30, see especially pp. 14–21.

14. I am indebted to Louis Henkin, a participant at the 1995 Conference on Confucianism and Human Rights, for reminding me of this background influence of F. D. R.'s "Four Freedoms" speech. See also Louis Henkin, *The Age of Rights* (New York: Columbia University Press, 1990), pp. 16–18.

15. See, for example, Adamantia Pollis, "Human Rights in Liberal, Socialist, and Third World Perspective," in Claude and Weston, *Human Rights*, pp. 146–56, which is a revised version of her original essay published in Peter Schwab and Adamantia Pollis, eds., *Towards a Human Rights Framework* (New York: Praeger, 1982), pp. 1–26.

16. Weston, "Human Rights," pp. 18–20.

17. See David Hollenbach, "A Communitarian Reconstruction of Human Rights: Contributions from Catholic Tradition," in R. Bruce Douglas and David Hollenbach, eds., *Catholicism and Liberalism: Contributions to American Public Philosophy* (Cambridge: Cambridge University Press, 1994), pp. 127–50. Weston himself says that "What is constant in this first-generation conception . . . is the notion of liberty, a shield that safe-guards the individual alone *and* in association with others, against the abuse . . . of political authority" ("Human Rights," p. 18, my italics).

18. For empirical data on this thesis and connection see, for example, Han S. Park, "Correlates of Human Rights: Global Tendencies," *Human Rights Quarterly* 9 (1987): 405–13, including references.

19. As Weston says, while these rights project "the notion of holistic community interests," each right also "manifests an individual as well as collective dimension."

"Human Rights," p. 20.

20. See Consultation Group on Universality vs. Human Rights, Sumner B. Twiss as principal coordinating author, with Abdullahi A. An-Na'im, Ann Elizabeth Mayer, and William Wipfler, "Universality vs. Relativism in Human Rights," in Kelsay and Twiss, *Religion and Human Rights*, pp. 30–59; see especially pp. 56–57; and Twiss and Grelle, "Human Rights," especially pp. 39–46.

21. Weston puts the point this way: "Essentially individualistic societies tolerate, even promote certain collectivist values; likewise, essentially communitarian societies tolerate, even promote certain individualistic values. Ours is a more-or-less, not an either-or, world." "Human Rights," p. 21.

22. The issues addressed in this paragraph are much more extensively developed and refined in my "Comparative Ethics and Intercultural Human Rights Dialogues." In that paper I argue that international human rights incorporate intercultural agreement on the importance of a sort of "homeostatic balancing" (in the words of Erich Loewy) of communal and individual interests for both liberal and communitarian societies and traditions. See Erich H. Loewy, *Freedom and Community: The Ethics of Interdependence* (Albany: State University of New York Press, 1993).

23. Strictly speaking, only states make formal human rights agreements, but arguably these states represent diverse cultural moral traditions.

24. For a similar approach to human rights justification, see Tore Lindholm, "Prospects for Research on the Cultural Legitimacy of Human Rights: The Cases of Liberalism and Marxism," in Abdullahi An-Na'im, ed., *Human Rights in Cross-Cultural Perspectives: A Quest for Consensus* (Philadelphia: University of Pennsylvania Press, 1992), pp. 387–426 (see especially pp. 395–401). Although Lindholm's justificatory strategy and my own two-level approach share significant similarities in aim and logic, there are also important differences.

25. I suspect that more could be done to develop the logic of this pragmatic and negotiated international consensus along the lines of, for example, John Reeder's version of neo-pragmatism, but I save this task for another occasion. See John P. Reeder, Jr., "Foundations Without Foundationalism," in Gene Outka and John Reeder, Jr., eds., *Prospects for a Common Morality* (Princeton: Princeton University Press, 1993), pp. 191–214.

26. For a critical assessment of the agenda of eco-Buddhism, see Ian Harris, "Causations and *Telos*: The Problem of Buddhist Environmental Ethics," *Journal of Buddhist Ethics* 1 (1994), an electronic journal available at *http://www.psu.edu/jbe/jbe.html*. For contrasting perspectives on the uses of human rights discourse *within* Buddhism, see Damien Keown, "Are There Human Rights in Buddhism?" and Kenneth Inada, "A Buddhist Response to the Nature of Human Rights," both in *Journal of Buddhist Ethics* 2 (1995).

27. During the 1995 Conference on Confucianism and Human Rights, a number of participants tended to interpret the international human rights consensus—which I regard as intentionally theory-thin—exclusively in terms of contemporary political philosophies in the American context (e.g., Rawls, Dworkin) and their strong commitments to certain understandings of the nature of the self, the meaning of rationality, and the

priority of the right over good. From the point of view developed here, however, these latter philosophies are no more than expressions of one particular cultural moral tradition's understanding of human rights at an internal level. It is a mistake to view this understanding as necessarily inscribed and operative at the international level. Such a view threatens to disrupt at the outset the attempt to investigate how the Confucian tradition might relate itself to the international human rights consensus understood as a theory-thin pragmatic moral agreement among diverse cultures.

28. The initial paragraphs of this section are drawn from Twiss and Grelle, "Human Rights," pp. 36–39. The first level of scholarly debate is represented in many anthologies, for example, Adamantia Pollis and Peter Schwab, eds., *Human Rights: Cultural and Ideological Perspectives* (New York: Praeger, 1979), and An-Na'im, *Human Rights in Cross-Cultural Perspectives*.

29. The second level of debate is well illustrated by the contributions in Rouner, *Human Rights and the World's Religions*.

30. See, for example, Alan Gewirth, *Human Rights: Essays on Justification and Applications* (Chicago: University of Chicago Press, 1982), and his more recent "Common Morality and the Community of Rights," in Outka and Reeder, eds., *Prospects for a Common Morality*, pp. 29–52, as well as the illuminating discussion and critique of foundationalist approaches to human rights in Michael Freeman, "The Philosophical Foundations of Human Rights," *Human Rights Quarterly* 16/3 (August 1994): 491–514.

31. For illuminating examples of particularist approaches, see Adamantia Pollis and Peter Schwab, "Human Rights: A Western Construct with Limited Applicability," in Pollis and Schwab, *Human Rights*, pp. 3–18, and Alison Dundes Rentelen, *International Human Rights: Universalism Versus Relativism* (Newbury Park, Calif.: Sage Publication, 1990).

32. Henry Rosemont, "Why Take Rights Seriously? A Confucian Critique," in Rouner, *Human Rights*, pp. 167–82; see also his "Interlude: Modern Western and Ancient Chinese Concepts of the Person," in Henry Rosemont, *A Chinese Mirror: Moral Reflections on Political Economy and Society* (La Salle, Ill.: Open Court, 1991), ch. 3.

33. Wm. Theodore de Bary, "Neo-Confucianism and Human Rights," in Rouner, *Human Rights*, pp. 183–98; the following quotations are from pp. 184 and 197, respectively. See also de Bary's *The Liberal Tradition in China* (Hong Kong: Chinese University Press, 1983; reprint New York: Columbia University Press, 1983) and his *Waiting for the Dawn: A Plan for the Prince* (New York: Columbia University Press, 1993).

34. My gratitude to my colleague Harold D. Roth for our discussions and courses together, which have focused in part on Confucian materials, especially Confucius, Mencius, and Wang Yang-ming, as well as excellent secondary sources, some of which I cite here.

35. Pier Cesare Bori, *From Hermeneutics to Ethical Consensus Among Cultures* (Atlanta, Ga.: Scholars Press, 1994), ch. 7 ("Human Rights and Human Nature"); the following quotations are from pp. 67, 69, and 70, respectively. In her contribution to the present vol-

ume, Irene Bloom discusses a functionally similar example with regard to a Confucian contribution to the 1950 UNESCO "Statement on Race."

36. *Mencius*, trans. D. C. Lau (London: Penguin Books, 1970), 1B:8 and 1B:12; see also 1A:7, 4A:1, 7B:14. If interpreted as a right, this notion of righteous revolt would appear to be a collective right regarding social and economic conditions.

37. Ann Kent, *Between Freedom and Subsistence: China and Human Rights* (Hong Kong and New York: Oxford University Press, 1993), ch. 2.

38. See de Bary, *The Liberal Tradition in China*, especially pp. 12, 20, 27, 32–33, 49–50, 85–85, for succinct summaries of these points; the following quotation is found on p. 85.

39. Kim Dae Jung, "Is Culture Destiny? The Myth of Asia's Anti-Democratic Values," *Foreign Affairs* 73/6 (November/December 1994): 189–94.

40. Tu Wei-ming, *Confucian Thought: Selfhood as Creative Transformation* (Albany: State University of New York Press, 1985), pp. 171–81; quotation from p. 180.

41. For example, Roger T. Ames, "Rites as Rights: The Confucian Alternative," in Rouner, *Human Rights*, pp. 199–216 (see especially pp. 203–09); Rosemont, "Why Take Rights Seriously?" especially pp. 175–76, and *A Chinese Mirror*, ch. 3; Tu Wei-ming, *Way, Learning, and Politics: Essays ont he Confucian Intellectual* (Albany: State University of New York Press, 1993), pp. 30–31; and Tu Wei-ming, Milan Hejtmanek, and Alan Wachman, eds., *The Confucian World Observed: A Contemporary Discussion of Confucian Humanism in East Asia* (Honolulu: The East-West Center, 1992), p. 17. From their contributions to the 1995 Conference on Confucianism and Human Rights and to the present volume, I gather that Tu may have changed his mind about this matter, while Rosemont has not.

42. See, for example, Hollenbach, "A Communitarian Reconstruction of Human Rights," and Alexander Ewen, ed., *Voice of Indigenous Peoples: Native People Address the United Nations* (Santa Fe, N.M.: Clear Light, 1994), Appendix B, pp. 159–74, which reprints the ext of the UN Draft Declaration of the Rights of Indigenous Peoples.

43. This is an indirect response to Henry Rosemont's paper in the present volume. I question the accuracy of the assumption that autonomy as Rosemont describes it is a strong premise of international human rights. Does the insistence on the importance of people's civil and political liberties presuppose a radically autonomous person? Cannot such rights construed as social enpowerments be compatible with a society based on a relational conception of the self? Though I agree that in a communitarian society there will be issues of how to balance civil-political liberties against social-economic rights, it strikes me that significant civil-political liberties can serve very well the pursuit of the social good in a communitarian society. This entire matter is discussed much more extensively in my "Comparative Ethics and Intercultural Human Rights Dialogue."

44. See Feinberg's justly famous and influential essay, "The Nature and Value of Rights," reprinted in his *Rights, Justice, and the Bounds of Liberty: Essays in Social Philosophy* (Princeton: Princeton University Press, 1980), pp. 143–55. Seung-Hwan Lee is one philosopher who makes excellent use of Feinberg in Seung-Hwan Lee, "Was There a

Concept of Rights in Confucian Virtue-Based Morality?" *Journal of Chinese Philosophy* 19/3 (September 1992): 241–61; see especially pp. 241–45; the following quotation is from p. 245.

45. I am perfectly willing to concede that claims implicit in social practices of the sort mentioned here are a far cry from recognizing international human rights. In order to close this gap a bit more, we need only to consider the functional requisites that must be addressed by any cultural moral tradition which hopes to maintain itself over time and serve its members in trying to lead a decent life: for example, security of the person, satisfaction of basic social and economic needs, some notion of fair procedure in dispute settlement, protection of "natural" interpersonal relations, etc. Whether or not these are given the status of explicit rights, a viable tradition will need to treat such items as deserving of priority, and that, combined with implicit rights or conceptual counterparts to rights in social practices, seems sufficient to permit a cultural moral tradition to at least make sense of the point and subject matter of human rights.

46. Lee, "Is There a Concept of Rights," pp. 246–50; quotations from pp. 246 and 248, respectively. See also Mencius, 2B:4 and 7A:33. See also Chung-ying Cheng's contribution to the present volume. Mark Unno has suggested to me that as a further response to those who find human rights discourse incompatible with Confucian thought, I mention the pragmatic situations faced by individuals who participate in social and cultural practices that bring together more than one set of moral discourses. One of his examples was that of a Chinese government official working in international trade who must at some level implicitly accept the discourse of human rights, since, for example, "most favored nation status" is inseparable from human rights issues. If this same official embraces or appeals to Confucian morality, then he or she must think about how human rights as a historical discourse is related to Confucianism. Prescinding from issues of using human rights in American foreign policy, I think that the general point is well-taken: namely, that real-life situations often compel consideration of how moral discourses can be negotiated in such a way that one acknowledges the fact that one may already be subscribing to the validity of these discourses in a practical sense. This point broadens and at the same time makes more vivid the importance of identifying compatibilities between the Confucian tradition and international human rights, as well as seeking a modus vivendi for how this tradition can participate on pragmatic grounds in international human rights consensus.

47. Certain of these appeals and lines of argument are developed by other papers in the present volume; see, for example, the contributions of Irene Bloom, Chung-ying Cheng, Wejen Chang, and John Schrecker.

48. Randall Peerenboom's interpretation of Confucius's philosophy as "anthropocentric pragmatism," as contrasted with the foundationalism of Huang-Lao, may lend some support to the acceptability of this pragmatic line of justification within the Confucian tradition; see R. P. Peerenboom, *Law and Morality in Ancient China: The Silk Manuscripts of Huang-Lao* (Albany: State University of New York Press, 1993), ch. 4. Here it might be

appropriate to mention that this particular strategy diverges from Peerenboom's own attempt to project a Chinese theory of rights in his "What's Wrong with Chinese Rights? Towards a Theory of Rights with Chinese Characteristics," *Harvard Human Rights Journal* 6 (1993), pp. 29–57.

49. My thanks to my colleague John P. Reeder for suggesting that I develop this recapitulation.

50. Here it is appropriate to cite Andrew Nathan's judgment that "there are common points between the Western and Chinese conceptions of rights, such as a belief in the social usefulness of free speech . . . [which] do constitute a basis for dialogue and possible mutual influence," as well as his view that, "This Chinese intellectual tradition contains many of the building blocks of a more liberal, pluralistic theory of rights, and the new opening to the West has made many of the resources of foreign intellectual traditions available for fresh consideration." Andrew J. Nathan, "Sources of Chinese Rights Thinking," in R. Randle Edwards, Louis Henkin, and Andrew J. Nathan, *Human Rights in Contemporary China* (New York: Columbia University Press, 1986), pp. 125–64; quotations from pp. 163–64.

2

Human Rights: A Bill of Worries

Henry Rosemont Jr.

Although the scholarly study of Confucianism in the West looks very different today than when it began with the first Jesuit mission to China, at least one feature of those studies has remained constant: Western investigators have sought similarities and differences between Confucian principles and those principles embedded in their own Western conceptual framework.

Originally that framework was Christianity, and beginning with Matteo Ricci, running through Leibniz, and even extending in some circles to the present, many scholars have declared Confucianism—in either its classical or Song formulations, or both—to be compatible with basic Christian principles and beliefs. Other scholars, beginning with Ricci's successor Nicolo Longobardi, running through Malebranche, and again, even extending to the present, found Confucian principles and beliefs sufficiently un-Christian to necessitate their rejection as a precondition for conversion. But however much these two groups differed in their analyses and evaluations, they shared the same presupposition in examining Confucian thought, namely, that the fundamental principles and beliefs of Christianity were universal, and, therefore, binding on all peoples.[1]

To be sure, not all Christians agreed on what the fundamental principles and beliefs of their faith were, or ought to be; there was much room for theological and metaphysical debate. But at least a few beliefs were indeed fundamental, paramount among them being the Passion of Christ—from which much else of Christianity follows.

A different conceptual framework is employec
Confucianism. Most Western scholars—and no†
ilarities and differences between Confucian m
beliefs and those embedded in a conceptual f†
concept of human rights. While Christian c
search, they no longer have pride of place in the gi⌐
logical studies.[2]

This change has been significant, and it is equally significant
scholars have argued cogently that much of Confucianism is compatible w..
the modern Western moral and political principles and beliefs centered in the
concept of human rights.[3]

What has not changed, however (or so it seems to me), is that contemporary scholars share a common presupposition, in this case the presupposition
that the rights-based Western conceptual framework is universal, and therefore
binding on all peoples.

To be sure, within this conceptual framework of rights, there is room for
legitimate disagreement (just as in the framework of Christianity). For those
who embrace deontological moral and political theories, especially of a Kantian sort, rights are absolutely central; whereas for most consequentialists, they
are more adjunctive. And rights theorists invoke, or deny, differing notions of
natural rights, of inalienable or defeasible rights, negative and positive rights,
rights as trumps, and much more.[4] But again, some things are fundamental,
paramount among them being that human beings are, or ought to be seen as,
free, autonomous individuals. If, for Father Ricci and his colleagues, the rejection of the Passion of Christ was tantamount to turning the world over to the
Devil, so today the rejection of the free, autonomous individual seems tantamount to turning the world over to repressive governments and other terrorist
organizations. But just as one can be skeptical of Christianity without endors-
ing Old Scratch, so too, I believe, can one be skeptical of a rights-based conceptual framework without giving any aid or comfort to the Husseins, Milos-
evics, or Li Pengs of this world.

My own skepticism is directed not toward any particular moral or political
theory in which rights play a role, but toward the more foundational view of
human beings as free, autonomous individuals on which all such theories more
or less rest.[5] The study of classical Confucianism has suggested to me that rights-
oriented moral and political theories based on this view are flawed, and that a
different vocabulary for moral and political discourse is needed. The concept of
human rights and related concepts clustered around it, like liberty, the individual, property, autonomy, freedom, reason, choice, and so on, do not capture
what it is we believe to be the inherent sociality of human beings; they have
served to obscure the wrongness of the radical maldistribution of the world's

—both intra- and internationally—and even more fundamentally, such
pts cannot, I believe, be employed to produce a coherent and consistent
ory, much less a theory that is in accord with our basic moral intuitions.[6]

I am not the only philosopher to study classical Confucianism who has
come to this (tentative) conclusion. Herbert Fingarette, for example, has said:

> I am quite prepared to attack the doctrine of individual rights—attack it at least to
> the extent of arguing that it is not so purely beneficent a doctrine as we tend to
> assume today. Along with its major benefits, it has profound potential as a social-
> ly disruptive and anti-human force. It is against the background of a Confucian vi-
> sion of human life that this corrosive effect of a rights-based morality comes clear-
> ly into focus.[7]

I have not, however, become highly skeptical of rights-based moral and
political philosophies solely from the study of the *Lun Yu* and related texts. I am
also a citizen of the United States,[8] and am increasingly struck by two unique
features of it: "rights talk" more thoroughly permeates our moral and political
discourse than in any other country, and second, we are the world's most morally conflicted society; which, to my mind, can hardly be merely a coincidence.

There are, of course, numerous conflicts in the rest of the world today, ranging from the mildly to the unspeakably violent: Israelis versus Palestinians, Irish
Catholics versus Irish Protestants, Russians versus Chechnyans, Hutus versus
Tutsis, Serbs versus Bosnians and more. These and other conflicts seem to defy
settlement because of the hatred that characterize them, hatreds rooted in
economic, cultural, and historical circumstances that are exceedingly difficult
to overcome.

The situation in the United States is rather different. To be sure, some mili-
tiamen truly hate anyone who works for, or supports, the government, and some
fundamentalists believe that the *Roe vs. Wade* decision was not simply wrong-
headed, but positively evil.

Yet the great majority of Americans are not—or at least not yet—so rigid
and narrow in their beliefs and attitudes. Although firmly in what is called the
pro-choice camp, I am acutely aware of the basic decency of most of the abortion opponents I know. I still believe affirmative action is needed, but know
nonracist, principled opponents of it. I do not hate these people, and certainly do not think they are bent on evil; many of them I respect and admire. Nor
do I think I am in the least bit strange in this regard: I would hazard the generalization that virtually every U.S. reader of this volume could and would
make the same statement.

If this all-too-facile view of American society is granted, we must address
the question of what causes these conflicts. Is there some *fact* about fetuses, or

women's bodies, such that if everyone was aware of them, the abortion controversy would be resolved? Do the arguments of either side display faulty premises or invalid reasoning? I think not. Rather do I think the conceptual framework of rights, within which human beings are seen as free, rationally choosing autonomous individuals, is at the heart of the problem. As soon as one side speaks of a right to individual life as basic, and the other claims as basic the rights of every rational individual to choose what happens to her body, an irreconcilable moral conflict is guaranteed.

A fairly similar case can be made for the issue of affirmative action, or welfare, capital punishment, euthanasia, or indeed virtually every moral and political conflict that is rending the American social fabric today. More generally, it has been uniformly presumed that individual rights and social justice are, or can be made, compatible concepts ("with liberty and justice for all"). But the evidence is mounting that such is not the case: a large number of very fine minds in the fields of law, politics, philosophy, and religion have grappled long and hard with these problems, with no consensus on how to solve any of them; indeed, virtually all of the conflicts have become even more intense, with dialogue giving way to diatribe, peaceful demonstrations to homicide.

One major reason for this lack of consensus, I submit, is the failure to make plausible the idea of extending the concept of basic human rights from the civil and political realms—where it originated—to the social and economic. If I am essentially a freely choosing autonomous individual, it is easy to understand my demands that, *ceteris paribus*, neither the state nor anyone else abridge my freedom to choose. But how do such essential individuals demand a job or health care or an education? There is a logical gap here, which no one has successfully bridged yet. It is difficult to argue, from the mere premise that every human being is a free, autonomous individual, to the conclusion that every human being has a right to employment. Something more is needed, but I myself cannot think of what that something would be, unless it conflicted with our image of the free, autonomous individual, which is the foundation of the concept of basic human rights.

That is to say, the many people who have called for "second generation" rights as enumerated in the 1948 United Nations Declaration have clearly been concerned with distributive rather than procedural justice, hence the call for social and economic rights. But jobs, adequate housing, health care, and so on, do not fall from the sky. They are human creations, and no one has been able to show how I can demand that other human beings create these goods for me without them surrendering the "first generation" or civil and political rights which accrue to them by virtue of their being free, autonomous individuals.[9]

Consider affirmative action again. One of the most well-known of rights theorists, Ronald Dworkin, has argued cogently that the right to equal consideration is the most basic of all.[10] Rhetoric aside, affirmative action, by defini-   57 tion, entails preferential treatment, hence the basic right of equal consideration will be considered only briefly for those on the wrong side of the preferences. It is in this way that not alone racists, sexists, and angry white males might oppose affirmative action; if one's central moral and political vision is grounded in the inviolable individual rights of free, autonomous individuals, the opposition can be highly principled.

As noted earlier, I have supported affirmative action, but I do not rely on the argument that because of past discrimination, the rights of women and minorities could somehow "trump" the rights of others. Nor do I claim that affirmative action is fair, because it obviously is not. Rather must I maintain that it is less unfair than the system of white male privilege that preceded it, but in order to make my argument at all compelling I must appeal to principles of distributive justice which do not square well with the notion that all freely choosing autonomous individuals have the same inviolable basic rights on which procedural justice rests.[11]

Of course not everyone would agree with Dworkin that the right to equal consideration is the most basic right of all. But most Americans must take it as among the more basic, because I can give no other explanation of why there is always such a hue and cry when the media report a new study which ostensibly shows that women do not do as well in some areas as men, or African-Americans as well as whites, Herrnstein and Murray's *The Bell Curve* being only the most recent example.[12] Some people hail these studies as the truth, others dismiss them as sexist or racist. But what is the fuss all about? In a truly decent society there would be interesting and productive work for everyone, and in such a society the obvious differences between people would not be of major consequence, no matter whether the differences were hereditary or environmental in origin. I personally do not believe these studies show what they are purported to show, but even if they did, my response would be: "So what?" If, however, I hold equal consideration as a basic individual right, then I must be greatly exercised to learn that some fundamental inequalities are genetically determined, for it *must* follow that not everyone can be considered equal in all ethically relevant respects.

These and similar issues do not regularly come to the surface in our discourse, and when they do, tend to be pasted over or dealt with in ways that are becoming increasingly *ad hoc*, which is, I maintain, a function of the pervasiveness of rights language in our moral and political deliberations; there doesn't seem to be any alternative. To take another example, there is growing worldwide concern about the loss of our woodlands and rain forests. One ingenious response to this concern has been to claim that while trees are not sentient creatures, corporations aren't either; and if the latter have rights, and hence legal standing, so too might trees.[13] Now I applaud any effort to rein in the rapacious lumber industry, but isn't there a hint of desperation in having to claim that trees have rights? This claim must also strike us as bizarre, because basic rights stem from our being freely choosing individuals, and trees are neither free nor decision-makers, at least according to our current botanical understanding.

The same may be said for the rights of animals, or the rights of the unborn to inherit a healthy and genetically diversified natural environment; animals and future generations aren't free either, and cannot make choices. Nor can any of these groups respect our rights, which further vitiates the plausibility of according them rights: the notion of reciprocal obligations to respect rights is lost in all these cases.

As an aside on this point, I would take a cue from the writings of Thomas Berry with respect to the spiritual dimension of our lives.[14] I believe we fundamentally misunderstand our human relations to trees, animals, our great-great grandchildren, and the natural world that sustains us by seeing them all as rival rights claimants. This view must see us as essentially distinct from the entire nonhuman world, in the same way that free, autonomous individuals are already cut off from each other in the original position. That each of us is theoretically an isolate can be seen from the fact that 99% of the time I can fully respect your first generation civil and political rights simply by ignoring you. You certainly have a right to speak, but no right to make me listen; here, too, reciprocity is lost.

Now to all of these objections to various facets of the concept of rights I have all too quickly sketched, replies can of course be made, and have been made. Yes indeed; on economic rights for instance, at least Rawls, Nozick, Sandel, and Sen will all reply to my worries.[15] The problem is that they all give different and incompatible replies, a not insignificant commentary given that it is now a quarter of a century since *A Theory of Justice* was published. To my mind, the belief that these differing views on economic rights vis-à-vis political rights will one day soon be reconciled is less a purely rational one, and more an article of faith.

And I would also maintain that even more pure faith is needed to believe that the justification for rights across domains can ever lead to a coherent and consistent overall theory. That is to say, even if it were possible, which I doubt, to reach consensus on a subtheory of economic rights for extant individual human beings within the context of civil and political rights, I doubt even more that the arguments supporting that subtheory could be made to square with arguments for the rights of human groups, animals, trees, the natural environment, later generations, and so forth. One argument for according rights to animals, for example, is that they can feel pain, hence have moral standing: we are enjoined, at the minimum, from inflicting pain on them, just as is the case with other human beings; and at the maximum, we may well have a moral duty to alleviate the pain of an animal, again, just as is the case with and for other human beings. This is in many respects a good and humane argument, but I fear that someone highly entitlement-oriented will one day extrapolate from it, and argue that because he is in significant pain when obliged to remain celibate for any period of time, he therefore has a right to a sexual partner, who will alleviate the pain far more rapidly and efficiently than a doctor.

In summary on these points, I believe it takes a great deal of faith, little warranted by the available evidence, to believe that within rights theory a consistent and coherent view will one day emerge; and to believe that such a view can be obtained between and across the manifold areas of rights theories requires a faith that would be the envy of every religious fundamentalist.[16]

For all of these reasons, I submit that neither the Confucian tradition nor contemporary American society are best served by scholars examining the Confucian corpus for precursors of the concept of human rights. Much more will be gained, I believe, by seeing the Confucian vision as an *alternative* to ours, and one that may, with emendations, be viable for the "global village" our planet is becoming. Other reasons could be proffered for this claim,[17] but I wish now to turn from the more philosophical dimensions of human rights to the more political, again, with a focus on the United States.

Let me juxtapose three of the claims advanced thus far: first, the United States is a highly conflicted society, morally and politically today, and is growing more so; second, the conflicts stem in important ways from the language of our moral and political discourse of rights; and third, the conceptual framework in which that discourse is embedded—the idea of the free, autonomous individual—does not yet, and perhaps cannot, provide a coherent and consistent vision for us.

If these claims have any merit at all, they suggest an immediate moral question: how can Americans justify insisting—by diplomatic, military, economic, or other means—that every other society adopt the moral and political vocabulary of rights? With our own ideological house falling apart, with no agreement on how to shore up its foundations, how can we demand the remodeling of other houses?

The questions become painful to contemplate when we face the reality that the United States is the wealthiest society in the world, yet after over two hundred years of human rights talk, many of its human citizens have no shelter, a fifth of them have no access to health care, a fourth of its children are growing up in poverty, and the richest two percent of its peoples own and control over fifty percent of its wealth.[18]

It will immediately be objected, correctly, that these injustices are not solely caused by the language and conceptual framework of rights, and, moreover, whatever problems the United States has, it is better off than any other society in the world. To the second objection, I can respond that "better off" almost always refers to possession of material goods, and it is largely because of hard work, fertile soils, natural resources, and diversity of hospitable climates that Americans own so much, not the belief in human rights. And if "better off" is intended in the social and political senses—we abolished slavery and permitted women to vote, etc.—then clearly we are not better off than most other industrial nations, and much more importantly, the social and political advances we have made have not led to a greater equalization of wealth. The abolition of slavery affected who was rich and who was poor to a certain extent, but did not disturb the growing concentration of wealth in fewer hands. And of course, the Nineteenth Amendment didn't affect the maldistribution of wealth at all.

The issue is by no means only of historical significance. Women and minorities have made, through intensive and extensive struggles, major advances in securing first-generation rights during the past thirty years. But these advances have more than been matched by decreases in the number of decent-paying jobs, declining union membership—from a third of the work force to only slightly more than 10 percent of it today—a rise in poverty, loss of community, reduced access to health care, and increasing concentration of wealth in the hands of the few.[19]

Which brings us to the first reply: rights talk, and the laws which are justified by rights talk, are not solely responsible for many of the iniquities plaguing the United States today, but they are surely partially responsible. As a free, autonomous individual, I have a fundamental right to choose how I will disburse my wealth, and will therefore vehemently oppose, and/or get around the payment of inheritance taxes. Cigarette companies have a right to contribute more to a political campaign than any of their working people earn in a year. Currency traders demand the right to withdraw as much money from a nation as they like, on a moment's notice, no matter how much havoc the withdrawal might have on the nation's economy. The lumber industry has a right to do whatever it pleases with the lands it owns except for what the government expressly forbids (and of course anything forbidden must involve an infringement of some basic rights). The legal thinking which has contributed to these current states of affairs is epitomized in a 1989 decision (DeShaney vs Winnebago County of Social Services):

> [The Due Process Clause's] purpose was to protect people from the State, not to ensure that the State protected them from each other. . . . Consistent with these principles, our cases have recognized that the Due Process Clauses generally confer

61

no affirmative right to governmental aid, even where such aid may be necessary to secure life, liberty, or property.[20]

If it now appears that I have descended to an anticapitalist diatribe, the appearance is intentional. The development of the conceptual framework of rights went hand in hand with the development of industrial capitalism, and nowhere else. To the extent that the vision of human beings as free, autonomous individuals provided an intellectual bulwark against the abuses attendant on the notion of the divine right of kings, it contributed measurably to enhancing the quality of life of many people. But if the Stuarts and their successors became increasingly limited in their ability to violate the liberty of English yeomen, they became equally limited in their ability to control the growing wealth of the bourgeoisie. Whatever else it has done, the concept of civil and political rights has consistently served to protect wealth, power, and privilege.

The myth of the free market[21] makes it difficult to appreciate how much the rhetoric and the laws surrounding first generation rights serve to enhance the power of, for example, large corporations. Consider one issue that has been pressed hard on China by the United States: intellectual property rights. Much has been made of the Chinese proclivity for pirating books, CDs, and tapes, and the failure of the Chinese government to take adequate measures to halt such activities.[22] Surely the Chinese look bad on this score, for shouldn't authors or musicians have a right to control their own creations, and derive a livelihood therefrom?

But pass from a book of poems or a rock album to new seed strains, animal genes, and medicines, and the situation begins to look a little different.[23] In the first place, the Chinese know full well they can't really compete with major electronics, biotechnology, and pharmaceutical research firms in the West. Even more important, we have moved from entertainment to necessities of life—food and medicine—and what intellectual property rights means is that those who have the rights can charge whatever they wish for the foods and medicines, which will almost surely be far beyond the means of the average Chinese peasant, now and in the future.[24] Against this background, the rhetoric of rights talk and free trade becomes less compelling, and the reluctance of the Chinese government to submit to U.S. pressure becomes much more understandable.

Over and above the questionable morality of this aspect of rights, I would also argue that industrial capitalism can never become the norm for most of the world's peoples, which should make rights talk even more suspect. This is a multifaceted issue, only one element of which I can take up herein, specifically again with respect to China.

In challenging the Chinese government for its human rights violations, we demand that they adopt rule by law, not by men. In one sense, this demand is ludicrous: the Chinese have a very sophisticated legal system, which they abide by fairly well. The problem is that the United States and a few other governments, and almost all of the multinational corporations—as well as exemplary groups like Amnesty International—do not like a number of Chinese laws, especially those involving counterrevolutionary activity, protection of state secrets, the regulation of trade, visa restrictions, and so forth.

Hence the demand must translate into an imperative to change Chinese laws. I will be the first to admit that a number of current laws do not conduce to the well-being of the average Chinese if they should run afoul of officialdom. As is fairly well known, *guanxi* is the universal lubricant for the machinery of all China, and those without much of it suffer. *Guanxi* is so pervasive in China, and has led to so much corruption, that the very word "corruption" seems to be too weak to describe the way the country operates today.

Yet I think we should pause before condemning *guanxi* altogether, and seek replacing it strictly with the rule of impersonal law. Despite the supposed success of the "economic reforms," and even allowing that GDP will continue to grow, and even believing—much more implausibly—that the government can develop an efficient system of taxation, I submit that China is, and will always be, a relatively poor country economically, sufficiently so that no government will ever be capable of providing adequate social services for its 1+ billion people. If this is so, then some other institutions are going to have to maintain responsibility for the care and nurturing of the young, the sick, the elderly, the unlettered, etc.

The family and village are two such institutions, and it is in them that *guanxi* is rooted. When you're in your prime, you care for the old folks, and will be cared for when your time comes. The healthy care for the sick, and the educated pass on to the next generation what was passed on to them. And these aren't necessarily profit-maximizing calculations either. You aren't attentive to your grandmother so that your (not yet born) grandchildren will be attentive to you; she's your grandmother, you love each other, and that suffices.

So finally I come to the conceptual framework of Confucianism, wherein rights-talk was not spoken, and within which I am not a free, autonomous individual. I am a son, husband, father, grandfather, neighbor, colleague, student, teacher, citizen, friend. I have a very large number of relational obligations and responsibilities, which severely constrain what I do. These responsibilities occasionally frustrate or annoy, they more often are satisfying and they are always binding. If we are going to use words like "freedom" here, it must be seen as an achievement, not a stative term, as Confucius suggests in describing the milestones of his life.[25] And my individuality, if anyone wishes to keep the   63 concept, will come from the specific actions I take in meeting my relational responsibilities: there are many ways to be a good teacher, spouse, sibling, friend, and so forth; if Confucian persons aren't free, autonomous individuals, they aren't dull, faceless automatons either.[26]

Furthermore, the language of Confucian discourse is rich and varied, permitting me to eulogize a Martin Luther King; it allows me a full lexicon to inveigh against the Chinese government for its treatment of Han Dongfang, Wei Jingsheng, Wang Dan, and others; I can express outrage at the rape of Bosnian women, and petition the governor of Pennsylvania to grant a new trial to Mumia Abu Jamal; I can, in sum, fully express my moral sentiments without ever invoking the language of human rights.

Perhaps, then—and this is my concluding plea—we should study Confucianism as a genuine alternative to modern Western theories of rights, rather than merely as a potentially early version of them. When it is remembered that three-quarters of the world's peoples have, and continue to define themselves in terms of kinship and community rather than as rights-bearers,[27] we may come to entertain seriously the possibility that if the search for universal moral and political principles is a worthwhile endeavor, we might find more of a philosophical grounding for those principles and beliefs in the writings of Confucius and Mengzi than those of John Locke, Adam Smith, and their successors.

Notes

1. Early Christian scholarship on China is well and sensitively narrated by David Mungello in his *Curious Land: Jesuit Accommodation and the Origins of Sinology* (Honolulu: University of Hawaii Press, 1989). A briefer account is in Daniel J. Cook and Henry Rosemont Jr., *Leibniz: Writings on China* (Chicago and LaSalle, Ill.: Open Court Publishers, 1994).

2. A typical example of this latter-day interest is Julia Ching, *Confucianism and Christianity* (Tokyo: Kodansha, 1977).

3. In the first instance the reference is to other papers in this volume.

4. I have taken up these differing notions of rights in "Rights-Bearing Individuals and Role-Bearing Persons," in Mary I. Bockover, ed., *Rules, Rituals, and Responsibility: Essays Dedicated to Herbert Fingarette* (LaSalle, Ill.: Open Court Publishers, 1991).

5. In the context of challenging this vision, it is irrelevant whether it is taken to be descriptive of human beings, prescriptive (how we should view human beings in doing political philosophy or conducting research in the social sciences), or whether the vision is simply a Western conceit, analogous to the visionary in Plato's Cave, Hobbesian capitalists in the state of nature, Rawlsian statesmen in the original position behind a veil of ignorance, or Quinean field linguists struggling to ascertain the meaning of "gavagai."

6. Or, to use Irene Bloom's phrase in her insightful analysis of Mencius in this volume, "foundational intuition."

7. Bockover, ed., *Rules, Rituals, and Responsibility*, p. 191.

8. From this point on, the line between scholarship and activism becomes blurred. The topic of the Conference, however, was such that the political world could not be ignored; virtually every conclusion drawn by the other participants in the Conference has political implications, as does the fact that at the last minute, several of the Chinese delegates from the Confucius Foundation did not attend. Thus I do not believe it necessary to apologize for writing this paper both as a philosopher, and as a U.S. citizen.

9. In using the terminology of first, second, and third generation rights I am following Sumner Twiss. See especially his contribution to this volume.

10. Ronald Dworkin, *Taking Rights Seriously* (Cambridge: Harvard University Press, 1977).

11. As Rawls states: "The aim is to use the notion of pure procedural justice as a basis of theory," in *A Theory of Justice* (Cambridge: Harvard University Press, 1971), p. 136.

12. Richard J. Herrnstein and Charles Murray, *The Bell Curve: Intelligence and Class Structure in America* (New York: Free Press, 1994). A useful antidote to such research is Richard Lewontin et al., *Not in Our Genes* (New York: Pantheon, 1985).

13. The *locus classicus* here is Christopher Stone, *Should Trees Have Standing? Toward Legal Rights for Natural Objects* (Los Altos, Calif.: William Kaufman Press, 1974).

14. Especially as found in his *Dream of the Earth* (San Francisco: Sierra Club, 1988).

15. Rawls, *A Theory of Justice*; Robert Nozick, *Anarchy, State, and Utopia* (New York: Columbia University Press, 1974); Michael Sandel, *Liberalism and the Limits of Justice* (Cambridge: Harvard University Press, 1982) and *Liberalism and Its Critics* (New York: New York University Press, 1984); Amartya K. Sen, *Collective Choice and Social Welfare* (San Francisco: Holden Day, 1970) and (with J. Dreze), *Hunger and Public Action* (Oxford: Oxford University Press, 1989), among other writings. For reasons of his own, and for reasons that overlap mine, Alasdair MacIntyre is as skeptical of rights talks as I am. See his *After Virtue* (1981), *Whose Justice? Which Rationality?* (1988), and *Three Rival Versions of Moral Enquiry* (1990), all Notre Dame, Ind.: Notre Dame University Press.

16. In "Moral Dilemmas and Consistency," *Journal of Philosophy*, 77, no. 3, March 1980, Ruth Barcan Marcus maintains that the existence of moral dilemmas within a moral theory does not establish that the theory is inconsistent. Even if her arguments were accepted, however (and there are good grounds for challenging them), they would not invalidate my skepticism about rights-oriented moral and political theories, because: (1) the dilemmas remain at least *prima facie* evidence of inconsistency; (2) there are a great many such dilemmas of this kind today; and (3) her arguments (quite properly) do not address my question of how free, autonomous individuals jump from first generation to second generation rights.

17. Some other reasons: (1) No Chinese graph from the classical era approximates the meaning of "rights," nor are there close analogues for related terms, such as "free-

dom," "liberty," "individual," "autonomy," "rationality," "choice," etc. (2) At most, then, the concept of rights might in some way be argued to be implicit in the classical texts, but except for serving political ends—as Twiss suggests in this volume—it is not clear what we would then be able to do philosophically with the implicit claim; (3) The more we look for rights talk in the Confucian corpus, the more difficult it is for us to be open to the texts for other visions.

18. To cite only a few sources for these figures: Andrew Hacker, "Who Should Go to College?" in the *New York Review of Books*, May 11, 1995; Noam Chomsky, *World Orders Old and New* (New York: Columbia University Press, 1994), especially ch. 2. A number of sources are cited in my *A Chinese Mirror* (La Salle, Ill.: Open Court Publishers, 1991).

19. Ibid., plus the Chomsky work cited above.

20. Cited by Randall Peerenboom in his excellent article, "What's Wrong with Chinese Rights?" in the *Harvard Human Rights Journal* 6 (1993): 43.

21. For the lack of competition in today's markets, see the analysis of Art Hilgard, "Unfree Trade," in the *Nation*, November 22, 1993. Also, Noam Chomsky takes up this idea in his *Secrets, Lies, and Democracy* (Tucson: Odonian Press, 1994), pp. 64–70.

22. For details, see my "Why the Chinese Economic Miracle Isn't One," in *Z Magazine*, October 1995.

23. Noam Chomsky has made this point well. See his *The Prosperous Few and the Restless Many* (Berkeley: Odonian Press, 1993), especially p. 12.

24. I've estimated the average annual income for 700 million Chinese peasants in 1993 at U.S. $145. See note 22 and *A Chinese Mirror* for details and sources.

25. *Lun Yu* 2:4.

26. A fuller account of the Confucian person is in *A Chinese Mirror*, ch. 3.

27. I have argued that one major strand of contemporary feminist philosophy also shares this vision. See "Classical Confucian and Contemporary Feminist Thought: Some Parallels, and Their Implications," in Douglas Allen and Ashok Malhotra, eds., *Culture and Self* (Boulder: Westview Press, 1997.

3

Human Rights: A Valid Chinese Concept?

Julia Ching

> It has been a long-cherished ideal of mankind to enjoy human rights in the full sense of the term. Since this great term—human rights—was coined centuries ago, people of all nations have achieved great results in their unremitting struggle for human rights. However, on a global scale, modern society has fallen far short of the lofty goal of securing the full range of human rights for people the world over. And this is why numerous people with lofty ideals are still working determinedly for this cause.[1]

The above statement sounds like a press release from the United Nations. It is actually the first paragraph from the preface to the White Paper on Human Rights issued by the government of the People's Republic of China in November 1991.

Having said this much, I might conclude right here with a resounding Yes to the question I have posed myself: "Are human rights a valid Chinese concept?" However, certain difficulties come to mind at once, such as the internationally known, abysmally bad record on human rights in China.[2] So I shall have to persist further in my examination of the problem. First, I offer a working definition of the term,"human rights," describe its essential contents briefly, and then go on to examine its viability for the Chinese situation, given both China's cultural heritage and its current political situation.

The Meaning of Human Rights

It is both easy, and difficult, to speak on human rights. It is easy because many people have some idea of what the term means. Yet it is also difficult because no one definition can adequately explain the term.

There is a problem, for example, with the word "rights": not just in Chinese translation, but also in Western languages. At first sight, the term represents legally protected entitlements of individuals in society. And many have the impression that certain rights taken for granted are a sacred legacy from the past.

Actually, history reveals that before the seventeenth century, European and even British society placed as much emphasis on duties as on rights. One owed duties to one's lord, to the king, the Church, and to God. *Rights*, belonged to the powers that be. Feudal lords claimed *les droits du seigneur;* kings claimed *divine* rights; the Church disputed these latter by invoking even higher rights received from the Supreme Being; and God, of course, was always sovereign in his unlimited rights and domains. Such was the state of affairs not only in Western Europe but also in much of the world where theistic religions reigned.

Historically, the dialectic was between the rights of rulers and the duties of subjects. Beginning with the seventeenth century, subjects or former subjects of the lords, kings, Church, and God began to assert their own rights—those claims that they demanded the law to protect. Rights, therefore, relied on law for enforcement: even such a fundamental right as that to life and security. Without the proper laws of the land, especially if chaos was the order of day, this right would have remained only a fiction even in our own Western society.

I turn now to the term "human" since by *human rights* we are referring to the "rights of human beings." I shall not dwell on the definition of a human being, since even this could be controversial. Depending on whether we opt for the biological (for example, the full genetic code), the philosophical (rationality, free will, self-consciousness), or some other model, there will always be problems regarding the boundary lines. For example, people question whether fetuses, or the comatose, should be considered human. And I sidestep the gender issue, by avoiding the use of the term, the "rights of man." But we can see how the extent of human rights depends on where the boundary lines are drawn.[3]

Human Rights: A Western Concept

I would like to describe human rights as a creature of recent birth with a fairly long lineage. Its mother is liberal moral and political philosophy—the French Enlightenment and liberal English thinking, among other things; its father is international law, while its midwife is revolution: first the Revolution of American Independence and then the French Republican Revolution of the late eighteenth century. Such papers as the American Declaration of Independence and the French Declaration of the Rights of Man and of the Citizen, may be considered its birth certificate. The ensuing Bills of Rights that became incorporated in many national constitutions worldwide, and especially the United Nations Universal Declaration of Human Rights (1948), might be described as its introduction to high society. But its ancestry includes further back, Stoic concepts of natural law and the traditions of Roman civil law on the continent and of the Anglo-Saxon common law to the extent that these lent protection to the rights of citizens and of individuals.[4]

The United Nations Charter of 1945 enjoins:

> universal respect for, and observance of, human rights and fundamental freedoms for all without distinction as to race, sex, language, or religion.[5]

So we may suppose that certain articles from the United Nations Universal Declaration on Human Rights (1948), that has been widely publicized, command a general consensus regarding the definition of these rights. I quote briefly here:

Article 1. All human beings are born free and equal in dignity and rights. . . .

Article 3. Everyone has the right to life, liberty and the security of person.

Article 5. No one shall be subjected to torture or to cruel, inhuman or degrading treatment or punishment.

Article 7. All are equal before the law and are entitled without any discrimination to equal protection of the law. . . .

Article 9. No one shall be subjected to arbitrary arrest, detention or exile.

Article 18. Everyone has the right to freedom of thought, conscience and religion. . . .

Article 19. Everyone has the right to freedom of opinion and expression. . . .

Article 20. (1) Everyone has the right to freedom of peaceful assembly and association.[6]

These examples constitute a statement of principles, which are generally what people refer to when speaking of "human rights" in the international arena. However, although enshrined by the authority of the founding nations of the United Nations Organization, the Declaration itself does not bear the signatures of all those nations participating in the international organization. The government of the Republic of China, which moved its seat to Taiwan, participated in the drafting of the Declaration, but the government of the People's Republic of China which has succeeded to its seat, has never signed this Declaration. The Declaration itself serves principally as a manifesto, in its own words, "a common standard of achievement for all peoples and all nations."[7]

The Declaration, including a Preamble and some 30 Articles, was drafted very much under the influence of the Western nations, in particular the United States of America, at the end of the Second World War. The social and economic rights were included at the insistence of the Communist nations, which, however, did not become signatories. There has been, understandably, discussion and argument as to whether the statement of rights represents a Western

69

conceptual construct with limited applicability, or whether it offers a solid core of principles that deserve the respect of all peoples and governments. I shall discuss some of these problems later, but offer those parts of the Declaration that I have quoted as examples of what is considered to be the *contents* of human rights. And these rights as "rights" are also considered—in the West— as universal and inalienable, to be enjoyed equally by all who are human, without which they cannot live a life deemed to be fully "human."

And here arises our problem. Are human rights mainly a Western ideological export (to accompany trade delegations) bolstered by subtle claims of Western political and cultural superiority? What validity can rights claim to have in non-Western cultures such as the Chinese?

These questions may be answered in two successive steps, which are not mutually exclusive: (1) seeking theoretical and historical justification within Chinese culture for a certain capacity to accept and adapt this concept, and (2) arguing from the language of today's Chinese constitution itself, to see whether it is in harmony with, or in opposition to, the spirit of human rights. In doing such, I shall compare Chinese ideas in some cases to Western concepts.

Human Rights and Chinese Culture

Let me begin by reporting some alternative interpretations.

The Debates

When we come to the topic of human rights and Chinese culture, we find at least two opposing interpretations. They concur that human rights are not historically a Chinese concept, but a Western import. The first interpretation regards attempts to introduce human rights into China as an unnecessary cultural intrusion into a culture and a society quite self-sufficient in its own pursuit of humane values and social harmony.[8] The second essentially maintains that Chinese civilization has nurtured for millennia a brutal political culture that has only commanded passive obedience without permitting the development of any real idea of civil rights and liberties. In this case, however, the conclusion may either be that the contemporary situation in China represents already a vast improvement on the traditional past,[9] or that these rights and liberties need to be properly developed and protected.[10]

But, granted the historically alien character of the concept of human rights, could we still argue the validity of extending it to the Chinese situation, on the basis that there is enough in the culture that could accept it?

Problems of Translation

70 A preliminary problem regards translation. The Chinese language does not

have an exact equivalent for the word "rights." This term is usually rendered as "power" (*quan*), a reminder that "might makes right"—in the East and the West. On the other hand, the term "human" in "human rights" is sometimes translated as "people" (*min*) or "citizens" (*gongmin*), rather than as individuals. This happens especially in the language of Chinese constitutions and politics.

Literally, "human rights" is translated as *renquan*, "human power," one reason why the struggle for human rights has been understood by the Communist state as a fight for political power, and therefore, a threat to the establishment. A less ambiguous term is the Chinese translation for "democracy," that is, *minzhu* (literally, the people as masters).

The Chinese Humanist Legacy: Positive Teachings

In the post-Christian West, liberal humanism has offered a climate of openness for the assertion and discussion of universal moral values. In China, where a Western ideology, Marxist-Leninism, nominally reigns as absolute dogma, some of the population still remember a native humanist tradition going back more than two millennia to Confucius and even earlier.

I have already mentioned how the United Nations Declaration places primary importance on every *individual's* human dignity, and the sanctity of human life. In China, tradition claims that an ancient sage-king refrained from a war of conquest with the words: "I would not shed the blood of one innocent human being even if that could gain me the world." Whether that was actually said is not so important, because the *belief* in the truth of the statement shows how important one individual human life was regarded through the ages.

In the West, people are accustomed to an image of Confucius as a wise man or a sage, teaching about how to live a virtuous life, much as did Socrates in ancient Greece. Socrates is regarded as a humanist; in fact, he was condemned by the state for misleading youth, turning them away from the gods of their fathers. Confucius had his own struggles with the state, but died a natural death. In a world where military valor was highly esteemed, he instructed the youth instead in the ideal of a humane person, who valued moral relationships above all else. Confucius seldom discussed religious matters and has generally been known as a humanist. Indeed, he transformed the particular virtue of *ren*, the kindness that characterized the man of high birth, into the universal virtue of humaneness that *makes* every person who practices it, a "gentleman" or *junzi* (literally, the prince's scion). Moreover, he distanced himself from the religion of antiquity, with its emphasis on divination and sacrifice—including human sacrifice, which he is reported to have condemned in strong terms. And Confucius's teaching of *ren* was extended to the political order, where it is defined as benevolent or humane government, as government of moral suasion, in   71 which the leader gives the example of personal integrity and selfless devotion to the people.

The Confucian teaching of moral relationships, defined as those between parent and child, ruler and minister, husband and wife, elder and younger siblings, and friends, appears to uphold a vertical hierarchy in society while urging responsibility and reciprocity. In many ways it did have this effect socially. Besides, the Chinese view of the human being tends to see the person in the context of a social network rather than as an individual. But the fourth- to third-century Mencius (372–289 B.C.) further developed Confucius's thought to articulate his conviction that every human being could become a sage. Implicit in this doctrine of the universal accessibility of sagehood, is a teaching of human equality, of what we may call, "moral equal opportunity." And we should remember that becoming a sage was tantamount to gaining the rights to kingship, since the most revered sages were the sage-kings of ages past.[11]

The United Nations Universal Declaration on Human Rights says that human rights should be protected by the rule of law "[if] man is not to be compelled to have recourse, as a last resort, to rebellion against tyranny and oppression."[12] In the case of China, there has been an age-old doctrine regarding the legitimation of power: that the ruler rules only by a divine mandate, called the Mandate of Heaven (tianming), which he could lose by misgovernment. Indeed, the Chinese word for revolution is literally, to "remove the Mandate" (geming).

Mencius, the best-known disciple of the Confucian school, even formulated a doctrine justifying tyrannicide, declaring that killing a "tyrant" is *not* killing a "king."[13] In an age when the altars of the earth and grain signify political authority, Mencius's words were: "The people come first; the altars of the earth and grain come afterwards; the ruler comes last" (7B:14).

And so Confucian China shares with Christian Europe the idea of vicarious authority in kingship. But the doctrine of tyrannicide, which developed so early in China, emerged only much later in Europe. The late sixteenth-century treatises to similar effect by an anonymous Huguenot author and by the Spanish Jesuit Luis Mariana, were either publicly burnt or condemned, although they continued to wield enormous influence.[14] In China too, some of Mencius's teachings were considered inflammatory. This was the opinion of the fourteenth-century founder of the Ming dynasty, who sought to delete from the Book of Mencius those passages that approved of tyrannicide.[15]

Implicit in the political teachings cited above is that government rests on popular consent. More explicitly, the fourth-century B.C. Confucian thinker Xunzi (Hsün-tzu) speaks of human beings coming together in society to achieve the strength and harmony without which they cannot conquer other beings, presumably, the birds and beasts.[16] Before him, the fifth-century B.C. thinker,

Mozi (Mo-tzu), already discussed the origin of social authority through a form of consent on the part of human beings who gather together to prevent disorder and injury by the election of wise leaders.[17]

A fourth-century-B.C. Legalist thinker, Han Feizi (Han Fei Tzu), a staunch defender of the ruler's rights, and an opponent of Confucian political philosophy, nevertheless also says that the people are the ones who make a ruler:

> In the most ancient times, when men were few and creatures numerous, human beings could not overcome the birds, beasts, insects, and reptiles. Then a sage appeared who fashioned nests of wood to protect men from harm. The people were delighted and made him ruler of the world, calling him the Nest Builder.[18]

The seventeenth-century English philosopher Thomas Hobbes's *Leviathan* came much later (1651); in it he describes everyone as at war against everyone else in a state of nature. Hobbes discerned in this the basis of natural right in the human desire to live. Aided by reason, which he calls the law of nature, human beings would agree to relinquish much of their sovereign right to all things in a contractual relationship to a state, while reserving certain individual liberties having regard to self-preservation. Hobbes cites interhuman conflict as what human beings wanted to avoid in joining together in political society, as did Mozi in China much earlier. But the other ancient Chinese thinkers go back to a more remote past, and conceive society to have begun in the human struggle with the nonhuman species. Implicitly, they are saying that the human family is one, and that human beings in a state of nature had rights and liberties that they freely surrendered for the good of the whole.

But if incipient ideas of human equality and popular sovereignty arose very early in Chinese thought, they did not lead to a political structure that protected human rights. The twentieth century has not seen the proper development of the institutions of participatory democracy which could assure human rights in China. Unfortunately, the danger remains that only another violent revolution could "rectify" the situation, and so far, revolutions have only replaced one set of authoritarian ruling elite with another.

In modern times the Chinese language had to coin a word for "freedom" (*ziyou*, literally, self-determination). The closest classical term was *ziran* (literally, the natural), connoting more a Taoist sense of harmony with nature than of Promethean self-assertion. Actually, the belief in human perfectibility, a cornerstone of Confucian philosophy, implied a belief in personal freedom. But this was more an interior, spiritual freedom to improve one's own moral character. The concept of freedom as a *right*, such as the right to freedom of thought and religion, to freedom of speech and assembly, was never clearly articulated until modern times, and then under Western influence.

Leading twentieth-century Chinese philosophers living outside China, where they breathe a fresher air, have agreed that traditional Chinese culture contains "seeds" for concepts like science and democracy, which have come more directly from the West. I am referring to such persons as Carsun Chang, Mou Zongsan, Tang Junyi, and Xu Fuguan.[19]

Chinese observers of the West have also pointed out what the West could learn from the East, in order to remedy an excessive individualism working against so-called family values, a litigious spirit promoting conflict rather than harmony, and especially in the United States, an unacceptably high crime rate. Other problems include an increasing gap between rich and poor in capitalist societies, a monopoly of political election campaigns by the well-to-do, and the social deprivation of various minorities, including Native Americans and Canadians. Meanwhile in China, the population has been able to maintain a high degree of self-discipline. And the peaceful, disciplined, and thriving societies in East Asian countries outside of China with very dense populations show how the people have maintained a sense of social harmony and family virtues. East Asians value what they call humaneness, or human warmth, which they find lacking in a system where human relationships have lost a personal touch. The West may yet have something to learn from the East here.

Legal and Political Heritage: Negative Developments

The concept of law (*fa*) is also understood differently in the Chinese cultural context. The Confucian society was governed by forms of decorum (*li*), a term rooted in ancient religion, and originally presuming a distinction between nobility and commoners. *Li* may be described as customary, uncodified law, internalized by individuals, and governing gentlemen in their personal and social lives, in their behavior toward the spirits as well as the rest of the world. For that reason, *li* has the extended meaning of "correct behavior." It was based on justice, rightness (*yi*), even humaneness (*ren*). A classical education was an education in the rites, one that prepared the young nobles for life. *Fa*, on the other hand, were customs, selected and codified, which became a penal code, to be applied to commoners who lacked the privilege of a ritual education.

The evolution of law in China may be described as the *devolution* of ritual (*li*) into law (*fa*) and of law into punishment (*xing*).[20] For this reason, law is regarded as having played a mainly penal role in Chinese society, protecting the rights of the rulers and enjoining passive obedience on the part of the subjects. Until today, the Chinese have feared the law, because law has been an arbitrary instrument in the hands of the rulers.

Traditional Chinese political thought also has always assumed that human beings would be governed by monarchies. Confucianism obviously preferred benevolent monarchs and had no use for tyrants, but Confucian ministers did not always have the power to make sure that tyrants were kept from the

throne. There were changes in the dynastic cycle but the individuals who acquired power were often of the wrong kind, even if they ruled in the name of the Mandate of Heaven. Unfortunately, in the light of historical events, this doctrine became understood by many totalisticly as a kind of historical determinism governing the rise and fall of political dynasties.

There had been critics of absolute power among traditional Chinese intellectuals. For example, student protests were known nearly two thousand years ago, in the second century C.E., when the Han dynasty capital witnessed an assemblage of 30,000 students at the Imperial College, quite a few of whom held mass protests and political demonstrations. Eventually, the state learnt from such experiences to give more importance to civil service examinations (for which China became famous) than to imperial colleges with large enrollments. But the year 1126 once more saw student petitioners at the Song dynasty palace gates in Hangzhou, protesting the removal from office of a much-loved figure at a time when the country was threatened by outside invaders. A riot ensued when their sympathizers came into conflict with soldiers. But the students achieved their political aims and were pardoned for making trouble. In modern times, student demonstrations on May Fourth, 1919, in support of "Mr. Science" and "Mr. Democracy" are especially remembered for having brought about national consciousness of needs and problems.[21] On April 18, 1989, student representatives recalled history when some of them made "petitions" to the government on their knees at the entrance to the Great Hall of the People in Beijing, on behalf of the thousands gathered during an all-day demonstration. After sixteen hours, the written petition was accepted, although nothing came of it.[22]

Unlike Thomas Hobbes, who believed that the people have no right to rebellion, another seventeenth-century English philosopher, John Locke, asserted in his *Second Treatise of Government* (1690), that subjects, like their rulers, have important and even absolute rights, such as to life, liberty, and property.[23] In the late eighteenth century, the idea of natural rights eventually contributed to the overthrow of two governments: George III's over the American colonies, and Louis XVI's in France, and became articulated in the statements proclaimed after these events.[24]

The situation in pre-modern China (long after the time of Mencius!) was quite different. Increasingly, critiques of power were made obliquely or in secret. A seventeenth-century Chinese thinker, Huang Zongxi, well known as a philosopher and intellectual historian, wrote a critique of despotism, *Mingyi daifanglu* (Plan for a Prince) which was not widely circulated until the early twentieth century. In it, he condemned rulers for regarding their domains as their private property, and their subjects as servants and slaves. He proposed that law (*fa*) be established for the interest of all rather than of the few, and that government be by laws rather than men. And he denounced laws that enslave

75

the people as "unlawful laws."[25] An important thinker and influential teacher, Huang was a philosopher of the school of the sixteenth-century thinker Wang Yang-ming, who placed emphasis on the human mind-and-heart (xin) as the seat of wisdom and goodness, the source, we may say, of human dignity and of potential sageliness. Yang-ming's philosophy has also been the principal inspiration behind contemporary Confucian thought, stimulated as well by ideas from the West.

Unfortunately in premodern and modern China, political power became more despotic as the voices of criticism and protest were increasingly stifled. This process continued under Communist rule, as a Western imported ideology—Marxist-Leninism—became used as a theory and practice of power on a scale hitherto unimagined, and by men often less competent and more ruthless than some earlier emperors. Decisions affecting the lives of the entire population continued to be made by the few, or rather, by the "one man," whether Mao Zedong or Deng Xiaoping, and without the benefit of such traditional institutional balances as the imperial censorate, which had been empowered to criticize the exercise of power in the days of the monarchy. As the media have been strictly controlled by the government, journalists have complained, as in May, 1989, that there had been more liberty before the Communists took power, even under the warlords. And it was for lack of a vehicle to communicate their complaints that the people made use of big wall posters, as in the late seventies, which however have since been outlawed.

Why was it that the Chinese had very early articulated ideas about human dignity and equality, but were unable to establish a political system that would protect this dignity and equality? This question has been troubling the minds of many contemporary Chinese intellectuals. The disintegration of feudalism in Western Europe was eventually followed by the empowerment of the propertied classes, whose assertions of their own rights eventually contributed to the extension of like rights to the whole population. In China, however, a system of enfeoffment started very early and was already disintegrating by the time of Confucius and Mencius. It came to a formal end when the country was unified by the sword under the First Emperor, a hated despot who burnt books and buried scholars (c. 213 B.C.E.).

In contrast with Western Europe, power in China became increasingly centralized in the hands of the monarch, rather than shared with others. A titled aristocracy, strong during the classical period (the time of Confucius and Mencius), when the country was divided into feudal states, lost its powers and privileges to a centralized absolute monarchy, never to regain them. A government-controlled education system and a civil service examination promoted the principle of merit, while monopolizing the supply of bureau-

crats, who were mere advisers and administrators, and, as the propertied class, never threatened rebellion. In this system there was never an independent judiciary, although the Censorate did serve as a channel for policy criticisms. In these circumstances the Confucian doctrine of benevolent government from above was insufficient to guarantee the rights of the subjects below, and the population was instructed more to preserve social harmony than to assert their own rights.

I think that philosophers like Mencius and Huang Zongxi demonstrate that the Chinese intellectual tradition was well prepared for accepting Western ideas regarding the legal protection of human rights. Witness the efforts of intellectuals in the late nineteenth and early twentieth century who sought to secure a constitutional form of government, first under a monarchy, and then under a republic. Witness too the final failure of the *monarchical* idea, after the fall of the Manchu dynasty (1911), in spite of efforts to restore it or to start a new one. The population was no longer wedded to the idea of dynastic rule.

Moreover, I feel assured by the recent expressions of popular dissent in China during the last decades that despotism, under whatever form, even when proclaimed in the name of the dictatorship of the alleged proletariat, is not loved. Human rights, on the other hand, have been very much in the consciousness of a people deprived of them. "We want to be human beings" was the rallying cry of the Tian'anmen demonstrations of 1989. There have been many smaller demonstrations in Beijing: demonstrations, or petitions, of individuals or groups, such as poor peasants, who went to the capital in search of justice and protection, as did their ancestors before them in the days of the monarchy. That they did so was proof that they believed in certain entitlements—even if they had received no Western education.

Human Rights and the Chinese Constitution

My discussion of the relevance of human rights in the light of Chinese culture might appear superfluous given the fact that the government of the People's Republic has recently declared itself in favor of human rights, explicitly in the White Paper of 1991, and certainly implicitly in its constitutions, especially that of 1982.

In this Communist China has followed the precedent of the Soviet Union, as well as that of the Republic of 1911 in eventually giving itself a constitution. China has promulgated several constitutions, three times (1954, 1975, 1978) before 1982. This reflects a need to find some instrument of legitimation, as each constitution lost credibility through its nonobservance by the previous party in power. The expectation seems to be that a government should exist for the protection of the people's rights; thus the 1982 constitution acknowl-   77 edges the "citizens' freedom of speech, of the press, of assembly, of association" and even describes such freedom as "inviolable."[26] In fact, we can compare, article by article, the 1982 constitution with those of the United Nations Universal Declaration and find close parallels.

> Article 35. Citizens of the People's Republic or China have the freedom of speech, of the press, of assembly, of association, of procession (*yu xing*) and of demonstration (*shiwei*).
> Article 37. The freedom of the citizens of the People's Republic of China is inviolable. . . .
> Unlawful deprivation or restriction of citizens' freedom of person by detention or other means is prohibited. . . .

The problem with all this is the supremacy of the Communist Party, enshrined in the constitution as the "dictatorship of the proletariat," with a resulting incongruity between the constitution and the system for enforcing it. My brother Frank, who served in China as a correspondent for the *Wall Street Journal* (1979–1983), was once briefly detained by Chinese security. While walking by their office on a city street, he chanced to see a notice of certain decrees and decided to note them down. This apparently attracted sufficient attention for him to be summoned inside for questioning. He was asked what he was doing, and why. He replied that he was taking notes of the published rules and regulations, which he found interesting because they limited the constitutional rights of freedom of speech, of assembly, of association, of demonstrations. When confronted with the fact of these laws and decrees, which could be found unconstitutional in a Western society, his interrogators were not amused. They even questioned his motives in noting things down, as though this itself might be an act of sabotage. If he was permitted to leave after an hour or so, it was because he was an American citizen, not a Chinese.

In this situation, it is noteworthy that a non-Chinese citizen could exercise his rights better than a Chinese, as the constitution specifically speaks of the freedom of its *citizens*. This is indicative also of the government's view that civil liberties are privileges bestowed by the state rather than natural rights, and this, in spite of the assertion in the constitution that all power comes from the people.

The country's leaders who proclaimed the 1982 constitution, had themselves suffered from random repression and lawlessness during the Cultural Revolution (1966–1976). Consequently the public had expected that they would set up a judicial system at a proper distance between the political and the administrative. The threatened loss of power in June 1989—accompanied perhaps by a genuine fear of another chaotic "cultural revolution"—led to the enactment of martial law without due observance of constitutional safeguards. In the process the military crackdown effectively trampled on the constitution itself.

There are those who say that for China, collective rights are more important than individual rights. This has also been the argument of the Communist government, which claims to have liberated the country from colonialism and imperialism, as well as what it calls the "feudalism" of past oppressions. However, what is implied is often that individuals should be sacrificed when necessary for the collectivity, and that those in power should decide what is good for that collectivity. The record of the Communist government speaks for itself in this regard. While it claims to have fought for the people's economic and social rights, the price it has exacted is far too great for the limited progress made to date. Dissidents comparing the present to the past usually find that there was less repression and more liberty *before* the Communist liberation than afterwards. The millions of refugees from mainland China who made the prosperity of Hong Kong also demonstrate their preferences for enjoying guaranteed liberties even under a colonial government to "legally possessing" those rights accorded by a government which is not responsible to the people whom it calls its own.

Before the Communists seized power, and in spite of great odds and many imperfections, the Republic of China had made halting but significant progress with its judiciary system. Today, we can take encouragement from those East Asian countries and regions where the democratic record has improved vastly. This is true of the situations in Japan (where the postwar democratic Constitution has survived all tests), and more recently in South Korea and Taiwan, countries with a deep background of Confucian culture that have experienced rapid economic modernization, accompanied by democratization and the more conscientious enactment and observance of human rights legislation. Taiwan, which still calls itself the Republic of China, is both a bastion of Chinese culture, and upholder of modern legal standards.

In conclusion then it can be stated quite confidently, in answer to the question with which we started, "Are human rights a valid Chinese concept?" that it has been shown to be so in at least three important respects:

1. Support for certain human rights concepts can be found in the writings of leading Confucian thinkers, early and late.
2. Most East Asian countries have been quick to endorse human rights and quite ready to claim them as their own.
3. East Asian countries historically much influenced by Confucian culture have demonstrated that the observance of democratic practices and human rights is not incompatible with, and can be beneficially adapted to, Confucian traditions.

If obstacles remain to the observance of human rights in China, they are 79 due not to any incompatibility of these concepts or practices with Confucian tradition, but to the misuse of political power in defense of entrenched repressive regimes.[27]

Notes

At the request of the Royal Society of Canada, I have previously prepared two reports: "Political Constraints to Freedom of Scholarship and Science: The Case of China," for a symposium held in Ottawa, 1991, and "Chinese Intellectuals Since Tian'anmen: The Continuing Difficulties," for the Society's Committee on Human Rights, when it was chaired by the late Hon. Walter Tarnopolsky, in 1992. The first is published in Constraints to Freedom of Scholarship and Science, ed. by Eve Kushner and Michael R. Dence (Toronto and Capetown: Royal Society of Canada, 1996). The second will be printed for circulation within the Society.

1. Given in the Chinese White Paper entitled, "Human Rights in China," published by the State Council's Newsroom. Preface. This appeared in *Beijing Review* (November 4, 1991), pp. 8–45. Its publication has led to a stream of discussions and books on human rights, usually supporting the government's line, but offering facts and explanations about human rights in general as well.

2. A recent Western work on human rights in China is *After the Event: Human Rights and Their Future in China*, ed. by Susan Whitfield, with contributions by Andrew J. Nathan, Jay Berstein, James D. Seymour, Chan Hong-mo, Liu Binyan, and others (London: Wellsweep Press, 1993). A somewhat earlier work remains useful: *Human Rights in Post-Mao China*, by John F. Copper, Franz Michael, and Yuan-li Wu (Boulder: Westview Press, 1985).

3. Traditionally, human rights have been spoken of as *natural rights* or *universal moral rights*, which are possessed by all, and in some sense inalienable and indefeasible, because deemed to belong to the moral nature of things, whether recognized as such everywhere or not.

4. Among the many books on human rights, one might cite for example, Eugene Kamenka and Alice Erh-soon Tay, ed., *Human Rights* (London: Edward Arnold, 1978). Includes international contributions from philosophers and legal experts.

5. Article 55, in Walter Laqueur and Barry Rubin, *The Human Rights Reader* (New York: New American Library, 1989), p. 196. Besides its Universal Declaration of Human Rights (1948), the United Nations has published International Conventions, such as *On the Prevention and Punishment of the Crime of Genocide* (1951), pp. 203–4, and organized International Covenants on Economic, Social, and Cultural Rights (1966), the Elimination of All Forms of Racial Discrimination (1969) and the like. Quite explicitly, it recognizes "the inherent dignity and . . . the equal and inalienable rights of all members of the human family" Preamble to the United Nations International Covenant on Economic, Social, and Cultural Rights, p. 225.

6. See Laqueur and Rubin, *The Human Rights Reader*, pp. 198–200. These are examples

of human rights in the civil or political domain, that reflect earlier discussions. There are other articles in the United Nations Declaration that have been called social and economic rights. See Maurice Cranston, *Human Rights Today* (London:, Ampersand, 1962), pp. 36–38.

7. Laqueur and Rubin, *The Human Rights Reader*, p. 198.

8. See, for example, James C. Hsiung, ed., *Human Rights in East Asia: A Cultural Perspective* (New York: Praeger, 1985), especially his own chapter, "Human Rights in an East Asian Perspective," pp. 3–17.

9. See the publications in the mainland, such as *The White Paper*, Section 2.

10. Ann Kent, *Between Freedom and Subsistence: China and Human Rights* (Hong Kong: Oxford University Press, 1993), especially ch. 2.

11 Consult Julia Ching, *Chinese Religions* (London: Macmillan, 1993). chs. 3–4.

12. Laqueur and Rubin, *The Human Rights Reader*, p. 197.

13. Consult the Book of Mencius 1B:8. In fact, the Chinese word for king (*wang*) contained philosophically the meaning of a *good* king, even an ideal king.

14. I am referring to the *Vindicae contra Tyrannos* (1579) and to Mariana's *De rege et regis institutione* (1598–99).

15. See the article by Chu Ron Guey in this volume and Julia Ching, *Confucianism and Christianity* (Tokyo: Kodansha International, 1977), p. 193.

16. "The Regulations of a King" in *Hsün Tzu: Basic Writings*, trans. by Burton Watson (New York: Columbia University Press, 1963), p. 46.

17. "Identifying with One's Superiors," in Burton Watson, *Mo Tzu: Basic Writings* (New York: Columbia University Press, 1963), pp. 34–35.

18. "The Five Vermin," in *Han Fei Tzu: Basic Writings*, trans. by Burton Watson (New York: Columbia University Press, 1964), p. 96.

19. Consult "A Manifesto for the Reappraisal of Sinology and Reconstruction of Chinese Culture," in Carsun Chang, *The Development of Neo-Confucian Thought* (New York: 1963), vol. 2, Appendix.

20. Consult Sa Meng-wu, *Zhongguo fazhi sixiang* (Chinese Thinking on Government by Law) (Taipei: Yenbo Press, 1978).

21. Julia Ching, *Probing China's Soul: Religion, Politics, Protest in the People's Republic* (San Francisco: Harper & Row, 1990), pp. 105–7.

22. Ching, *Probing China's Soul*, p. 18.

23. See Laqueur and Rubin, *The Human Rights Reader*, p. 62.

24. The American Declaration of Independence (1776) puts it this way: "We hold these truths to be self-evident, that all men are created equal, that they are endowed by their Creator with certain unalienable rights, that among these are life, liberty, and the pursuit of happiness." See Laqueur and Rubin, *The Human Rights Reader*, p. 107.

25. *Mingyi daifanglu*, Sibu beiyao edition, ch. 1–3. For complete translation see Wm. Theodore de Bary, *Waiting for the Dawn: A Plan for the Prince* (New York: Columbia University Press, 1993).

26. Articles 35 and 37 of the 1982 Constitution. Consult Ching, *Probing China's Soul*, p. 168. However, certain rights permitted earlier were struck out, such as the right for workers to strike, and the right to air grievances on wall posters and to privacy in correspondence.

27. An earlier version of this paper was presented on a panel at an NGO forum during the United Nations Social Summit (March 1995) organized by the Religious Consultation on Population, Reproductive Health and Ethics (Washington D.C.) in Copenhagen, Denmark.

4

On the Rites and Rights of Being Human

D. W. Y. Kwok

This essay is written with an awareness that the literature on human rights in traditional Chinese civilization is legion and already highly sophisticated. Indeed, like ideas of science and democracy and their relationships to traditional Chinese civilization, the topic of human rights in Chinese civilization presents great complexity. This essay focuses on a few notions around the Chinese idea of "being human" or "behaving as a human being" (*zuoren*), an idea which reveals a preponderant concern with "rites," rather than "rights." The discussion of "human rights" vis-à-vis Chinese tradition needs to develop this idea of rites in order to provide a meaningful background.

The idea that a human being is born with rights is of a distinctly Western origin, traceable to seventeenth-century views of natural law and natural rights, if not earlier ones. Its absence in traditional Chinese thought and culture is commonly accepted, to be sure; yet, on this question, there are two distinct views.

One group, consisting mainly of philosophers who argue on linguistic grounds as to whether there is any adequate Chinese translation of "rights,"[1] maintains resolutely that there is no evidence for the presence of "human rights" in Chinese tradition. Members of this group also say that China was a society steeped in Confucian rites and as such possessed a civilization of several thousand years that was superior in its achievement of "human harmony." This being the case, China has no need for a Western notion of human rights that takes as its starting point the autonomy of the human being. Here then we have an outright encomium of Chinese culture, set in contrast to the contemporary moral chaos of Western society and its contentious individualism, for which China's approach to human harmony is seen as the right and timely antidote.

Comforting as it may be to those who believe that China's Confucian past has a singular and immediate contemporary relevance, this view is weak on the historical side. China's response to the inroads of modernism since the early nineteenth century holds no lessons for this group, whose moral idealism overlooks the critical historical changes that have taken place in the fabric of Chinese society. One critic of the views of this group charges that such idealization of the Chinese past has often led their advocates to create a "Nowheresville."[2]

Another group holds the view that any society, whether or not it has any native term for "human rights," nevertheless has its own notions of "right" and "rights." Were it not to have such views, that society could not conduct the exchanges and agreements necessary for maintaining social order.[3] Compared to the first group, this view is moderate, pointing out that, for such a rites-centered civilization as that of China, it does not mean that the society was devoid of the notion of "right"; rather, that the society has placed above such notions of "right" those ideas of "rites" which governed moral behavior. This view, allowing for the existence of notions of "rights" in the Chinese past, even if they were of secondary importance, holds much more promise for the resolution of our current concerns on whether China could and should develop human rights for its present and future.

The reason for bringing up these contrasting views before considering the question of "rites" versus "rights," is to avoid the simplistic dichotomizing of Western society as driven only by individualism,[4] and Chinese society as pursuing only human harmony. Historically, can we really say that the former does not show concerns with rites and mores, and the latter does not evince an appreciation of individualism? Some forms of the Western tradition's valuing of human rights are in the form of a belief that arches over and includes social rites and customs. Chinese tradition, on the other hand, has steadfastly refused to erect a belief or an ism above its valuation of human selfhood (individuality) and moral behavior. Such a relative difference can easily become a stark contrast of mutual opposites.

The Rites of Being Human

China's traditional civilization has always boasted of its special distinction in knowing how to be human (*zuoren*). Not only has it placed a premium on being human, but it has also claimed that its humanistic civilization was superior in the world.[5] Here we must make clear that the traditional civilization we refer to is one informed by Confucianism with its singular insistence on the definition of the human being. Whether being human was a question of "rites" or of law was argued over during the philosophical contentions of preunification China. Eventually Confucian and Mencian interpretations of human efficacy in terms of rites (*li*), with its web of human connectedness, won out over the specificities of legal definitions of prescribed human conduct. This was the outcome of a process which took much time as well as thoughtful, deliberate choice. For our present purpose, however, we will look particularly at the place of the "individual" and the "self" in this tradition.

Among the thinkers of the classical age, Xunzi came close to offering a view of natural equality of human origins, as when he said, "Heaven and Earth [nature] are the origin of life; ancestors are the origin of species." He pointed out, in this way, that life is endowed by nature, and all newly born belong to the same species. But then he also said, "Where is life without Heaven and Earth? Where is birth without ancestors?"[6] While the first parts of the two passages quoted seem to offer a view of natural equality, the second parts betray the higher importance Xunzi attached to life and being human. It was the ancestors who created the human species, and, while all humans were "born equal," they were "equal" in the sense of being equally human and different from animals. Moreover, only humans could recognize ancestors. Thus ancestors took precedence over nature. Thus also filial piety quite rapidly became a core value in the Chinese web of interpersonal relationships, an axis linking the individual human being, his family, and his society. By the Han dynasty, filial piety had already become institutionalized as a criterion for selection of persons into officialdom.

Such an "individual," then, from birth heads into a network of clan and kin relations guided by the spirit of interpersonal or interhuman regard (*ren*). There is no room for, nor is there anyone to encourage, such a person to develop and proclaim self-centered individualism. Although under such Confucian exhortations as "cultivate the self" (*xiushen*) and "restrain the self to restore the rites" (*keji fuli*), there is an awareness of the "self," this self-awareness is occasioned by the need to "behave as a human being" (*zuoren*), which in turn means to fulfill the five Confucian cardinal relationships: parent and child, ruler and minister, husband and wife, elder and younger, and friend and friend.[7] Of these five relationships, three refer to blood relations, and the other two, even though appearing to be outside of the family, are often given familial equivalents—pater/ruler (*fujun*) and brother/friend (*wuxiong*, *laodi*). Such a way of "behaving as a human being" allows little room for the individual to make any special claim on behalf of his/her own rights and privileges. The only way to be a "good person" (*haoren*) is within this network of behavioral rites.

By the time of the North-South Dynasties, the three hundred and fifty years between the Han and the Sui-Tang, this person enveloped in the web of rites received a liberation of the self unprecedented in Chinese history. The Daoist outlook of Laozi and Zhuangzi replaced for many the views of Confucius and the Duke of Zhou. The natural self became a philosophy and way of life. Ruan Ji of the Seven Sages of the Bamboo Grove was, in thought and deed, thoroughly averse to rites and family. One example was Ruan Ji's continuing to play a game of chess after hearing of his mother's death. This liberation of the self manifested clearly in literature and in philosophy. Tao Qian (375–427), the statesman-recluse, is perhaps the most successful example of the achievement of a "self" liberated from worldly attachments. Even during this age in which there was such free vent of the self, however, this tendency produced no doctrine that might be labeled as "individualism."

By the same token, the six hundred years after Buddhism's entry into China saw this religion of compassion influence many aspects of Chinese life. It promoted the individual quest for deliverance, while holding the state, the king, or the heads of families in no particular reverence. Among the enormous changes it wrought in Chinese culture, Buddhism added to Chinese sensibilities the dimension of kindness and compassion, qualities which address the relationships among common people and, poignantly, regard by human beings for all sentient things around them. These two relationships—among ordinary people and all sentient beings—are absent in the cardinal relations emphasized in early Confucianism.

The Sui-Tang period following this period of vigorous Buddhist faith and a revived Daoist tradition not only rebuilt an empire on the Qin-Han model but continued the open, extroverted, and broad-spirited ways of this intervening age. The poetry of Li Bo breathed the spirit of the unrestrainable individual, even though at times it sighed the messages of social tribulation. Du Fu, though reputed to be China's poet with a social conscience, still managed to impart a strong impression of the individual's sensibilities.

From the late Tang through the Song, Confucianism came to be revived and reached its completion as Neo-Confucianism with Zhu Xi in the twelfth century. Zhu Xi's annotation of the Four Books lifted their position well above the older importance of the Five Classics, although both sets of texts became Neo-Confucian canons and were designated as "required readings" for the imperial civil service examinations from then on. As such, these works acquired the status of official works. A new orthodoxy now once again habituated the Chinese to "behaving as human beings" according to even more detailed rules and rites. One might say that the Four Books taught people how to behave, and much in this corpus emphasizes "self-perfection" and "self-restraint" (*xiusheng, keji*).

Further, the Neo-Confucianism of Song and Ming also probed the individual human psyche. In spite of this, however, one must also admit society from the Yuan and Ming periods on became even more adept at ... aging human beings. What was in theory "humane rule" became in practice "ruling human beings" (*renzhi bian cheng zhiren*).

The foregoing historical sketch of Chinese tendencies in the matter of "behaving as a human being" (*zuoren*) bespeaks on one hand the strong point of traditional Chinese in its humanistic emphasis, and on the other its weak point in circumscribing the individual within the cardinal relationships and the web of clan-kin interests and ties. There are, however, other "cardinal" concerns in human and social life, most notably the relationships between a human and the world of matter. Thus, even in modern Chinese society, a Chinese often finds it difficult and awkward to relate to strangers.[8] As for the question of the human-thing relationship, as it involves utility and profit (*li*), it had always been shunted in favor of Mencius's *yi* (right impulse). As this human-thing relationship has everything to do with a culture's compatibility with a modern scientific worldview, its disregard in traditional Chinese culture has also meant the lack of development of any principles of science in the past, Joseph Needham's colossal twenty-plus volumes on *Science and Civilization in China* notwithstanding.

A few years ago, in an essay on *he* and *tong* (harmony and identity), I ventured the following view on this correlative set of values.[9] It is stated with deceptive simplicity in the *Analects* of Confucius as *"Junzi he er bu tong, xiaoren tong er bu he"*[10] (The sovereign man harmonizes but does not identify; the petty man identifies but does not harmonize), has always pointed to the direction that Chinese moral concerns have taken. *He* envelops all manner of logical opposites, and the superior person harmonizes them with his magnanimity. *Tong* describes the fretful and petty concern with exact identities and is clearly calculative. However, while this *he-tong* correlation illustrates China's moral inclinations, it may also explain a peculiar Chinese cosmological preference for seeing the cosmos as a harmony of patterns, *wen* (*wen*ming for civilization, *wen*hua for culture, tian*wen* for astronomy, ren*wen* for humanities). And *tong*, on another level, means the measurement necessary to illustrate equality and/or difference, contrast and inherence—essential elements of the scientific method. This *he-tong* correlation, then, while illustrating the moral rites of being human in China, also goes some distance toward explaining why China did not produce modern science, capitalism, or even natural rights philosophy, all of which require a certain abstraction and identification (*tong*) of thought and ideas.

Human Rights?

So far we have stated that all societies possess some views of "rights" and that Chinese values were determined by the rites of moral behavior and not based on any abstract beliefs of rights. Thus, it is not that China's civilization of several thousand years did not recognize individuality, but that it did not feel compelled to turn individuality into a belief in individualism; not that it did not have the wisdom for science and technology, but that it never "discovered" scientific principles and laws; not that it did not know how to make money and become wealthy, but that it did not produce capitalism; not that it did not know how to behave as human beings (*zuoren*), but that it did not formulate any belief in human rights. Yet, such a society is not without its awareness of rights, duties, and privileges. A few examples follow:

> Mencius said to King Xuan of Qi, "One of Your Highness's ministers once entrusted his wife to a friend while going on a trip to Chu. Upon his return, he found that his wife had been neglected. What is to be done?" The king said, "Dismiss him."[11]

Here is a clear case of the interaction of "right" and "duty." The person who promised a friend to look after his wife had the "duty" to perform his task, and the friend who entrusted his wife to someone's care had the "right" to expect good care. A similar case is mentioned in the *Mencius* about accepting the care of another person's stable animals.[12]

Then again, Mencius thought that people had the right to remonstrate against bad government, as when he had this to say to Duke Mu of Zou: "During this disastrous year of starvation, the old and weak among your people are moaning and groaning in the ditches; the strong have fled in all directions. They number in the thousands. Yet your granaries are packed and coffers full. Your officials do not report such affairs to you, thus cheating you and debasing those below them. . . . Alas, the people now have a right to show their opposition."[13]

Xing Yitian cites numerous cases from the Qin-Han period which evoked an awareness of human rights.[14] He cites examples of Qin law which do not approve extraction of confession through torture, Han laws forbidding arbitrary entry into people's residences by officials, laws against infanticide, laws against reducing punishment for the killing of slaves and the like. However, the cases valuing human life are limited only to human beings and not to a generalized humane outlook on all living forms. Just as Dong Zhongshu of the Han had said, "Because humans derive life from Heaven, they are different from other life forms."[15] Again, "Heaven and Earth issue forth their essence to create life, that which is precious is endowed in humans."[16]

The relationship between "right" and "duty" in any viable social sense is always close and dynamic. Thus the Confucian injunction of "serving when one excels in learning" (*xue er you ze shi*)[17] is not unrelated to the numerous cases in Chinese history when daring censors remonstrated against misdeeds of their emperors. Of course, these censors had no constitutional right to protect them in the performance of such acts; theirs was a moral pathos nurtured in their Confucian learning. Whether a censor acted to protect his name or save his head by such acts depended on his own moral self-respect and not on any constitutional stipulation. Thus in Chinese historical annals, cases of censors losing their heads while keeping their reputations intact are as replete as cases of heads intact and reputations lost. Then again, those who listened to such censorial entreaties were often acclaimed as *mingjun* (enlightened rulers), those who would not were called *hunjun* (befuddled rulers). All such cases point to the dynamic relationship between a sense of right and a sense of duty.[18] When a ruler trespasses, one must admonish. When he repeatedly listens but does not heed, he should be deposed," said Mencius.[19] The *Mingyi daifang lu* (A Plan for the Prince) of Huang Zongxi of the late Ming is a treasure trove of the Confucian political conscience as it addressed "right" and "duty" and the listening or unheeding prince.[20]

The examples cited above, resonant as they are of "right" and "duty," are nevertheless insufficient proof of the existence of human rights in the Chinese tradition. Even if the Confucian universe were still intact, perhaps the right-duty correlation could suffice to inform human relationships in Chinese society. But, even so, it is hard to imagine who would come forth in such relationships to *claim* his or her rights? Confucian society as a communitarian society is not composed of unassailable *individuals*; rather, it is a clan-kin society of interrelated individuals. C. K. Yang points out, "Self-cultivation, the basic theme of Confucian ethics . . . , did not seek a solution to social conflict in defining, limiting, and guaranteeing the rights and interests of the individual or in the balance of power and interests between individuals. It sought the solution from the self-sacrifice of the individual for the preservation of the group."[21]

The relationships in Confucian society are as complex as they are difficult to untangle. Between individuals, moreover, there is no completely equal position, whether in relation to the law or in relation to a father or ruler. The lack of equality between man and woman goes without saying. It is precisely because of this lack that there were grounds for feminine protest.

Su Dongpo, famed statesman and man of letters of the Song, had a maidservant by the name of Chun Niang. On the occasion of Su's giving Chun Niang to a certain Mr. Jiang, the maid could not tolerate the humiliation and committed suicide by dashing her head against a tree. Before she did so, she left a poem entitled "Thanking and Bidding Farewell to Master Su:"

To be human at all let one not be a woman,
A hundred year's bitterness or happiness determined by someone else.
Only today do I know the baseness of being human,
Hard it is to murmur the resentments of this meager life.[22]

With such social gradations, then, "rights" could not be accorded everyone, nor could they be accorded every *min* (people or citizen). The former is undoubtedly a human being,but the latter is not necessarily a *min*. For this reason, only those situated above could have a "right"—right of the prince, right of the patriarch, right of the ruler (*jun quan, fu quan, zhi quan*)—and such rights as those of the people, sons and self rule (*min quan, zi quan, zizhi quan*) are not encountered in past historical pages. Ju Tongzhu's *Chinese Law and Chinese Society*[23] presents with some detail such a system of graded laws in Chinese society, proving adequately that no evidence exists for any autonomy of individual human rights.

Why insist on the absence of human rights concepts in traditional China and at the same time show that notions of "rights" were nevertheless present? Such a position encompasses the two contrasting views presented at the beginning of this paper. It is important to point out the paramountcy of a morality based in rites which governed behavior in traditional China; it is also necessary to point out the secondary position of the notions of "rights" in such a society and, for our current purpose, to explore whether these formerly weak and negative "rights" views could be transformed sufficiently to support a modern society based on equal individual rights as well as of the groups they form. Answers can be sought from philosophy, sociology, political science, and legal studies. Here we have tried to see the question in light of certain historical aspects.

In recent years, as moral chaos seems to increase in Western societies, certain writers blame such confusion on the unbridled individualism of the West. At the same time, the increase of litigation and litigiousness in modern society has also occasioned a tendency to look for answers to conflict resolution in nonindividualist, or at least less individualistic, societies such as China. These tendencies naturally gladden those who sing only the praises of "rites." Yet, this latter view is unhistorical and unrealistic, in that it sees only the good side of such rites-centered society and not the deleterious side that accompanies the institutionalization of the practices of rites. This produces a self-deluding idealism built on past examples of uncertain applicability to a rapidly changing present. The result is not unlike that of trying to carry water on both ends of a bamboo pole.

What this essay tries to point out is *not* that China did not have a fine and exquisite tradition, or that its primary value of rites-based morality is not of some value. What it wants to convey is both the reason for and the limitation that attaches to this fine tradition. As we can see historically, the liberated approaches to the self took place outside the web of Confucian relationships and at a time when the Confucian polity was in eclipse. Even then, this liberated awareness and appreciation of the self did not lead to the establishment of either a *belief* or a code which can be labeled as individualism or a code of human rights.

Either way, a mode of human behavior based in rites and not on laws, or a spiritual liberation that neither recognizes nor makes any moral claims, both leave themselves open to authoritarian and despotic rule. Sometimes they even serve as ideological sanction for wielders of despotic authority. Human conduct based on morality naturally introduces and encourages judgments based on considerations of good or bad, kindly or rapacious, lofty or base. Though there is nothing wrong in wanting to scale moral heights—in itself a noble pursuit—when such aspirations after long centuries of institutionalization came to serve the ambition to scale the political heights, the continuing moral idealization of the process, along with the cultural idealism of moral harmonium, often have covered over political struggles of an unequal nature in the high reaches of society.

Chinese dynastic changeovers were the results of real power struggles and contentions. Seldom if ever were they based on any principled stand or philosophical "orthodoxy." They were instead invariably nasty occasions of bloodletting. In such struggles one detects not even a faint suggestion of the moral concerns taught by Confucius and Mencius. Whence the mandated prince? The long continuum of Chinese imperial monarchies was the product rather of a belated appropriation of moral values by the victorious power.

When this traditional China entered its century and a half of modernization, both its past culture and its despotic polity came to be shattered from internal as well as external factors. Concurrently throughout this long period efforts arose to establish a new culture, or to reform and renew the old culture (New Confucianism), while China underwent repeated political revolutions, three in the twentieth century, four if one counts the Cultural Revolution. Yet, at twentieth century's end China has still not shaken its authoritarian polity, and the people still cry out for the arrival of science and democracy. One also hears in these cries the yearnings for laws and rights that safeguard human decency.

If, then, the Chinese traditional civilization adept at "behaving as human beings" has any relevance and contribution to the increasingly global civilization of the present, it will depend on whether it can broaden its own basic view of what constitutes a human being and endow this person with legal rights the protection of which he or she can effectively claim when necessary.

Notes

First written in Chinese with the title "Zuoren yu renquan" (Behaving as a Human Being and Human Rights), this essay was read at a conference on human rights in Berkeley in spring 1994. At the conference, "Confucianism and Human Rights," in August 1995 in Honolulu, Professor Wm. Theodore de

D. W. Y. KWOK

Bary asked that the oral version of it be presented in English. This written version in English remains an essay in the original French meaning of essai.

1. Henry Rosemont, Jr., "Why Take Rights Seriously? A Confucian Critique," and Roger Ames, "Rites as Rights: The Confucian Alternative," in Leroy S. Rouner, ed., *Human Rights and the World's Religions* (Notre Dame, Ind.: University of Notre Dame Press, 1988), pp. 167–82 and 19–216, respectively; Chad Hansen, "Punishment and Dignity in China," in Donald Munro, ed., *Individualism and Holism* (Ann Arbor: University of Michigan Center for Chinese Studies, 1985), pp. 359–83.

2. Joel Feinberg, "The Nature and Value of Rights," *Journal of Value Inquiry* 4 (1970): 243–47.

3. See for instance Alen Gewirth, "Rights and Virtues," *Review of Metaphysics* 38 (June 1985): 739–62; Daniel A. Putnam, "Rights and Virtues: Toward an Integrated Theory," *Journal of Value Inquiry* 21 (1987): 87–99.

4. See Alasdair MacIntyre, *After Virtue* (Notre Dame, Ind.: University of Notre Dame Press, 1984). MacIntyre excoriates the moral chaos of the West and attributes it to its insistence on individual human rights; he praises, by contrast, Asian emphases on custom and harmony.

5. John C. H. Wu, "The Status of the Individual in the Political and Legal Traditions of Old and New China," in Charles A. Moore, ed., *The Chinese Mind* (Honolulu: University of Hawaii Press, 1967), p. 346. Wu maintains that, outside of China, no other society of the world has so preponderantly pressed the law into service of filial piety.

6. Both passages from the "Lilun" (On Rites) chapter of the *Xunzi.* Present translations are made from the *Zhuzi jicheng* (Collectanea of the Philosophers) edition, vol. 2 (Beijing: Zhonghua shuju, 1986, 1988), p. 233.

7. Ruey Yeh-fu, "The Five Social Dyads as a Means of Social Control," *Journal of Sociology*, no. 3 (April 1967, Taipei), 53.

8. See Jin Yaoji, "Rujia xueshuo zhong de geti yu qunti" (Individual and Group in Confucianism), *Zhongguo shehui yu wenhua* (Chinese Society and Culture) (Hong Kong: Oxford University Press, 1992), p. 12.

9. D. W. Y Kwok, "Ho and T'ung in Chinese Intellectual History," in Richard J. Smith and D. W. Y. Kwok, eds., *Cosmology, Ontology, and Human Efficacy: Essays in Chinese Thought* (Honolulu: University of Hawaii Press), pp. 1–9.

10. *Analects* 13:23 in *Zhuzi jicheng,* cited, pp. 296.

11. *Mencius* 2A:6 in *Zhuzi jicheng,* cited, pp. 83–84.

12. *Mencius* 2B:4 in *Zhuzi jicheng,* cited, pp. 157–58.

13. *Mencius* 2A:6 in *Zhuzi jicheng,* cited, p. 94.

14. Tianfu [pen name of Xing Yitian], "Zhongguo gudai falü zhong de renquan" (Human Rights in Ancient Chinese Law), *Lishi yuekan* (Historical Monthly), no. 7

(1990), pp. 128–32.

92

15. "Dong Zhongshu zhuan" (Biography of Dong Zhongshu), in *Hanshu* (History of Former Han), *juan* 56 (Beijing: Zhonghua shuju ed.), p. 2516.

16. Dong Zhongshu, "Renfu tiansu" (Humans in the Destinies of Heaven) chapter, *Chunqiu fanlu* (Luxuriant Dew of the Spring and Autumn Annals), in "Hanwei congshu" (Taipei: Xinxing shuju, 1966), vol. 2, p. 296.

17. *Analects* 19:13 in *Zhuzi jicheng*, cited, p. 405.

18. See D. W. Y. Kwok, "Protesting tradition and Traditions of Protest," in Kwok, ed., *Protest in the Chinese Tradition* (Honolulu: Center for Chinese Studies, University of Hawaii, 1989), pp. 1–7.

19. *Mencius* 5B:9 in *Zhuzi jicheng*, cited, p. 430.

20. See Wm. Theodore de Bary's treatment and translation of this classic under the title of *Waiting for the Dawn* (New York: Columbia University Press, 1993).

21. C. K. Yang, *Chinese Communist Society: The Family and the Village* (Cambridge: M.I.T. Press, 1959), p. 172.

22. Cited in Huang Yanli, "Kanghun, zishu, yu nüxing buping" (Resisting Marriage, Asserting Independence, and Inequality for Women), *Mingbao* (March 1994), pp. 24–25.

23. *Zhongguo falü yu Zhongguo shehui* (Hong Kong: Longmen shudian, 1967).

5

Fundamental Intuitions and Consensus Statements: Mencian Confucianism and Human Rights

Irene Bloom

If I were to ask you to imagine that Mencius is alive again, you would probably resist the idea, despite the fact that you have more than once heard him
invoked in recent discussions of the prospects for democracy and human rights
in China. Considering, however, that Mencius once was willing to travel thousands of *li* to discuss such matters as humaneness and humane government, we
might ourselves go to some imaginative lengths in order to draw him more
fully into our discussions of Confucianism and human rights. His world was
different, as was his language: the modern terms *quanli* and *renquan*—rights and
human rights—and *pingdeng* and *zunyan*—equality and dignity—were not part
of his vocabulary. But in a deeper sense many of his concerns seem related to
our own: his sense of common humanity, his discovery of a moral potential
common to all human beings, his devotion to the idea of "natural nobility," his
concern with the responsibilities rulers have for the well-being of the people,
his insistence on the limits of power—with what rulers should decline to do
out of respect and compassion for the people.

You will perhaps warn that we would have to be prepared to brief Mencius
on developments in China over the course of more than two millennia—no
easy matter. True enough, but the difficulty should not be exaggerated. An obvious starting point would be to apprise him that the Warring States period
ended shortly after his own time (or, at least, that the warring states he knew
are no longer the relevant contenders). Follow this by recounting the story of
imperial China and of modern China, coming at last to the epochal Chinese

encounters with the West and Japan in the nineteenth and twentieth centuries, the demise of imperial China in 1911, two world wars, and the revolution of 1949. The historical account concludes with the assurance that the empire has finally been unified (depending, of course, on how under present circumstances he might choose to define *tianxia*—all-under Heaven—and how he would construe "unity"). Once having brought him up to speed on the language of human rights, and supplied him with the Chinese text of the Universal Declaration of Human Rights and the major human rights conventions, we conclude the briefing by acquainting him with a debate that has been going on in recent years in China and the West.

Here, we allow, is the crux of the matter: in China and also in the West there have lately been those who, for different reasons, have voiced the concern that "human rights" is a Western idea without relevance to or resonance in the Chinese tradition. The implications of this assertion are complex, bearing as they do on matters ranging from internal politics and international relations to political and moral philosophy—even the understanding of culture itself. If the assertion should be found to be valid, then promoting human rights in a Chinese context may be regarded as an inappropriate attempt to foist non-Chinese values on Chinese people—like "climbing a tree to seek for fish," you might say, or perhaps "even worse." But in order to determine whether such an assertion of unbridgeable cultural difference *is* actually valid, it is necessary to deepen the discussion. If there is to be any hope of arriving at a more refined understanding of where today's China stands in relation to its own past, philosophical as well as historical, and in relation to the past and present of the rest of the world, a minimal requirement is that we acknowledge the full complexity and immense resources of what is sometimes too broadly characterized as "the Confucian tradition" or even "the Chinese tradition."

To Mencius, who disclaimed a fondness for argument, yet was compelled to argue by the desperate circumstances in which he lived, we are obliged to argue that the circumstances of the world are once again desperate. Scholars of the late twentieth century are no less disposed to argue than were the scholars of his own time, perhaps with similarly ominous results. Still, even if our contemporaries cannot otherwise agree on valid characterizations of "the Chinese tradition," or on appropriate judgments about its most prominent ideas and institutions, there is widespread agreement in acknowledging Mencius as the source of some of the most enduring dispositions and commitments of that vast company of Confucian scholars (*ru*) who over the course of centuries did so much to define Chinese culture, to identify the role of the scholar in public life, and to animate and exemplify a characteristically Chinese sense of humaneness and humanity. So we can give Mencius the satisfaction of knowing that we take him seriously in thinking through possible Confucian responses to human rights ideas.

What elements in human rights thinking seem consonant with classical Confucianism and congenial to a Mencian spirit, and what might Mencius find incompatible with his own thought? What might seem to be a promising (we hesitate to use the word "profitable") approach to these issues when we consider the future of China and of the world at large? Until he arrives, and has completed his briefing, we might try to make an effort to reach some tentative conclusions.

Fundamental Intuitions and Consensus Statements

Mencius, given his profound concern with the issue of human nature, would no doubt have been interested to learn that when a group of international experts came to drafting a statement on human nature and racial difference for the UNESCO "Statement on Race," published in July 1950, they settled on the incisive observation of Confucius in *Analects* 17:2, "By nature close together; through practice set apart."[1] Just eight characters in Chinese, eight words in English translation, this apparently simple affirmation from more than two millennia ago was evidently chosen because it seemed aptly to express a modern sense of human equality and relatedness—one that allows for both similarity and difference. Part of the effectiveness of this statement was no doubt its spareness and brevity: had it been more elaborate or explicit, it might have lost its transparency,[2] openness, and useful ambiguity.

But whatever it was that commended this statement of Confucius to the purposes of a UNESCO panel, it is clear that it has had a larger significance in the context of the long and argumentatively rich Confucian tradition. This is because, in its context, it is not a consensus statement but, almost the opposite of that, a fundamental intuition whose ambiguities, while presumably unintended, became, over time, the occasion for a variety of interpretations. The consensus statement, in other words, recognizes differences but encourages convergence; the fundamental intuition is born of conviction but, as a focus of centuries of reflection, becomes hospitable to divergence. But pointing to these two guises of a single truth invalidates neither the consensus statement, on the ground of its scant acquaintance with changing historical contexts, nor the fundamental intuition, on the ground of its relative openness to reinterpretation over time. Both play a role in the still ongoing history of ideas.

This leads to the central argument of this essay—namely, that just as human rights thinking represents only a *part* of morality rather than an entire moral system, so human rights thinking and activity in the world today draw and, indeed, depend upon the diverse moral understandings and energies of people of different cultures. However important a document it is, there is no one in the world who initially or primarily learns his or her moral values from that prototypical consensus document, the Universal Declaration of Human Rights. At the same time there are many whose understanding of the Universal Declaration, as of other human rights instruments and of human rights ideas more broadly, is informed and energized by religious and moral attitudes much older, more complex, and more diverse. Rather than seeing cultural and religious diversity as, ipso facto, constituting an impediment to (or a counterargument against) the twentieth-century consensus represented by human rights, it seems more fruitful to acknowledge that this diversity may be potentially supportive of human rights thinking—not in every way, but often in very significant respects.[3]

The shared element in the consensus statement represented by *Analects* 17:2 (as it is found in a UNESCO document) and the fundamental intuition represented by *Analects* 17:2 (as it appears in its original context) is a belief in some significant similarity among human beings—a recognition that opens up the possibility of thinking in terms of a common humanity. This, I shall argue, is the single most important connecting link between traditional philosophical and religious ideas and contemporary human rights documents: the former, with their fundamental intuitions, provide insight into the human condition and into the human capacity for mutual respect and regard; the latter, as consensus statements, draw specific consequences for civilized behavior—that is, defining behavior that human beings in the twentieth century can consider worthy of the designation "humane." The consensus statements are designed to bolster this move by promoting appropriate legal sanctions in the national and international spheres.

One way of approaching Mencian Confucianism and its bearing on human rights thinking both in China and in the world at large is to examine some of its fundamental intuitions. In particular, I propose to examine the Mencian perspective on a common human moral potential and its relation to the modern concept of equality, as well as the Mencian view of the "nobility of Heaven" and its relation to modern ideas of human dignity. In both cases I shall set Mencian views alongside Confucian views in order to suggest what appears to be the trajectory from a more aristocratic ethical perspective toward one that involves a deeper persuasion of a common humanity.

Human Moral Potential and the Concept of Equality

Returning to *Analects* 17:2 as a point of departure, it is understandable that a statement suggesting the intuition of a common human nature might capture the attention of contemporary readers precisely because it seems to suggest modern notions of equality. It is, of course, important to keep in mind that in

97

a tradition as ancient as Confucianism, a statement like this one was more embedded, and its significance was more particular. The language of Confucius is dynamic and relational; almost invariably he seems to be visualizing a process of development rather than some essential reality. The phrase he uses in 17:2 does not mean that he finds that human beings are "equal" in the sense of being *identical* by nature but, rather, that they are *close together* (*xiangjin*). There is a commentarial tradition that finds in the eight characters *xing xiang jin ye, xi xiang yuan ye* a perception on his part that all human beings share a moral potential and that their commitment to developing this potential determines more than anything else what they will be as persons.

This is a view which, in the context of the ancient world, may be seen as distinctly egalitarian. The idea of a fundamental similarity among human beings is a new development in China during the period from the sixth to the third centuries B.C.E. Closely identified with Confucius, and even more with Mencius, it sets the classical Confucian tradition apart from certain other traditions that were also evolving during the "axial age"[4]—the Upanishadic tradition in India, for example, or the Platonic tradition in Greece. The emphasis on a common human moral potential implies a respect for persons that goes beyond, and tends to undermine, class distinctions. It is also one that would be utterly incompatible with views based on a notion of natural *in*equality—the Indian concept of *varna* or caste, for example, or the Platonic idea of souls that are qualitatively distinct. Given the immense importance of moral potential, Confucius, and later Mencius, would argue urgently that it should not be slighted, damaged, or neglected. Confucius's saying that, "In education there should be no class distinctions"[5] accords with this respect, as does his openness to offering instruction to anyone,[6] and his sensitivity to the moral sensibilities of the common people.[7]

However, recognizing a common humanity and a similarity in moral potential implies no commitment on the part of Confucius to ultimate equality of treatment because he recognizes that the many variables involved in the process of human development may lead to different behavioral outcomes. Both parts of the statement in *Analects* 17:2—the conviction of a fundamental similarity among human beings and the perception that individuals distinguish themselves through their personal development—are equally significant. Donald Munro has observed that a distinction can be drawn between natural equality and evaluative equality. Confucius and Mencius, he suggests, demonstrate a belief in natural equality along with a moral perspective that entails evaluative *in*equality. A corollary of the notion that human beings enter the world with a similar endowment and potential is that this potential is realized to different degrees. Value attaches more to the achievement that a completed being represents than to the potential with which he began,[8] so that people may be similar at the outset of their lives but nonetheless deserving of different treatment as they live out their lives.

In the *Mencius* the egalitarian theme is further deepened, and the emphasis on moral competence is even more pronounced. In many encounters, especially those with rulers, a familiar pattern presents itself: Mencius's interlocutor poses a question in such a way that he seems, either through moral inertia or psychological avoidance, to be locating a problem beyond the sphere of his own control. Mencius then pointedly redirects attention from what might *appear* to be beyond human control to what, given the exertion of moral effort, is actually *within* human control.[9] The exchanges with rulers typically reflect the immediate concerns of some justifiably uneasy rulers about how to quiet their own sense of anxiety or foreboding, how to rule successfully, and even how to avert regicide. Almost invariably the Mencian answers to these questions turn on the ruler's need to cultivate and exert his own moral potential. Present in the thought of Confucius, this idea becomes not only more explicit in the thought of Mencius but fundamental to his concept of the person: with Mencius, the source of this human moral potential is specifically located and, at the same time, its presence is generalized.

From the conversations of Confucius, it emerges unmistakably that the individual's moral potential is important. But what is its source? Is it the *de*— virtue or moral force—that Confucius discovered in himself and whose origin, he believed, was Heaven?[10] Perhaps, but Confucius never assured his listeners that they also possessed this *de* and had only to develop it or "pile it up." Perhaps it was uncertainty about the source of moral potential that prompted Confucius's disciples to inquire so persistently about *ren* or humaneness and a disinclination on his part to be too specific about that source that explains his laconic responses. Certainly, it is characteristic of him to speak of *ren* or humaneness as difficult and challenging, as, for example, when he says, "Unbending strength, resoluteness, and reticence are close to humaneness."[11] Zengzi, in a famous statement in the same vein, speaks of *ren* as a lifelong burden, demanding breadth and fortitude.[12]

In one of his more encouraging moments, Confucius confirms that humaneness is not far away: "If I want humaneness, then humaneness is there."[13] But where *is* Confucius when we really need him? Given all of the difficulties, how does one summon forth such "unbending strength"? When Confucius insists that he himself is neither sagely nor humane but simply learns without flagging and teaches without growing weary, the response of Gongxi Hua is understandable. "This," he says, "is precisely where we disciples are unable to learn from your example."[14] When Yan Yuan asks about humaneness and is given the reply, "Through mastering oneself and returning to ritual one becomes humane," it is, again, hardly surprising that he ventures to ask for some specifics. 99

Confucius's answer seems no more specific and hardly less imposing: "Look at nothing contrary to ritual; listen to nothing contrary to ritual; say nothing contrary to ritual; do nothing contrary to ritual."[15] Small wonder that at one point in his short life Yan Yuan would sigh deeply and say, in regard to the Way of Confucius, or his personal example, "I look up to it and it becomes higher still; I delve into it and it becomes more impenetrable; I look at it in front of me, and suddenly it is behind me."[16]

With Mencius, our sights become fixed. His instructions are clear and explicit. We are not told about subjects on which he "seldom spoke,"[17] nor is he depicted as in the slightest respect elusive. In the dialogues between Mencius and rulers in the opening books of the *Mencius* he is straightforward and forthcoming—actually, almost unrelenting —in purveying his advice and admonitions. In supporting and demonstrating his argument for moral competence, Mencius must apparently persuade his interlocutors that they are, in fact, *able* to do what they *should* do—that it is within their capacity. Many of these rulers seem to make a study of moral weakness; Mencius makes it his business to correct for that, but he evidently cannot do so by invoking, with Confucius, the demanding requirements of unbending strength, perseverance, self-discipline, and fortitude. One suspects that, had Mencius emulated Confucius in recounting the many arduous prerequisites for humaneness and picked up Zengzi's punning image of *ren* as a burden, he might have lost his audience among these rulers.[18] Perhaps realizing this, he argues not as a moral elitist who presents the requirement to work indefatigably at something exceedingly difficult, but as one more grounded in a common life who understands and defends the expansive moral potential found in a common humanity.

A kind of prefiguring of this argument as it will later appear in its fully developed form is found in the conversation with King Xuan of Qi in *Mencius* 1A:7,[19] in which Mencius claims to have discerned the king's capacity for commiseration in the story of his having spared an ox from being sacrificed. The king's moral fortitude is, by his own admission, open to some question; in fact, the special impact of this story may be contingent on the fact that he seems otherwise so deficient in virtue that to a less purposeful teacher than Mencius the case might have been hard to sustain. Finding in this gesture on the part of the king a sign of his "inability to bear" the agony of the ox, Mencius interprets the compassionate response as "the working of humaneness" (*ren-shu*). What he is after here—his solution to the problem of moral weakness, apparently—is the extension of an altogether natural sense of kindness and compassion, something that he supposes almost anyone would have experienced in the course of family life. Having brought home to the king that the compassion he showed for an animal must obviously be extended to human beings, he continues:

By treating the elders in one's own family as elders should be treated and
this to the elders of other families, and by treating the young of one's own
the young ought to be treated and extending this to the young of other people's
families, the empire can be turned around on the palm of one's hand. . . .

Thus if one extends his kindness it will be enough to protect "all within the four
seas," whereas if one fails to extend it, he will have no way to protect his wife and
children. The fact that the ancients so greatly surpassed others was nothing other
than this: that they were good at extending what they did.[20]

Humaneness is no longer a burden requiring "unbending strength," now the
empire can be turned around on the palm of one's hand through an impulse as
natural as extending the scope of a normal human disposition to commiseration. This is a different sort of strength—more underlying than overwhelming—but we may be assured of its efficacy because it is, after all, what distinguished the ancients.

An argument taking essentially the same form, and repeating some of the
same language, is found in what is unquestionably the most famous passage in
the *Mencius*—the one with the unforgettable image of a child on the verge of
falling into a well. Here the interlocutor is not identified, but this time it is evidently not a ruler. Mencius begins with the affirmation—central both to his
moral philosophy and to his concept of the person—that, "All human beings
have a mind that cannot bear to see the sufferings of others." In his view,

The ancient kings had a commiserating mind and, accordingly, a commiserating
government. Having a commiserating mind and effecting a commiserating government, governing the world was like turning something around on the palm of
the hand.

Here is why I say that all human beings have a mind that commiserates with
others. Now[21] if anyone were suddenly to see a child about to fall into a well, his
mind would always be filled with alarm, distress, pity, and compassion. That he
would react accordingly is not because he would use the opportunity to ingratiate
himself with the child's parents, nor because he would seek commendation from
neighbors and friends, nor because he would hate the adverse reputation.[22]

Mencius does not need to tell us what the person watching the imperiled child
will do: we fill this in out of our own humanity. We have no doubt what any
human being in this situation could reliably be expected to do. Psychologically
speaking, this is all familiar ground: we have responded similarly in the course
of our own ordinary experience. Then Mencius takes a crucial step, turning the
negative "shuddering qualm"[23] that expresses our fear for the child's life into a
positive empathetic response: the mind that "cannot bear" to see the sufferings
of others. This mind is the mind of *compassion*, he explains, and it is a mind that
belongs to everyone.

One who lacks a mind that feels pity and compassion would not be human. One who lacks a mind that feels shame and aversion would not be human; one who lacks a mind that feels modesty and compliance would not be human; and one who lacks a mind that knows shame and dislike would not be human.[24]

In what follows these four—compassion, shame, modesty, and the sense of right and wrong—are identified as the "four sprouts" or "four beginnings" that Mencius believes are present in all human beings. As sentiments, as promptings of the mind or heart, these inclinations exist at the outset of an individual's life as a potential that is there to be realized in the normal course of human experience. The sense of compassion is the sprout of humaneness; the sense of shame, the sprout of rightness; the sense of modesty, the sprout of ritual decorum; and the sense of right and wrong, the sprout of wisdom.

Human beings have these four sprouts just as they have their four limbs. For one to have these four sprouts and yet to say of oneself that one is unable to fulfill them is to injure oneself, while to say that one's ruler is unable to fulfill them is to injure one's ruler. When we know how to enlarge and bring to fulfillment these four sprouts that are within us, it will be like a fire starting to burn or a spring finding an outlet. If one is able to bring them to fulfillment, they will be sufficient to allow him to protect "all within the four seas;" if he is not, they will be insufficient even to enable him to serve his parents.[25]

Here the characteristic Mencian affirmation is repeated: "*All human beings have* a mind that cannot bear to see the sufferings of others" and "Here is why I say that *all human beings have* a mind that commiserates with others." It is reiterated in the conversation about human nature recorded in 6A:6 where the disciple Gongdu reports on several views of human nature (*xing*) that differed from the one advanced by Mencius, particularly in emphasizing "external" determinants of human propensities rather than "internal" ones, as Mencius did. Defending his sense of natural tendencies shared by all human beings by virtue of their humanity itself—in other words, deriving from *within*—Mencius replies:

As far as the natural tendencies are concerned, it is possible for one to do good; this is what I mean by being good. If one does what is not good, that is not the fault of one's capacities. The mind of pity and commiseration is possessed *by all human beings;* the mind of shame and aversion is possessed *by all human beings;* the mind of respectfulness and reverence is possessed *by all human beings;* and the mind that knows right and wrong is possessed *by all human beings.* The mind of pity and commiseration is humaneness; the mind of shame and dislike is rightness; the mind of reverence and respect is ritual decorum; and the mind that knows right and wrong is wisdom. Humaneness, rightness, ritual decorum, and wisdom are not infused into us from without. We definitely possess them. It is just that we do not think about it, that is all. Therefore it is said, "Seek and you will get it; let go and you will lose it."[26]

The affirmation becomes consistently stronger: what were "sprouts" or "beginnings" in the context of 2A:6 are recognized in 6A:6 as "natural tendencies" (*qing*) or "capacities" (*cai*) that "we definitely possess." "Humaneness is the human mind,"[27] as he later puts it, and "Humaneness is what it means to be human."[28]

Several points are worth making here about Mencius's view of human moral potential: that it is shared by everyone, that it derives from sources based in common human experience, that it must be recognized and extended, that recognizing and extending it are as essential to one's own well-being as to the well-being of others, and that it can be injured or even lost. What is perhaps most striking about this view from the point of view of comparative philosophy is its metaphysical weightlessness: that is, Mencius asserts very little at a metaphysical level, making only the most minimal claims about an ultimate source for this moral potential. It is not that human beings are "created" by God, out of God, or in the image of God, nor that they are similar by virtue of standing in a certain relation to God or to ultimate reality. Rather, in this biological, familial, and social view of human nature, they are *procreated*, nurtured in families, and naturally given to interaction with others, and it is through these mundane human interactions that their distinctively human ability and knowledge develop:

> What people are able to do without having learned it is good ability (*liangneng*). What they know without having to think about it is good knowledge (*liangzhi*). There are no young children who do not know to love their parents, and there are none who, as they grow older, do not know to respect their older brothers. To be affectionate toward those close to one—this is humaneness. To have respect for elders—this is rightness. It is just this that is shared by everyone in the world (*wu ta da zhi tianxia ye*).[29]

Humaneness, along with its complement, rightness, is understood by Mencius as something natural, something shared by everyone in the world through the experience of growing up in a human family. The same message that was conveyed to King Xuan of Qi at the beginning of the book is repeated toward the end, but now it is directed not only to a king but, potentially, to everyone: becoming humane is within the competence of everyone and depends only on extending the affection and respect that are felt for those nearby in ever widening concentric circles of concern.

This version of equality differs in obvious respects from Western views which turn on the idea that human beings are born possessed of the faculty of reason—a view that was common to Stoic philosophy, the medieval scholastics, and many of the natural law philosophers of the seventeenth and eighteenth centuries. However, the differences, while significant, should not be exaggerated. John Passmore even suggests that *Analects* 17:2 ("By nature close together; through practice set apart") "could well be interpreted in a Lockian

103

sense,"[30] while there are echoes of the characteristic Mencian affirmation of humaneness in the views of the Cambridge Platonists and Richard Cumberland, with Ralph Cudworth arguing that "There is . . . a principle of common sympathy in everyone,"[31] and Cumberland that "There are in mankind, considered as animal beings only, propensities of benevolence to each other."[32] "In many respects," Passmore continues, "Confucianism stands very close to the characteristic teachings of the eighteenth century, which was, it is worth noting, fascinated by Chinese civilization."[33]

Both the Chinese and the Western idea of equality drew attention to what was found to be similar among human beings and to what was found most valuable. It is probably fair to say that, of the two concepts, the Chinese idea was, down to the eighteenth century, both the more inclusive, in that it emphasized human moral potential rather than the faculty of reason (which, it might be argued, appears to be differentially endowed), and the more influential in terms of political and social life, in that it had such profound ramifications in Chinese institutions, especially the civil service examination system and the educational system associated with it.

It is fascinating to note that Western thought may be said to have come closest to Chinese thought at just the point when the two were about to diverge again, especially in the political sphere, as the Western notion of equality found its way into legislative formulations in the eighteenth and nineteenth centuries from the Bills of Rights of several of the American states to the Declaration of the Rights of Man and the Citizen (1789) and, later, to several of the national constitutions enacted during the nineteenth century. In these documents the idea of equality would be associated with "equality before the law" and the "equal protection of the law," and thus, over time, "equality" would gain new meaning and fresh potency.

The Nobility of Heaven and Human Dignity

Pingdeng, the modern Chinese term for "equality" found in the Universal Declaration, does not occur in the *Analects* or the *Mencius*, nor does *zunyan*, the modern Chinese term for "dignity."[34] It is noteworthy that classical Greek lacks a term for "dignity," and, as Herbert Spiegelberg has observed, the Latin word *dignitas* is not applied to human beings. He adds that "there is no Latin phrase *'dignitas humana'* before the papal encyclicals of the last century."[35] In other modern languages too the more particular term "human dignity" appears rather late, the first occurrences of the German compound *Menschenwürde* being found, for example, only in the late eighteenth century.[36] It would appear that, "it was not until well into the Enlightenment that the 'dignity of man' as such became a current phrase."[37]

Still, it would be hard to deny that, even before the term gained political significance, the psychological and moral sense to which the term "human dignity," or *zunyan*, would later be applied can be discovered in philosophy and literature. Certainly both Confucius and Mencius display a deep concern for what, through modern eyes, can be recognized as "human dignity." Often statements having to do with human dignity are cast in a way that suggests that this dignity is contrasted with, and in some cases may cast some doubt upon, aristocratic dignity.[38] For example, Confucius says,

> Wealth and honor (*fu yu gui*) are what people desire, but one should not abide in them if it cannot be done in accordance with the Way. Poverty and lowliness are what people dislike, but one should not depart from them if it cannot be done in accordance with the Way. If the noble person (*junzi*) were to depart from humaneness, how could he fulfill that name? The noble person does not abandon humaneness for so long as the space of a meal. Even when hard pressed he is bound to this; even in times of danger he is bound to this.[39]

The "honor" to which Confucius refers in this case is part and parcel of the aristocratic dignity conferred by rulers. He does not simply deny this honor or wealth, nor does he say anything that would suggest that they harbor some taint or are necessarily compromising. Still, one must forego them if acquiring or retaining them would involve departing from the Way, just as one must accept poverty and lowliness if avoiding them would entail departing from the Way. The "noble person," or *junzi*, is, of course, noble according to the Confucian understanding of the term—noble in character rather than by hereditary status. For the morally noble person to depart from humaneness would mean a change in his entire orientation to the world and in the way he is known in the world. Neither change would be acceptable.

In the quotation we have just been considering, I have translated *wu hu cheng ming* as "how could he fulfill that name?" (meaning, "how could the noble person still be called a noble person if he were to depart from humaneness?"). An alternative rendering is that of D. C. Lau: "in what way can he make a name for himself?"[40] (meaning, "how can he fulfill his reputation?").[41] There is a distinction between the two translations, but the point in either case is that one's "name"—how one is known in the world—is extremely important in a Confucian context. Good actions are not discounted, as they might be by many Christian thinkers, because they are done out of a sense of *amour propre* or of how one is regarded by others;[42] rather, one's reputation is recognized as a factor in moral motivation and as a valid concern. Mencius does not suggest that one acts primarily for the effect the action will have on one's reputation—he specifically excludes *ming* as the motive that would prompt *all* human beings from saving a child from falling into a well[43]—but this does not mean that sensitivity to the effect an action would have on one's reputation invalidates that action as a *moral* action, as it would for Kant, for example.

The reasons for this are no doubt complex, and go to the heart of Confucian ethical thought, but at least one part of the explanation may be that Confucius and Mencius and the classical Confucians generally have no conviction of an afterlife—nothing comparable to the Christian idea of an infinite career of the soul, still less to the Hindu or the Buddhist idea of successive lifetimes. There is no larger life or greater spiritual realm for which this present life is a preparation. Rather, we find a perspective that might be characterized as "we pass this Way but once" (perhaps even, "one person/one lifetime"). In this perspective, reputation *matters*. One's "name" or "reputation" is, after all, not only an expression of the way one is regarded in the world during one's lifetime, but it becomes, in all likelihood, a form of immortality, the resonance or remainder that follows as a life beyond life.

Mencius has a similar intuition about the relation between aristocratic dignity and what might be called "human dignity," but he makes the distinction rather more pointedly:

> There is the the nobility of Heaven [or, natural nobility, *tianjue*] and the nobility of man (*renjue*). Humaneness, rightness, loyalty, and truthfulness—and taking pleasure in doing good, without ever wearying of it—this is the nobility of Heaven. The ranks of duke, minister, or high official—this is the nobility of man. Men of antiquity cultivated the nobility of Heaven, and the nobility of man followed after it. Men of the present day cultivate the nobility of Heaven out of a desire for the nobility of man, and once having obtained the nobility of man, they cast away the nobility of Heaven. Their delusion is extreme, and, in the end, they must lose everything.[44]

Confucius, while not denying aristocratic dignity in favor of moral nobility, tacitly recognizes the possibility that fitting into the social order and following the Way may sometimes involve competing claims. With Mencius, there is, again, no overt denial of aristocratic dignity, but there is far greater specificity about the source of the discrepancy. "The nobility of Heaven" (or "natural nobility") derives from fitting into the natural order by following through on the moral potential that, we now learn, is an endowment that human beings receive from Heaven. The "nobility of man" is of a different order—not necessarily antithetical or inimical to "the nobility of Heaven" but only accessory to it and purely transient. Those who sacrifice the "nobility of Heaven" on the belief that the "nobility of man" is sufficient are delusional, having failed to understand the larger context in which their lives are led.

The point is sharpened still further in the following passage in which Mencius is quoted as saying,

In their desire to be honored (*yuguizhe*) all human beings are of like mind.[45] And all human beings have within themselves what is honorable. It is only that they do not think about it, that is all. The honor that derives from men (*ren zhi suo gui zhe*) is not the good honor (*lianggui*). Whom Chief Zhao honors, Chief Zhao can also debase. The *Classic of Odes* says: "We have been plied with wine, And satisfied with virtue."

To "satisfy with virtue" means that one is satisfied with humaneness and rightness, and therefore does not crave the flavors of the meat and grain served by men, and when a good reputation and widespread esteem accrue to one's person, one does not crave the elegant embroidered garments worn by men.[46]

Mencius's use of the term *liang* in the phrase I have translated, sparely, as "good honor" is noteworthy. It is the same word he used in explaining the source of human moral potential, a potential that *all* human beings share through an endowment of Heaven expressed in their "good ability" and "good knowledge."[47] In the present context Mencius uses the term *liang* to identify the "good honor" that *all* human beings have within themselves.[48] It is clear from the fact that this honor is contrasted with "the honor that derives from men" that it is an honor endowed by Heaven or Nature. Even now, aristocratic honors are not denied, but in being associated with sensual indulgence they are heavily discounted in comparison with the moral satisfactions of humaneness and rightness.

This evidence, as well as other evidence in the text, suggests that a genuine—and, ultimately, powerful—concept of human dignity took form in the thought of Mencius. As in the case of Mencian equality, Mencian dignity is based on moral potential and, more particularly, on the psychological awareness of that potential within the minds of individuals. In the passages quoted above, we have seen Mencius drawing more and more explicit contrasts[49] between aristocratic dignity, which may be morally vacant (if it does not actually degenerate into an *ig*noble nobility), and human dignity. In other exchanges, some of them apparently more personal in nature, he speaks of a person's capacity to affirm his own humanity by asserting himself as a moral agent:

I desire fish, and I also desire bear's paws. If I cannot have both of them, I will give up fish and take bear's paws. I desire life and I also desire rightness. If I cannot have both of them I will give up life and take rightness. It is true that I desire life, but there is something that I desire more than life, and therefore I will not do something dishonorable in order to hold onto it. I detest death, but there is something I detest more than death, and therefore there are some dangers I may not avoid. If among a person's desires there were none greater than life, then why should he not do anything necessary in order to cling to life? If among the things he detested there were none greater than death, why should he not do whatever he had to do to avoid dan-

107

ger? There is a means by which one may preserve life, and yet he does not employ it; there is a means by which one may avoid danger, and yet he does not adopt it.[50]

The sense of dignity that comes through in this statement is strong; one is perhaps inclined to think this is the kind of nobility to be found only in a few. But Mencius's vision is more encompassing, as is evident from his conclusion:

> Thus there are things that we desire more than life, and things that we detest more than death. It is not only exemplary persons who have this mind; all human beings have it. It is only that the exemplary ones are able to avoid losing it, that is all.
>
> Suppose there are a basketful of rice and a bowlful of soup. If one gets them, one may remain alive; if one does not get them one must die. If they are offered contemptuously, a wayfarer would decline to accept them; if they are offered after they have been trampled upon, a beggar would not demean himself by taking them. And yet when it comes to ten thousand bushels I accept them without regard for ritual decorum and rightness. What do the ten thousand bushels add to me? Is it for the sake of beautiful dwellings that I take them, or for the service of wives and concubines, or for the recognition of those afflicted by poverty? What formerly I would not accept even if it meant my death, I now accept for the sake of beautiful dwellings. What formerly I would not accept even if it meant my death, I now accept for the service of wives and concubines. What formerly I would not accept even if it meant my death, I now accept for the recognition of those afflicted by poverty. Could this not have been declined as well? This is what is called losing one's original mind (*shi qi benxin*).[51]

Now the wealth and status that are often the seal of "the nobility of man" begin to look even more problematical. Now they *are* morally vacant. What the wayfarer and the beggar know not to do because it would entail a loss of dignity, the man of wealth and status has forgotten. We may well feel embarrassed by this man and his all too understandable memory loss amid material gain. Mencius may well have intended to evoke some such response through the use of the first person pronoun ("Is it for the sake of beautiful dwellings that I take them. . . ?) which seems to make this man more immediately present and strangely insinuating as a reproof and a warning.[52] Human dignity can be lost, but, as the witness of the wayfarer and the beggar is there to show, with great poignancy, it cannot be taken away.

One final point should be made about the Mencian idea of dignity, and that concerns its political implications. I have focused here on "human dignity"—the dignity that human beings have by virtue of their humanity—as contrasted with "aristocratic dignity"—the dignity that rulers and elites claim based on their roles in the political and social order. This is also the way the distinction has been analyzed in terms of Western thought in light of the history of the con-

cept in the Enlightenment and post-Enlightenment period when the notion of "human dignity" may be seen to have evolved in parallel with democratic thought, as a *denial* of aristocratic dignity.[53] In the case of classical Confucian thought, of course, we are examining a perception that emerged very early, at a time when social mobility was producing a telling effect in Chinese society, but many centuries before there was any serious challenge to monarchical rule per se. In China during much of the "axial age" the two notions of dignity, while distinguishable, seem to have coexisted. Always, however, "human dignity"—or, to put it in Mencian terms, "natural nobility" or "the nobility of Heaven"—are recognized to be primary and authentic, whereas the "nobility of man," at times becoming a kind of simulacrum, might be subject to corruption.

The idea of "natural nobility" or "human dignity" seems to have emerged alongside the egalitarian idea that human moral potential is a natural endowment that all human beings share and, as I have suggested, to have involved a recognition of the importance of the psychological awareness of that potential on the part of individuals. Just as human moral potential is understood by Mencius to dispose human beings to interact harmoniously with one another, so the Mencian notion of dignity, allied to this understanding, seems to involve a self-consciousness on the part of human beings that they are both capable and worthy of respect. I would suggest that human dignity in this context involves an appreciation on the part of individuals of their own moral potential, a claim for respect from others, and a corresponding duty and disposition to show respect for others—all in light of the awareness of a common humanity. The degree of respect that is to be shown may vary in accordance with the specific relationships between individuals—depending on kinship ties, gender, age, and social position—and the particular behaviors required vary as well. But always there is a basic respect required from each human being toward every other human being as a condition of their common humanity.

Where the requirement of mutual respect is forgotten, it is natural that the parties involved in the transaction should feel that their dignity has been assaulted. This may happen in the sphere where "aristocratic dignity" pertains, as is illustrated in some of Mencius's exchanges with rulers in which he speaks with stunning forcefulness about issues that bear on the dignity of ministers. This is evidently what is at issue when Mencius says to King Xuan of Qi:

> When the ruler regards his ministers as his hands and feet, the ministers regard the ruler as their stomachs and hearts. When the ruler regards his ministers as dogs and horses, the ministers regard the ruler as just another person. When the ruler regards his ministers as dirt and grass, the ministers regard the ruler as a bandit and an enemy.[54]

In what follows it emerges that this dire situation arises when a king's actions contravene the courtesies prescribed by ritual and specific to the particular relationship between ruler and minister. In this case the king's disregard for the dignity of ministers may be described as an affront to "aristocratic dignity"—in other words, to the dignity that belongs to ministers *qua* ministers. But the psychological and moral principle here is more general than that: there is a consistent sense, in the *Mencius*, that the claim to receive respect from others and the disposition to behave respectfully toward them are both psychologically and morally correlative. This is as true of ordinary people, including wayfarers and beggars, as it is of ministers and kings. Politically speaking, this concept of human dignity may not be either subversive of monarchical rule or necessarily conducive to democratic government per se, but few would deny that it provides a firm basis for a critique of cruelty, oppression, and misrule in both its active and passive forms. It is surely consistent with, though not generative of, many of the democratic ideas and values that would evolve in subsequent centuries.

The point of the imaginative exercise entertained at the outset of this essay, followed by an exploration of two of Mencius's fundamental intuitions, was to suggest that, complex methodological strategies notwithstanding, this is actually the way a philosophical tradition is generally reclaimed and revivified and the way it comes to figure in moral education. For scholars, historical research may go some considerable way toward illuminating the circumstances in which a figure like Mencius worked and in which his thought evolved; in our own time we have seen the way gradually being opened to more nuanced understandings of how ideas figured in their original context.[55] But if we want to come closer to that thought—to evaluate it and truly to repossess it—we will need to consider what bearing it has had on later times and what possibilities it appears to have for the present. This is even more obviously true when one considers the role of traditional moral thought in the larger perspective of an evolving cultural life.

Mencius would no doubt have a legitimate complaint that the above analysis, in focusing on the issues of human moral potential/equality and natural nobility/dignity, omitted much in the *Mencius* that would naturally come to mind as consonant with human rights thinking, including the idea of "the people as fundamental" (*minben*), the emphasis on the importance of the people's economic livelihood,[56] and the strong valuation of education.[57] He might also note that his insistence on the responsibility of the ruler for the well-being of the people received virtually no attention here, even though the text that bears his name attests that this represented a conviction so deeply held that it produced a clear (and, for more than a few rulers, a decidedly unsettling) justification for deposing a ruler who demonstrably "despoils humaneness and rightness."[58] There is much else that could also have been discussed in regard to

Mencian thought and human rights.

The reason for having focused on moral potential/equality and the nobility of Heaven/human dignity is that these two ideas are so clearly at the heart of both Mencian Confucianism and contemporary human rights thinking. Again, this is not to suggest that Mencian Confucianism was generative of democratic ideas or of human rights thinking, but, rather, that its fundamental intuitions—with their crucial affirmations of human equality, responsibility, relatedness, and respect—are consistent with and morally and spiritually supportive of the consensus documents that figure so importantly in our emerging modern civilization.

Notes

1. See *Sources of Chinese Tradition*, compiled by Wm. Theodore de Bary, Wing-tsit Chan, and Burton Watson (New York: Columbia University Press, 1960), p. 25, n. 2.

2. By using the word "transparency," I do not mean to imply that those who adopted Confucius's statement necessarily had a clear understanding of *his* intention in uttering it but, rather, that they almost certainly had a clear understanding of *a* meaning.

3. In some instances there appear to be conflicts involved, one of the more famous of which surfaced in the concerns of some adherents of Islam over Article 18 of the Universal Declaration, which deals with religious freedom and, specifically, the freedom to convert to another religion. Even here, there may be creative approaches to an apparent conflict. See, for example, David Little, Abdulaziz Sachedina, and John Kelsay, "Human Rights and the World's Religions: Christianity, Islam, and Religious Liberty," in Irene Bloom, J. Paul Martin, and Wayne L. Proudfoot, eds., *Religious Diversity and Human Rights* (New York: Columbia University Press, 1996), pp. 213–39.

4. Karl Jaspers, "Die Achsenzeit," in *Vom Ursprung und Ziel der Geschichte* (Zurich: Artemis Verlag, 1949), ch. 1; trans. by Michael Bullock as *The Origin and Goal of History* (New Haven: Yale University Press, 1953). The concept of the "axial age" is discussed in Benjamin I. Schwartz, "The Age of Transcendence," in the symposium, "Wisdom, Revelation, and Doubt; Perspectives on the First Millennium B.C." in *Daedalus*, Spring 1974. See also Benjamin I. Schwartz, *The World of Thought in Ancient China* (Cambridge: Belknap Press of Harvard University Press, 1985), pp. 2–3 and p. 423, note 2.

5. *Analects* 15:38.

6. *Analects* 7:7.

7. *Analects* 2:3 and 9:26, for example.

8. Donald J. Munro, *The Concept of Man in Early China* (Stanford: Stanford University Press, 1969), esp. chs. 1 and 4.

9. One example is Mencius's conversation with King Hui of Liang in 1A:3 in which he insists that the king, in arguing that he has done his duty by transferring grain supplies to areas of shortage due to famine, has seriously underestimated both his duty and his own moral capacity. Another example is the famous discussion in 1A:7 where

Mencius impresses on King Xuan of Qi the distinction between "not doing something" and "not being able to do it."

10. *Analects* 7:22.

11. *Analects* 13:27. Translation adapted from D. C. Lau, *The Analects* (Harmondsworth: Penguin, 1979), p. 123.

12. *Analects* 8:7. Here, Zengzi is, of course, drawing attention to the fact that *ren* (humaneness) and *ren* (a burden) are homophones.

13. *Analects* 7:29.

14. *Analects* 7:34. Translation adapted from D. C. Lau, *The Analects*, pp. 90–91.

15. *Analects* 12:1.

16. *Analects* 9:10. And this was, after all, from someone in whom Confucius could find "no fault" (*Analects* 8:21).

17. Cf. *Analects* 5:12, 7:20, 9:1.

18. If even King Hui of Liang found Mencius's views to be "impracticable and remote from actuality," one can imagine the reactions of some of the other rulers whom Mencius admonished in an even more combative spirit. See the biography of Mencius in *Shiji* 74; translation by D. C. Lau in his translation of *Mencius* (Harmondsworth: Penguin Classics, 1970), p. 205.

19. By saying that the fully developed argument will appear later, I simply mean later in the received *Mencius* text. I make no assumptions about the order of composition or compilation of the chapters or their authenticity, leaving these complex issues to the detailed scholarship of E. Bruce Brooks and Taeko Brooks.

20. *Mencius* 1A:7.

21. At the beginning of the passage Mencius recalls that the ancient kings had this "mind that cannot bear to see the sufferings of others." Here he affirms that people of the present also have it.

22. *Mencius* 2A:6.

23. I. A. Richards' phrase in *Mencius on the Mind* (London: Kegan Paul, Trench, Trubner, 1932), p. 19.

24. Ibid.

25. Ibid.

26. See also the statement attributed to Confucius at the end of *Mencius* 6A:8.

27. *Mencius* 6A:11.

28. *Mencius* 7B:16.

29. *Mencius* 7A:15. My translation of the Chinese word *liang* is inadequate, but I have not found a way to express it more aptly. Frequently the *liang* in *liangneng* and *liangzhi* is translated, following several Neo-Confucian thinkers, as "innate." But this seems to miss the sense in which Mencius uses the term here because the term seems to hover between nature and nurture—or, rather, to obviate the distinction. Although his translation is periphrastic, W. A. C. H. Dobson was obviously trying to capture this sense of

a good that is "given" when he rendered the opening lines of the passage: "The abilities men have which are not acquired by study are part of their endowment of good. The knowledge men have which is not acquired by deep thought is part of their endowment of good." See W. A. C. H. Dobson, *Mencius* (Toronto: University of Toronto Press, 1963), p. 148. An alternative translation of the last line of the passage would be: "and requires nothing more than to be extended to everyone in the world."

30. John Passmore, *The Perfectibility of Man* (London: Gerald Duckworth, 1970), p. 160.

31. British Museum Add. MSS. 4983,83; quoted in Passmore, *Perfectibility of Man*, p. 160.

32. Richard Cumberland, *A Philosophical Inquiry Into the Laws of Nature*, first published in Latin in 1672, trans. John Towers (Dublin: 1750), p. 211; quoted in Passmore, *Perfectibility of Man*, p. 160.

33. Passmore, *Perfectibility of Man*, p. 160. In Passmore's view:

> Confucius, like the eighteenth century, seeks the perfection of man through the exercise of virtue, a virtue with two aspects, knowledge and humanity (*ren*). Knowledge, for Confucius as for the eighteenth century, is first and foremost knowledge of mankind (*Analects* 12:22). He defines "humanity" as "earnestness, liberality, truthfulness, diligence and generosity" (17:6)—typical eighteenth-century virtues. The "heavenly law" of the Confucianists is, furthermore, very like the God of the deists, an impersonal governor of the Universe. What happened in the seventeenth and eighteenth century, one might almost say, is that European thought became Confucianised. Not, of course, that this is a correct historical account of what happened, if we are thinking in terms of "influences." Confucian-type ideas—originating, as we have suggested, in Greek sources, Platonic, Stoic, or Epicurean—were already abroad before Confucius was translated. But Confucianism served as living proof that the love of neighbours was not a peculiarly Christian doctrine. (Ibid.)

34. While *pingdeng* is found in none of the texts of classical Confucianism and may have its origin in Buddhist texts, *zunyan* is found in chapter 14 ("On Attracting Scholars") of the *Xunzi*. In John Knoblock's translation the passage reads: "There are four techniques for being a teacher, but a superficially broad general acquaintance is not one of them. One who requires deference, is majestic in manner (*zunyan*), and instills a fearing respect may properly be regarded as a teacher." John Knoblock, *Xunzi: A Translation and Study of the Complete Works*, vol. 2 (Stanford: Stanford University Press, 1990), p. 209. *Zunyan* in this context would appear to have more the sense of an imposing presence than of moral nobility.

35. Herbert Spiegelberg, "Human Dignity: A Challenge," in *Human Dignity—This Century and the Next: An Interdisciplinary Inquiry into Human Rights, Technology, War, and the Ideal Society*, ed. by Rubin Gotesky and Ervin Laszlo (New York: Gordon and Breach, 1970), p. 42. Spiegelberg also points out that, "At the beginning of the Renaissance Pico della

Mirandola's famous oration is entitled 'De dignitate hominis,' but neither this phrase nor 'dignitas humana' appears in the text" (ibid.).

36. Spiegelberg, p. 42.

37. Ibid.

38. In distinguishing between "dignity" and "human dignity" as those terms evolved in the modern Western European context, Herbert Spiegelberg makes the point that *human* dignity is "a very different matter." "It implies the very denial of an aristocratic order of dignities. For it refers to the minimum dignity which belongs to every human being qua human. It does not admit of any degrees. It is equal for all humans" (Spiegelberg, "Human Dignity," p. 56). I am inclined to think that in the perspective of Confucius or Mencius, an aristocratic order of dignities is clearly called into question but not explicitly *denied*. As the following quotation from the *Analects* 4:5 suggests, the problem arises mainly when the world's honors are perceived to conflict with the individual's sense of what is right.

39. *Analects* 4:5.

40. D. C. Lau, *Analects*, p. 72.

41. James Legge explicitly rejects the validity of translating *ming* as "reputation," however. James Legge, trans., *Confucian Analects* in *The Chinese Classics*, vol. 1 (Oxford: Clarendon Press, 1893), p. 166, note 5.

42. John Passmore makes the interesting point that one of the new directions charted by Locke was his recovery of the idea of the importance of reputation:

> Even more shocking [to Scholastic theologians, Calvinists, and others] than the elevation of habits, derived from education, to being both necessary and sufficient for virtue in the fullest sense of the word, was Locke's belief that shame and reputation were the instruments by which men were to be educated into virtue. "Shame and reputation" [referring to Locke's essay *Some Thoughts Concerning Education*, 1693]—in short that *amour propre*, that concern for one's position in the world that Christian moralists united in denouncing. . . . It is clear enough what Locke is doing. Not only enlightened self-interest—*amour de soi*—but even a concern for reputation—*amour propre* [a distinction made famous by Rousseau]—were to lose their old terrors. In some ways, indeed, we are back in the atmosphere of Homeric Greece. Reputation and shame are the important things; if a man can learn to feel ashamed at the right moments there is no need to fear for his virtue. Passmore, *Perfectibility of Man*, pp. 162–63.

43. See the quotation from 2A:6, above.

44. *Mencius* 6A:16.

45. Legge's translation (*The Chinese Classics*, vol. 2, p. 419) reads: "To desire to be honorable is the common mind of men."

46. *Mencius* 6A:17.

47. In 7A:15.

48. Sparely, and no doubt inadequately, translated here as "good," the word *liang* is sometimes translated as "innate," though this translation has been contested because it could be understood to imply something static and fixed. Since *liang gui* or "good honor" is obviously related to human moral potential, it shares in the dynamic quality of *liang neng* and *liang zhi*.

49. I do not mean to suggest that the order of the passages as given here suggests anything about a progression or development in Mencius's thought. The order is my own.

50. *Mencius* 6A:10.

51. Ibid.

52. James Legge's comment on this passage (*The Chinese Classics*, vol. 2, p. 413) is:

> There is here a contrast with the case in the former paragraph, which was one of life or death. The large emolument was not an absolute necessity. But also there is the lofty, and true, idea, that a man's personality is something independent of, and higher than, all external advantages. The meaning is better brought out in English by changing the person from the first to the third.

I agree with Legge's perception about Mencius's "lofty and true idea" but not with his decision to forget Mencius's use of the first person pronoun and change to the third person in English.

53. Spiegelberg, "Human Dignity," p. 56.

54. *Mencius* 4B:3. In the remainder of this exchange, King Xuan, apparently missing the point here, or seeking to evade it, changes the subject to ask, "According to ritual, a minister wears mourning for a ruler he has once served. How must one behave in order for this practice to be followed?" The response from Mencius is withering:

> When a minister whose admonitions have been followed and whose advice has been heeded, with the result that benefits have extended down to the common people, has reason to depart the state, the ruler sends an escort to conduct him beyond its borders. He also prepares the way for him at his destination. Only after he has been gone for three years without returning does the ruler repossess his land and residence. This is called the threefold courtesy. When a ruler acts in such a way, the minister will wear mourning for him. Now, however, a minister's admonitions are not followed and his advice is not heeded, with the result that benefits do not extend down to the common people. When he has reason to depart, the ruler tries to seize and detain him. He also tries to place him in extreme jeopardy at his destination. He repossesses his land and residence on the day of his departure. This is known as being a bandit and an enemy. What mourning should there be for a bandit and an enemy?

55. Many scholars working today are making important contributions; I refer particularly to the exhaustive and very creative work of E. Bruce Brooks and Taeko Brooks of the Warring States Working Group at the University of Massachusetts, Amherst, which is soon to be published.

56. *Mencius* 1A:3, 1A:7.

57. *Mencius* 1A:3, 1A:7.

58. *Mencius* 1B:8.

6

Confucian Theory of Norms and Human Rights

Wejen Chang

Initially a concept derived from Western liberalism and constitutionalism, "human rights" is now accepted by many, and its scope has been expanded to include a lengthening list of different types, or "generations," of rights, characterized as "civil and political," "social and economic," and "developmental and collective."[1] The Confucians, for their part hoping to help humans live a good, human way of life, developed a fine theory of norms for that purpose, yet we do not find in the Confucian classics a term that is close to "human rights." To my mind this raises two questions: is Confucianism conceptually compatible with "human rights"? and is the Confucian theory of norms practically conducive to a good, human way of life if it does not recognize "human rights"? In this study I shall first take a close look at that theory of norms and then try to answer these two questions.[2]

The basic guiding principle for a person to behave as a human being in human society, according to Confucius, is humanity or to be humane (*ren, jen*), from which all social norms are developed. In his view people need this principle more than water and fire.[3] If a person is completely without this principle what, asked Confucius, does that person have to do with rites and music (as social norms)?[4] None will have any effect on him, he will cause problems not only to society but also to himself—he will be unable to remain long either in difficulty or in comfort.[5] For a gentleman the principle is even more important—he should not deviate from it for even as short a moment as it takes to eat a meal;[6] he should never do harm to it even for the preservation of his own life; rather, he should sacrifice his life to uphold it.[7]

What is humanity? On different occasions Confucius explained it in different terms, each emphasizing one or more of its aspects and ramifications. One of the more fundamental explanations is that to be humane is to love all human beings (*ai ren*).[8] This idea is supported by several of his other statements. In one of them he characterized a person as humane if he is able to practice five virtues (respect, tolerance, trustworthiness in word, diligence in action, and kindness) in his relation with all the people of the world.[9] In another, he praised Guan Zhong as humane for helping assemble the feudal lords nine times to maintain the authority of the Zhou dynasty, repel the aggression of the barbarians and thus save Chinese civilization, to the benefit of all the people.[10] This idea of love of all human beings was accepted by all Confucians as central to the concept of humanity. Mencius not only endorsed this idea but emphasized that to be humane is the way to be a human being.[11]

Nevertheless to be humane is not easy. Apart from Guan Zhong and a few of the persons in ancient times Confucius did not readily praise people as being humane.[12] It is particularly difficult, Confucius said, in the sense of practicing universal love, widely sharing one's bounty with the people and bringing help to them, as it was even for the sage-kings Yao and Shun.[13] It was probably in this sense that Confucius modestly declined to claim being humane.[14] Nevertheless, he insisted that one should try. It will be a long journey, but anyone can take it by oneself without outside assistance.[15] The starting point is not far away—once one puts one's mind to take the journey one is already there,[16] and once on the road, no one, as far as Confucius knew, would lack the strength to continue.[17]

Exactly how, then, can one try to be humane—how is one to behave oneself and love all human beings? Confucius suggested that there are certain rules to follow and that one can find these rules by oneself, or one can follow the rules found by others. This leads to an elaborate theory of norms. It begins with the simple observation that human beings are by nature similar, although they can become different due to different life experiences.[18] All men, sharing a similar human nature, can look into their own hearts and find there some basic feelings toward other human beings. This is particularly true of filial piety toward one's parents and a brotherly affection toward one's siblings. That is why these two feelings are said to be the very essence of humanity.[19] And it is presumed that with these feelings one should naturally know how to treat one's parents and siblings and, by extension, other human beings.

This line of thinking was followed and spelled out in more interesting language by Mencius. According to him human beings have a common (not just similar) nature, which is good.[20] He illustrated this by his celebrated reference to the pity and alarm one feels on seeing a child about to fall into a well. In addition to this "heart of pity," Mencius asserted that human beings also have "the heart [feeling] of shame," "the heart of courtesy" and "the heart of right and wrong." These four "hearts," or natural feelings, are, according to him, the seeds of behavioral rules or social norms—from the heart of pity grows the virtue of humanity; from the heart of shame, rightness; from the heart of courtesy, ritual decorum; and from the heart of right and wrong, wisdom. Because everyone has these four "hearts" just as everyone has four limbs, Mencius said, all one need to do is to develop them in order to have these virtues.[21] Thus, he alleged, the norms are intrinsic to humans, not imposed on them from outside.[22] It follows that to be humane—and to be righteous, etc.—are not difficult.[23] According to him, human beings have an inborn ability—while young, they naturally love their parents, when older, they naturally respect their elder brothers.[24]

A second way to find the guidelines for humanity, suggested Confucius, is to examine another set of feelings—desires and aversions. This self-scrutiny will lead one to recognize a pair of basic principles: negatively, telling one not to impose upon others what one does not desire oneself;[25] positively, telling a person who wishes to establish himself and reach his goals, to help others in establishing themselves and reaching their goals as well.[26]

This idea that one can "find" guidelines for personal behavior in one's own heart is a Confucian innovation. Ancient Chinese believed that norms were based on the will of Heaven and the wishes of gods and ghosts. To make human relations the basis of norms is a significant departure. It makes norms more understandable and predictable but also gives rise to some problems. First, it lets every individual ascertain his own rules of behavior, which may not correspond to the norms followed by others. This is why Zhuangzi, an advocate of absolute subjective standards, denied the possibility of widely applicable social norms. Confucius was not caught in this trap, however, because he believed that all human beings are by nature similar. When one treats others according to Confucius's pair of basic principles, one's actions should be appreciated by those affected by it. Indeed, if most human beings to a large extent partake of this "similar nature," a shared sense of right and wrong can be derived from it and a set of values and norms based on Confucius's principles can become acceptable to most people.

If human nature is similar and the pair of principles suggested by Confucius is generally acceptable, would his theory lead to indiscriminate, universal love, an idea advocated by Mozi? Mencius criticized that idea as a proposition leading to denial of the special relationship between parents and children.[27] Confucius had no aversion to that idea but, as we have seen earlier, believed it almost impossible to implement universal love.[28] In any event, he never insist-   119 ed that one should treat all people alike, because he knew that people in different relationships have different feelings and will behave differently. For instance, a person is required to observe three-years mourning for the death of a parent, based on the fact that an infant is unable to leave his parents' bosom before the end of his third year and would normally feel sorrow for a like period after their deaths.[29] As this situation is unique, and not found in other relationships, it was not required that one observe the same lengthy mourning on the death of anyone other than one's parents.

Moreover, Confucius recognized not only that rules governing different relationships differ, but also that in many relationships parties may follow different rules. Take again the example of the parent-child relationship. We find in *The Analects* many prescriptions for a child's behavior toward a parent, but few for parents toward their child. The same is true of *Mengzi, Xunzi*, and other Confucian classics. The trouble is, if parties may follow different rules in their interaction, the relationship can become unbalanced and unfair—giving one party more of the benefits and the other more of the burdens. In fact, a system of norms supporting this kind of relationship between the authorities on the one hand and the common people on the other was developed later in China.

This was not the system of Confucius's time, however, and certainly not the system he wished to help build. Once more let us look at the parent-child relationship. When Confucius said a father should behave as a father and son should behave as a son,[30] he obviously implied that the relationship is reciprocal and conditional—only when a father behaves as a correct father can a son be expected to behave as a correct son.

On many occasions Confucius discussed with his disciples the meaning of filial piety, often emphasizing respect.[31] Once he remarked that a filial child should "never be defiant."[32] What did he mean? Realizing this problem and fearing that the remark might be misconstrued, he hastened to explain that what a child should never defy are the rites that govern the parent-child relationship—a filial child should, while the parents are alive, serve them according to rites and, after their death, bury them according to rites and revere them according to the rites.[33] But does not respect entail obedience? Confucius's answer is indirect and ambiguous: If one's parent is about to commit a wrong, one should gently advise against it; if the advice is not accepted, one should be respectful and not defiant, fearful of the consequences but never resentful.[34] This instruction might lead some to think that children were expected to be subservient to their parents. But that was not the understanding of Mencius, Xunzi and the authors of *The Record of Rites*.

Mencius's view is modest. He suggested that when a parent is wrong, a child should try to influence the parent and cause a correction. Shun, who succeeded in making his unloving father happy with him, was used as an example and hailed by Mencius as a son of truly great filial piety.[35] In addition, Mencius emphasized something more positive. A truly great deed of filial piety, according to him, is to bring honor to one's parents, and again he used as an example the case of Shun, who honored his father as the father of the Son of Heaven.[36]

Xunzi was more radical. In general he emphasized reciprocal conditions in all human relationships—for instance, while a son should be respectful and loving, a father should be tolerant and benevolent.[37] Therefore, he thought unconditional obedience was typical of a petty person, and specified three circumstances in which a filial son shall not obey his parents—if obedience will put them in danger or bring disgrace upon them or make oneself appear bestial. Then he went on to say that in a case where a son ought to obey but nevertheless disobeys, he is not filial; in a case where a son ought not to obey but obeys, he is not right; only a son who knows the distinction between what ought and ought not to be obeyed and is capable of carefully making this distinction when he acts, can be called a son of great filial piety. Hence he concluded, "One should obey what is right but not [necessarily] one's father."[38]

In fact, sometimes simple disobedience was not enough. A truly filial son should prevent his parents from doing wrong. Xunzi tells a story about Confucius being asked by Duke Ai of Lu: "If one obeys his father, is he a filial son. . . ?" The question was repeated three times but Confucius gave no answer. Then after coming out of the court Confucius told Zigong about the encounter and asked what he thought. Zigong said, "One who obeys his father is a filial son. . . . What is there for you, sir, to answer?" "You are indeed too young to know," said Confucius, "If a father has a son who would argue with him, he would not fall into impropriety. . . . Hence if one simply obeys his father, how can he be considered filial? . . . Only the person who carefully scrutinizes what is to be obeyed can be considered filial."[39]

The Book of Filial Piety records a slightly different version of that story, showing Confucius more strongly displeased by Duke Ai's question.[40] It also emphasizes that the ultimate expression of filial piety is to establish oneself, implement the Way, leave a good name after one's death, and thus bring honor to the parents.[41] For that final objective, different rules are spelled out for the emperor, the feudal lords, the ministers, the intellectuals and the commoner to follow, each thereby fulfilling what it means to be filial.[42]

The same themes are repeated in *The Record of Rites*—one should not merely obey one's parents but should help them to follow the Way. A filial son of the highest order will bring honor to his parents, one on the next level will not shame them, one on the lowest level will merely take care of their basic needs.[43] Then the book goes further, stressing that in making even the slightest move, a truly filial son will not forget his parents—he will do nothing wrong that would invite disgrace upon his person, the physical body given by his parents.[44] Furthermore, *The Record of Rites* says that one will be considered unfilial if one fails to conduct oneself in everyday life with dignity, to serve one's ruler loyally, to execute one's official duties with respect, to be trustworthy among friends, and to be courageous on the battlefield.[45] Thus filial piety becomes an all-embracing principle, guiding every aspect of one's behavior. Obedience to one's parents becomes only a small, rather unimportant aspect of it.

Nevertheless, two questions remain. First, why should filial piety be given so much emphasis? Neither Confucius nor any of his followers gave an explicit answer. But they all seemed to agree on three premises—that one owes one's very existence to one's parents, that the sacrifices of the parents in raising a child are extreme, and that one should repay that debt.[46] It follows that one should be grateful toward, most of all, one's parents and do everything one can to return their favor. Second, why in the Confucian classics is there so little prescription for the behavior of parents toward their children? The answer, it seems, is in an assumption that parents naturally love their offspring and they know what is best for them. That assumption must have been so widely accepted in ancient times that no proof was considered necessary.

Inequality in the relationship between persons on different levels of the political hierarchy is a more serious problem. At Confucius's time there was not only an hereditary aristocracy but also a hereditary bureaucracy. That resulted in a high concentration of power and privileges in a few families. Confucius did not criticize that system, but tried to instill the idea that the power and privileges were not free of costs. He not only emphasized that a ruler should behave as a ruler and a subject as a subject,[47] implying that the relationship should be conditional and substantially reciprocal, but also spelled out in considerable detail how it should work. Let us first look at the norms he suggested for someone in government employment. He said that in serving a ruler a subject should be loyal,[48] dedicated to his assignment,[49] and act according to certain rites;[50] that an official should never deceive his ruler but should courageously stand up to him;[51] that those in government should do their best in carrying out their responsibilities and resign their posts if they fail;[52] and that a great minister should serve his ruler according to the Way and, when that is no longer possible, relinquish his office.[53] From these remarks it is obvious that in Confucius's mind there is a distinction between the ruler and proper governance, and that for an official the paramount loyalty should be to the latter, not the former.

On the other hand, according to Confucius, the ruler must follow more numerous and stringent norms in relation to his subjects. Generally speaking, he must comply with certain rites in employing the service of his subjects.[54] But to govern well requires more. He must establish himself as an example for his subjects and, for this purpose, he must above all correct himself because to govern is to correct, to rectify.[55] If a ruler leads the people by being correct himself, who would dare to be incorrect?[56] But if a ruler is himself incorrect, how can he correct others?[57] In fact, if a ruler is himself correct, people will follow him without being so ordered, but if he himself is incorrect people will not follow him regardless of being ordered.[58] If he is not greedy, people will not steal even if he rewards theft.[59] The moral force of a ruler is like the wind, that of the common people is like the grass, when the wind blows over it, the grass is sure to bend.[60]

What is "correctness (*zheng*)"? As discussed above, Confucius believed that there can be widely accepted standards based on the similar human nature and shared experiences. It should follow that what is in accordance with these standards is correct. Nevertheless, we find no definition of "correctness" in *The Analects*. From his various remarks on government we get the impression that to be correct a ruler must have certain attitudes and take certain responsibilities. First of all, he should "rectify the names"—establish a set of standards.[61] Then he should conduct himself with dignity.[62] He should be filial to his parents and kind to his children.[63] He should be respectful to the worthy and tolerant to the masses.[64] He should reward the good and be sympathetic toward the less able.[65] He should observe the rites and be righteous and trustworthy.[66] He should personally lead the people in their work, labor for them, and never be tired of the effort.[67] He should lead the officials, forgive their small mistakes, and promote those with merits.[68] He should tax the people lightly.[69] He should enrich them.[70] He should educate them.[71] He should banish unrestrained music and distance himself from persons who use crafty language.[72] He should elevate the righteous to correct the crooked.[73] He should be generous but never wasteful, dignified but never arrogant and awe-inspiring but never ferocious.[74] He may have desires but should never be greedy and he should work hard and never complain.[75] He should never cruelly impose penalties without attempting first to reform the people, never expect results without first giving warning, never be slow in giving orders but quick in demanding the meeting of a deadline, and never be miserly in rewarding the people.[76] He should realize that while it is not easy to be a subject, it is more difficult to be a ruler, and he should never take satisfaction as ruler from the mere fact that his words are never disobeyed.[77]

Taking a closer look at *The Analects*, we might find more to add to this list of what Confucius considered the responsibilities of a ruler. But what we have already seen is enough to show that, comparing the responsibilities imposed on the ruler with those required of a subject, the relationship involves mutual obligations.

Mencius went still further with this idea of reciprocity in political relationships. First of all, his assumption that human nature is good and his theory that

123

one can find norms of behavior in one's own heart imply that human beings are morally equal. If one properly develops one's four "hearts," or innate moral feelings, one can be just as good as the next person. Thus Mencius quoted Cheng Xian and Yan Yuan. The former, an official of the state of Qi, reportedly said: "He [Duke Jing of Qi] is a man, but so am I, why should I be afraid of him?" Yan Yuan, one of Confucius's disciples, was said to have mused "What kind of person was Shun, and what kind of person am I? Anyone who wants to do something of significance, should aspire to be like him."[78] In fact, Mencius even maintained that everyone could become a Yao or a Shun.[79] In other words, the potential for moral development was the same in all.

Still, this idea of human equality seems to be in conflict with the fact that in any society some have to rule while others are to be ruled. Mencius recognized that fact, saying that society needs rulers just as it needs farmers, potters, blacksmiths and so on. Classifying some persons as rulers and others as the ruled is meant to achieve an effective division of labor. The two classes do different jobs and receive different rewards. The ruler, who has to perform more difficult tasks and take greater responsibilities than the ruled, is rewarded more. It is only fair.[80]

If human beings are essentially equal, a basic requirement of all social norms must be that in human relations the parties should interact with mutual care and respect. To make this point clear Mencius started with the general principle of reciprocity: one who treats others with care and respect is usually loved and respected by others. Therefore, if one suffers an outrageous offense, one should reflect on one's own behavior—am I unkind, discourteous, or disloyal?[81] This emphasis on reciprocity is especially strong in Mencius's discussion of the relationship between the ruler and his subjects. Generally, he observed, "If a ruler treats his subjects as his hands and feet, they will treat him as their belly and heart; if he treats them as his horses and hounds, they will treat him as a stranger; if he treats them as mud and weeds, they will treat him as an enemy."[82]

How did Mencius think a ruler should treat his subjects? He told the ruler to share what he likes together with the people, so as to let them have a similar enjoyment.[83] As one can enjoy life only when one has enough for one's basic needs, a ruler should begin by providing the common people with enough farming land and letting them have time to put it to good use. He should avoid overexploiting them and, when they have leisure, let them be taught proper norms at public schools.[84] This is a tall order, but the task, according to Mencius, is actually not difficult. All a ruler needs to do is look into his own heart and understand how the people would feel. If he can, in caring for his own elders, think of the elders of others, and in caring for his own youngsters, think of the youngsters of others, the world can be turned around as if on the palm of his hand.[85]

Traditionally the Chinese believed that a ruler held power and authority because of a mandate from Heaven. But Mencius observed that for this the approval of the people is necessary.[86] In fact, he said, quoting *The Classic of Historical Documents*, "Heaven sees through the eyes of the people, Heaven hears through the ears of the people."[87] That is why he maintained that the people is of the greatest importance, the state comes next and the ruler last.[88] Therefore, he argued, one who wins the hearts of the people wins the empire and one who loses the hearts of the people loses it.[89] As to how one can win the hearts of the people, Mencius advised that in general, the ruler should be correct and humane, thus setting himself as an example for the people.[90] More specifically, he should accumulate and provide what the people need and avoid imposing upon them what they dislike.[91] If incapable of leading and caring for his subjects, a ruler should bear the responsibility of the undesirable results.[92] For a tyrant who neglects and abuses his subjects, exile or even regicide is justifiable.[93]

To prove his points Mencius surveyed past history and asserted that each of the Three Dynasties had won the empire by being humane and lost it by being cruel and irresponsible.[94] Indeed, *The Classic of Historical Documents* is full of passages[95] showing that what the people desire is always obliged by Heaven[96] and that if a ruler treats his people well, they follow him; if he treats them poorly, they become his enemies.[97] The lesson is clear: The relationship between the ruler and his subjects is not a simple one of dominance and submission. It is, in a substantive sense, reciprocal and conditional.

Mencius gave even greater emphasis to reciprocity in the relationship between the ruler and the intellectuals who, as a class gained political importance during his time. In principle, he argued, an intellectual seeking government service is, as a person, equal to the ruler.[98] Indeed, among the three things generally esteemed in the world, the ruler, who usually has only his governing position, is less respectable than the intellectual who possesses the other two—virtue and seniority.[99] Therefore, a ruler should never summon the intellectuals. If he wants their advice, he should go to them as a student.[100] When an intellectual talks to a ruler, he should not be awed by the trappings of the ruler's position, because these are trivial things which he should disdain.[101] If a scholar is invited to serve the ruler, he should do so only if the invitation is offered with respect, and the ruler agrees to follow his advice.[102] When he is in service he should guide the ruler to the Way—to become humane[103]— and resign his office if his advice is ignored.[104] He should not, of course, quit without trying to change the ruler's behavior. It is for the scholar-official to correct the wrong in the heart of the ruler.[105] Without that, a state is sure to fall.[106] In other words, ultimately scholar-officials serve something higher than the ruler—they serve the best interest of the state. And for that purpose they cannot simply be subservient to the ruler.

Xunzi also believed that the relationship between the ruler and the people should be reciprocal. But he encountered more theoretical difficulties with this because of his belief that human nature is evil—selfish and ungrateful[107]—and that the human individual is incapable of meeting his own needs, except by living in a group.[108] Since human nature is evil, one cannot find norms in one's own heart and, without norms, individuals, in their effort to satisfy their desires, will compete and struggle with one another, thus causing tumult and making everyone's life difficult.[109] To avoid this, sages of the past devised controls over human nature and attempted to transform it. These controls are the rites, which should regulate everyday human interactions and form the basis of laws and other social institutions.[110]

If, however, norms cannot be found in people's own hearts but have to be imposed on them,[111] there is an implication of a need for authoritarianism. Yet Xunzi himself denied this. He identified as "sages" only the good "former kings" of ancient times and the rites only as "the Ways of the former kings," as recorded in the classics.[112] Moreover, while believing that everyone can, through education, become a sage,[113] he did not, like people of later times, undiscriminatingly call all rulers "sages." Second, in *Xunzi*, the rites (*li*) are connected with "rightness" or "what is right" (*i*). Thus the rites are not just arbitrary creations of the sages but are in agreement with the common sense of rightness. This is why Xunzi said "The essence of rites is their agreement with [what is felt to be right in] the people's hearts. As long as there is such an agreement, a rite is acceptable even though it is not recorded in the books of rites."[114]

What is the right relationship between a sagacious ruler and his subjects? Xunzi gave the ruler more responsibilities than Confucius and Mencius did. According to him a ruler is to raise the people just as parents are to raise children. He is to remove what is harmful and increase what is beneficial to them. He will protect them like infants.[115] But this does not mean that he is to embrace them and feed them; it means that he will give them the means and the time to take care of their basic needs, refrain from competing with them and over-exploiting them, choose the right persons to be their officials and, finally, teach them the norms.[116] To accomplish all these it is unnecessary for him actually to do the work. What is crucial is for him to cultivate himself— to learn and observe the rites. The ruler is like a container and the people are like the water it contains; if a container is square the water in it will conform to that shape.[117] In other words, if the ruler is good, the people will be like him. Moreover, not only will they become good, but they will love him like a parent and honor him like a god.[118]

Again there seems to be an authoritarian implication. But to liken the ruler to a parent, even a god, was not new with Xunzi. *Mengzi, The Classic of Historical*

Documents and *The Classic of Odes* also say that good rulers should be like parents to the people and take care of them like infants.[119] And, of course, the term "Son of Heaven" (*tianzi*), widely used in all ancient works, had something of a supernatural connotation. Yet Xunzi said only that under a sage-king the people only needed to follow his moral example,[120] and he regarded most rulers as ordinary men. With ordinary rulers the people need not be subservient but only deal with him in accordance with the rites.[121] And high officials should be even more independent. When a ruler is wrong and is endangering the state, they should remonstrate with him and resign their posts if he refuses to listen. Still better they should argue with him and commit suicide if they are ignored. It will be even better if they can lead other officials in persuading him to take their advice. Best of all, would be to take his power and use it to save the state from disaster.[122] Xunzi also asserted, "Heaven gives life to people not for the sake of the ruler; it established the ruler for the sake of the people."[123] Again he said, "The ruler is like a boat, the people are like water. While the water floats the boat, it can also capsize it."[124] This shows his strong advocacy of a reciprocal and conditional relationship between the people and the ruler.

Now let us consider another way Confucius suggested for a person to become humane. Although anyone could look into one's own heart and find the norms, this is not readily done by people who lack the habit of careful introspection. For them it is easier to follow established norms. By Confucius's time these had been formulated as "the Way" (*dao*), morality (*de*), regulations (*zheng*), penal proscriptions (*xing*), and the rites. The last were in his opinion particularly useful. According to him, if one disciplines oneself and acts according to the rites, one will become humane;[125] and if the people are guided by moral principles and made to conform to the rites, they will not only have a sense of shame but also rectify themselves.[126] Thus, if those in high positions love the rites, the people will be easy to employ,[127] and government in general will no longer be difficult.[128] There are only brief passages in *The Analects* suggesting some of Confucius's views on the rites, for instance, that they are not mere formalities;[129] that they can be products of custom[130] as well as authoritative action;[131] that not all of such products are good;[132] that the good ones are based in human feelings and reason;[133] that they stylize behavior,[134] just like the final touches of color added to a painting;[135] and that they help define social classes.[136]

One passage records that Confucius was asked by Lin Fang, a disciple, about the essence of the rites. "What a great question!" the Master exclaimed and went on to say: "With the rites, it is better to err on the side of frugality than on the side of extravagance; in mourning, it is better to err on the side of grief than on the side of formality."[137] What is essential is that the rites should express genuine feelings. Thus he emphasized that when one worships a god or the spirit of an ancestor, one should do it as if the god or ghost were actually there to register one's own feelings. If one cannot feel wholeheartedly involved, the rite would best not be performed at all.[138]

What should be the genuine feelings behind the rites? In addition to grief, joy, and so on appropriate to the occasion, Confucius emphasized one that is essential to all the rites—reverence and respect. This is clear from his advice on how one should worship gods and spirits. Similarly, a child, in performing the rites of filial piety, should not merely provide parents with physical care but should do so with respect and in a cheerful manner.[139] Respect is also required of an official in carrying out his duties[140] and of a ruler in governing his people.[141] Zichan won Confucius's praise for being respectful in serving his superiors,[142] and so did Yan Pingzhong for being good in making friends and remaining respectful toward them.[143] Indeed, everyone should conduct oneself in a respectful manner.[144] If a person performs a rite without respect, what is there about him for others to observe?[145]

Mencius also valued the rites. He even considered that under some circumstances observing the rites was more important than obtaining food and sex.[146] But Xunzi was even more emphatic. Because if people could not find norms written in their own hearts, they would need objective rules to guide them. Rites defined each individual's role or duty (*fen*)—his share of the responsibilities each has in the life of the group.[147] Thus, the rites served as standards for judging whether the behavior of a person is in accordance with his *fen*, just as a scale is used to check weight, a measuring square to check right angles, a compass to check circles and a carpenter's line to check straightness.[148]

How should one's *fen* be defined? Xunzi suggested one's conduct and abilities as the determining factors.[149] Thus, whether one is to be a member of the ruling class or one of the ruled should be determined by whether one is able to observe the rites and follow the right way. If the son of a king, a minister, or a lower official is unable to do so, he should be assigned the status of a commoner; if the son of a commoner is able to do so, he should be made a minister or a lower official.[150] Thus Xunzi was ready in some cases to replace the existing hereditary aristocracy with a meritocracy.

Although Xunzi gave greater weight to the rites and discussed them more than Confucius and Mencius did, the most comprehensive Confucian discussion of the rites is to be found in *The Record of Rites* (Liji), which asserts that without the rites no other norm can be effective, no individual behavior or public affair can be performed properly.[151] Therefore, the book makes an in-depth study of many aspects of the rites, including their origins, objectives, characteristics, rationales, applications, potential effects, and relationships to other norms. Most of its conclusions support the basic points made by Confucius, Mencius, and Xunzi, but some passages also shed new light on those points. Most rites are said to originate from the need to give expression to human desires and feelings,[152] but in a restrained and moderate way.[153] Many of these were created by rulers; but in some cases, even the common people participated in their creation.[154] Thus, an act in agreement with what is right could be made a rite even though it was not created by the former kings.[155]

The ultimate objective of the rites, as spelled out in *The Analects*, is to achieve harmony.[156] *The Record of Rites* also lists this as one of the objectives[157] and characterizes this harmonious condition as "one of great rapport" (*da-shun*), in which human beings get along well not only with one another but also with gods and spirits.[158] For this purpose, the rites are designed to define every person's position and role in a group,[159] to prescribe how one should interact with others,[160] to avoid overdoing things and to prevent other forms of excess,[161] thus making behavior more reasonable, predictable and even elegant.

In *The Record of Rites* there is an overarching principle called "the way of the measuring square" (*qie jiu zhi-dao*)—what a person dislikes in his superiors, he should not display in the way he treats his inferiors; what he dislikes in his inferiors, he should not display in the way he serves his superiors; what he hates in those who are before him, he should not therewith precede those who are behind him; what he hates in those who are behind him, he should not therewith follow those who are before him.[162] It is, of course, basically the same as Confucius's more concise principle of reciprocity.

Underlying the rites is also a spirit of gratitude and humility that guides their implementation. As one's life and welfare depend on many other people and things, one should be grateful for them and repay the benefits one receives. Thus, *The Record of Rites* says that if one receives a favor and fails to return it, one is in violation of the rites.[163] This is why one should be filial to one's parents and grateful to others. It also explains why emperors of ancient times would at the end of each year offer sacrifice to the spirits of myriads of things that benefited people, including the cat that killed field mice and tigers that killed wild boars that destroyed harvests.[164]

Likewise the great kings of the three ancient dynasties, Xia, Shang, and Zhou, began their government by paying respect to their wives who helped extend their family line and sons who were descendants of their ancestors. He who respected his own wife and sons, would then disrespect nobody.[165]

From this general principle that people should show each other mutual respect springs a set of specific rules governing their relationships. The relationship between the ruler and the ruled is particularly problematic because they are usually perceived as being in unequal positions. *The Record of Rites* recognizes this,[166] but like *The Analects*, *Mencius*, and *Xunzi*, it makes far greater demands on the ruler than the ruled. The ruler, it says, should aspire to be hu-   129 mane, protect the people like infants, appreciate what they desire, and shun what they are averse to.[167] Specifically, he should institute measures to provide the common people, as well as officials, with the means of livelihood;[168] give special care for orphans, widows, and the handicapped;[169] refrain from over-taxing the people and making excessive demands on their labor;[170] cut down on government expenses and luxuries unless he is sure that the people will not go hungry even during drought and flood[171] and, finally, cultivate himself and make himself a model for the people, educating them according to the Way and correcting them with the rites so that they will have a sense of right and wrong.[172] When he treats the people in this manner, they will reciprocate by treating him like a parent.[173] But in the final analysis, the actions of people are more important, since the ruler, according to *The Record of Rites*, exists for the sake of the people and will be removed when they decide to do so.[174]

Reciprocity is stressed even more in the relationship between the ruler and his officials. About the ancient rite requiring an expatriate minister to mourn the death of his former ruler, *The Record of Rites* says that the expatriate should comply with the rite only if his former ruler had treated him according to the rites. Thus where a ruler had initially employed a subject as if to place him on his own lap [like a pet] and then later dismissed him as if to throw him out into deep water, the mourning rite is not applicable. What is there to mourn for? It would be enough, *The Record of Rites* suggests, for the expatriate to re-frain from leading the army of a foreign state to invade that of his former ruler.[175] This is a stronger position than that taken by Mencius in his version of the same story.[176] But *The Record of Rites* even goes further to say that when the ruler is wrong, his ministers should not only advise correction but take action themselves to bring it about. Such action is hailed as "a service to the state" (*sheji zhiyi*).[177]

Thus far we have analyzed two sets of rules in the Confucian theory of norms—first an internal set which can be discovered by anyone looking into one's own heart, second an external set which is established by persons with some special authority. In this latter set of defined norms there are several subgroups including the rites, which were most cherished by the Confucians. The other subgroups, as Confucius spoke of them, were government regula-tions (*zheng*) and punitive measures (*xing*), which he thought less effective than moral suasion and the rites.[178] He did not in *The Analects* discuss law (*fa*).[179] Mencius had little to say about law, but he did point out that neither laws nor moral virtues could be effective without the other.[180] Xunzi gave law some status as a subcategory of the rites, but warned that law should not be applied mechanically.[181] Among the Confucian classics *The Classic of Historical Documents* and *The Rites of the Zhou Dynasty* are noteworthy for their considera-

tion of the criminal law. Here we shall only analyze a few points in those two works and similar discussions in *The Analects, Mencius,* and *Xunzi* that are relevant to this paper.

In *The Classic of Historical Documents* a crime is described as a voluntary and intentional act[182] that violates norms established by Heaven and its human agents.[183] As crimes harm not only the immediate victims but society as a whole, they must be prevented. Therefore while punishments serve the need for retribution, their more important goals are to let the people live in peace and the state grow in prosperity, while, above all, educating the people in public morality.[184] This last objective was of the utmost importance to the legal theory of the Confucians. They made moral education a precondition for administration of criminal justice. *The Analects* records advice for the authorities to grieve, not to rejoice, when they succeed in uncovering a crime, since it is because those in high places have lost the Way that the people have long been left in the wilderness, without knowing the right course to take.[185] Xunzi tells a story wherein Confucius refused to hear a suit between a father and son, and blamed the authorities for failing to teach the two parties how to behave properly in their respective positions. Reportedly the Master said, "When the entire army is routed, the retreating soldiers should not be executed; when the legal system is not in order, the people should not be punished."[186] Xunzi himself endorsed the same idea and suggested a series of measures for the education of the people, emphasizing particularly that the ruler should establish himself as a model.[187] From these materials we can see that, contrary to a widespread impression, the Confucians did not belittle law, but simply regarded it as a norm of limited scope. Their discussions of it did not address many of the problems referred to above, but even in their narrow application of it to social outcasts, the Confucian law was to be guided by the principle of fairness and compassion.

To achieve these latter objectives the handling of the judicial process was of great importance. It is discussed in some detail in *The Classic of Historical Documents*. At a trial both parties must be heard, witnesses and evidence must be examined, and groundless accusations rejected.[188] There should be a period of five or six days between the hearings and the announcement of a sentence, during which the judge should impartially deliberate all relevant factors.[189] If the alleged crime is caused by factors beyond the control of the accused, he shall not be considered guilty.[190] If there is doubt about whether a person should be punished, he should be spared. The principle should be: Rather than punish one innocent person, it is better, and less serious, for one guilty person to go free.[191] For the same reason, punishment for one person should not extend to his relatives or any other innocent person.[192] After a sentence prescribing capital punishment is declared, it should, according to *The Rites of the Zhou Dynasty,* be automatically reviewed by higher judicial officials, and appeals brought to the emperor himself.[193] In deciding difficult cases the emperor should consult high officials first, then lower officials and, finally, if necessary, the opinions of the people.[194]

In assessing a punishment *The Classic of Historical Documents* suggests many ways of ensuring that it will fit the crime.[195] Cruel punishments are not permissible.[196] If an act is not committed with criminal intent but results from negligence, the punishment should be reduced.[197] Also when there is doubt about whether a punishment is appropriate it should be reduced.[198] *The Rites of the Zhou Dynasty* extends this principle further to grant reductions to those who cannot appreciate the consequences of their action and to pardon the very young, the very old and the mentally retarded.[199] Most of these ideas are in agreement with what Confucius, Mencius, and Xunzi advocated. Behind them is the distinctive Confucian principle that even criminals should be treated fairly and with compassion.

Having looked closely at the Confucian theory of norms, I shall now address the questions raised at the outset of this paper. First of all, we notice that the Confucians not only did not talk about "human rights," they did not talk about "rights" at all. One may wonder how the ancient Chinese, who entered into contracts and committed torts and crimes as most of the people do, could do without a concept of "rights;" yet whenever a person claims a certain "right," his claim can be fruitful only if others concerned are willing to honor it. The West looks at the relationship from the side of the claimant and gives great weight to his claim; the Confucians looked at it from the other side and considered the willingness of other people to accommodate the claims. Thus, it is not that the Confucians did not think a person could claim something as his due. He could, and it was called his entitlement or "share" (*fen*). But *fen* is not just another name for *right*. While a right can be an outcome of human interactions, a gift from society or, as some may say, a natural endowment; a *fen* is strictly a societal product—a person's *fen* is a share of what is created by the joint efforts of many members in a society, which they see fit to let him enjoy. The validity of a *fen* is thus dependent on the good will of those concerned; a person is not born with a *fen*, his *fen* is what his society allows or assigns to him.

The Confucians recognized that to live a good, human life, a person must have a share of society's wealth (in a broad sense, including goods, services, and relationships) to meet his physical, psychological, and intellectual needs. They specifically mentioned the need for food, clothing, shelter, sexual partnership, and education. Claims to such wealth are nowadays called "social and economic *human rights*," but the Confucians did not think it meaningful to say that a person can make such claims simply because he is a human being. Instead, they considered those who might be affected by such claims, arguing that because they and the claimant share a common or similar human nature, they should appreciate his basic needs and honor any reasonable claim of his.

What are known as "civil and political *human rights*" today were not discussed by the Confucians, but they did look from a different angle at the problems arising from relationships between persons of different statuses and positions. They argued that the relationships should be equitable and reciprocal but, again, they underscored that it was not enough for a person or group simply to demand certain treatment; all concerned, especially those in power, had to be taught self-restraint and respect for such persons or groups, yet they knew that such teaching is difficult and that is why they promised it on the assumption of a common or similar human nature and emphasized consensual rites as the norm. The presumption was needed to provide a conceptual basis for their advocacy of compassion, fairness, and reciprocity in human relationships; the grounds for this was their belief that among all possible norms rites based in human feelings are the most effective in cultivating humility in oneself and respect for others.[200]

Thus although the Confucians did not talk about "human rights," they maintained that people should treat each other as fellow human beings and help one another to live a good, human way of life. This idea is clearly compatible with the concept of "human rights." In fact, we may say that Confucian norms could promote all types of human rights because, in the *Record of Rites* depiction of a Confucian utopia, where the highest principle of humanity would prevail, everyone has a proper share of this world's wealth and treats his fellow humans with respect and love.[201]

Now for our second question: Is the Confucian theory of norms, in practice, conducive to a good, human way of life (effectively protecting all "human rights")? To find an answer I shall first make a comparison. The Western practice of calling certain claims "human rights" seems to me to have two benefits: it makes clear to people what they can claim, and it elevates the claims to a seemingly superior moral status, encouraging people to assert and struggle for them. But the practice also leads to some problems. First, beyond certain minimum standards, people in different times and circumstances may disagree on what a good, human way of life should be. As a result, the list of "human rights" has to be frequently reconstructed and the meaning of the various rights constantly reinterpreted. Second, the idea that certain rights are "human"—that a human being is born with them—is fictive. To insist on labeling some claims as "human" and, by implication, natural, inherent, and sacrosanct, while they are not universally acceptable, will inevitably lead to confrontation between its claimants and opponents and, in such a confrontation, the result may depend less on the merit of a claim than on the ability and resources of a claimant to influence the decision-making process.

On the other hand, the usefulness of the Confucian norms, teaching people mutual respect and guiding them to amicable resolution of their differences, seems to me timeless and universal. Indeed, if people are successfully 133 taught to appreciate one another's needs and respect one another's proper "shares," there should be no serious differences and no need for anyone to assert and fight for his "rights"—there should be, not confrontation, but harmony. Yet this approach has its problems also. It makes a person less certain about what he can and cannot expect from society. Thus, if Confucian norms are not yet completely accepted and observed, a person may get either more or less than his proper share. Correction of the inequity is usually slow. Unaccustomed to being assertive, those who get less are often unable to stand up and demand their due. If, eventually, their suppressed resentments explode, there is a revolt, bringing disaster to society.

In current discussions of human rights there are those who advocate the universal validity of that concept and those who emphasize particular cultural traditions that uphold different views of what a good, human way of life should be. My conclusion is that Western and Confucian ideas are conceptually compatible but practically different. I am inclined to think that because each of the practical approaches has its problems, neither is sufficient to conduce to a good, human way of life. Fortunately the two approaches are not mutually exclusive but can be complimentary—people can first learn the Confucian norms and become compassionate and respectful toward one another and then be assured that they have certain "rights" which they can, when necessary, assert and defend. People would then have the benefits of both approaches but the problems of neither. Thus I would recommend this two-step approach to both those who live in the Confucian tradition and those who are more accustomed to the Western idea of "human rights," hoping that the combined wisdom of the East and the West could enable us to better achieve our common objective.

Notes

1. See John P. Humphrey, "The International Law of Human Rights in the Middle Twentieth Century," in Richard B. Lillich and Hurst Hannum, ed., *International Human Rights: Problems of Law, Policy, and Practice* (Boston: Little, Brown, 1995), pp. 1–13. Sumner B. Twiss studied the further development and added a third type, or "generation," of human rights—the claims for global redistribution of power, wealth, and the common heritage of humankind. See his paper in this volume.

2. I shall confine this study to the early Confucian classics where the Confucian theory of norms was developed and largely perfected. My focus will be on the *Analects*, *Mencius*, and *Xunzi*, but several other works reputedly edited or written by Confucius or his disciples will also be consulted, including *The Classic of Historical Document*, *The Classic of Poetry*, *The Classic of Filial Piety*, *The Rites of Zhou*, *The Record of Rites*, and *The Zuo Commentary*.

3. Liu Baonan, *Lunyu zhengyi* in *Xinbian zhuzi jicheng* (Taibei: Shijie, 1978), p. 347 (ch.

15 "Wei Linggong," para. 35).

4. Ibid., p. 44 (ch. 3 "Bayi" sec. 3).

5. Ibid., 75 (4 "Liren" 2).

6. Ibid., 76 (4 "Liren" 5).

7. Ibid., 337 (15 "Wei Linggong" 9).

8. Ibid., 278 (12 "Yan Yuan" 22).

9. Ibid., 371 (17 "Yang Huo" 5).

10.Ibid., 311 (14 "Xian wen" 16); 314 (14 "Xian wen" 17).

11. Jiao Xun, Jiao Hu, *Mengzi zhengyi* in *Xinbian zhuzi jicheng* (Taibei: Shijie, 1978), p. 350 (ch. 8 "Li Lou xia" para. 28), 575 (14 "Jinxin xia" 16); 592 (14 "Jinxin xia" 31).

12. See *Lunyu zhengyi*, 92–93 (5 "Gongye Chang" 8); 386 (18 "Weizi" 1).

13. Ibid., 133 (6 "Yong ye" 30).

14. Ibid., 152 (7 "Shu er" 34).

15. Ibid., 262 (12 "Yan Yuan" 1).

16. Ibid., 150 (7 "Shu er" 30).

17. Ibid., 77 (4 "Li Ren" 6), 121 (6 "Yongye" 12).

18. Ibid., 367 (17 "Yang Huo" 2).

19. Ibid., 4 (1 "Xue er" 2).

20. *Mengzi zhengyi*, pp. 434–35 (11 "Gaozi shang" 3); 51 (11 "Gaozi shang" 7).

21. Ibid., 138–40 (3 "Gongsun Chou shang" 6).

22. Ibid., 446 (11 "Gaozi shang" 6).

23. Ibid., 298 (7 "Li Lou shang" 11).

24. Ibid., 138 (3 "Gongsun Chou shang" 6).

25. *Lunyu zhengyi*, 263 (12 "Yan Hui" 2); 343 (15 "Wei Linggong" 24).

26. Ibid., 33–134 (6 "Yong ye" 30).

27. *Mengzi zhengyi*, 269 (6 "Teng Wengong shang" 9).

28. *Lunyu zhengyi*, 133 (6 "Yong ye" 30).

29. Ibid., 380–82 (17 "Yang Huo" 18).

30. Ibid., 271 (12 "Yan Yuan" 11).

31. Ibid., 15 (1 "Xue er" 11); 25–27 (2 "Wei zheng" 7–9); 406 (19 "Zizhang" 18).

32. Ibid., 25 (2 "Wei zheng" 5).

33. Ibid.

34. Ibid., 83 (4 "Li ren" 18).

35. *Mengzi zhengyi*, 314 (7 "Li Lou shang" 28).

36. Ibid., 378 (9 "Wan Zhang shang" 4).

37. Wang Xianqian, *Xunzi jijie* in *Xinbian zhuzi jicheng* (Taibei: Shijie, 1978), p. 153 (ch. 12 "Jundao").

38. Ibid., 347 (29 "Zidao").

39. Ibid., 347–48 ("Zidao").

40. Xing Bing, *Xiaojing zhengyi*, in Ruan Yuan, ed., *Shisanjing zhushu* (Taibei: Yiwen, 1965), p. 48 (ch. 15 "Jianzheng").

41. Ibid., 11 (1 "Kaizong mingyi").

42. Ibid., 11–27 (2 "Tianzi"; 3 "Zhuhou"; 4 "Qing daifu"; 5 "Shi"; 6 "Shuren").

43. Kong Yingda, *Liji zhengyi*, in Ruan Yuan, ed., *Shisanjing zhushu* (Taibei: Yiwen, 1965), p. 820 (ch. 24 "Ji yi").

44. Ibid., 821–22 (24 "Ji yi").

45. Ibid., 821 ("Ji yi").

46. See *Xiaojing*, 11 (1 "Kaizong mingyi"); Qu Wanli, *Shijing quanshi* (Taibei: Lianjing, 1983), p. 387 ("Liao o"); *Liji zhengyi* 469 (10b "Li qi"); 500 (11b "Jiao tesheng"); 813 (24 "Ji yi"), 819 (24 "Ji yi"); 821 (24 "Ji yi").

47. *Lunyu zhengyi*, 271 (12 "Yan Yuan" 11).

48. Ibid., 62 (3 "Ba yi" 19).

49. Ibid., 348 (15 "Wei Linggong" 38).

50. Ibid., 62 (3 "Bayi" 18).

51. Ibid., 318 (14 "Xian wen" 22).

52. Ibid., 351 (16 "Ji shi" 1).

53. Ibid., 251 (11 "Xian jin" 24).

54. Ibid., 62 (3 "Bayi" 19).

55. Ibid., 274 (12 "Yan Yuan" 17).

56. Ibid.

57. Ibid., 289 (13 "Zilu" 13).

58. Ibid., 286 (13 "Zilu" 6).

59. Ibid., 274 (12 "Yan Yuan" 18).

60. Ibid., 275 (12 "Yan Yuan" 19).

61. Ibid., 280–83 (13 "Zilu" 3).

62. Ibid., 35 (2 "Wei zheng" 20).

63. Ibid.

64. Ibid., 401 (19 "Zizhang" 3).

65. Ibid.

66. Ibid., 284 (13 "Zilu" 4).

67. Ibid., 279 (13 "Zilu" 1).

68. Ibid., 280 (13 "Zilu" 2).

69. Ibid., 268 (12 "Yan Yuan" 9).

70. Ibid., 287 (13 "Zilu" 9).

71. Ibid.

72. Ibid., 339 (15 "Wei Linggong" 11).

73. Ibid., 35 (2 "Wei zheng" 19).

74. Ibid., 417 (20 "Yao yue" 2).

75. Ibid.

76. Ibid., 418 (20 "Yao yue" 2).

77. Ibid., 290 (13 "Zilu" 15).

78. *Mengzi zhengyi*, 188–89 (5 "Teng Wengong shang" 1).

79. Ibid., 592 (14 "Jin xin xia" 31).

80. Ibid., 214–30 (5 "Teng Wengong shang" 4).

81. Ibid., 350 (8 "Li Lou xia" 28).

82. Ibid., 322 (8 "Li Lou xia" 3).

83. Ibid., 27–30 (1 "Liang Huiwang shang" 2); 58–65, 69–77, 77–83 (2 "Liang Huiwang xia" 1, 2, 4, 5).

84. Ibid., 32–35, 40–41, 56–58 (1 "Liang Huiwang shang" 3, 5, 7); 196–97, 205–14 (5 "Teng Wengong shang" 3).

85. Ibid., 47–52 (1 "Liang Huiwang shang" 7).

86. Ibid., 379–81 (9 "Wan Zhang shang" 5).

87. Ibid., 381.

88. Ibid., 573 (14 "Jin xin xia" 14).

89. Ibid., 295 (7 "Li Lou shang" 9).

90. Ibid., 309 (7 "Li Lou shang" 20).

91. Ibid., 324 (8 "Li Lou xia" 5).

92. Ibid., 83–84 (2 "Liang Huiwang xia" 6).

93. Ibid., 86 (2 "Liang Huiwang xia" 8).

94. Ibid., 289–90 (7 "Li Lou shang" 3).

95. See Qu Wan-li, *Shangshu jishi* (Taibei: Lianjing, 1983). For the rise and fall of the Xia dynasty: pp. 25 ("Yao dian"); 37, 42 ("Gao yao mo"); 191 ("Duo shi"); 214, 216 ("Duo fang"); 279 ("Yu Xia shu"). For the rise and fall of the Shang dynasty: pp. 78–79 ("Tang shi"); 272–73 ("Tang Zheng"), 191 ("Duo shi"), 216 ("Duo fang"), 205 ("Jun shi"); 197–98 ("Wu yi"); 162, 163 ("Jiu gao"); 105, 107 ("Wei zi"); 112 ("Mu shi"). For the rise and fall of the Zhou dynasty: pp. 200, 201 ("Wu yi"); 277 ("Da shi"); 208 ("Jun shi"); 190, 193 ("Duo shi"); 217 ("Duo fang"); 113 ("Mu shi").

96. This observation appears in "Da shi," a missing part of *The Book of Historical Documents*. It is quoted in *Zuozhuan*. See Hong Liangji, *Chunqiu zuozhuan gu* (Beijing: Zhonghua, 1987), p. 633 ("Zhaogong yinian").

97. Gao You, annotator, *Lüshi chunqiu* in *Xinbian zhuzi jicheng* (Taibei: Shijie, 1978), p. 246 (ch. 7 "Lishulan, yongmin").

98. *Mengzi zhengyi*, 188–89 (5 "Teng Wengong shang" 1).

99. Ibid., 154 (4 "Gongsun Chou xia" 2).

100. Ibid.

101. Ibid., 596–98 (14 "Jin xin xia" 34).

102. Ibid., 509–10 (12 "Gaozi xia" 14).

103. Ibid., 503 (12 "Gaozi xia" 8).

104. Ibid., 509 (12 "Gaozi xia" 14).

105. Ibid., 309 (7 "Li Lou shang" 20).

106. Ibid., 515 (12 "Gaozi xia" 15).

107. *Xunzi jijie*, 289–90, 293–94, 296–97 (23 "Xing e").

108. Ibid., 104 (9 "Wang zhi"); 113, 116 (10 "Fu guo").

109. Ibid.

110. Ibid., 231, 243 (19 "Li lun"); 291–92 (23 "Xing e"); 266 (21 "Jie bi").

111. Ibid., 250 (19 "Li lun"); 350 (30 "Fa xing").

112. Ibid., 7 (1 "Quan xue"); 77, 89 (8 "Ru xiao").

113. Ibid., 7 (1 "Quan xue"); 295–96 (23 "Xing e").

114. Ibid., 324 (27 "Da lue"). It should be noted here that Xunzi distinguished the human heart (*ren xin*), by which he seemed to mean something with a capacity for making judgments, from human nature (*ren xing*), which he said is characterized by selfishness and ingratitude and is therefore evil.

115. Ibid., 248 (19 "Li lun"); 104 (9 "Wang zhi"); 156 (12 "Jun dao"); 147 (11 "Wang ba"); 116–17 (10 "Fu guo").

116. Ibid., 122–23 (10 "Fu guo"); 139–40 (11 "Wang ba"); 191–92 (15 "Yi bing"); 330–31 (27 "Da lue"); 158, 161–63 (12 "Jun dao"); 134–36, 145, 159 (11 "Wang ba").

117. Ibid., 154 (12 "Jun dao").

118. Ibid., 117 (10 "Fu guo"); 147 (11 "Wang ba").

119. *Mengzi zhengyi*, 237 (5 "Teng Wengong shang" 1); 68 (2 "Liang Huiwang xia" 3); *Shangshu jishi*, 116, 120 ("Hongfan"); 150 ("Kanggao"); 175 ("Zhaogao"); *Shijing quanshi*, 307 ("Nanshan youtai"); 500 ("Jiongzhuo").

120. *Xunzi jijie*, 167, 168 (13 "Chen dao").

121. Ibid., 152 (12 "Jun dao").

122. Ibid., 165–66 (13 "Chen dao").

123. Ibid., 332 (27 "Da lue").

124. Ibid., 97 (9 "Wang zhi").

125. *Lunyu zhengyi*, 262 (12 "Yan Yuan" 1).

126. Ibid., 22 (2 "Wei zheng" 3).

127. Ibid., 329 (14 "Xian wen" 41).

128. Ibid., 80 (4 "Li ren" 13).

129. Ibid., 53 (3 "Bayi" 12); 375 (17 "Yang huo" 9).

130. Ibid., 173–74 (9 "Zi han" 3).

131. Ibid., 354 (16 "Ji shi" 2).

132. Ibid., 174 (9 "Zi han" 3).

133. Ibid., 380–382 (17 "Yang huo" 18).

134. Ibid., 155 (8 "Tai bo" 2).

135. Ibid., 48–49 (3 "Bayi" 8).

136. Ibid., 41, 43, 69 (3 "Bayi" 1, 2, 22).

137. Ibid., 44 (3 "Bayi" 4).

138. Ibid., 53 (3 "Bayi" 12).

139. Ibid., 26, 27 (2 "Wei zheng" 7, 8).

140. Ibid., 7–9 (1 "Xue er" 5), 348 (15 "Wei Linggong" 38).

141. Ibid., 112 (6 "Yong ye" 2).

142. Ibid., 101 (5 "Gongye Chang" 17).

143. Ibid., 101 (5 "Gongye Chang" 18).

144. Ibid., 329 (15 "Xian wen" 42).

145. Ibid., 74 (3 "Ba yi" 26).

146. *Menzi zhengi*, 474 (12 "Gaozi xia" 1).

147. *Xunzi jijie*, 104 (9 "Wang zhi"), 115 (10 "Fu guo"), 231. (19 "Li lun").

148. Ibid., 20 (2 "Xiu shen"); 115 (10 "Fu guo"); 135 (11 "Wang ba"); 236–37 (19 "Li lun").

149. Ibid., 96 (9 "Wang zhi"); 113, 118–119 (10 "Fuguo"); 144 (11 "Wang ba").

150. Ibid., 94 (9 "Wang zhi").

151. *Liji zhengyi*, 14–15 (1 "Quli shang").

152. Ibid., 416 (9 "Li yun"); 947–48 (35 "Wen shang"); 961–62 (38 "Sannian wen").

153. Ibid., 120, 125, 127, 135, 142, 175 (4 "Tan Gong xia"), 852–53 (28 "Zhongni yanju").

154. Ibid., 146 (3 "Tan Gong shang"); 189 (4 "Tan Gong xia"); 414 (9 "Li yun"); 667, 671, 679–80 (19 "Yue ji").

155. Ibid., 15–16, 37, 38 (1 "Quli shang"); 112 (3 "Tan Gong shang"); 164, 173 (4 "Tan Gong xia"); 439 (9 "Li yun"); 684 (19 "Yue ji"); 750 (21 "Za ji xia"); 854 (28 "Zhongni yan ju").

156. *Lunyu zhengi*, 16 (1 "Xue er" 12).

157. *Liji zhengyi*, 813 (24 "Ji yi").

158. Ibid., 440 (9 "Li yun").

159. Ibid., 846 (26 "Jing jie"); 848 (27 "Aigong wen"); 853 (28 "Zhongni yanju").

160. For how man and woman should interact, see *Liji zhengyi*, 37 (1 "Quli shang"), 520 (12 "Neize"); for how husband and wife should interact, see ibid., 533–34 (12 "Neize"), 849 (27 "Aigong wen"); for how a son should treat his parents, see ibid., 517–21 (12 "Neize"); for how a daughter-in-law should treat her parents-in-law, see ibid., 518, 522 (12 "Neize"); for how parents-in-law should treat a daughter-in-law, see ibid., 521 (12 "Neize"); for how a man should behave when he lives with his parents and several wives, see ibid., 521 (12 "Neize"); for how the sons of the wife and the sons of the concubines should interact, see ibid., 522 (12 "Neize"); for how the wife of the eldest son and the wives of the other sons should interact, see ibid., 522 (12 "Neize"); for how a person should interact with a senior, see ibid., 18, 19, 31, 34, 35, 36, 40–43 (3 "Quli shang"); 628, 635 (17 "Shao yi").

161. Ibid., 125, 127, 133, 135, 142 (3 "Tan Gong shang"); 164, 172 (4 "Tan Gong xia"); 847 (26 "Jing jie"); 852–53 (28 "Zhongni yanju"); 863, 865 (30 "Fang ji").

162. Ibid., 987 (42 "Daxue").

163. Ibid., 15–16 (1 "Quli shang").

164. Ibid., 819 (24 "Ji yi"); 500 (11 "Jiao tesheng").

165. Ibid., 849 (27 "Aigong wen").

166. Ibid., 671 (19 "Yueji").

167. Ibid., 984, 986, 987 (42 "Daxue").

168. Ibid., 214–15 (5 "Wangzhi").

169. Ibid., 266, 267 (5 "Wangzhi").

170. Ibid., 246, 247 (5 "Wangzhi").

171. Ibid., 238 ("Wangzhi").

172. Ibid., 397, 398 (8 "Wenwang shizi"); 654 (18 "Xueji"); 927 (33 "Zi yi").

173. Ibid., 914 (32 "Biao ji").

174. Ibid., 933 (33 "Zi yi").

175. Ibid., 173 (4 "Tan Gong xia").

176. Mencius was once asked by King Xuan of Qi how an expatriate should mourn the death of his former ruler. He replied, "In the case where a subject, whose advice has been accepted by the ruler to the benefit of the people, has a reason to leave the state, if the ruler sends someone to escort him beyond the border and to prepare a welcome for his arrival in the state he is going to and finally takes over his land only if after three years he decides not to return, these are known as the three courtesies. If the ruler behaves in this way, then it is the subject's duty to mourn after his death. Today, when a subject leaves because his advice is rejected to the detriment of the people, the ruler ties him up, makes things difficult for him in the state he is going to, and confiscates his land the day he departs. Such a ruler can only be called a robber and an enemy. What mourning is there for a robber and an enemy?" Mengzi zhengyi, 322–23 (8 "Li Lou xia" 3).

177. Ibid., 630 (17 "Shao yi").

178. Lunyu zhengyi, 22 (2 "Wei zheng" 3).

179. The character fa only appears twice in Lunyu. In the first instance (9 "Zi han" 24) it refers to exemplary words (fa yu zhi yan), in the second (20 "Yao yue" 1) it refers to official measurements (fa du).

180. Mengzi zhengyi, 284 (7 "Li Lou shang" 1).

181. Xunzi jijie, 96 (9 "Wangzhi"); 151–52 (12 "Jundao"); 173 (14 "Zhi shi"); 329 (27 "Da lue").

182. Shangshu jishi, 86 ("Pangeng shang"); 100 ("Gaozhong tongri"); 163 ("Jiu gao"); 218 ("Duo fang"); 275 (A quotation from "Tai jia" in Mengzi zhengyi; 133 (3 "Gongsun Chou shang" 4).

183. Ibid., 74–75 ("Gan shi"); 94 ("Pangeng zhong"); 112 ("Mu shi"); 152, 153, 154 ("Kang gao"); 248, 249 ("Fei shi").

184. Ibid., 253, 254, 257 ("Lüxing"); 91 (Pangeng zhong); 154 ("Kang gao"); 230 ("Li zheng").

185. Lunyu zhengyi, 407 (19 "Zi zhang" 19).

186. Xunzi jijie, 342–43 (28 "Youzuo").

187. Ibid., 189–91 (15 "Yi bing"); 300–301 (24 "Junzi").

188. Shangshu jishi, 257, 259, 260, 261 ("Lüxing").

189. Ibid., 150 ("Kang gao").

190. Ibid., 22 ("Yao dian"); 149 ("Kang gao").

191. This principle is quoted from "Xia shu," a missing part of The Book of Historical Documents. See Chunqiu Zuozhuan gu, 587 ("Xianggong ershiliu nian").

192. This principle is a missing part of "Kang gao" of *The Book of Historical Documents* quoted in *Chunqiu Zuozhuan gu*, 347 ("Xigong sanshisannian").

193. Jia Gongyan, *Zhouli zhengyi*, in Ruan Yuan, ed., *Shisanjing zhushu* (Taibei: Yiwen, 1965), pp. 528–31, 539–40, 475–76 (5 "Qiuguan").

194. Ibid., 525.

195. *Shangshu zhengyi*, 257, 259 ("Lüxing").

196. Ibid., 22 ("Yao dian"); 87 ("Pan geng shang"); 177 ("Zhao gao").

197. Ibid., 149 ("Kang gao").

198. Ibid., 258 ("Lüxing").

199. *Zhouli zhengyi*, 539–40 (5 "Qiuguan").

200. *Liji zhengyi*, 847 (26 "Jingjie").

201. Ibid., 413 (9 "Liyun").

7

Transforming Confucian Virtues into Human Rights: A Study of Human Agency and Potency in Confucian Ethics

Chung-ying Cheng

Sociopolitical Background: Political Patriarchy in China

In my view the ancient Chinese people's belief in the consanguinity of heaven and man as reflected in the Classic of Poetry (*Shijing*) and the Classic of History (*Shujing*) has provided a metaphysics of man which explains the rise of both "ancestor worship" in China,[1] and the political patriarchy in China since before the time of the Xia. Historical research has now traced a line of development in Chinese society as follows: first came familial patriarchy, then clan patriarchy, and finally state patriarchy over groups with different surnames (*yixing*). What made this "patriarchy" political was the reformulation of family morals and possibly even clan morals into a system of rites (*li*), applicable to a larger society under the political control of an enfeoffed aristocracy.[2]

The basis for the rites (*li*), however, is virtue (*de*), which qualifies the ruler for the Mandate of Heaven in the sense that it both legitimates his rule and effectively secures his rule. In this sense virtue (*de*) is nothing less than an outward conformity with the sentiments among the clans and people and an inward cultivation of qualities in the ruler which make him care for the people. Rites are designed or evolved to preserve the ethos of self-discipline on the one hand and social harmony and political order on the other. In the unity of virtue and rites one thus finds both the metaphysical unity of heaven and man and the unity of ruler and people, based on a belief in the consanguinity of Heaven and man. It is important to recognize that nowhere in Chinese history or philosophy was a ruler considered, or would he consider himself, to have his primary obligation to Heaven and not to the people. Heaven is only the de jure basis for political rule; the de facto foundation of rule, among Confucians, is always the people. This is true from the time of Yao and Shun, in the subsequent Zhou culture, and down through Confucian tradition.

The ritualization of human relationships and human transactions may not have been completed until Duke Zhou in the twelfth century B.C.E. and may not have been written down in the form of the book of "Ceremonial Rites" (*Yili*) and "Institutes of Zhou" (*Zhouguan* or *Rites of Chou, Zhouli*) until late in the Warring States (*Chan guo*) Period.[3] From a modern moral point of view, we have in the practice of virtue and rites a morality of devotion to the common good based on the universal practice of virtue as exemplified by the ruler. We may therefore regard the system of rites as a paradigm of a community-based ethics of virtue.

The world of rites is based on a discovery of human relationships and thus of a capacity for human relationships, reflecting an awareness of feeling-directed sociality on the one hand and abilities-based humanity on the other, both of which culminate in Confucius's moral humanism of virtue. Both sociality and humanity are experiences of a holistic human existence extending in time and space; hence with it comes an ideal of human culture which is an expression and valuation of human creativity. Based on this experience the lifeworld of an individual is also extended, and there is no urgent motive for radical transcendence into another world. Even death as an event acquires a proper place in this world of cultural values as articulated in the rites of ancestral worship and the virtue of respecting the old and commemorating the historically remote. This is the basic reason why the secular becomes the sacred. If the ruler is able to practice virtue and secure the rites, he is able to rule effortlessly. But in order to secure rule by rites rooted in virtue, the ruler also has to provide for the livelihood of the people as a basis for their practice of virtue and rites.

Based on this perception of virtue and rites and their relationship, in confronting the problem of how to establish good government, Confucius wished to restore Zhou culture and society by restoring the spirit of rites. Hence his famous statement in defining humaneness (or cohumanity, *ren*) as disciplining oneself and restoring the rites (*keji-fuli*).[4] Realizing that the ancient rites would not be easily restored, Mencius no longer speaks of rites as a system but instead speaks of four cardinal virtues, of which ritual decorum is only one among four. Although both Confucius and Mencius failed to induce or convince a ruler to put their philosophies into practice, their position and understanding nevertheless represent the very essence of the deep sentiment of the people of the time. At the same time they have addressed the deeper problems of political rule. In the fourth century B.C.E. Mencius was specially alert to the issue of   143 political patriarchy, the issue as to how the ruler could provide for the well-being of the people so that the people could be taught moral cultivation and the development of humaneness on both the individual and social levels. Again, although Mencius's words on welfare planning did not receive any serious consideration or produce any significant results in small states, such as Teng and Song, whose rulers were attracted to what Mencius had to say regarding "humane rule" (ren-zheng), he nevertheless identified the central concern of any society or state for the internal practice of virtue and its external institutionalization in a social system.[5]

Given what has been said about rites and virtue, to speak of rule by the Mandate of Heaven as if it were a religion of magic and the ruler an emperor-magician does not convey much about Confucian statecraft based on rites and virtue.[6] It is true however that in later history rites and virtue degenerated into something else. Laozi says that "When the great Way is abandoned, the virtues of humaneness and rightness appear" and "When the Way is lost, virtue appears; when virtue is lost, humaneness appears; when humaneness is lost, rightness appears; when rightness is lost rites appear."[7] In this there may be an element of truth. Yet Laozi did not realize that when the rites are lost, legalist laws and systems, as well as techniques (shu) appear. When finally settled in the larger unified order of the Han empire, political rule was founded on a subtle combination of Confucianism, Daoism, and Legalism and this combination has lasted to this day as part of an implicit Chinese way of political thinking. On this basis we may be able to explain why rights could be seen as implicit in the social duties and political obligations derived from Confucian virtues and rites, while yet they may still need to be developed in the modern situation.

Regarding the last point, it can further be said that both Mozi and Xunzi shared with Thomas Hobbes (1588–1678) the view that the original natural state among men before government arose was a state of war of everyone against everyone else. Mozi suggested that it was the discovery of the principles of "universal love" (jianxiangai) and "mutual benefit" (jiaoxiangli), deriving from the will of Heaven (tian-zhi) that led to the rise of government under a sage-ruler, who had become aware of these principles. Similarly, for Xunzi it was the realization by sage-kings of the benefits to be derived from social principles of "differentiation" (fen) and "collectivity" (qun), which persuaded people to accept patriarchy or monarchy. Here there is no Rousseauistic idea of giving up one's right of self-government in exchange for protection, as an explanation of the rise of sovereign power in kingship. Thus the rights of man have never occupied a prominent place in Chinese thinking, because the Chinese and Western conceptions of the rise of government differ. However, this is not because there is nothing whatever like human rights in the Chinese tradition.

Some notion of the natural right to change a government for the well-being of the people, was conceived by Mencius, based on his view of human nature as an embodiment of the Mandate of Heaven from which people are entitled to claim what is originally intended for them by Heaven. This is a prime case of deriving a right from human nature conceived as virtue.[8]

Duties and Rights of the Human Person

In Confucianism, the ruler and his government are given the role of making the moral transformation of society and individual possible. There is thus a strong sense of duty prevailing among the governing class, and the ruler and those under him would think of their responsibility for governing also as an entitlement, insofar as the responsibility could not be discharged without the authority. For the ruler to define his identity in terms of ruling means his duties are also his rights; on the other hand, for the ruler to define his identity as serving the interests of the people means his rights are also his duties.

When we extend this relation between duties and rights to people in general, we can see how a Chinese might see his rights as his duties and define his own self in terms of his entitlements to consideration by the ruler who has duties as the content of his consciousness. This would explain why Chinese culture under the influence of Confucianism has not had a sense of free-standing human rights. They have had however a sense of human rights implicitly defined in terms of the self in relation to virtues. What then is the Chinese concept of self in relation to virtues?

As the collective experience of society and community has overwhelmed individual experience, the reality of individual life has been dominated by concerns about the preserving of human relationships so as to secure one's place in society and community. This is how rites and virtue arose together in ancient Chinese culture. Consequently, the primary or immediate consciousness of a human person has been one's power or ability to develop family and community order and harmony as a base for developing oneself as an individual. It has not been to assert oneself first against some political authority outside one's direct concern. In other words, the primary or immediate concern of the self has been that of virtue, for virtue has been conceived as the power of harmonization both within a person (in the form of mental attitudes) and without a person (in the form of institutions); hence they take the form more of a duty rather a right. For virtue to be virtue is to fit the individual into the social whole, to be achieved by cultivation and transformation of oneself. Virtue is precisely the power of self-cultivation and self-transformation toward the goal of social and even political integration.

Among all the specific virtues conceived by the Confucians there is none which does not also take the form of a duty, since it is this sense of the har- 145 monization of parts within a whole which preempts virtue as a duty. Consider the virtue of humaneness (*ren*). It is the expression of humanity in a self as a sense of co-humanity with others. It is a duty from which the whole society will benefit. Even though it requires self-cultivation, its aim is not to secure the interests of the individual alone. On the contrary, it is a way of making the individual available to a society, possibly even, as Mencius would see it, to enable a man to become a sage-king. Even as the virtue of proper behavior in the form of ritual decorum (*li*) it is a duty to both self and society which prompts this cultivation. So too with other Confucian virtues.

When the duties attached to virtues are performed, one naturally receives a place of dignity and respectability in society. A virtuous man, becoming known, would even receive political respectability and accommodation as well. This means that the duty conception of virtues serves to protect the individual in society and community. Perhaps the only way to be so protected is that one would have the right to do more of the same, namely the right to develop oneself as a moral person.

Given this understanding of the Confucian self, one may venture the philosophical question as to whether we could view virtues as rights rather than as duties. I do not see why this could not be so if we take a correlative point of view. A virtue is required of a person in his conduct toward another person or toward himself. There is no reason why one could not be both the agent and recipient of virtues. In other words, we could see society itself as having the duties of virtues for the benefit of the individual. In this sense an individual might expect such duties to be performed for him so that these duties could become recognized as personal rights. Thus a theory of explicit virtues could be turned into a theory of implicit rights if it could be seen as a theory of correlative duties among members of a community. The only thing lacking would be an explicit assertion of these rights as a basis for their political recognition. This of course would take a revolutionary development of society and politics to achieve.

Seen in this light we can see how rights consciousness could arise in contemporary China and even approximate the Western model since the political structure and political culture would change accordingly. But set against the background of Chinese history and Chinese culture and assuming the prevailing preoccupation with Confucian virtue-consciousness, the rights movement would not have the same momentum as it has had in the modern West nor would its content be as sharply defined as in the West. If we could speak of human rights with Chinese characteristics, it would be a theory of human rights based on the Confucian theory of human nature and human virtues. This same theory would of course temper our understanding and practice of democracy, as it is seen in Japan and Taiwan. One could not expect simple Westernization with the importation of abstract concepts into an ongoing, self-sustaining culture. According to Alasdair MacIntyre, the modern West, in developing notions of rights and utilities, has lost its Aristotelian tradition of virtue ethics, which he wants it to relearn or recapture. In my view, for modern Chinese, the point would be how to preserve the Confucian virtues, while at the same time extrapolating from them an ethics of rights for modern society.[9]

Human Rights and Rational Liberation from Tradition

Even though the Hegelian theory and history of universal freedom[10]—a concept of freedom confined to individuals—is an inspiring doctrine, a fundamental problem is posed by its lack of consideration for how individual freedom protected by law may interfere with the moral development of individuals and society. For example, the freedom not to work or the freedom not to take care of one's parents might lead to serious problems of moral development for both individuals and society. There must always be a new sense of freedom to be realized in the future as there will be a new sense of value based on the overall experience of history and culture.

Rational liberation of Chinese society from its traditional heritage has been a constant theme among Chinese intellectuals since the time of the May Fourth Movement. Theoretically speaking, rational liberation in the sense of overcoming historical customs and conventions toward a more open, more explicit, and more orderly procedure for public policy making and governmental accountability is certainly desirable, and few people doubt that this is a sound way to become democratic and to secure the implementation of human rights in a modern setting. Yet there is no reason why rational liberation should take only one unique form, and there must be room, and even respect, for different forms of rational liberation so long as equality, self-respect, and respect for human dignity are recognized as the essential bases for the universalization of human rights and democracy across nations and cultures.

It has been suggested that the Confucian social duty of mutual respect and mutual help between friends (one of the cardinal relationships regarded as horizontally equal) may be a native source for an ethics of equal human rights with Chinese characteristics. Thus even in Confucianism there is this dimension of human rights, but this being the case does not imply that other Confucian virtues are necessarily incompatible with human rights. For instance, the Confucian aspiration to secure a proper place in society according to one's ability and merit can be considered a human right too. Human rights should not be conceived only as leveling down, but rather as raising people up. Human rights should support the moral development of man and society rather than being disruptive of society. Human rights should extend to and include 147 all the virtues that contribute to the full development of the human person and human society. In this sense both the Chinese humanistic tradition of virtues and the Western rationalistic tradition of human rights could go hand in hand for the creation of a self-sustainable and ecologically sound social order in the century to come.

The Transformation of Virtues Into Rights

How then do we actually characterize the transformation of Confucian virtues into human rights in a modern society? I offer the following observations.

First, we must recognize that virtues are the products of efforts issuing out of the internal abilities and propensities of a person in response to external stimuli, especially the needs and feelings of other people in the community. In Confucianism this presupposed a theory of human nature, which it went on further to articulate. Virtues in this sense have always been community-oriented and community-based. But this is not to say that virtues are mere conventions of community behavior, but only that virtues serve the interests of the social order and community harmony (i.e., the common good) and perhaps the improvement of such conventions. In this sense virtues represent the individual creative inputs into the community serving the needs of both the community and individual selves. They are composed of both self and community and serve the two together.

Second, virtues, insofar as they are community-nurtured and community-oriented, represent a duty of the self to the community and a duty of the community to the self. The duty consciousness comes from a vision of the perfect union or unity of self and community in which both their needs are realized. The oughtness of these virtues derives from the actual understanding of one's ability to choose this vision, in fulfillment of one's own need for rational consistency and natural self-realization; that is, the sense of oughtness arises out of a sense of consistency between what one has been and what one could be, and thus the need to maintain this consistency becomes the sense of oughtness as obligatory. Thus what the self owes to the community for the fulfillment of perfect virtue and what the community owes the self on the same account, become the duty consciousness of the self and the community, by which the virtues become duties.

Third, the duty consciousness of virtues is sometimes attended with a sense or an expectation of their public utility. This is implicit in the Confucian distinction between private interest and public utility. Hence the virtues which are premised on a public consciousness and the consciousness of public utility (*gongli* versus private desires or *siyu*) deserve to be respected and even secured, as being based on good will toward the public (common) good, it being in the interest of the public that such virtues should be protected. The question is how this public consciousness is to be expressed or articulated as a public concern of the community. One criticism that can be lodged against Chinese traditional society is the lack of such expression, in that public consciousness has not been rationally propounded as a main part of the educational system, and has not become a virtue independent of loyalty to the ruler or of filial piety toward parents. Without rational recognition of this public consciousness there can be no public sense of duty or public recognition of the implicit rights of the virtuous person as a virtue-performer or practitioner.

Fourth, related to this is the point that the individual as a member of the community is also the indirect beneficiary of the virtuous action of any other individual, even though that may not be intended by the agent. If the public good or utility is to be protected, all indirect interests of the individual in society which result from the obtaining of this public utility should also be protected. In this sense the individual's claims to this public utility, which logically justify the existence of this public utility, should be recognized as an integral part of the virtue; and this is precisely how rights could be constituted and recognized, namely, rights as implicit claims to public well-being so that one may perform and cultivate virtues for the public welfare. The very existence and importance of public virtues implies or entails a recognition of the rights of the individual. Thus we see how rights could be born from virtues: they could be born both from the duty consciousness of the individual to the public or community in developing and perfecting or refining virtues, and from the claims to public utility that give a reason for defining and performing these virtues.

Fifth, there is a final stage in the transformation of virtues into rights, namely the removing of intervening powers and authorities which may distort or dominate the public interest, and thus prevent the realization of the public interest in favor of the interests of the ruler. In so far as the private interests of a ruler or a ruling class usurp the public interest or create a condition (often in the form of institutionalization) for protecting their own existence, there is a need to remove such distortion and domination by preventing selfishness and partiality on the part of the ruler in both his personal attitudes and social instruments. This includes institutions that are not in the long-term interests of the public (even though sometimes there are enlightened despots who bring about the public good and do not work only for their private interests, there is no guarantee that the outcome would always be in the public interest). Often the conflicts of public interest with the ruler's private interests are so severe that the ruler comes to use his power in his own defense against the people, and thus becomes oppressive. The need to protest and even fight against an oppressive ruler is obvious. Not so clear is that oppressive condi-   149 tions may call for awakening the implicit consciousness of rights as individual claims for virtuous actions on the part of individuals, in order to defend the community against the selfish interests of a ruler. Thus revolutions become needed, as has happened many times in both Western and Chinese history.

In an earlier article,[11] I have discussed how the Western conception of rights is explicitly formulated in Bills of Rights, as documents resulting from successful rebellions against encroachments on the public interest that serve the private interests of the ruler or the ruling class. Of course, in the dynastic changes in Chinese history it was mostly the collective rights of survival which were fought over in confronting corrupt or irresponsible rulers. Even in the 1911 Revolution we can see that the revolution against the Manchus was conducted for the collective survival of a people. At that time Dr. Sun Yatsen spoke for the power of democracy or people's power (*minquan*), but this *minquan* revolution has not been completed, even after the lapse of eighty years. This is partly from the fact that "the people" (*min*) in the *minchuan* revolution was still conceived as the collective right of national survival; neither Dr. Sun Yatsen's doctrine of the people-power-ism (*minquan zhuyi*) nor Mao Zedong's new democracy (*xinminzhuzhuyi*) confronted the issue of the individual's claims to rights as against the powers of government, which should constitutionally and effectively protect the rights of people. True, in the writing of Chinese constitutions the protection of rights has always been acknowledged, but in actual practice they have often not been observed. This is because a consciousness in the form of public interest against private interests has not been effectively established through law, education, and the personal commitment of leaders. To overcome this the explicit promotion of a rational way of thinking in regard to rights could be very useful.

To conclude from the above, we may recognize that the Confucian conception of the limitation of the ruler's power for the well-being of people does imply a kind of democratic consciousness and an acknowledgment of the political rights of the people. The following often ignored passage from Mencius calls for the ruler's acknowledgment of such political rights on the part of people:

> If those close to a ruler recommend the talent of a person (to be appointed), it is not to be agreed to. If all those in the rank and file also recommend the talent of a person, it is still not to be agreed to. It is not until all the people in the state recommend the talent of a person that a ruler, taking a close look and finding the recommendation to be correct, will then make the appointment. If those close to a ruler recommend dismissal of a person, it is not to be listened to. If those in the rank and file also recommend dismissal of a person, it is still not to be listened to. It is not until all the people in the state recommend the dismissal of a person that a ruler, taking a close look and finding the recommendation to be correct, will then order the

dismissal. If those close to a ruler recommend the execution of a person, it is not to be listened to. If all those in the rank and file also recommend the execution of the person, it is still not to be listened to. It is not until all people in the country recommend execution of the person that the ruler, taking a close look and finding the recommendation to be correct, will then order the execution. In this way it is the people of the country who order the execution. It is in this way that a ruler can be said to be a parent to the people.[12]

Two observations may be made on this passage: First, it is the people's judgment that should be decisive. Presumably it is not just a few people but at least a majority of people that should be consulted. Second, that the ruler has "to take a close look" (*cha*) suggests that he has to be rational and fair in rendering final judgment regarding the merits and demerits of a given person. In other words, rationality and justice must be applied. This implies that a person is always entitled to his own respect, of which he cannot be deprived simply by the opinions of others. It also implies the right of innocence until proven guilty by due process. Nevertheless, there is still a problem in that no effort is made explicitly to articulate this right, and no consequent effort to secure its enforcement and practice.

To summarize, the possible transformation of Confucian virtues into rights can be described as follows: the cultivation of virtues by individuals-in-community should lead to an awakening of duty consciousness in an individual to the community and the public, which in turn should call forth an awareness of the individual's legitimate potential for participating in public affairs (no individual can be separated from the public). But claims to such participation on the part of the individual require participation also in an independent rational discourse on the public interest. It further calls for a consciousness of the need for the ruling political power to conform to the public interest. Should rulers fail to conform to the public interest, protest and revolution against usurpation and oppression may well ensue, with the attendant assertion of peoples' rights against political encroachment. As a result of such protest or revolution there could finally come a positive, explicit, and written declaration of individual human rights, including both rights as freedoms and rights as virtues.

Notes

1. See my article "Dialectic of Confucian Morality and Metaphysics of Man, A Theoretical Synthesis," in *Philosophy East and West* 21, no. 2 (1971): pp. 111–23.

2. The legends in the founding and formation of Chinese society and Chinese culture are mentioned in the Historical Records (*Shiji*); these can be traced to the tribe-clans of culture heroes such as Youzaoshi, Suirenshi, Fuxishi, and Shennongshi, which eventually evolved into clan-states such as the Kingdoms of Yellow Emperor, Yao,

Shun, and Yü (Dynasty of Xia, twenty-first century to seventeenth century B.C.E.) which gradually unified various tribes. From Xia on, Chinese culture flourished in terms of the rituals and rites that governed basic human relationships and ceremonial occasions. These were not only for the maintenance of political control but for the creation of a social order that would give meaning to human life and activities. In this sense the ritual culture of the Zhou is an achievement of Chinese culture, which both embodied an understanding of humanity and human relationships, and successfully developed a form for realizing such an understanding. In the rites there is already a recognition of virtue (*de*) as a way of achieving social order and political control.

3. There are controversies over the dates of these two ritual texts. The third book of rituals, *Liji* (Records of Rites), is recognized as a later work of Confucians in the Warring States Period, composed of various Confucian discussions of the meaning of different rites.

4. See *Analects* 5:12.

5. See *Mencius*, ch. 3 Tien Wen Gong. One may easily see how difficult it was for the Mencian program of social and political reform to meet the objective needs of the time when many agents of change contributed elements of instability and uncertainty.

6. See Clark Butler, *History as the Story of Freedom* (Amsterdam and Atlanta: Philosophy in Intercultural Context, Editions Rodopi, 1995), ch. 7: China and Divine Emperorship, pp. 149–66.

7. See the *Daode jing*, chs. 18 and 38.

8. In conceiving the rise of the state from the discovery of sagely principles, not simply as a matter of brutal conquest or by contract in exchange for the pursuit of self-interest through pragmatic rationality, as suggested in Leviathan, Chinese philosophers, somewhat like Aristotle, came to see governance as the best expression of collective wisdom and conscience, which should guard its legitimacy on the basis of its attention to the needs and life conditions of the people. If these conditions were not met, political chaos would ensue, people would rise to take over, and there would be a competition for a true ruler to take over for the benefit of the people. This can be seen in the dynastic cycles in Chinese history. It becomes a struggle for power on the pretext of fulfilling the mandate (*ming*) or virtue (*de*) of Heaven. In this recycling of Chinese political power we can see the plausibility of a mix of the Hobbesian view and Confucian or Mo-ist views.

Insofar as the present moment of human society can be seen as a departure from an ideal order of harmony, and human society can be seen as arising from principles of wisdom, the Confucian memory (not just a projection) of a golden past seems to be a natural reminder and even implicit critique of the problems of the present. This warrants the employment of history for the service of the future.

This may explain the immanent coherence of the Chinese cultural experience as the basis of its development, not its transcendence, but it may also explain why the immanent coherence of the culture sometimes fails to meet the challenge of the times. Eventually, in the May Fourth, 1918, Period when political and social pressures mounted, the tradition was emotionally rejected in favor of a rational reconstruction in which what was alien and transcendent gradually became absorbed into the immanent whole. In my view, China has now gone beyond the stage of rejection of the past and has begun a stage of the rediscovery of its tradition for the purpose of integrating the traditional and the modern. In this manner a golden age may again become projected, but in the future, not in the past.

9. See Alasdair MacIntyre's *After Virtue* (2d ed.; Notre Dame, Ind.: University of Notre Dame Press, 1984), chs. 2, 4, and 16.

10. See Hegel's *Lectures on History of Philosophy*, trans. by J. Sibree (London, 1857); E. S. Haldane and F. H. Simson translation is in 3 vols. (London, 1892–1896, reprint, 1955).

11. See my article "Human Rights in Chinese History and Chinese Philosophy." *Comparative Civilizations Review*. no. 1 (1979): 1–20.

12. See *Mencius* 1:7 Lianghuiwang.

8

Might and Right: The "Yellow Emperor" Tradition as Compared with Confucianism

Yu Feng

As an encouraging and laudable development, more and more people have come to the realization that Asian traditional values may contribute to the enrichment and improvement of a universal concept of "human rights" whose current interpretation is still primarily set in Western terms.

Although Confucianism is undoubtedly the most significant social and political tradition in China, and in the whole of East Asia as well, it is not the *sole* tradition that may be relevant to our discussion of human rights. As is well known, Taoism and Buddhism also have their own view on human freedom.[1] What I shall discuss here, however, is another early tradition that was significant in shaping the Chinese political tradition during the past two millennia, though it has only begun to be recognized by most modern scholars.

As we examine Chinese history, we can discern a pattern of political activity that Chinese rulers, assisted by the ruling elite, regularly practiced in formulating policies, strategies, and tactics. Although most of these rulers openly claimed to be followers of Confucianism, the principles underpinning their political practices could be called, in important respects, not Confucian. Zhu Xi (Chu Hsi), the great synthesizer of Song Neo-Confucianism, repeatedly spoke to the effect that no emperor in Chinese history since the Han dynasty had really practiced the Confucian way of governance. Some emperors had been lauded by historians for having governed well, e.g., Li Shimin (Li Shih-min), the second emperor of the Tang dynasty, yet their supposed Confucian Kingly Way (*wangdao*) or "Government by Rightness" was according to Zhu Xi no more than "hypocritical humaneness and rightness" and, in reality, they based their policies on unyielding calculations of their own interests.[2]

I think this is no overstatement. But what was the tradition that actually functioned behind all this? In Zhu Xi's terminology, it is called *badao* or "Government by Might," in contrast to the Confucian "Government by Rightness."[3] For a long time, the *badao* has been understood as the principles of "Legalism." However, the politics the Chinese emperors adopted seemed to be more moderate then Shang Yang's doctrine that put strong emphasis on *yanzing junfa* or strict laws and severe punishment. The unearthing of the *Four Texts of the Yellow Emperor (Huangdi sijing*, for convenience referred to here as the *Four Texts*) in 1973 provides us an unexpected and valuable clue to a better understanding of this non-Confucian political tradition.[4] The *Four Texts* is a quadripartite work written in the Warring States period and ascribed to the "Yellow Emperor," a legendary king of remote antiquity.[5] It focuses on the "art of rulership," and elaborates a set of guiding principles, policies, strategies, tactics, and ways of spiritual cultivation for a supreme ruler to achieve a successful government. It has many ideas in common with some Pre-Qin works later labeled as either "Taoist" or "Legalist," especially with the *Works of Guanzi (Kuan Tzu)* and the *Works of Han Feizi (Han Fei Tzu)*. However, it also shows clear differences from the policies of punishment-priority propounded by such "extreme Legalists" as Shang Yang, as well as from the naturalism and individualism taught by such "extreme Taoists" as Zhuang Zi. The *Four Texts* may best represent the political tradition that Chinese rulers of the imperial period covertly followed, i.e., "Government by Might."

What then are the distinct features of the political thought taught by the *Four Texts*? We can understand it better by comparing it with Confucianism. The terms "Government by Rightness" and "Government by Might" themselves may express the fundamental difference. Confucianism is an ethical-political philosophy based on a series of moral categories. The main stream of Confucianism, especially those who follow Mencius, places emphasis on the motives for political action. Rulers should do what conforms with the moral imperative regardless of whether or not it will be practically successful.[6] By contrast, the *Four Texts* pay more attention to outcomes. A policy is good only if it is successful. In the *Four Texts*, we frequently find such terms as gains (or *de*), losses (or *shi*), success (or *cheng*), and failure (or *bai*). To borrow Zhu Xi's words, it "discusses right and wrong from the perspective of success and failure."[7] This tradition is conspicuously pragmatic.

Furthermore, according to Confucianism, all members of society, both the ruler and the common people, need moral cultivation in order to initiate the process of transforming society into a better one. The *Four Texts*, by contrast, are meant for the supreme ruler and the ruling elite only. One can hardly find   155 in the *Four Texts* any advice for the common people. The Confucians were primarily scholars, although some were also officials at different levels. The authors of the *Four Texts* and similar works were primarily statesmen on the top level, or at least they based themselves on the experiences of such top statesmen as Guan Zhong (Kuan Chung) and Zi Chan (Tzu Chan).[8] This explains why Confucianism is an overt tradition and the political thought represented by the *Four Texts* is a covert one. For a supreme ruler, the art of rulership should not be exposed to the multitude but be kept secret.

Chinese politics during the imperial period was not monolithically Confucian. There have been two political traditions: the overt "Government by Rightness" and the covert "Government by Might." Therefore, the totalitarianism or autocracy manifest in Chinese history would relate rather to the latter than to the former.

To be sure, the tradition represented by the *Four Texts* openly acclaims the peerless power and indisputable authority of the supreme ruler. The Yellow Emperor himself is portrayed as a perfect exemplar of such values. He claims that: "It is I alone who rules over all-under-Heaven."[9] The totalitarian nature of this tradition predetermines that it cannot be congenial to the modern concept of human rights.

On the other hand, the affirmation of a supreme ruler as the center of politics does not necessarily involve political arbitrariness and the abuse of power. The "Yellow Emperor" tradition is not one that absolutely relies on might alone. In fact, the *Four Texts* and similar works advocate on the one hand the supremacy of the king or emperor; and on the other hand the need to restrain his power and warn him against its abuse. In so doing, they engage in some discussion of rights that are not irrelevant to the present study of human rights. I will very briefly analyze these discussions under four aspects that contrast with Confucianism.

Benefiting the People

The concept of human rights is closely linked to the issue of human nature. Unlike the Mencian theory of human nature that man is innately endowed with such qualities or potentials as humaneness (*ren*), rightness (*yi*), trustworthiness (*xin*), or loyalty (*zhong*),[10] the *Four Texts* assumes that the innate nature of human being, as well as all other living beings, is contentious and aggressive.[11] All things seek to enhance their own survival. They seek to run after material gains and avoid harm to their lives.

In this regard, a ruler is no different from any ordinary person. Both want to satisfy their material desires. With peerless power, the ruler of course enjoys himself better than the farmer. However, if a ruler wants to sustain his enjoyment longer, he has to acknowledge the rights of his subjects for subsistence as well as for a better livelihood. The second text says,

> As people are brought to life, through hardship they manage to secure food and bear descendants. If there were no mating, there would be no descendants—such a situation [i.e., to have none such] would fail to abide by [the principle of] the earth. If people were not supplied with food, there would be no people at all—such a situation would fail to abide by [the principle of] heaven. (2.2.5; OT 84a)

The people's need to survive, though narrowly understood as the right to have mates, to sustain simple reproduction and to have food, are in accord with the principles of heaven and earth. A government that does not follow them is called "perverse" (*ni*) and will suffer loss.[12] If the ruler cannot provide governance that meets well the basic needs of his people, his reign will be greatly endangered.

The *Four Texts* discusses thoroughly the relationship between taking and giving. The ultimate aim of government is for a ruler to get more from his people. To achieve this, however, he has to take less at first, e.g., to reduce taxes and the use of corvée labor, and even to "give" something. In case of natural disasters, he should let people enter forbidden areas such as royal parks to fish and hunt.[13] Only when the people become rich, will the ruler be able to take more from them. It is necessary for a ruler to lead a relatively frugal life in the beginning. The *Four Texts* warns:

> The accumulation and hoarding of gold, pearls, and jade is a source of resentment. If a ruler (indulges) in traveling about with a numerous retinue of beauties, musicians, and playthings, it becomes a cause for disorder. If he harbors the sources of such resentment, he nurtures the basis of disorder, and even if there are sages (to help him), such a ruler cannot be saved. (1.5.15; OT 46a-b)

This does not mean, however, that a ruler cannot enjoy life. When the people are rich, he will be able to take more from them. Then, he can lead a luxurious life without jeopardizing his reign. The *Four Texts* says:

> A ruler who knows [the art of rulership], though he indulges in (the pleasures of) hunting, does not neglect (state affairs); though fond of drinking and eating, he does not disregard (state affairs); though enraptured by beauties and treasures, he is not bewildered (by them). (1.4.8.; OT 30b)

How is this so? Just because he gives and takes in due time. In this sense, the *Four Texts* says: "If one takes and gives properly, he is a king; if not, he is dying."[14]

In the *Four Texts* we find an "inaugural speech" of the Yellow Emperor in which he states that he has affection for his people.[15] This affection, different from the moral and spiritual concept of humaneness (*ren*), is openly pragmatic. 157

He says: "because I harbor intimate affection for my people, they do not run away from me." Furthermore, this affection is not linked with moral and spiritual values but only material benefits. The government should benefit the people. Then people will fight for the government.[16] This art of rulership reminds us of a famous story about Wu Qi, an eminent statesman and a renowned commander during the Warring States period. Once a soldier suffered from an ulcer and Wu Qi sucked out the pus for him. The mother of that soldier, however, cried with grief, saying, previously Wu Qi did the same for her husband, so her husband fought forward resolutely until he was killed by the enemy. Now Wu Qi, by sucking out the pus, was hoping her son would do the same for him as well.[17] Advice similar to this of purposively benefiting the people can also be found in the *Works of Guanzi* and the *Works of Han Feizi*.[18]

The relationship between the ruler and the ruled should be reciprocal or of mutual benefit. This is one of the basic points of the Yellow Emperor tradition.

Since human nature is to seek gain and avoid harm, the most effective means of government, according to the *Four Texts* as well as many other statesmen/thinkers of ancient China, is the use of rewards and penalties. However, there are apparent differences between them. While most recommend keeping a balance between reward and penalty, Shang Yang believes that there should be more punishments than rewards, and the ratio should be nine to one.[19]

The author of the *Four Texts* and many other ancient Chinese thinkers had a deep conviction that the improvement of the people's livelihood was the key factor in the success of a state. Only after this goal was achieved, could a country be successful in military contention with other states, and it be possible for the people to follow moral doctrines and rites.[20] In other words, the "might" of the government is based on a prosperous and stable economy so that most of the common people can enjoy life. The present attitude toward human rights of the Chinese government, giving priority to the "rights of subsistence," may well have its historical root in this tradition.[21]

Confucianism also teaches that the government should benefit people. However, there are two major differences between Confucianism and the *Four Texts*.

First, the *Four Texts* pays due attention to the material aspect when benefiting people is discussed. To benefit people is to enrich the people materially.[22] There is no mention about their mental development and about their education in the *Four Texts*. Confucianism considers that both the material and spiritual aspects are important. In a certain sense, the spiritual or educational aspect is more significant for a nation.[23] One of the most important tasks of a government is to educate the people.[24] Therefore, people not only have the right to physical subsistence, but also have the right to receive education in order to achieve a complete development and to pursue "Perfect-Manhood"

(*chengren*).[25]

Second, as mentioned above, the *Four Texts* bases its theory on the calculation of interests. When the ruler benefits the people, he expects repayment from them. On the contrary, Confucianism believes that the politics of benefiting people is deduced from the premise that human nature is innately good. Interests or gain are not the concern of the gentleman but only of the "small man."[26]

Abiding by Laws

The acceptance of human rights is often, if not always, accompanied by acceptance of the spirit of law. Since people are equally entitled to the same rights, they should be equal before the law. Without a legal system, it is impossible to safeguard human rights.

Can a polity of autocracy share the spirit of law? Generally not. An autocrat is by nature both the lawmaker and the supreme head of government, hence, he is inclined to act above the law. It is expected that the ruler may require his subjects to obey the laws strictly, but not that these laws constitute any restriction upon himself. The ruler and the ruled can hardly be equal before the law.

The *Four Texts*, however, sets forth a compromise position between the absolute authority of the ruler and the spirit of law. On the one hand, it advocates that the king should have such a supreme authority that the dukes and ministers cannot compare themselves to him.[27] On the other hand, it warns the supreme ruler not to act beyond the laws and regulations. A ruler "formulates laws but dares not violate them. Once the laws have been established, he dare not abrogate them."[28]

Why is the law so immutable and sacrosanct? The answer is found in the first sentence of the *Four Texts*:

It is out of the Way (*Tao*) that laws come into existence.[29]

The Way, according to the *Four Texts*, is the ultimate source of the universe as well as the fundamental principle of change and transformation for all things to follow.[30] Specifically, as the Way in government, laws and regulations, it is the objective standard that the ruler must obey. Otherwise, his government will fail and his reign will come to an end. This is the lesson of history. There were indeed many rulers in history who ignored or abrogated laws to satisfy their personal desires and favorites. Such dictatorial actions, however, have always led to great losses or the utter ruin of governments and dynasties. Therefore, a ruler must learn to obey the Way and laws, and to give up his personal preferences. The third text says:

In general, one must not discard laws and replace them with personal desires. 159

Personal desires must not be used (as standards of conduct). Otherwise disasters will befall. (3.18, OT 149b)

The *Four Texts* emphasizes the distinction between public (*gong*) and private (*si*). *Gong* in this context means objective standards rather than public interests. The *Four Texts* often resorts to metaphors and similes in comparing laws and regulations to yardsticks, rulers, compasses, scales, and other tools (1.1.7, OT 4b-5a; 1.5.11, OT 42b-43a). With the establishment of objective criteria, the ruler can maintain order and control over his domain, no matter how numerous and complex the affairs of the state may be. In this manner, a ruler may handle state affairs at ease and without any perplexities. The third text says:

> To measure with surveying equipment will avoid mistakes. To observe (heavenly bodies) with astronomical instruments will remove perplexity. A country governed according to laws will not be in disorder. (3.5, OT 144a-b)

For his own long-term interest, the ruler must restrain personal desires and abide by the law. A number of pre-Qin works consider the laws as objective standards as opposed to personal favoritism, and use the same metaphors to compare laws and regulations as yardsticks, rulers, compasses, scales and other tools.[31] Han Fei states:

> The law does not fawn on the noble; the string does not yield to the crooked. Whatever the law applies to, the wise cannot reject it nor can the brave defy it. Punishment for a fault never skips ministers, reward for good never misses commoners.[32]

However, it is the *Four Texts* that clearly state that the ruler himself must abide by law. The ruler holds the ultimate state power yet he cannot wield this power in an unlawful way. His personal desires or favorites must yield to *gong* or the objective standard. This restriction is obviously protective of the rights of the masses of people even in the structure of autocracy.

Early Confucianism also stressed that a ruler should not let favorites influence his governance of the country but should follow objective principles. The *Book of Odes*, a Confucian Classic, includes a song in which God admonishes the king of Zhou (Chou):

God spoke to King Wen of Zhou, . . .

> Do not rely on your own views and wits,
> But follow Principles (*ze*) of Mine.[33]

In Confucianism, however, the *ze* primarily refers to the ethical principles represented by the Rites (*li*), i.e., the guiding rules for the proper behavior of people in different social statuses and in different contexts, not universal laws. According to Confucius, the legal system is an important and effective means of government, but the Rites are more significant and far-reaching. He said:

Lead the people with governmental measures and regulate them by laws and punishment, and they will avoid wrong-doing but will have no sense of honor and shame. Lead them with virtue and regulate them by ritual decorum (*li*), and they will have a sense of shame and, moreover, set themselves right.[34]

Confucius criticized many rulers who violated the Rites because of their unlimited and often personal desires. He called for conquering selfish desires and returning to ritual decorum (*keji fuli*).[35] By contrast, the *Four Texts* only sporadically mention such rules of the Rites as the colors for official dress that distinguish the different social statuses.[36] Instead, the *Four Texts* places emphasis on the legal system.

Nonassertion, the Ideal of Rulership

For Confucianism, the ideal ruler or sage-king is a perfect exemplar of high virtue, and he is diligent in both moral cultivation and state governance. A famous Confucian motto is found in the *Book of Changes*:

As Heaven keeps active and vigorous, a gentleman makes unremitting efforts to improve himself.[37]

When the ruler can set a moral example for his people to follow, the country will naturally order itself.

In the *Four Texts*, however, the sage-king should be an exemplar of nonassertion (*wuwei*). It says:

Therefore, he who has mastered the Way, while investigating the affairs of All-under-Heaven, holds no opinion and occupies no place; he does not do anything and is selfless.[38]

Why and how should he be so? This question can be answered from different angles.

First, as the above quotation indicates, nonassertion is the best way for a ruler to get true information needed for his government. If the ruler shows any prejudice, he will not be able to see things objectively; if he exposes his opinions prematurely, his subjects will tend to hide their own real views. Instead, he should get rid of any self-preconception and keep tranquil in the process of investigation. Then he will be able to know the situation correctly and nothing can hide the facts and escape from his judgment. The second text says:

If one wants to know with certainty what are the gains and losses, one must examine names and investigate forms. Forms always settle themselves; hence, I keep myself in quietude. Affairs always carry themselves out; hence, I need not take any action. Be quiet and motionless. What is coming will present itself; what is leaving will go away by itself. Can I keep to oneness? Can I stop? Can I dispel self-interest? 161

Can I dispel self-centeredness and pay respect to principles? I shall be silk-like and hair-like as if I do not exist. Then, even when all the myriad things come forth, I will not fail to respond to any one of them.   (2.15.1; OT 141a-142a)

Second, since the laws are already well publicized, most state affairs can be handled automatically by the respective officers in accordance with the respective provisions of the laws. There is no need for the ruler himself to micromanage affairs in detail.

Third, unlike a tyrant who arbitrarily makes all the important decisions by himself, an ideal ruler will not initiate anything for policy and strategy making. Instead, he will depend on his aides, i.e., the most capable ministers and intelligent advisors. The *Four Texts* states that the relationship between the ruler and his ministers should be as student and teacher, or at least as friend to friend.[39] He should listen to their advice with deep respect although he makes the final decision himself. The Yellow Emperor was described as such a ruler. He always consulted his advisers, such as Li Mo, Guo, Tong, Yan Ran, etc. before making a significant decision. Thus, nonassertion means to avoid arbitrary decisions.

Fourth, nonassertion also implies a nonintervention policy in economic development. A successful ruler will not mobilize the masses of people for war or undertake big projects if this will have a bad effect on agriculture. He will not micromanage the economy but let people develop by themselves. The third text says:

Heaven has light and does not worry that people might live in darkness. The "hundred surnames" can open doors and windows to get light, and heaven need not do anything. The earth possesses [plentiful resources] and it does not worry that people might live in poverty. The "hundred surnames" can cut down trees and chop firewood to become rich, without the earth doing anything. (3.42; OT 158a-b)

A ruler should follow the example of heaven and earth, i.e., not to do anything but just let people do what they can. The *Four Texts* suggests that the restrictions imposed on markets and on state borders should be lifted to stimulate the free development of the economy.[40] This is the easiest and best way for development.

Fifth, nonassertion implies a strategy and tactics in preparation for attack. When there is no chance to attack, the ruler must be patient and prepare. The ruler assumes the posture of nonassertion (*wuwei*) so that he can act with potent efficacy when the appropriate moment is at hand. In addition, the *wuwei* strategy will make the enemy relax his vigilance. The *Four Texts* provides rulers with an example of this strategy as successfully practiced by Da Ting, a legendary king of remote antiquity:

He stood as if he were afraid to stand, and he moved as if he could not move. When he was about to engage in a fight, he looked as though he dared not engage in a fight. When he knew everything, he looked as though he knew nothing. By observing weak conduct, he became strong. He waited for the deterioration of those who held to male conduct and then defeated them. (2.14.3; OT 138a-b)

Finally, nonassertion is the way for a ruler to keep in good health. The country is so vast and state affairs so numerous for the ruler to handle, that he will soon get exhausted and fall into illness if he tries to micromanage all affairs himself. The purpose of governance is to take more from the people and to enjoy material pleasures himself. Thus, he should avoid exhausting his energy so that he can enjoy longer life.

Nonassertion is both a device of the ruler and a restriction on the ruler. Within the framework of autocracy, there could hardly be a more optimal way for government than nonassertion (wuwei). In theory however, people, even though they would not have the rights of direct political participation, would have an opportunity to express their ideas and influence the final judgment of the ruler. If they all think a certain person is good and capable because of his experience and achievements, he would automatically be promoted to a proper position in government; if they all think a certain minister is bad and incapable because of his poor performance, he would automatically be dismissed from his position. Furthermore, people would also have the opportunity to choose their own ways of economic development and the government should not intervene.

Although Confucianism stresses activism (youwei) while the Four Texts prefers nonassertion, their differences should not be exaggerated. The convergence between the two traditions is evident. Confucianism also teaches that one should follow the will of people in government,[41] and promote the worthy.[42]

Development, Achievements, and Deterioration

The Four Texts was written at a time when the feudal system, a combination of autocracy and aristocracy, was being replaced by a highly centralized bureaucracy. Based on the political experience of prominent statesmen of the time, such as Guan Zhong and Zi Chan, it outlines the foundation of a "mild" autocracy. The political application of the Yellow Emperor tradition by Chinese rulers, together with the pervasive social influence of Confucianism, brought about some positive results in Chinese history.

The relationship between overt Confucianism or "Government by Rightness" and the covert Yellow Emperor tradition or "Government by Might" is a complex one. Adherents of each held opinions opposed to each other, and at least once there was an open debate between Confucians and the "Yellow

Emperor Scholars" in the Han dynasty.[43] However, they combined in many ways to shape a "mild" or moderate autocracy characteristic of Chinese imperial politics.

One of the greatest achievements of the Yellow Emperor tradition is found in the early period of the former Han dynasties. Guided by the so-called Huang-Lao (Yellow Emperor and Lao Zi) teachings, the government reduced taxes and corvée labor to the benefit of the people, and adopted an appeasement policy in foreign affairs. The Han dynasty quickly restored the exhausted economy and became a super power in the world of that time.[44]

During the reign of the Emperor Wu of the Han dynasty, Confucianism gradually came to replace the ideas of the "Huang-Lao" as the guiding principle of politics. However, the Yellow Emperor tradition carried on, as we see from the continuing tension between it and Confucianism, as for instance in the Han History (Hanshu) records of Emperor Xuan's criticism of the heir apparent:

> Our Han dynasty has established a system of government whose foundation combines Government by Might and Government by Rightness (bawangdaozazhi). How could we rely on moral education (only) and follow the way of government of the Zhou dynasty (government by means of rites and ceremonies)? Moreover, the stupid Confucians do not understand the current affairs of the state; they are fond of praising the old system and criticizing the present one. In so doing, they cause confusion among people about names and realities so that people are unable to know what to follow. How could these Confucians be appointed and relied on?[45]

The politics of the Tang dynasty, the next golden age of imperial China, was also influenced deeply by the Yellow Emperor tradition. Under the reign of Li Shimin, we find an attempt to institutionalize the theory of wuwei by establishing a sophisticated bureaucracy consisting of three principal departments: the Imperial Secretariat, the Imperial Chancellery and the Secretariat of State Affairs.[46] When an important matter came up, the emperor would not respond himself. Instead, the Imperial Secretariat would discuss the matter, make suggestions, and then write drafts of imperial decrees on behalf of the emperor. Then, the draft would be passed on to be checked by the Imperial Chancellery. If the latter agreed, all the emperor needed to do was to sign the draft and it would be passed onto the Secretariat of State Affairs for implementation. Only if the Imperial Chancellery and the Imperial Secretariat could not reach agreement, would the emperor read the report from the two departments and make his own judgment. Moreover, his judgment would not be the final decision. It was still subject to review by the Imperial Chancellery. If the emperor's judgment was rejected, he would preside at a meeting with the heads of the three departments for further discussion. According to the historical

records, Li Shimin openly encouraged his ministers to propose and criticize.

He set a good example of "nonassertion" for the ruler and the political stability and economic prosperity of the Tang dynasty was the outcome of the most advanced political system in the world at that time.

Although the political practice of late Imperial China was not always as good as that of the early Han and early Tang, Chinese autocracy was not as notoriously had as some modern totalitarian systems. Under the influence of both the "Government by Rightness" and "Government by Might" traditions, the common people not only had the right of subsistence which, though meager by modern standards, might have been second to none in the world then. Also people enjoyed the right to receive an education, and an opportunity to become members of the ruling elite if they passed the civil service exams successfully. There were quite a few stupid or even half insane emperors in the first millennium of imperial China but there were not many tyrants. Confucianism and the Yellow Emperor tradition together reduced the possibility of tyrannical government.

An obvious deterioration followed after the Tang dynasty. The authority of the emperor gradually became overpowering while the role of ministers declined. In the Ming dynasty, the position of chief minister was finally abolished and there was no longer a balance between the emperor and his ministers. Meanwhile, the place and spirit of law declined. Emperors no longer observed the principle taught by the *Four Texts* that both the ruler and the ruled should obey the laws and regulations. Instead, they openly went beyond the laws. The art of rulership was reduced to a series of tactics and intrigues marked by the establishment of secret police.[47]

Of course the Yellow Emperor tradition is far from a perfect political philosophy. As mentioned above, this theory supports openly the distinction between a supreme ruler and his subjects, in fundamental contradiction to the modern concept of equality. In this regard, Confucianism may have been a little better. However, we must keep in mind that the concept of human rights is one of the significant achievements of the enlightenment movement in the West although some ideas may be traced back to the Greek tradition. We should compare it with its Western counterpart in approximately the same period of history. Since the Chinese "Government by Might" was not a brutal autocracy resorting to bloody punishment only, but a relatively "mild" one that acknowledged certain rights of the multitude for subsistence and also because Confucianism created a certain social mobility throughout the examination system, the Chinese dynastic system could last for over two millennia.

The emphasis on the rights of subsistence and for a better livelihood in the *Four Texts* is not an obsolete idea, especially for developing countries where a considerable portion of the population is not yet free from starvation. In addition, the warnings against and apparatus to control the abuse of power by the   165 top leadership, which should not try to micromanage the state, may also have some relevance to modern politics. However, the *Four Texts* fail to pay attention to other aspects of human rights beyond these primary rights. By contrast, Confucianism concerns both the spiritual and material development of man, esteems both individual dignity and the interdependence of members in society. It possesses abundant ideas on human rights that the peoples of modern society may inherit.

Notes

This paper is based in part on research jointly conducted by me and Professor Leo S. Chang of Regis College.

1. For example, Zhuang Zi (Chuang Tzu), the great Taoist master, imagines a mysterious state beyond society, time, and space, where people can enjoy maximum freedom and fully realize their original nature. See *The Complete Works of Chuang Tzu*, trans. Burton Watson (New York: Columbia University Press, 1970), pp. 33–34.

2. *Zhuzi Yulei*, or *The Classified Utterances of Master Zhu* (Taipei: Zhengzhong Book Store, 1982), pp. 5149, 5167.

3. See "Letter to Chen Liang," *Zhongguo zhexueshi Ziliaoxuanji* or *Selected Materials of the History of Chinese Philosophy* (Song, Yuan, and Ming volume) (Taipei: Jiuxi, 1978), p. 257. The distinction between *badao* and Confucian *wangdao* was already set up in the Han dynasty, as we have seen above.

4. A number of "Silk Manuscripts" were found in a Han tomb near Changsha, the capital city of Hunan province. Among them, there are four texts that precede version B of the *Book of Laozi*. Although it is not unanimously agreed, many scholars believe that they constitute a single work, i.e., the *Four Texts of the Yellow Emperor*, which is mentioned in the *History of the Former Han Dynasty*, but disappeared sometime around the sixth century C.E. For details of the excavation, see the Hunan provincial Museum and IAAS (Institute of Archaeology, Academia Sinica): "Excavation of the Han Tombs Nos. two and three at Mangwangdui, Changsha," *Wenwu*, 218 (1974) 7:39–48. For English translation, see *Zhongyingduizhao Huangdisijing Jinzhujinyi* or *The Four Classics of the Yellow Emperor with Current Annotation, Interpretation, and English Translation* (Changsha: Yuelu Press, 1993).

5. While some scholars suppose that it was written in the early Han dynasty, most scholars believe that it was composed in the Warring States period. See ibid., pp. 5–20.

6. See *The Works of Mencius*, James Legge, trans., *The Chinese Classics*, vol. 2, p. 175.

7. "Letter to Chen Liang," cited above, note 3.

8. Guan Zhong was an adroit chief minister of Qi in the seventh century B.C.E., and he assisted Duke Huan of Qi in achieving overlordship. Zi Chan was appointed the chief minister of Zheng in 551 BC, and he initiated a series of political reforms that enabled the state to survive in a very difficult situation.

9. 2.4.1, OT 95a, the *Four Texts*. (The first number indicates text; the second num-

ber indicates section; the third number indicates paragraph; OT means original Chinese text; the number is the line number and a and b respectively indicate above and below.)

10. *The Chinese Classics*, p. 419.

11. *Four Texts*, 1.1.3, OT 1b; 2.6.2., OT 1107a-b.

12. Ibid., 1.6.12, OT 55b-56a.

13. Ibid., 3.29, OT 153a-b.

14. Ibid., 3.17, OT 149a-b.

15. Ibid., 2.1.2–3, OT 78b-80a.

16. Ibid., 1.3.3, OT 17b.

17. *Shiji juan* (chuan) 65: "Sunzi Wuqi liezhuan," or *The Records of the Grand Historian* (Taipei: Qiye Book Store, 1976), p. 2166.

18. The first chapter of the *Guanzi* states this. For Han Fei's idea of benefiting the people, see Hsiao-po Wang and Leo S. Chang, *The Philosophical Foundations of Han Fei's Political Theory* (Honolulu: University of Hawaii Press, 1986), pp. 117–31.

19. Duyvendak: *Book of Lord Shang*, pp. 201–2.

20. *Four Texts*, 1.3.4, OT 17b-18b; ch. 1 of the *Works of Guanzi*.

21. The official response of the Chinese government to the Western criticism, issued by the Information Office of the State Council, begins chapter 1 with the following analysis: "It is a simple truth that, for any country or nation, the right to subsistence is the most important of all human rights, without which the other rights are out of the question." *Human Rights in China* (Beijing: Foreign Language Press, 1991).

22. *Four Texts*, 1.3.6, OT 19b-20a.

23. *Analects of Confucius* 12:7 records a conversation between Zi Gong (Tzu-kung) and Confucius:

> Tzu-kung asked about government, Confucius said, "Sufficient food, sufficient armament, and sufficient confidence of the people." Tzu-kung said, "Forced to give up one of these, which would you abandon first?" Confucius said, "I would abandon armament." Tzu-kung said, "Forced to give up one of the remaining two, which would you abandon first?" Confucius said, "I would abandon food. There have been deaths from time immemorial, but no state can exist without the confidence of the people." Quoted from W. T. Chan, *A Source Book in Chinese Philosophy* (Princeton: Princeton University Press, 1969), p. 39.

24. *Analects of Confucius*, 13:9, James Legge, trans. *Chinese Classics*, vol. 1, pp. 266–67.

25. Cf. 13:13. Legge renders this as "complete man." I propose "Perfect Manhood" as possibly better.

26. Cf. 4:16, *Analects*, p. 170.

27. *Four Texts*, 3.15, OT 148a-149a.

28. Ibid., 1.1.1, OT 1a-b.

39. Ibid.

30. See last text.

31. Cf. *Shen Pu-hai*, tr. by G. C. Creel (Chicago: University of Chicago Press, 1974), pp. 356–57; *The Book of Lord Shang*, tr. by Duyvendak, p. 262; *Shenzi (Sheng Dao)*, in *Zhuzijichang (Complete Works of Various Masters)*, ed. by Guoxuezhenglishe, p. 11.

32. *The Complete Works of Han Fei Tzu*, tr. by W. K. Liao (London: Authur Probsthain, 1939), vol. 1, p. 45.

33. See James Legge, *Chinese Classics*, vol. 4, p. 454. I have revised the translation.

34. *Analects of Confucius*, 2:3, quoted from *A Source Book in Chinese Philosophy*, p. 22.

35. Ibid., 12:1, p. 38.

36. *Four Texts*, 1.3.4, OT 18a.

37. *Xiang*, quoted from Gong Dafei and Yu Feng ed., *Chinese Maxims*. (Beijing: Sinolingua, 1994), p. 71.

38. *Four Texts*, 1.1.5,; OT 3b-4a.

39. Ibid., 3.9, OT 145b-146a.

40. Ibid., 1.3.3, OT 16a.

41. Legge, *Chinese Classics*, vol. 2, pp. 165–66, 299–300.

42. Ibid., p. 199.

43. *Hanshu* 58: "Rulin liezhuan" (2d ed.; Taipei: Hongye Book Store, 1974), p. 911.

44. Cf. *Shiji*, p. 1417.

45. *Hanshu* 9: "Yuandi benji," (Hongye ed.), p. 77.

46. Cf. Edwin O. Reischauer and John K. Fairbank, *East Asia, the Great Tradition* (Boston: Houghton Mifflin, 1958), p. 168.

47. The *Four Texts* objection is to political conspiracy, see 2.14.3, OT 139b.

9

Rites and Rights in Ming China

Ron Guey Chu

On August 6, 1995, a large rally was held at Peace Square in Hiroshima to commemorate the fiftieth anniversary of the dropping of the atomic bomb. After Prime Minister Tomiichi Murayama delivered his keynote speech, condemning the forthcoming nuclear testing by the French in the South Pacific, the mayor of Hiroshima, Takashi Hiroaka, followed with equally strong words against nuclear weapons and with a proposal to create a nuclear free zone in East Asia. In his appeal to ban all nuclear weapons in the region, he invoked the Confucian ideal of humaneness (*ren*), asserting in essence that nuclear weapons are inhumane. While Confucian rhetoric alone may not suffice to bring about any concrete result today, in premodern East Asia Confucian values and rituals set the standard for civilized behavior in both the domestic and international arenas, and it is to what survives of this that Mayor Hiroaka no doubt appealed.

This paper focuses on one specific aspect of this ritualized civility, and attempts to show how, in an ethic of virtue embodied in the practice of rites, the ritual process could operate to establish a certain power for the individual in Ming China, safeguarding the individual's right to perform the ritual and to decide how the ritual is to be performed. By examining four episodes in the Ming dynasty (1368–1644) wherein emperors and Confucian scholars bitterly clashed over rituals, I will argue that ritualization empowered the individual and thus contributed to the maintenance of meaningful political and social life. A consequence of this ritual empowerment, I will argue, served to check the imperial authority and to foster a kind of "constitutional culture,"[1] by which to limit or modify dynastic rule.[2]

Rites occupied a place of special importance in traditional China because of their transformative power to maintain social and political order. Among these, the sacrificial rite to Confucius was particularly important to the state because of its use by emperors to legitimize their claim to rule. Since the first emperor of the Han dynasty (206 B.C.E.–220 C.E.), Gaozu, offered a sacrifice to Confucius in 195 B.C.E., it had become a tradition for every emperor to announce his accession to the throne in a grand ritual at the Confucian Temple. Moreover, the emperor exercised the authority to canonize outstanding scholars in the Confucian Temple. Through this process he attempted to exemplify, and thus to define, the state ideology. By the seventh century the performing of this sacrificial ritual to Confucius was no longer reserved to the emperor or Confucius' descendants alone, but was extended to schools on the county and prefectural levels, where scholar-officials were allowed to perform the oblation ritual (*shidian*) twice a year in spring and autumn. By granting this access to rituals, the emperor was able to extend the scope of his ritual authority to his own political advantage, but his doing so through a system of state (quasi-public) schools also opened the door for contestation between the emperor and his ministers or other officials over the proper conduct of ritual prescriptions and canonization.

The Prohibition on Sacrifice to Confucius Outside the Capital, 1369–1382

When Ming Taizu ascended the throne in 1368, he soon offered a grand sacrifice (*tailao*) of an ox, sheep and pig to Confucius at the Imperial College.[3] By conforming with this long-standing ritual tradition, he also exposed himself to being regulated by it. Thereafter, Taizu's reign was marked by continuing and concerted efforts to establish such Confucian institutions as the civil service examination system and an official school system, so as to promote Confucianism in a form suited to his own interests. In 1369 however he suddenly issued a decree, prohibiting the performance of the oblation ritual to Confucius except in the capital and at Confucius's birthplace, Qufu. His action amounted to making the Confucian ritual an exclusive privilege of the emperor and the descendants of Confucius, denying the right of participation that every Confucian scholar had enjoyed for more than a thousand years.[4] Moreover, in thus deciding to break with a long-standing ritual tradition, Taizu did so without observing the rite of due process through discussion and debate at the imperial court. Consequently, this Confucian ritual was no longer performed in local schools.[5] In his decree Ming Taizu maintained that in the hierarchy of state rituals the sacrifice to Confucius, like the sacrifice to Heaven, was the most supreme ritual and thus should be the sole privilege of the emperor. Therefore, he concluded that the Imperial College (*Guoxue*) at the capital was the only proper place for performing the oblation rite for Confucius and that no person other than himself and Confucius's own descendants should perform it. To support his view, Taizu cited Confucius's own sayings in the *Analects* about ritual decorum and principle. To justify his prohibition he especially drew on Confucius' saying, "To sacrifice to a spirit not one's own is obsequiousness."[6]

The Confucian ritual classics may appear to support Taizu's view because ritual duties and rights are defined therein strictly in terms of status in the official hierarchy. Accordingly, the lowest-ranked officers (*shi*) and commoners were allowed to offer sacrifice only to their own ancestors, certainly not to Confucius, the supreme sage.[7] However, in imposing this ritual prescription literally, Taizu effectively invalidated ritual precedents and practices that had prevailed officially for the past seven hundred years.[8] Moreover, the political implication of this prohibition was quite transparent. To restrict access to this ritual would necessarily translate into a lowering of Confucius's political significance. In the ritual world of the time, Confucius received the highest ritual honors, equivalent to those paid to Heaven, and unquestionably higher than what the deceased members of the royal family were entitled to. Thus, to disallow the peoples' paying of such high ritual respect to Confucius was to suggest that Confucius no longer occupied a moral authority equal to Heaven, that is higher than the emperor. In other words, constitutionally speaking, it closed off appeal to a higher authority than the ruler and dynastic law, which means one could not invoke that higher authority in challenging or criticizing imperial decisions.

Protests and dissent against the ban soon broke out at the imperial court. Minister of Justice (*Xingbu shangshu*) Qian Tang presented a memorial, in which he argued, "Confucius left his teachings for scholars of a thousand generations and all under Heaven follow his teachings. Therefore, all the people under heaven should be able to sacrifice to him. The ritual of paying tribute to the source (*baoben zhili*) cannot be abolished."[9] Further, the assistant minister Cheng Xu concurred in a memorial which said, "Confucius established his teaching in accordance with the Way. The sacrifice that all people under heaven make is not directed to Confucius personally, but rather to his teachings and to the Way."[10] Ming Taizu apparently was not persuaded, and two years later (in 1371), Prime Minister Song Lian (1310–1381) presented a memorial to plead for the restoration of the universal sacrifice to Confucius.[11] Offended by Song Lian's open criticism of the ban, Ming Taizu banished him to a remote post.

What later prompted Taizu to restore the "universal sacrifice" (*tongsi*) to Confucius is not clear. In 1382 he decreed that the biennial sacrifice to Confucius be resumed in county and prefecture schools. In the same edict, Taizu acknowledged that Confucius was as great as Heaven and Earth and that all under heaven could and should express their gratitude to the Source (*baoben*) in ritual.[12] We do not know whether he came to this conclusion because he realized that rituals widely performed would serve his own political ends better. By embracing the principle of universal sacrifice for Confucius, however, Taizu acknowledged that Confucius, like Heaven and Earth, claimed a higher authority than the emperor. Not only did he acknowledge this, but he personally demonstrated his submission and humility at the oblation rite for Confucius in a ceremony to commemorate the reopening of the Imperial College at the end of 1383. Wearing a ceremonial robe, he held a *gui* tablet, and during the ceremony bowed four times to Confucius, in accordance with ritual prescriptions.[13] In this ritual contestation then, over the issue of moral authority, the supremacy of Confucius survived the challenge. As long as scholars's ritual access to Confucius could not be denied by imperial authority, they could claim partnership with the emperor as the defenders of Confucian teachings and preservers of the social and cosmological order.

Removing Mencius from the Confucian Temple in 1372

While official canonization of outstanding Confucian scholars in the Confucian Temple had been the prerogative of the emperor, the process leading up to it practiced in Ming times, as before, had required collective, open discussions and debates in the Board of Rites (*libu*) in order to seek out "public opinion" (*gongyi*).[14] The opinion in question was considered to be "public" in the sense of being openly aired and debated; it was not a private decision of the emperor, but rather a public one reached at the imperial court in open discussion with court officials, who regarded themselves as the natural spokesmen of the scholar-officials at large. While this "public opinion" may not be as open or public as the informed discussion which modern media may sometimes allow, the process to ascertain it was as open and public as one could imagine possible under dynastic rule. Because Ming Taizu did not show sufficient respect for this due process when he ordered the tablet of Mencius to be removed from the Confucian temple in 1372, a great uproar erupted at court, which resulted in perhaps the most serious challenge to his authority made during his reign.

According to the *Ming History*, one day Taizu was reading the *Book of Mencius*. When he got to the passage where Mencius said that if a ruler treated his ministers like grass and dirt, the ministers should regard the ruler as a robber,[15] he became furious, and said, "This is not a proper thing for a minister to say."[16] Then he added, "If this old man were still alive today, how could he escape death?"[17] As it happened, the time to perform the Confucian sacrificial ritual was approaching. In his rage Taizu ordered the spirit tablet of Mencius to be removed from the Confucian Temple so that Mencius would not receive ritual honors at the ceremony. The emperor's action also meant that Mencius was in effect decanonized. The next day a state astrologist reported that an eclipse occurred in the star of culture (*wenxing*), signifying a bad omen.[18] Taking heed of the omen, Taizu soon restored Mencius to his proper place in the Confucian sacrificial ritual.[19] Another account reports that a thunderbolt struck the residential quarter of the emperor in the imperial palace, which persuaded the emperor to rescind his decree.[20] However, the *Ming History* provides us with a more gripping account. As Taizu anticipated that his action would invite remonstration from the ministers, he decreed that anyone who remonstrated with him over this matter would be insulting the emperor himself, and would be punished with death. Minister of Justice Qian Tang, however, was not deterred by the threat. When he presented his memorial of remonstration to the court he brought along a coffin with him. Qian declared, "To die for the sake of Mencius would be a glorious death." The emperor was moved by Qian Tang's sincerity and spared him.[21] Yet another source, less plausibly, dramatizes the scene by informing us that Taizu was enraged by this show of insubordination on Qian's part and ordered his guards to shoot arrows at the offending remonstrator. Qian Tang willingly bared his chest to receive the arrows, but miraculously was not hurt at all.[22]

Although Taizu seems to have given in to this strenuous protest from his minister, he was determined to set Mencius straight. Soon he ordered Hanlin Academician Liu Sanwu (1313–1399) to purge passages in the *Mencius* that were offensive and improper in his view. An expurgated edition was published under the title, *Mengzi jiewen* (Selected Texts of *Mencius*), and was authorized for use as one of the standard texts for the civil service examinations.[23] But this move likewise met with strong opposition and was rescinded about twenty years later. From this ritual confrontation and its aftermath, it is clear that Mencius had won a permanent place in the Confucian ritual and in the minds of scholars. The political outcome of this episode was that no emperor thereafter in Chinese history ever attempted to bypass the due process of consultation and debate, so as to ascertain "public opinion" in such a matter whenever he contemplated major changes concerning the sacrificial ritual to Confucius. In this regard, the ritual tradition and its specific prescriptions were not subject to the arbitrary or whimsical desires of the emperor. Insofar as faithful observation of the ritual tradition was required and any major alteration of it necessitated open consultation between the emperor and his ministers, one may say that rituals obtained something of the status of a basic "constitution," and that any clash over rituals at court tended to foster and uphold a "constitutional culture" limiting the exercise of dynastic rule.

Reform of the Confucian Temple in 1530

When the Ming emperor Wuzong died without a successor in 1521, his cousin Zhu Houcong was installed as the eleventh emperor Shizong (r. 1521–1567).[24] Soon after ascending the throne, Shizong decided to grant imperial titles to his deceased father and to place the latter's spirit tablet in the Imperial Ancestral Temple (zongmiao). Thereupon a contentious debate known as the Great Rites Controversy (Daliyi) broke out between the emperor Shizong and the court ministers. When the controversy finally ended three years later, the opposing ministers paid dearly for their dissent. Eighteen ministers were flogged to death in public and more than a hundred of them were thrown into jail. The event proved to be an opportunity for a very determined emperor to show how he could exercise his power ruthlessly.

Basically the controversy was concerned with whether a successor to the throne had to be a descendent of the emperor or not. Shizong insisted that he could inherit the throne without having first been designated heir apparent; the majority of the ministers at court strongly disagreed with this, insisting that he should have been adopted into the family of the preceding emperor if he were to come into the throne legally.[25] In order to deal with this institutionally and to set the record straight on his own terms, Shizong, when he finally got his way by sheer force, turned his attention to the compilation and codification of court rituals. Under his auspices, two ritual texts, Dali jiyi (1525) and Minglun dadian (1528), were compiled and declared to be canonical with respect to ritual practice.

In 1530 the same emperor boldly decided to reform the sacrificial rituals to Confucius.[26] Perhaps learning from his previous experience, Emperor Shizong this time invited the Han-lin academician Zhang Cong to present a memorial that met with his prior approval and then ordered an open debate to be held at court. This far-reaching memorial, also known as Reform of the Confucian Temple (Kongmiao gaizhi), stirred up as much emotion and opposition at court as had the previous ritual confrontation less than a decade before. Fortunately, no blood was spilled this time. The opposing view was represented by academician Xu Jie (1503–1583), joined by Wang Rumei and a contingent of censors led by Li Guan. The issue proved so contentious that Shizong felt compelled to order at least three debates held in the Board of Rites.[27]

The strongest criticism focused on the question of whether to take away Confucius's title of nobility. Instead of referring to Confucius as Culture King

(Wenxuan Wang), the proposed reform suggested that Confucius should be called the "Former Sage and Master" (*xiansheng xianshi*). Because the level of ceremonial honors in rituals was determined by the status of the person to whom the rite is directed, the intention of the emperor to demote Confucius in the ritual hierarchy was quite apparent. Ever since the Tang dynasty in the seventh century when the Confucian ritual had been officially codified, the "middle sacrifice" (*zhongsi*), was prescribed for Confucius. This was below the sacrifice performed in honor of Heaven and the imperial ancestors, but was above the ritual reverence paid to kings and emperors of previous dynasties.[28] Therefore, to reduce Confucius to the status of a master teacher, rather than one of royal rank, had real implications. This lower ritual status for Confucius would be translated into diminished authority for him, with less of a need for him to be respected in the mind of the reigning emperor. If Confucius's status in the ritual hierarchy were to be below that of the emperor, Confucian scholars at court would find it difficult to invoke Confucius's moral authority in arguing against what they considered to be errors or abuses in the exercise of imperial authority. No wonder that Xu Jie insinuated in his memorial that the emperor was "robbing" Confucius of his noble title.[29] For this remark, Xu Jie was stripped of his official title, thrown into prison, and tortured. Later he was demoted to a local post.[30]

In the same memorial, Xu Jie cited the precedent established by the founding emperor of the Ming dynasty, Taizu, and argued that because Taizu had abolished noble titles for all deities in 1370, but not for that of Confucius, this precedent should be respected and Confucius not be reduced to the status of a commoner (*ren Kongzi*).[31] Li Guan not only invoked the authority of the founding emperor as a precedent, but also sought to invoke the views of the entire Neo-Confucian tradition in making his case. He said that all Confucian thinkers from Luo Congyan and Zhou Dunyi in the Song, down to contemporary scholars, all had agreed that Confucius deserved to be treated as a king, even though uncrowned. The emperor remained unpersuaded and dismissed Li Guan as censor.[32]

These instances of ritual contestation occurred because rituals mattered in Ming China. For the emperor, the Confucian ritual legitimized his authority to rule and helped to bring about social and ideological harmony. However, the ministers at court and, by extension, the Confucian scholarly community in general were not silent or passive partners in the ritual process. They too had a stake in the rituals and demanded to be heard from on ritual matters. Perhaps as the outcome of that process the emperor and the ministers more often than not agreed on how to conduct the rituals. But when disagreements and conflict did occur, the consequences were usually serious. As the Great

Rites Controversy indicates, the debate over the succession rite could have jeopardized the legality of the succession of Emperor Shizong and impaired his authority. Whether scholars were allowed to perform the libation ritual privately or what kind of ritual honors Confucius should receive were questions that might not entail immediate consequences or political repercussions, but for Confucians the basic issue here was the higher authority and moral status of Confucius in relation to the emperor, that is, as a limitation on imperial power and authority.

The longstanding ritual tradition first and foremost safeguarded the individual's right to perform rituals, and in this sense had a significance comparable to the exercise of religious freedom. Even the most tyrannical ruler could not simply abrogate this right by a stroke of the brush or impress of the imperial seal. The same ritual tradition also required the ruler to seek out and show respect for "public opinion" as expressed in open scholarly discussion concerning significant ritual matters. Scholars thus had a channel through which to express their views freely and even to subject the emperor to some test. While these "rights" were not absolute and martyrdom was sometimes the price one had to pay for insisting on them, we should not underestimate how important the ritual system was to the safeguarding the right of scholars and officials to express themselves on fundamental issues in traditional Chinese society.

Notes

1. I use this term in the sense expressed by Louis Henkin in his "Elements of Constitutionalism," Occasional Paper Series, November 1992, Center for the Study of Human Rights, Columbia University; i.e., as a moral culture supportive of a duly constituted order and process, restraining the arbitrary exercise of power.

2. For a discussion of the religious and cosmological context of Confucian rituals see my paper, "The Appropriation and Contestation of Sacrificial Ritual in the Confucian Temple in Ming China," paper presented at the Conference on State and Ritual in East Asia, Paris, College de France, June 28–July 1, 1995.

3. Pang Zhonglu, *Wenmiao sidian kao*, 1878 edition, 4:1a.

4. In 630 the Tang emperor Taizong decreed that all counties and prefectures should establish Confucian temples in their schools. This proclamation established the official legitimacy of the "universal sacrifice" (*tongsi*) to Confucius, which meant that every Confucian scholar could and should make sacrifice to Confucius. See *Wenmiao sidian kao*, ch. 2. However, before this practice was institutionalized in the seventh century, Confucian scholars had performed the ritual privately since the Han dynasty. See discussion of this issue in Huang Jinxing, *Yuru shenyu* (Taipei: Yunchen, 1994), p. 149.

5. Ming Taizu's edict is cited in part in Huang Jinxing, *Yuru shengyu*, p. 149. The complete edict is found in *Da Ming jili*, ch. 16.

6. *Analects* 2:24.

7. *Book of Rites*, ch. 2, "Summary of Ceremonies," part 2, section 20. See Wing-tsit Chan, trans., *Neo-Confucian Terms Explained* (New York: Columbia University Press, 1986), p. 152.

8. The biannual oblation rite had been performed in county and prefecture schools ever since the Sui dynasty (581–618). See *Wenmiao sidian kao*, 2:9b.

9. *Ming shi* (Beijing: Zhonghua shuju), 1974, ch. 139, p. 3981, biography of Qian Tang.

10. Ibid., p. 3982.

11. *Wenmiao sidian kao*, 4:2a-3a.

12. *Ming Taizu shilu*, ch. 144, p. 2263–64.

13. *Wenmiao sidian kao*, 4:4b.

14. See Cheng Minzheng's memorial, ibid.

15. *Mencius*, 4B:3.

16. *Ming shi*, ch. 139, p. 3982, biography of Qian Tang.

17. Quan Zuwang, *Jiqi ting ji*, Sibu congkan ed., 35:3a, "Pian Qian Shangshu zheng Mengzi shi."

18. The literary star refers to the constellation of six stars, which is believed to preside over man's destiny. See *Shiji* about the literary star that predicts disaster in the examination hall. See Fei Tingyu, *Dongguan zhouji*, cited in Wang Xinglin, Xu Tao, *Zhongguo minjian xinyang fengsu zidian* (Beijing: Zhongguo wenlian chuban gongsi, 1992), p. 161.

19. Ibid.

20. *Wenmiao sidian kao*, 4:3b.

21. *Ming shi*, ch. 139, p. 3982; *Wenmiao sidian kao*, 4:3b.

22. *Wenmiao sidian kao*, 4:3b.

23. See my article, "Cong Liu Sanwu de *Mengzi jiewen* lun junquan de xianzhi yu zhishi fenzi zhi zizhu xing," *Bulletin of Chinese Literature and Philosophy* 6 (March 1995): 173–97.

24. L. Carrington Goodrich and Chaoying Fang, eds., *Dictionary of Ming Biography* (New York: Columbia University Press, 1976), pp. 315–22.

25. See Carney T. Fisher, *The Chosen One: Succession and Adoption in the Court of Ming Shizong* (Sydney: Allen and Unwin, 1990).

26. For a discussion of the ritual reform, see Huang Jingxing, *Yuru shengyu*, pp. 133–63.

27. *Wenmiao sidian kao*, 4:11b-13b. See Huang Jinxing, *Yuru shengyu*, pp. 138–42.

28. See Li Linfu et al., eds., *Tang liudian*.

29. His memorial is in *Shijing Tangji*, ch. 6, quoted in Huang Jinxing, *Yuru shengyu*, p. 141.

30. There seems to be a question of Xu's motivation in attacking the reform measures. See *Dictionary of Ming Biography*, p. 572. However, it is interesting to note that he

later regained the favor of Shizong and became a Grand Secretary in 1552 under the emperor he had severely criticized some twenty years earlier.

31. Huang Jinxing, *Yuru shengyu*, p. 140.

32. *Wenmiao sidian kao*, 4:12a.

10

Confucianism and Due Process

Alison W. Conner

Eight years after the Beijing massacre of 1989, the human rights situation in the People's Republic of China (PRC) continues to draw criticism from the international human rights community. Not only the events of June 4 but also the political crackdown that followed have increasingly focused attention on China's criminal justice system—and its failure to meet or provide for the due process standards contained in international covenants.[1]

In response to its critics, the PRC authorities have asserted the legitimacy of a distinctive approach to human rights, based at least in part on historical and cultural factors.[2] According to the 1991 white paper on human rights, for example, the human rights situation is "circumscribed by the historical, social, economic and cultural conditions of various nations and involves a process of historical development."[3] China's representative to the 1993 Vienna conference expressed the same idea in stronger terms: "The concept of human rights is a product of historical development. . . . Countries at different development stages or with different historical traditions and cultural backgrounds also have different understanding and practice of human rights."[4]

Although the 1991 white paper maintains that a country's human rights situation should not be judged in total disregard of its history,[5] the PRC has relied less than some other countries on the argument that rights are culture-specific.[6] Indeed, its representatives do not seek to defend the administration of criminal justice in the PRC by arguing that China is simply following its own historical tradition. To the contrary, they maintain that they have worked to replace the traditional (and defective) Chinese system with modern institutions that can properly protect the rights of the accused.[7] According to this view, the persistence of certain abuses or problems (if acknowledged at all) has its roots in "feudalism," and any such recurrences are labeled "feudal vestiges."

It is true that a comparison of China's traditional and modern justice systems reveals many apparent similarities, including the characteristics most troubling to human rights observers. Both systems are at least partly inquisitorial, and the role of law is arguably the same: to enhance the power of the state and encourage the people to carry out its policies rather than to protect their rights.[8] Jerome Cohen has suggested other parallels between the contemporary and traditional criminal justice systems, including the long detention of suspects, the lack of a privilege against self-incrimination, the absence of counsel, the possible presumption of guilt, and the emphasis placed on confessions.[9] These shared characteristics might lead one to conclude that—even if no direct link exists between the two systems—China's legal tradition offers little in the way of due process values for the modern PRC to draw upon and in fact might contribute to the abuses China is charged with today.

But perhaps these surface similarities disguise even greater differences between the past and the present systems, leading us to gloss over traditional notions of due process. Thus, despite earlier criticism of Qing law and practice, more recent research has discerned some principles of due process or a "fair trial." It would therefore be a mistake "to overgeneralize and assume that China's legal tradition is wholly without support for due process values."[10] The purpose of this essay is to analyze some aspects of that tradition for the due process values they contain. Of course, it would be quite pointless to search China's past for analogues of today's standards, which have been enumerated in international covenants and whose content is now well defined.[11] But did imperial China develop any other concepts of due process—or are such values alien to the Chinese tradition?

This essay will focus on Qing procedure, particularly on the law governing confessions and the use of torture, which would raise basic issues of due process in any system. To suggest—as some earlier commentators have—that no principles operated in the traditional criminal justice system and that the procedures were arbitrary, or to imply that the facts could only be extracted through torture ("trial by confession"), is to say that a fundamental part of Qing criminal procedure was both irrational and unfair. I do not believe that this was the case. But could there be any place for "due process" in a system that relied so heavily on confessions and torture?

The Qing Law of Confession and Torture

There can be no doubt that, throughout the imperial period, Chinese proce-dure attached tremendous importance to obtaining confessions from the accused,[12] by torture if necessary. By Qing times the rules on confessions had become less flexible, and the exceptions narrower, than during the early impe-rial period. The accused's confession was ordinarily required in order to close a case—the necessity to obtain one is stressed in all the magistrate hand-books—but by then the requirement may also have been taken for granted, as no provision of the Qing Code[13] plainly stated it.[14]

But even during the Qing period a confession was still not required in every case, and the law clearly provided for at least three exceptions. First, certain classes of people could never be interrogated under torture (the old, the young, the disabled, and members of the eight privileged classes), out of con-sideration for their position or compassion for their age or infirmity; therefore no confession was required from them. The second exception applied when one of the co-offenders was at large but the others had been captured. Ac-cording to the Qing Code, if the absent offender's guilt was clear from all evi-dence, a final determination of fact could be made for him even in his ab-sence—and therefore without a confession.[15]

The third exception provided for the case in which a seemingly guilty accused was "tricky and obstinately refused to confess," or persisted in plac-ing the blame on someone else, presumably even under torture. Tang law made clear that such a defendant could be convicted on the evidence, but under the Qing Code the case had to be either memorialized to the emperor or forwarded to the Board of Punishments, depending on the punishment involved.[16] If an obviously guilty defendant would not confess even under torture, then the authorities had to release him or make another exception to the confession requirement—and the Qing authorities apparently preferred the latter.

In all other cases, confessions were necessary to close a case. Qing law thus made obtaining confessions a central goal for officials handling cases, a con-cern vividly reflected in the handbooks written by magistrates and legal secre-taries to advise their colleagues.[17] In theory, requiring confessions should have provided the highest protection for the innocent, since (with only the excep-tions discussed above) no one could be convicted without admitting his guilt. In practice, of course, this insistence on the confession led inevitably and fatal-ly to the use of torture, as did the requirement of a "complete proof" in the European inquisitorial system.[18] In China, as in Europe, there developed a jurisprudence of torture rather than simply of confessions or proof: the law of confessions was in reality the law of torture.

181

Thus, the Qing Code and various administrative regulations contained numerous provisions on torture, which both sanctioned its use and sought to place restrictions on it. Above all and by definition, the Code limited any use of torture to the formal judicial process: "Examination by torture is something that takes place during the trial."[19] Moreover, interrogation by torture could be conducted only under the supervision of the magistrate. Constables and runners were supposed to be punished severely if they put pressure on the accused to confess to crimes of which they were innocent.[20]

Under Qing law also judicial torture of whatever kind could be applied only when there was a certain amount of evidence in the case. The required standard of proof was stated in slightly different form throughout the Code and administrative regulations. Thus, according to the official commentary to Article 404:

> If the guilt of the accused has already been established, but the accused is crafty and blames another person and will not confess, interrogation by torture may be applied.

The use of pressing sticks to squeeze the ankles or fingers, a more serious form of torture, required a similar standard: "If the official does not obtain a truthful deposition, only then may he apply the sticks one time."[21] In serious cases where "the evidence is already clear and they have been repeatedly investigated but they will not reveal the true facts," then the official might resort to pressing sticks.[22] Administrative regulations provided a similar standard: "If it really is the guilty person and the evidence is clear and certain but the offender's testimony is crafty and lying," then officials would avoid punishment for the use of legal instruments of torture. Under all these provisions, therefore, the accused's guilt should already have been established before an official employed torture to obtain a confession.[23]

Qing rules also attempted to prevent the uncontrolled application of legal torture and to keep it within clearly defined limits. Most of the law on torture is therefore devoted to spelling out restrictions on its use. First, the Qing Code set limits, if rather broad ones, to the people torture could be administered to, so members of certain groups (the very old, the very young, the disabled, pregnant women, and the eight privileged classes) were exempted from torture. Such persons were not only deserving of compassion, but they were also permitted to redeem most punishments, so the application of torture would have been exceptionally harsh in the Chinese view.[24]

Second, only specified instruments of torture were legally permitted: pressing sticks, finger compressors, the cangue, and bamboo sticks and boards.[25] All these instruments had to conform to dimensions prescribed in detail by the Qing Code and were required to bear the seal of the magistrate's superior officials. A magistrate was forbidden to manufacture any of these instruments himself, nor could he use the double cangue, a wooden frame, or any other instrument of torture whether or not specifically prohibited by the substatutes. (It was, however, permitted to twist someone's ears, force him to kneel on chains, press his knees, or slap him with the palm of the hand.)[26]

Third, as both the Code and administrative regulations made clear, the severest forms of legal torture, such as pressing sticks, were reserved for the most serious cases. "The official may deliberate and use pressing sticks" only in cases of robbery and homicide.[27] The law also regulated the number of times the pressing sticks could be used during interrogation:

> Only if the person on whom it is permitted to use the pressing sticks fails to give a true statement (*bude shigong*) may the pressing sticks be applied one time. If he refuses once again to make a truthful statement, they may be applied once more. It is absolutely not permitted for the official applying torture to use them many times arbitrarily.[28]

The Code also placed limits on the amount of ordinary torture that could be administered, although by Qing times these proved very broad indeed, particularly when compared to earlier restrictions. Under the Tang Code, for example, a defendant could not be beaten more than three times for a total of 200 blows during a period of sixty days, and only for more serious crimes. If the crime was punished by beating only, the number of blows could not exceed the number given in punishment.[29] But the Qing Code contained no comparable article. Instead, the *Qing Legal Treatise* set the limits of torture at thirty blows of the heavy bamboo daily, with no other restrictions or limits provided by law.[30]

The rules summarized above represent the most important of the Qing Code's numerous and complex restrictions on torture. Severe penalties were provided for their violation, and attempts were also made to monitor compliance by officials. Qing law required magistrates to complete a register established by the governor or governor-general detailing in what cases, on whom and for what reasons they had conducted interrogations with pressing sticks and how many times they had used torture. All such reports had to be investigated by their superiors, and magistrates could be demoted for falsifying this data (e.g., reporting that they rarely used torture but in fact using it frequently).[31] Articles 413 and 396 of the Code also provided severe punishment for officials who used torture illegally and thereby caused someone's death, with the severity of the punishment turning on whether the person accused proved to be innocent or guilty.[32]

Although the handbook authors never directly questioned the necessity for confessions, they did often question the absolute necessity for employing torture to obtain them. Thus, though no statute clearly required that officials begin with less drastic methods, most handbook authors advised magistrates to do so. According to Huang Liuhong, for example:

> The magistrate should consider the use of torture as a last resort, to be avoided especially when he is angry or incensed. There are many cases in which suspects make false confessions and admit nonexistent crimes under torture, but as soon as the torture is over they retract their confessions. These confessions, made by suspects for fear of suffering, are not valid. When the cases are transferred to the superior yamen, the suspects will loudly cry injustice, and what will the superior official think of the magistrate?
>
> The extraction of confession by torture is tantamount to the obstruction of justice, and the rendering of judgment based on personal prejudice results in perversion of the law. Such practices are not proper conduct in the administration of public affairs.[33]

Many other officials were also loath to use torture, as the handbooks show, because they recognized its cruelty or considered it unlikely to produce the right results. According to the legal secretary Wan Weihan, "The hearing and settling of cases does not lie in using torture to interrogate and seek a confession; it consists of calmly analyzing whether [the statements] are true or not." In the same work he also wrote that:

> You must examine their words, study their demeanor and search out the true loot and witnesses; only then can you settle the case. You may not lightly use torture to interrogate so as to cause injustice.[34]

The magistrate Yuan Shouding stressed the inherent cruelty of torture and the irrevocable harm its application might cause. Officials, he wrote:

> cannot hurriedly use the bamboo on people. Once ordinary people have been beaten they feel the blows their whole lives. . . . I have seen innocent people beaten, and their parents, wives and children all look at each other and cry; although comforted they still are grieved, and because of that sadness they sicken and die or kill themselves.[35]

One cannot, of course, conclude from a reading of the statutes or even the handbooks that magistrates necessarily complied with the rules. Despite the severe legal penalties, restrictions on torture were often violated, at least by the mid-nineteenth century and the widespread breakdown of central authority in China. Even Alabaster, not the harshest observer of the Qing system, remarked that illegal forms of torture were fairly often applied on the grounds of "necessity"—and the higher authorities acquiesced in their use or at least looked the other way.[36] Magistrates must have found it especially tempting to use torture when there was very little evidence, and not simply when there was a great deal of evidence and the accused's guilt seemed certain. Even the most conscientious magistrates might find it difficult to control the illegal application of torture by their runners and constables. It is thus far from clear that the Code restrictions provided an effective system for preventing abuse of power, much less direct protection for an accused.[37]

True Confessions?

Although the Chinese sanctioned the use of torture, one should not assume that they were therefore willing to accept false or unreliable confessions. Indeed, the only issue that preoccupied handbook writers as much as how to elicit confessions was how to ensure their reliability. The Qing authorities saw the truth of the final statements (however obtained) as not simply one factor in the justice or injustice of the decision, but as the crucial factor, and—unlike some earlier French jurists—they did not maintain that no innocent person would ever confess falsely, even under torture.[38] As the advice in handbook after handbook confirms, even those officials who employed torture were concerned that the results be reliable and realized that in some circumstances they never could be.

Qing rules effectively required the magistrate to discover the truth, and confessions alone, without supporting evidence, would rarely have been sufficient to dispose of a case. Officials trying cases were required by administrative regulations to obtain all the important depositions or suffer administrative penalties. They were also to be punished if they failed to discover the "true facts" of a case (*buneng shengchu shiqing*), of which the defendant's statement formed a critical, but by no means the entire, part.[39]

Handbook writers all advised trial officials to obtain the depositions and real evidence in their cases first, particularly when they involved robbery or homicide. Next, the real evidence, the various depositions and the offender's statement had to be compared to ensure that there were no discrepancies or omissions. "The oral depositions must be in agreement with the injuries and the weapon used."[40] And after the defendant had been questioned on all points, "[o]ne by one compare [his answers] with the depositions of the neighbors, witnesses, and relatives of the defendant to see whether they are in agreement."[41] Everything in the case should fit together in a coherent whole. As one magistrate advised:

> Obtain the depositions on the basis of the original complaint and decide the case on the basis of the original depositions. If from first to last they are as one and from beginning to end everything is in agreement, then the case will be as a single thread.[42]

To reach a safe decision, therefore, magistrates had to be convinced that they had indeed obtained the truth as well as a confession.

If, however, a magistrate was careless or too quick to settle cases on the basis of a confession alone, he still faced scrutiny from his superiors. All serious cases were required to be reviewed at the provincial level, which could involve a trial de novo. The most serious cases were in turn forwarded to the Board of Punishments in Beijing for individual handling, and in cases involving capital punishment only the emperor could grant final approval of the sentence and its execution.[43] As a result, even an apparently straightforward case was reviewed and the defendant's confession taken more than once and—most importantly—by different officials.

During this obligatory review, superior officials could reject the magistrate's decision on a variety of grounds, most of which involved the accuracy of the evidence or the accused's confession. According to the legal secretary Wang Youhuai, the main reasons a case might be overturned by higher officials included:

> If the report or complaint and the depositions did not correspond; if the injuries as described in the inquest form and the descriptions in the "Instructions to Coroners" were not in agreement; if the injuries and the instruments used to commit the crime did not correspond; or if they did not correspond with the defendant's statement; if there were omissions or errors; if the facts in the depositions were hasty and confused or contradicted each other; if the depositions were not thorough but were careless and inaccurate; if the facts in the earlier and later depositions differed; if on retrial there was retraction of testimony from the first report; or if the matter was without reason and without testimony and evidence.

In all these instances, said Wang, the decision would be reversed—and the magistrate, who was responsible for the original and unsatisfactory trial, would also be disciplined for his "careless and hasty settling of the case."[44]

Furthermore, the defendant himself could in theory retract his confession at any time. Article 416 of the Qing Code required the presiding official in all serious cases to summon the accused and his family to inform them of the decision and punishment and to obtain a written declaration of acceptance or disagreement. If the defendant refused to accept the result of the trial (thereby retracting his confession), the officials were required to listen to his reasons and offer a retrial.[45] In addition, Article 411 provided that if at any time during the routine review conducted by superior officials the accused repudiated his confession or his relatives complained of an injustice on his behalf, those officials were also required to reinvestigate the case under threat of punishment.[46] Even before passing final sentence at the assizes, the judges had to be convinced that the confession had not been obtained solely because of torture, as the official commentary makes clear:

> If during the time of the Court Assizes, the accused who must have his sentence executed repudiates his original confession, or his family states in a complaint that there

has been an injustice, the officials charged with the revision of the judgment must immediately proceed to a new investigation to get the details.[47]

According to Shiga, a provisional sentence based on a confession that was later retracted could easily be overturned once the accused repudiated it.[48]

Traditional Due Process

As many scholars have noted, the Qing authorities placed a higher priority on substantive than on procedural justice. Indeed, Shiga has argued that a Qing trial did not constitute an "adjudication" of legal issues but was instead an attempt to determine the truth of the matter before the court.[49] This in part explains the confession requirement, for obtaining a true confession was essential to achieving that goal. Because officials hearing a case were required to obtain the truth, they were in effect made guarantors for obtaining the correct result. Officials could be punished as well as demoted if it later turned out that they had failed to do so, whether through misfeasance or malfeasance; even following the required procedures was not sufficient to protect an official if he nevertheless failed in this duty.

Nevertheless, as the discussion of confessions illustrates, both the Qing Code itself and the administrative regulations supplementing it contained numerous rules of procedure: even the use of torture was subject to very detailed restrictions. Trial officials were also required to follow procedure in conducting inquests, handling suspects and witnesses, and in the general disposition of cases at each stage of development. Great weight was attached to an official's compliance with the proper procedures. Jones has emphasized, for example, how necessary it was for "an ambitious magistrate to get every procedural step right from the examination of the corpse to the precise form for recommending the sentence."[50] As a consequence, all these rules of procedure constituted an internal check on officials, limiting their actions.[51]

Moreover, the obligatory review system discussed above meant that all serious cases were subject to a series of thorough reviews before a final decision could be taken. Protest by a defendant or his family could also lead to a reopening and review of the case.[52] Capital cases were reviewed the most thoroughly, reconsidered to the very top of the system; under ordinary circumstances, the traditional Chinese authorities were cautious about carrying out the death penalty, and perhaps only ten percent of those marked off for execution were actually executed during the late Qing.[53] In Bodde's view, the review system in general and the review of death penalty cases in particular constituted a form of due process that "certainly deserves admiration and respect."[54]

The Qing system therefore exhibited a greater concern for procedure than might at first be apparent, and official behavior was subject to clearly prescribed legal limits. The intent of these rules—though in practice this was not always achieved—was to limit arbitrary action on the part of officials. Indeed, Shiga concludes that, because of the detailed statutes and the system of obligatory review, arbitrary manipulation of the law by officials was "almost impossible."[55] Although these rules set forth the duties of officials (and were addressed to officials) they nevertheless created certain expectations, if not actual rights, in the people that officials would act in conformity with the rules and procedures.

Of course, the gap between such traditional Chinese concepts of due process and a modern rights-based approach is not a simple one to bridge. As all commentators have pointed out, the relationship between law, the state, and the individual were quite different in imperial China than in the modern West, and the state's "principal motive was efficient administration and political stability, not concern for the rights of the individual."[56] The Qing Code was really in its entirety administrative law, directed toward and administered by regular officials; it was not designed directly to protect the rights of individuals, who received only an indirect or "reflective benefit."[57] Adherence to these rules, moreover, was ensured not by empowering a litigant to dispute a decision's validity, but by the imposition of disciplinary sanctions on officials who broke the rules.[58] Perhaps for that very reason, the traditional system provided neither the best possible safeguards against abuse nor the most consistent protection for an accused; after its use of torture this constitutes the system's greatest weakness.[59]

It cannot be denied that confessions played a central role in the Qing criminal justice system, signifying both acceptance of (or consent to) the decision and a confirmation of the "true facts" of the case. As in Europe, the confession requirement doubtless magnified the prosecutorial bias of Qing procedure and moreover led inevitably to the use of torture in judicial proceedings. No doubt the best magistrates complied with the rules and were loath to use torture, but it was sanctioned by the system and employed by many, and the literature provides plenty of examples of false confessions. Alford's detailed study of the famous Yang Naiwu and Xiao Baicai case illustrates that the system of review could indeed work—but the false confessions were corrected and justice done only after many levels of review.[60] For much of the Qing dynasty, the prevailing practices may not have been so cruel as they have often been depicted, but torture remained, as Alabaster said, a "blot which could not be overlooked."[61]

Nevertheless, confessions must be seen in the context of the many procedural rules set forth in the Code and administrative regulations. Trial officials were made personally responsible for discovering the truth in their cases, not protected simply by compliance with the proper procedure. There did, moreover, exist an elaborate system of review, not only of an accused's confession but of the entire case. The Qing system was therefore based on detailed rules, even if bureaucratic ones; it was neither arbitrary nor unregulated, and it embodied a clear conception of what constituted a "fair trial." Perhaps this traditional notion of due process, with its emphasis on good administration by good officials, should be characterized as "Confucian" in the broadest sense—while the harshest elements of the system (including, most obviously, torture) should be viewed as Legalist. If the PRC has so far inherited the worst of its criminal justice past, as Jenner argues,[62] perhaps now is the time to review the best of that tradition.

Notes

1. See, for example, the discussion of the post-1989 criminal justice system in Lawyers Committee for Human Rights [Timothy A. Gelatt], *Criminal Justice with Chinese Characteristics* (New York, 1993). The 1996 amendments to the PRC's criminal procedure law represent an improvement in the criminal process, but most human rights commentators agree that they still fall short of international standards.

2. See the discussions in Ann Kent, *Between Freedom and Subsistence* (Hong Kong: Oxford University Press, 1993); and Michael C. Davis, ed., *Human Rights and Chinese Values* (Hong Kong: Oxford University Press, 1995).

3. Information Office of the State Council, *Human Rights in China* (Beijing: Foreign Languages Press, 1991), p. ii.

4. Liu Huaqiu, "Proposals for Human Rights Protection and Promotion," speech in Vienna, 1993, *Beijing Review*, June 28–July 4, 1993, p. 9.

5. *Human Rights in China*, p. ii.

6. Such as Singapore, which relies heavily on "Confucian" values to justify its stance. But in China, as some scholars have argued, "the government's residual loyalty to Marxist thought is inconsistent with the adoption of this cultural approach, especially since so much of it is based on semifeudal thought in Asia." Yash Ghai, "Asian Perspectives on Human Rights," in James T. H. Tang, ed., *Human Rights and International Relations in the Asia-Pacific Region* (London: Pinter, 1995), p. 59.

7. See the 1992 white paper, *Criminal Reform in China* (Beijing: Foreign Languages Press, 1992), for a defense of the PRC system. Although at times PRC spokesmen have also suggested that China's legal traditions might be relevant at least to an understanding of the current system. See, for example, Jerome Alan Cohen, "Introduction," in Cohen, Edwards, and Chen, eds., *Essays on China's Legal Tradition* (Princeton: Princeton University Press, 1980), pp. 4–5.

8. Jerome Alan Cohen, *The Criminal Process in the People's Republic of China, 1949–1963: An Introduction* (Cambridge: Harvard University Press, 1968), p. 7.

9. Jerome Alan Cohen, "Due Process?," in Ross Terrill, ed., *The China Difference* (New York: Harper, 1979), p. 256.

10. Ibid.

11. In the provisions of the Universal Declaration of Human Rights and of the International Covenant on Civil and Political Rights. See, for example, Haji N. A. Noor Muhammed, "Due Process of Law for Persons Accused of Crime," in Louis Henkin, ed., *The International Bill of Rights: The Covenant on Civil and Political Rights* (New York: Columbia University Press, 1981), pp. 139–65.

12. Alison W. Conner, "The Law of Evidence during the Ch'ing Dynasty" Ph.D dissertation, Cornell University, 1979; "True Confessions: Chinese Confessions Then and Now," in publication.

13. The *Da Qing luli huitong xinzuan* [Comprehensive New Edition of the Qing Code] (Beijing, 1873; reprint ed. in 5 volumes, Taipei: Wen-hai, 1964). Referred to herein as the "Qing Code" or the "Code" and cited below as DQLL.

14. The confession rule appears only indirectly, as for example in the fifth substatute to Article 31:

> "If all the offenders are present [i.e., not at large] the presiding official is to interrogate them carefully and separately and it is absolutely necessary to get their confessions. Officials definitely may not cite the article on 'When all the evidence is clear, judgment is to be pronounced' [in Article 31, second substatute] and hastily petition to settle the case"   DQLL 1:502.

Thus, if the trial official had all the defendants in a case appearing before him, he was required to obtain their confessions. Shiga says the principle never appeared in law because it was viewed as self-evident. Shuzo Shiga, "Criminal Procedure in the Ch'ing Dynasty: With Emphasis on its Administrative Character and Some Allusion to its Historical Antecedents," *Memoirs of the Research Department of the Toyo Bunko* 32 (1974): 1–45 and 115–38, p. 120.

15. DQLL 1:497–98.

16. Although here too it seems that the accused was ultimately convicted according to the evidence, for all the evidence and facts (*zhongzheng qingzhuang*) were required to be forwarded or memorialized for the final determination. DQLL 1:502.

17. Although most such handbooks were general works on local administration, legal matters formed such an important part of a magistrate's duties that they nearly always contained substantial sections devoted to the hearing of suits and handling of cases.

18. As this brief discussion illustrates, the Qing system of confession and judicial torture offers many striking parallels to the European system of complete proof and the resulting torture. See John H. Langbein, *Torture and the Law of Proof: Europe and England in the Ancien Regime* (Chicago: University of Chicago Press, 1977), pp. 3–17.

19. DQLL 5:3562 (Official Commentary to Article 404).

20. DQLL 5:3507 (Article 396).

21. DQLL 1:220 (second substatute to Article 1). "Pressing sticks" (*jiagun*) were wood-

en compressors designed to squeeze the accused's ankles or fingers. See Justus Doolittle, *Social Life of the Chinese* (New York: Harper, 1865; reprint ed., Taipei: Ch'eng-Wen, 1966), vol. 1, pp. 36–37, for descriptions of pressing sticks and other forms of torture.

22. DQLL 5:3510 (first substatute to Article 396).

23. DQLL 5:3510–11.

24. DQLL 5:3561–64 (Article 404)

25. DQLL 5:3512 (Article 396, third substatute); they also had to conform to the dimensions prescribed in detail by the first and second substatutes of Article 1. DQLL 1:219–21.

26. DQLL 1:219–21 (first and second substatutes to Article 1). Derk Bodde and Clarence Morris, *Law in Imperial China* (Cambridge: Harvard University Press, 1967).

27. DQLL 1:219 (first substatute to Article 1); the first substatute to Article 396 provided the penalties for using them in other cases. DQLL 5:3510.

28. DQLL 1:219–20 (second substatute to Article 1).

29. Bodde and Morris, *Law and Imperial China*, p. 98. *Tanglu shuyi* [Tang Code with Commentary] (Taipei: Zhonghua, 1983), pp. 552–53 (Article 447).

30. Even during the Qing, however, a corresponding reduction from the punishment (if the defendant was found guilty) might still be allowed to take into account the torture applied to him during interrogation. *Qing shigao xingfazhi zhujie* [Legal Treatise from the Qing Draft History, Annotated] (Beijing: Falu chubanshe, 1957), p. 108; Ernest Alabaster, *Notes and Commentaries on Chinese Criminal Law* (1899; reprint ed. Taipei: Ch'eng-wen, 1967), p. 18.

31. DQLL 5:3510–11 (first substatute to Article 396).

32. DQLL 5:3507 (Article 396); DQLL 5:3707–08 (Article 413).

33. Huang Liuhong (Djang Chu, trans. and ed.), *A Complete Book Concerning Happiness and Benevolence: A Manual for Local Magistrates in Seventeenth-Century China* (Tucson: University of Arizona Press, 1984), p. 278.

34. Wan Weihan, *Muxue zhuyao* [Essentials for Private Secretaries] in *Jumu xuzhi wuzhong* [Five Essential Works for Legal Secretaries], vol. 269 of *Jindai Zhongguo shiliao congkan* (Taipei: Wen-hai, year?), p. 20.

35. Yuan Shouding, in *Muling shu* [Writings for Magistrates], 18:29b.

36. Alabaster, *Chinese Criminal Law*, p. 17.

37. See, for example, the analysis in Judy Feldman Harrison, "Wrongful Treatment of Prisoners: A Case Study of Ch'ing Legal Practice," *Journal of Asian Studies* 23 (1964): 227–44.

38. A. Esmein, *A History of Continental Procedure* (London, 1913), p. 262.

39. *Qinding libu chufen seli* [Imperially Endorsed Regulations of the Board of Civil Office] (1843; reprint ed. Taipei: Ch'eng-wen, year?), 48:4b-5a.

40. *Muling shu*, 19:7a.

41. Ibid., 17:21a.

42. Ibid., 19:2b.

43. Bodde and Morris, *Law in Imperial China*, pp. 115–17.

44. Wang Youhuai, *Banan yaolue* [Summary of Important Points for Handling Cases] (Preface, 1793), in *Rumu xuzhi wuzhong*, pp. 44a-b.

45. DQLL 5:3719–20.

46. DQLL 5:3627.

47. Ernest Alabaster, "Dips Into an Imperial Law Officer's Compendium," *Monumenta Serica* 2 (1936): 426–36, at 431.

48. Shiga, "Criminal Procedure in the Ch'ing Dynasty," p. 132.

49. Ibid., pp. 122–23.

50. William C. Jones, "Introduction," *The Great Qing Code* (Oxford: Clarendon Press, 1994), p. 15.

51. Shiga, "Criminal Procedure in the Ch'ing Dynasty," p. 132.

52. See the discussion in Jonathan K. Ocko, "I'll Take It All the Way to Beijing: Capital Appeals in the Qing," *Journal of Asian Studies* 47 (1988): 291–315.

53. Bodde and Morris, *Law in Imperial China*, p. 142, citing the Qing jurist Shen Jiaben.

54. Ibid.

55. Shiga, "Criminal Procedure in the Ch'ing Dynasty," p. 128.

56. R. Randle Edwards, "Civil and Social Rights: Theory and Practice in Chinese Law Today," in Edwards, Henkin, and Nathan, *Human Rights in Contemporary China* (New York: Columbia University Press, 1986), p. 45.

57. See the discussion in Jones, *The Great Qing Code*, at pp. 9, 13–14.

58. Shiga, "Criminal Procedure in the Ch'ing Dynasty," p. 132.

59. Harrison, "Wrongful Treatment of Prisoners," p. 243.

60. William P. Alford, "Of Arsenic and Old Laws: Looking Anew at Criminal Justice in Late Imperial China," *California Law Review* 72 (1984): 1180–1256.

61. Alabaster, *Chinese Criminal Law*, p. lxii.

62. W. J. F. Jenner, *The Tyranny of History* (London: Allen Lane, 1992), ch. 7.

11

The Concept of Popular Empowerment (Minquan) in the Late Qing: Classical and Contemporary Sources of Authority

Joan Judge

This discussion of "rights thinking" in early twentieth-century China focuses on editorials that appeared in the late Qing reform newspaper *Shibao* (founded in Shanghai in 1904). The *Shibao* journalists did not write extensively or explicitly about human rights (*renquan*) per se. In conceptualizing a new sphere of negotiation between ruler and ruled in early twentieth-century China, however, they advocated the assertion of *minquan* which they related to the principles of the "Declaration of the Rights of Man" and to the urgent need to develop constitutional rights in China. *Minquan* is frequently translated as popular rights, the term used for the *Jiyū minken undō* (Popular Rights Movement) in Meiji Japan in the 1880s, or as democracy when referring to Sun Yat-sen's Three People's Principles. In an effort to emphasize the complexity and uniqueness of this concept as it was used in late nineteenth- and early twentieth-century China, I will translate it instead as "popular empowerment"—a term which encompasses some but not all of the connotations of "popular rights" or "democracy." An analysis of the use and definition of this term in journalistic essays of the last Qing decade reveals the extent and limitations of reformist thinking related to the issue of human rights in this period.

The term *minquan* was one of three new or newly interpreted concepts which the reform publicists used to define a new "middle realm" of political interaction in early twentieth-century China. While these journalists continued to envisage this arena in terms of the dynastic structure and the fundamental principles of classical Chinese theory, they represented it as the site of a radically new politics of contestation. Through the assertion of *minquan*, this new mode of politics would shift the locus of authority from the closed world of dynastic imperium into the open realm of popular politics. The journalists further defined this new realm in terms of the nation (*guojia*) and public opinion (*yulun*). Encompassing both the dynasty and society but not exclusively identified with either, the nation represented the arena where state and society would meet and negotiate China's destiny under the authority of the constitution. Public opinion would serve as the tribunal of this new national realm and the voice of the emerging popular empowerment.

The *Shibao* journalists' appeal to these newly defined concepts—popular empowerment, the nation, public opinion—reflected their exposure to Western social and political theory. Their study of the new learning expanded their cultural horizons, impelling them to challenge familiar Confucian social and political constructs and to reorient their political vision. Rather than continue to look backward to the golden age of high antiquity for revelations concerning dynastic restoration, they began to look outward to new models of national reform and forward to the establishment of Chinese constitutionalism. At the same time, however, the reform publicists had not become as totally alienated from the Confucian tradition as the iconoclasts of the May Fourth period would be some five or ten years hence. Trained in the classical texts, they lived sufficiently within the Chinese cultural tradition to see it not as a monolithic entity but as an arena of tensions, alternatives, and conflicts that left room for the integration of new ideas.[1] Continuing to uphold the classical constructs as their own most enduring points of reference, they infused these age-old precepts with a radically new spirit and fused them with constitutional principles. The result was tension rather than synthesis, with the editorialists themselves often incognizant of the contradictions that arose as they continued to uphold the inherited ideal of harmony between ruler and ruled while promoting the confrontational new mode of public politics.

This tension is reflected most clearly in the journalists' equation of modern Western constitutionalism with China's "ancient constitutionalism"—the classical theory of the people as the foundation of the nation (*minben sixiang*).[2] An element in many of the Thirteen Classics and expounded upon in the Confucian *Analects*, this theory asserts that the key to genuine leadership is the manifestation of virtues which benefit the people.[3] Mencius (371–289 B.C.E.), who became one of the greatest theoreticians of *minben* thought, emphasized the ruler's responsibility in tending to the welfare of the people as a means of ensuring stability and prosperity in the polity. Despite this original focus on the role of the ruler, this theory was later appropriated by generations of social critics from Qu Yuan (339–c. 278 B.C.E.) of the Warring States period to

Huang Zongxi (1610–1695) and Tang Zhen (1630–1704) of the Ming and

Qing dynasties, who read it as an assertion of the primacy of the people. The richest source of positive social images in the Chinese tradition, this theory provided writers like Qu, Huang, and Tang with the means of denouncing autocratic authority and calling attention to the unjust sufferings of the people.[4] Following in the line of these critics, the late Qing reformists appealed to the theory of the people as the foundation of the nation in promoting their own political vision, claiming that contemporary Western and ancient Chinese constitutionalism shared the same ultimate ideals: the unification of ruler and ruled, social welfare, and popular participation in the political process.

In constructing and validating their constitutional claims, the journalists also appealed to the age-old concept of *gong*. Intimately connected to *minben* thought in the Confucian discourse, the concept of *gong* is rich in classical resonances and multiple historical meanings. It appears in classical texts such as the "Evolution of Rites" of the *Record of Rites*, where it refers to what is shared in common among members of society, and it is also prominent in the texts of seventeenth-century writers like Huang Zongxi and Lü Liuliang, who criticized the state for not satisfactorily serving the public interest.[5] In Confucian and Neo-Confucian texts *gong* is conceived in a dichotomous relationship with *si* (meaning privateness and self-regard, wickedness or unjustness [*buzheng*]), and it is understood that the individual must subordinate his or her selfish desires to the good of the community or *gong*.[6] Definitions of *gong* thus range from openness and publicness to the ethical principles of moral equality (*pingfen*), justice (*zheng*), and fairness (*gongping*).[7] In order to reestablish the principle of *gong* in their age and lay the foundation for an open and just middle realm, the reform journalists invested this classical concept with new valences of meaning by associating it with the nation rather than the dynasty, and with the expansion of popular empowerment and the expression of pubic opinion.

Seeking both to recover obscured age-old ideals and to apply contemporary political solutions to the problems of the age, the new publicists thus appealed to a fusion of old and new cultural and political constructs, combining classical conceptions of society and justice with Western notions of constitutionalism, nationalism, and civil rights. While they followed the Confucian literati practice of attempting to inspire change by contrasting a troubled present with an idyllic past, they further extended this juxtaposition of past and present by equating the "glory" of the modern constitutional nations with China's golden antiquity. Advocating the principles of appropriateness and the golden mean in the Inaugural Statement to *Shibao*, for example, Liang Qichao quoted the *Record of Rites* and Confucius alongside Charles Darwin and Herbert Spencer.[8] Another editorialist promoted democratic constitutionalism by likening Montesquieu's advanced views on democracy to those of Mencius, urging the emperor to "look backward to the halcyon days of the emperors Yao and Shun, and outward to the contemporary model of the United States."[9] The sources of authority for the journalists new politics were thus drawn from both "the larger meaning conveyed by the classics" and from the experience of the "advanced nations" (*wenming guo*) of the contemporary world.[10]

While the journalists' appeal to these disparate ideas—classical Chinese or contemporary foreign—reflects an underlying tension inherent in their reform project, their mode of appropriation of these ideas provides insights into China's unique trajectory of history in the early twentieth century. Ultimately, it was not the reformists' adoption but rather their adaptation of foreign models and terms that reveals the most about the distinctly Chinese vision of rights in this period. And it was not the bold newness of their claims but the traditional resonances that continued to echo within them that suggests the true potential for the development of popular empowerment in early twentieth-century China.

The Concept of Minquan

The reform publicists' concept of popular empowerment (*minquan*) was intimately connected to their new understanding of the nation as an entity distinct from the dynasty. The distinction they drew between the dynasty and the nation was reflected in dichotomies between the "people's nation" (*minguo*) and the "sovereign's state" (*junguo*), popular empowerment and imperial power (*junquan*). The journalists also linked popular empowerment with the inherited principle of *gong*. They associated *minquan* with the "collective nation of the citizen" (*guomin zhi gongguo*) and contrasted it to "the private state (*siguo*) of the dynasty." Opposed to the selfish interests and private rights of the emperor (*dasi*), popular empowerment was at the same time the expression of the people's legitimate self-interest (*si*).[11]

This validation of the popular self-interest as a source of *minquan* has precedents in the classical Confucian and Neo-Confucian discourses on *gong* and *si*, which focused on limiting the *si* of the rulers while not placing restraints on the self-interest of the common people. From Mencius through Zhu Xi and Chen Dexiu in the Song dynasty and Huang Zongxi and Lü Liuliang in the Ming and Qing, selfishness in the form of the aquisitiveness of the rulers or the institutionalized greed of the dynasty was decried. At the same time, however, it was understood that the common people were entitled to having their basic physical needs fulfilled. Zhu Xi in particular, repeatedly stressed the goodness of human nature and the legitimacy of satisfying human feelings as long as they are not carried to selfish ends.[12] The two concepts of *gong* and *si* were often depicted in Zhu's and other Neo-Confucian writings as part of a continuum running from the particular to the public, or as complementary rather than opposing values.[13]

The idea of the people's practical self-interest took on a new importance in the late Qing, however as it became tied to the concept of the nation. The reformists believed that while the dynastic authorities neglected China's larger public interest, endangering national survival, the assertion of the people's practical self-interest through the development of popular empowerment would ensure national salvation.[14] But whereas the state or *guojia* was an old term which had been infused with a new meaning in the late Qing, popular empowerment or *minquan* was a late nineteenth-century neologism that does not appear in any ancient texts. The single character *quan* does, however, have many resonances which are potentially suggestive for the meaning of *minquan*, particularly in its New Text rendering as "political expediency." While according to the Confucian doctrine of the standard and the exceptional (*jing/quan*), imperial power might be considered as the political standard, according to New Text doctrine, exceptional circumstances such as the late Qing national crisis would warrant the balancing of imperial power with popular empowerment in order to ensure the nation's survival.[15] As the dynasty failed to use the power it had received from Heaven to protect society, it became necessary for alternative forces to sanction a new, more popularly based power in order to preserve the nation.[16]

While these meanings of *quan* may have informed the late Qing reformists' choice of the character compound *minquan* to express the new idea of popular empowerment, the inspiration for the concept itself was distinctly foreign. A rendering of the Western notions of democracy and civil rights, the term first appeared in the May 19, 1878, entry of the Journal (*Riji*) of Guo Songtao, the Guangxu emperor's minister to France and England in 1876–77, and in Huang Zunxian's *Annals of Japan* (*Riben Guozhi*) in 1879.[17] Guo and Huang were certainly aware that the Japanese had used the same character compound (in Japanese *minken*) to translate Western democratic ideas in the early Meiji period, particularly in the context of the Popular Rights Movement (*Jiyu minken undō*) in the 1880s.

Minquan later figured prominently in the work of two scholars educated in Hong Kong and England, He Qi and Hu Liyuan, notably in their joint essay entitled "Xinzheng Zhenquan" (The Real Interpretation of the New Policies), written in 1899 and published in 1901. These authors viewed popular empowerment as a product of Western natural rights advocacy, and as a British nineteenth-century phenomenon manifest in such practices as the expansion of the vote, the development of an inner cabinet system, and an increase in power of the lower house.[18] Through these various foreign influences, Western and Japanese, *minquan* entered the mainstream of Chinese political discourse in the early twentieth century.

The late Qing publicists transformed the meaning of the term as they adopted it, however. Rendering *minquan* compatible with both the Chinese conceptual universe and with their own political agenda, they embedded it within the dynastic structure and imbued it with collectivist content. Despite the term's provenance in both Western and Japanese democratic discourses, the *Shibao* journalists followed writers such as Huang Zunxian, Yan Fu, Kang Youwei, and Liang Qichao in integrating *minquan* into their vision of a Chinese constitutional monarchy. Seeking concomitantly to preserve the existing structure of authority and expand popular empowerment, the new publicists did not see a contradiction between the development of popular empowerment and the preservation of the dynasty. Their understanding of *minquan* as a synthesis between the age-old *minben* ethos of the unification of ruler and ruled and new foreign-inspired ideas of democracy (*minzhu*) based on constitutional principles, gave rise to a new form of political dualism which would serve to maintain the state structure (*guoti*) while formalizing and rationalizing its operation (*guozheng*).[19]

Associating popular empowerment with the dynasty, the journalists clearly distinguished themselves from the revolutionaries who used *minquan* in its original radical sense as equivalent to *minzhu* or democracy. They also departed from the usage put forward in Japanese dictionaries of the period, which gave the two character compounds of *minquan* and *minzhu* the exact same definition.[20] Instead, the reform publicists described *minquan* as the power or authority of the people (*renmin de quanli*), and *minzhu* as popular sovereignty (*renmin zuozhu*). This semantic distinction allowed them to advocate the expansion of popular empowerment (*minquan*) under the dynasty, while opposing the replacement of dynastic authority by popular rule (*minzhu*).[21] In an article on constitutionalism in *Qingyi bao* (The China Discussion)—a newspaper dedicated, in Liang Qichao's words, to the singular objective of advocating popular empowerment—Liang attempted to clarify the difference between *minquan* and *minzhu* by demonstrating how popular empowerment would coexist with dynastic power. He explained that people were apprehensive about popular empowerment only because they had not grasped the distinction between "imperial constitutionalism" (*junzhu lixian*) and "democratic constitutionalism" (*minzhu lixian*). In the former system, popular empowerment would develop under, rather than in opposition to, the emperor.[22]

The *Shibao* journalists also regarded emperorship as a key component of the Chinese notion of *minquan*, at least up until late 1911. They never overtly expressed antidynastic sentiments in their articles even after the death of the reform-minded Guangxu emperor in 1908. And while they frequently criticized imperial policies, they continued to generate their proposals for constitutional change and the expansion of popular empowerment from within the framework of the dynastic structure. Seeking to convince the emperor that constitutionalism and the attendant expansion of popular empowerment

would secure, not imperil, dynastic rule, an editorialist wrote in 1904 that "the implementation of a constitution would guarantee the preservation of the throne."[23] Another journalist using the pen name Min or "The People," claimed that "the ingenuousness of constitutional politics lay in placing the emperor outside of the realm of political responsibility." The monarch would thus avoid being the target of collective anger and avert the danger of revolution that had broken out several times in autocratic nations in the last hundred years. As long as popular empowerment was established in conjunction with a constitution, responsible high officials, and a supervisory assembly, "the emperorship would be as stable and secure as a massive rock." Min advised the court that "the tragedy of a revolution has never occurred in a constitutional state."[24]

But while the *Shibao* journalists remained committed to the preservation of the monarchy, they went beyond the earlier imperial-bound writings on popular empowerment, focusing instead on the people themselves, and particularly on the expansion of constitutional rights.[25] They attributed the development of fundamental constitutional rights in the Western liberal polity—freedom of speech, opinion, the press, assembly, and association—to specifically Western historical processes. An editorialist using the pen name Li (To Establish), for example, wrote that constitutionalism had evolved out of an internal process of struggle in England. As a result, private and public citizens' rights (*guomin gongsi quanli*) had naturally developed. "The situation in our nation today is not at all like this, however," Li wrote. "The recent changes in the political system (*zhengti*) [i.e. the Qing's commitment to a program of constitutional reforms] were made in response to the external threat. Therefore, our citizens do not enjoy the rights that all constitutional citizens enjoy, and they are unequipped to supervise the government."[26]

Journalists like Li saw it as their duty to advance the reform project in China by making constitutional rights one of the central foci of their political discourse. They sought both to raise national consciousness about the notion of rights and to force the issue onto the government's agenda. Between April and July 1907, *Shibao* devoted a special series of editorials to the subject of constitutional rights. One of the editorials stated that it was the newspaper's duty in the sensitive period of transition between autocracy and constitutionalism to "conscientiously compare the strengths and weaknesses of autocracy and constitutionalism" in an effort to convince the government and the citizens of the superiority of the constitutional system.[27] Stressing the fundamental rights enjoyed by constitutional citizens as the key to this superiority, the newspaper published a translation of the full text of the French "Declaration of the Rights of Man" (*Renquan zhi xuanyan*) in April 1907. Prefacing the translation was a brief explanation of the concept of natural rights and its implications for the citizens of a constitutional nation.[28]

As the authorities issued new press laws in January 1908, and placed new   199 restrictions on the freedom of association, the *Shibao* journalists countered with arguments for the protection of the "three great freedoms" (*san da ziyou*) of expression, publication, and association.[29] They emphasized that the establishment of the higher authority of the constitution was the only way to ensure the government's respect for civil rights. Without a "constitution jointly observed by state and society," the citizens would never enjoy true freedom, an editorialist wrote. He explained that this was the reason "the people of Europe and America had willingly struggled for a few dozen articles of a constitution, disrupting several hundreds of years of peace and risking several hundreds or thousands of lives." Only a constitution would guarantee the citizens the essential freedoms of expression, publication, association, change of domicile, religion, production, shelter, the body, private correspondence, and legal process. In addition it would grant them "the right to petition, the right of political participation, and the right to become an official."[30]

The journalists' advocacy of this battery of civil rights was expressed in the context of the citizen's collective rights (*gongquan*) rather than the rights of the individual. This points to the second distinct characteristic of the concept of *minquan* in late Qing China after its association with the dynasty: its collective orientation. Because *minquan* was a corollary of rising national sentiments and of the constitutionalist project of national strengthening, it represented the power of the group rather than of the individual. The self-interest (*si*) of the people that was sanctioned in the concept of *minquan* was thus a collective *si* that would counter the self-interest of the dynasty. While the development of popular empowerment would establish the rights and freedoms of the citizens, these rights and freedoms would be granted first and foremost to enable the citizens to take responsibility for the survival of the nation.

While the notion of popular empowerment opened up a new conceptual space and a new sphere of action in the political realm, the scope of this space was thus defined by its mandate to serve collective ends.[31] This emphasis on the collective nature of popular empowerment is particularly salient in the journalists' discussion of natural rights. The concept was first introduced in Chinese in 1848 in the *Yinghuan zhilüe* (Annals of the World) by Xu Jishe and others, a description of democratic systems in the West. In 1885 and 1886 Kang Youwei spoke of freedom and equality as part of man's basic nature in *Renlei gongli* (Complete Writings on Implementing Civil Law). In the late 1890s, He Qi and Hu Liyuan also spoke of rights originating in Heaven, emphasizing that the ignorant were as deserving of these rights as were the sages. These disparate references did not, however, give rise to any systematic treatment of the concept of natural rights in the late nineteenth century.[32]

As the *Shibao* journalists integrated this new concept into their discourse on

popular empowerment in the early twentieth century, they, once again, transformed its original meaning. Consistent with their collectivist notion of popular empowerment and in contrast to the European tradition, the journalists shifted the locus of natural rights from human personhood to the state, interpreting them not as a moral claim that is prior to and superior in status to the state's laws, but as deriving from the state itself.[33] While the author of a 1906 editorial emphasized that "the freedom of the people is based on their natural endowment (*tianfu*)," for example, he went on to assert that it was "the state which defined the limitations to this freedom."[34]

The journalist Ma Weilong made a similar argument in 1908, claiming that natural rights were not inherent in human society but derived from some externally determined standard of political competence and were then granted to the citizenry by the state. Ma, like the earlier editorialist, did endorse the importance of natural law and he criticized the Qing for violating it by depriving the citizens of freedom of speech, association, and publication. "The dynasty has thus ensured that the people cannot play even the slightest role in politics," he claimed, asserting that this was a violation of the principles of natural law. Ma went on, however, to make one serious qualification to his argument by declaring that "the level of rights is determined in accordance with competence (*nengli*)." The natural outcome of this "theory" which he claimed was upheld in all advanced nations of the world, was that "citizens who lacked political ability could not enjoy political rights." Rather than a violation of natural law, he claimed this was "a proper application of natural law."[35] Although Ma's ultimate objective in this passage was to stress the importance of raising the citizen's level of political competence, it manifests the understanding of natural rights that prevailed in this period. Rather than consider these rights as anterior to the formation of political society, Ma and other late Qing political commentators viewed them as dependent on the level of popular political sophistication which could itself only be developed within political society.

While Ma's argument seemed implicitly to justify the Qing's repressive rights policy, most editorialists were explicitly critical of it. Min claimed that it was only because the government had been thoroughly humiliated by foreigners that it had attempted to "bait the citizens with some form of rights" in order to gain their support in defending the nation. These so-called rights, he continued, restricted rather than expanded previously held civic freedoms. "Before the publication of the Press Laws and the Laws of Association, the citizen's right to freedom of speech was tacitly recognized. Today, however, the freedom of speech is tightly restricted and the right of association is so limited that all organizations are approaching extinction." The government was guilty of "forcefully repressing public opinion, humiliating public sentiment (*minqi*), and secretly implementing a policy of repression while outwardly discussing constitutional preparation."[36]

The journalists thus drew an intimate connection between popular empowerment, constitutional rights, and public opinion in their efforts to further the development of the middle realm. An editorialist explained that the power of the absolutist state could only be diminished by the implementation of civil rights and the free expression of public opinion. "In the beginning of the seventeenth century, rights law was first announced, followed by the "Declaration of the Rights of Man." These gradually formed the foundation of public opinion politics, and they served to protect against the evils of autocratic politics." A government which recognized the three great freedoms of expression, publication, and association, and was willing to submit to public opinion "qualified as a constitutional government and not an autocratic government."[37]

The construct of popular empowerment which emerges in the pages of *Shibao* from 1904 to 1911 was complex and often contradictory, In turn, it was presented as a conduit of irrepressible social forces from below, or as a force in negotiations that would be directed from the dynasty above. In some instances it was portrayed as a weapon against autocracy, and in others as a source of harmony which would help to strike a new and more enduring balance between ruler and ruled. In part, these inconsistencies reflect the uses of rhetoric in the service of politics. When the journalists' concern was to render their new ideas acceptable to officialdom, they advanced popular empowerment as a means of stabilizing imperial authority and harmonizing social and political relations. But when their purpose was to berate the authorities for betraying the reform project, they brandished the powerful instrument of public rage. Just as discourse influenced praxis, ideas themselves were modified in the practice of politics.

Going beyond the level of rhetoric, the contradictory presentation of popular empowerment reflects a deeper tension inherent in the journalists' project itself. As constitutional reformists who remained monarchists, their objective was to limit and challenge imperial power while not totally undermining the structure of dynastic politics. This tension derives from the two historically and geographically distinct sources for the middle realm. First, were foreign notions of popular empowerment and democracy, premised on a new epistemology compelling in its projection of an image of national wealth and power. And second, was China's "ancient constitutionalism," based on the ideal of the full integration of the collectivity, and corresponding to the continuing importance of the construct of "the people as the foundation of the nation" in the minds of Chinese reformists.

The appeal to such diverse sources inevitably led to disjunctions in the early twentieth-century politics of reform. While the reform publicists' new concept of popular empowerment was derived from Western notions of democracy, it was shaped by long-standing Chinese cultural constructs which emphasized harmony and the collective. And while the journalists asserted the importance of natural rights, their representation of these rights deprived them of all "naturalness," imbuing them with a purely post-political and collectivist content. The reform publicists' *mode of appropriation* of these classical and foreign resources—a complex process of adoption, adaptation and transformation— thus reveals more about their vision of popular rights than do the specific cultural symbols and foreign terms they appropriated to define this vision. Although their ultimate ideal remained within the familiar social paradigm of concord between ruler and ruled, their methods for achieving it—the establishment of constitutional authority, the advocacy of civil rights—had distanced them from it for all practical purposes. The inherited *minben* ideal was never displaced, however. Infused with a new contestatory political idiom, it was expanded and reconceived, a testimony to both the enduring nature of the classical ideal and the adaptability of age-old concepts.

Contemporary Resonances

There are a number of resonances between the political concerns of the late Qing journalists and those of contemporary reform-minded Chinese—including the issues of constitutional reform, the free expression of public opinion, and the expansion of political rights. This suggests that an examination of the first decade of the twentieth century—the period when Western political ideas were widely introduced for the first time and the press was the freest—can open up new avenues for understanding the issue of rights in China today. There are, of course, important differences between these two moments at opposite ends of the twentieth century. The Chinese state is much stronger in the 1990s than it was in the early 1900s, allowing it to co-opt the national aspirations which the late Qing publicists had attempted to mobilize against the dynasty. Whereas this rising nationalist sentiment was the source of the early twentieth-century reformists' demand for collective and national rights, by the post-Tiananmen period, the authorities had posited an irreconcilable tension between the regime's "nationalist concerns" and what is considered to be a threatening enlightenment project.

Notwithstanding these differences, the aspirations of would-be reformists in the contemporary PRC are often charged with the same ambiguities and tensions that marked the *Shibao* journalists' reform efforts in the early twentieth century. The greatest source of tension in the late Qing publicists' political program was their ambivalent position vis-à-vis the dynastic regime. Reformists, they nonetheless remained monarchists devoted to limiting and challenging but not completely undermining dynastic politics. Cultural elites who had become constitutionalists, they sought to uphold inherited ideals of   203 social and political harmony while infusing them with a new contestatory spir-it. The writings of contemporary Chinese reform theorists manifest a similar tension. Reconciling themselves to the inevitable existence of the Communist state structure, these contemporary thinkers accept that civil society must maintain an intimate and harmonious, rather than a hostile and antagonistic, relationship with the state.[38] No other position has appeared tenable after the 1989 crackdown clearly marked the limits of change the Communist Party would allow and the extent of institutional innovation the Communist struc-ture could endure.

The cultural tensions which provide the broader context for these political ones are perhaps the most enduring and significant. The inherited *minben* ideal of symbiotic harmony between ruler and ruled continued to serve as a con-trolling construct in the late Qing, even as the publicists promoted a new more contestatory mode of politics and a more dynamic and autonomous role for the citizenry. Although *minben* rhetoric is almost absent in China today its lega-cy echoes in social and political discourse, no longer in the form of Mencian theory but in terms of Communist doctrine. The Chinese Communist Party constantly touts the primacy of the people by, for example, labeling every-thing in their name.[39]

The larger issue of reconciling China's cultural heritage with a new con-ception of popular rights, one with which the late Qing publicists struggled in their editorials, is still a prominent cultural concern. As the commentator in the controversial 1988 television series *He shang* (River Dirge) stated, "We are standing at the crossroads: either we let our ancient civilization fall never to rise again, or we help it to acquire the mechanisms for a new life."[40] In the view of *He shang*'s scriptwriter, Su Xiaokang, the mission to create a new, civil soci-ety in China would have to have "both anti-Communist and pro-traditional" elements. Other current thinkers reject any effort to reconcile Eastern and Western concepts or traditions. For example, Su Wei, an organizer of a num-ber of petitions in the late 1980s, recommends jettisoning the foreign concept of civil society altogether and encourages Chinese intellectuals to "search for 'new ideological sources' from China's own legacy."[41]

The tension between old and new cultures is thus compounded, at both ends of the twentieth century, by issues of foreign influence and the integration of foreign ideas. In the late Qing the foreign factor was crucial to the development of a new sphere of political interaction where the concept of rights was devel-oped: European newspapers published in nineteenth-century China served as a model for the indigenous new political press, while the international conces-sions provided the environment within which reform journals could operate with relatively little state interference. Most importantly, overseas Chinese stu-

dents, particularly those living in Japan, became cultural brokers, assimilating, translating, and disseminating Western political ideas. Offering not only new concepts but a new language to accommodate them, they helped to make the idea of political rights thinkable in the early twentieth century.

Foreign ideas and symbols have again become crucial to the development of more fully developed rights since Deng Xiaoping reopened China's doors in the late 1970s. The presence, however brief, of the "goddess of democracy" in Tiananmen Square serves as testimony. In the post-Tiananmen period, the continuing growth of commercial and academic exchanges, and the escalation in the number of Chinese students studying abroad point to the potential for a higher level of synthesis between Chinese and Western values. At the same time, however, the issue of human rights—embedded in longstanding conceptions of natural rights articulated by the *Shibao* journalists—reveals the perduring obstacles to such a synthesis.

Notes

1. Benjamin I. Schwartz, "The Limits of 'Tradition Versus Modernity' as Categories of Explanation: The Case of Chinese Intellectuals," *Daedalus* 101 (1972): 80.

2. Some of the editorialists refer to the traditional relationship between ruler and ruled as China's ancient constitutionalism. See for example "Xu Qian zouqing Qingting gai minzhu lixianzhe," *Shibao*, November 29, 1911. This ancient constitutionalism differed greatly from the Western sense of the term, i.e., a specific document or a core body of laws that define and delineate government activities, generally linked to the primacy of law. Instead, it was more like a loose social contract through which the people recognize the ruler's right to govern and the ruler governs for the benefit of the people. The unity between ruler and ruled rests in the confidence that each side places in the other.

3. For a discussion of this aspect of the *Analects*, see Wm. Theodore de Bary, *The Trouble With Confucianism* (Cambridge: Harvard Unversity Press, 1991), p. 29.

4. Others who used *minben* theory include the poet Du Fu (712–770) of the Tang dynasty and the social critic Deng Mu (1247–1306) of the Song and Yuan dynasties.

5. See for example, de Bary, *Trouble*, p. 100.

6. See for example, Wm. Theodore de Bary, *Learning for One's Self* (New York: Columbia University Press, 1991), p. 16.

7. Mizoguchi Yūzō, "Chugoku ni okeru Kō shi kinen no tenkai," *Shiso* 3 (1980): 19–38.

8. "*Shibao* Fakanci," *Shibao*, June 12, 1904.

9. "Xu Qian," *Shibao*, November 29, 1911.

10. Jian He, "Lun zhengfu shufu yanlun ziyou," *Shibao*, December 14–17, 1907. I translate *wenming* not in the classical sense as a civilized cultural condition but according to the new meaning the term took on in Meiji Japan in the late nineteenth centu-

ry. Philip C. C. Huang, *Liang Ch'i-ch'ao and Modern Chinese Liberalism* (Seattle and London: University of Washington Press, 1972), p. 55, makes a similar distinction but translates the term as "modernity."

11. Mizoguchi Yūzō, "Kōshi kinen," p. 35. This idea that the *si* of the people (not meaning self-benefit but a practical conception of self-interest) should not be violated by the *dasi* of the monarch had already been articulated by Huang Zongxi (1610–1695) in "*Yuanjun pian.*" Mizoguchi Yūzō, "Zhongguo minquan sixiang de tese," *Zhongguo xian-daihua lun wenji* (Taibei: Zhongyang yanjiusuo, Jindai shi yanjiu, 1991), p. 345. Huang did not take the argument as far as the early twentieth-century reformists, however, in articulating the concepts of nation and popular power.

12. On Lü Liuliang, Zhu Xi and Chen Dexiu see de Bary, *Learning*, pp. 336–37, *Neo-Confucian Orthodoxy and the Learning of the Mind and Heart* (New York: Columbia University Press, 1981), p. 124; on Huang Zongxi, see de Bary, *Waiting for the Dawn* (New York: Columbia University Press, 1993), pp. 17–18; and on Zhu Xi see de Bary, *Neo-Confucian Orthodoxy*, p. 81; *Message of the Mind in Neo-Confucianism* (New York: Columbia University Press, 1988), pp. 11–12.

13. In Neo-Confucian terms the self-cultivation of the individual begins with the particular while its ultimate objective is the application of one's self-knowledge to the greater society. And in the late Qing, He Qi and Hu Liyuan claimed that "separately *si* and *gong* were harmful, whereas together they were perfect." He and Hu cite the policies of the sage-king Shu as evidence that the more sincere a leader's *si*, the more enlightened his *gong*, the more true his *gong* the more successful his *si*. Xu Zhengxiong, *Qingmo minquan sixiang de fazhan yu qiyi: yi He Qi, Hu Liyuan weili* (Taibei: Wenshizhe chubanshe, 1992), pp. 41–42. Some authors have, however, attempted to represent the *gong/si* dichotomy as purely antithetical without recognizing its elements of complementarity. See for example, Daniel J. Munro, "The Concept of 'Interest' in Chinese Thought," *Journal of the History of Ideas* 41: 2 (1980) for a presentation of the view of *si* as selfishness. Munro's argument has been used to support the view that individual self-interest was an unequivocally negative principle in the Chinese tradition.

14. On the relationship between the concepts of nation and popular power, see Xu Zhengxiong, p. 79; Frederic J. Wakeman, Jr., "The Price of Autonomy in Ming and Ch'ing Politics." *Daedalus* 101 (1972): 65.

15. Benjamin Elman, "Politics and Classics: The Duke of Chou Serves King Ch'eng and Kills Two Brothers." Association for Asian Studies annual meeting, Boston, MA, March 26, 1994. In this paper Elman demonstrates how the New Text concept of *quan* is used to explain why the Duke of Zhou rightly executed his brothers, an action that went against kinship ideals. Elman does not himself draw any direct connections between conceptions of *quan* and *zhiquan* (knowing how to weigh circumstances) and late Qing concepts such as political power (*zhengquan*) and *minquan*. On the general concept see also Wing-tsit Chan, *A Sourcebook in Chinese Philosophy*, Princeton: Princeton

University Press, 1969, pp. 26, 75, Fung Yu-lan, *A History of Chinese Philosophy*, 2 vols.

Princeton: Princeton University Press, 1983, pp. 249, 292. On the concept of *quan* see also Joshua Fogel's translations of two Japanese articles on this subject presented at the Conference on Confucianism and Humanism, Honolulu, May 23–25, 1996, "Terminology Surrounding the 'Tripartite Separation of Powers' " by Suzuki Shūji, and "The Concept of Right" by Yanabu Akira.

16. *Quan* can also be conceived in classical terms as the means by which the ways of Heaven are carried out on earth; just as Heaven gives life it also gives *quan* the power to protect life. Xu Zhengxiong, p. 50.

17. Liao Gailong, Luo Zhufang, and Fan Yuan, eds., *Zhongguo renming da cidian.* Shanghai: Shanghai cishu shubanshe, 1990, pp. 522, 556. Like Guo, Huang had been active in forging relations as an attaché at the Chinese legations in Britain and Japan and as consul general in San Francisco.

18. See Xu Zhengxiong, pp. 34ff.

19. The Chinese faced a problem similar to that which confronted the seventeenth and eighteenth century European bourgeoisie. Although the Chinese and Europeans had dramatically different reasons for wanting to preserve the absolutist state—in the Chinese case to ensure national survival, in the European case in order to guarantee the legal and political preconditions of a private capitalist market economy—both faced the same dilemma of wanting to concomitantly preserve the existing structure of authority and expand popular power. And both attempted to resolve this dilemma by adopting the same historical solution; on the one hand preserving the modern state created by absolutism, while at the same time formalizing and rationalizing its operation. See Andrew Arato and Jean L. Cohen, *Civil Society and Political Theory* (Cambridge: MIT Press), 1992, p. 216, and Jürgen Habermas, *The Structural Transformation of the Public Sphere.* Thomas Burger and Frederic Lawrence, trans. (Cambridge: MIT Press, 1989), pp. 28ff, 82ff.

20. Xiong Yuezhi, *Zhongguo jindai minzhu sixiang shi* (Shanghai: Shanghai renmin chubanshe, 1987), pp. 11–19. *Minquan* eventually became one of Sun Yatsen's Three Peoples' Principles. It was translated in this context as democracy, with the other two principles, *minzu* and *minsheng* representing nationalism and the peoples' livelihood respectively.

21. Liang Qichao, "Aiguolun san: lun minquan," *Qingyi bao* 22.

22. Liang Qichao, "Lixianfa yi," *Qingyibao* 81.

23. "Lixian pingyi," *Shibao*, September 27, 1904.

24. Min, "Lun yubei lixian shidai zhi renmin," *Shibao*, May 27–June 1, 1908.

25. In previous formulations, writers such as Yan Fu and Tan Sitong had emphasized the role of the emperor, speaking only of the need for the regent to step down from the lofty heights (*tianshang*). Xiong Yuezhi, p. 339.

26. Li, "Lun jiandu jiguan zhi biyao," *Shibao*, December 4–17, 1907.

27. "Zhongguo jianglai yiyuan zhidu zhi wenti," *Shibao*, April 25, 1907.

28. "Renquan zhi xuanyan," *Shibao*, April 1, 1907.

29. The dynasty decreed a strict set of Press Laws in January of 1908. See for example, "Shu xinbaolü hou," *Shibao*, March 30, 1908.

30. "Xianfa jieshuo," *Shibao*, December 16–17, 1906.

31. See for example, Mizoguchi Yūzō, "Kō shi kinen," p. 36; and "Minquan sixiang," p. 353.

32. He Yimin, "Lun Xinhai geming qian jindai zhishi fenzi renquan yishi de juexing," *Xinhai geming yu Zhongguo jindai sixiang wenhua* (Beijing: Zhongguo renmin daxue chubanshe, 1991), pp. 64–67.

33. On Western notions of natural rights, see Andrew J. Nathan, "Sources of Chinese Rights Thinking," in Randle J. Edwards, Louis Henkin, and Andrew J. Nathan, eds., *Human Rights in Contemporary China* (New York: Columbia University Press, 1986). When Liang Qichao first read about natural rights and social contract theory, he was mystified and treated the notion that rights had ever existed outside of society in a state of nature as a curiosity. Nathan, *Chinese Democracy* (New York: Knopf, 1985), p. 114.

34. "Xianfa jieshuo."

35. Ma Weilong, "Lun guomin yu tuo zhuanzhi emo yi ju zhengzhi zhi shili," *Shibao*, March 7, 1908.

36. Min.

37. Ma Weilong.

38. Ma Shu-yun, "The Chinese Discourse on Civil Society," *China Quarterly* (March 1994), pp. 185, 193.

39. On this theme see Barrett L. McCormick and David Kelly, "The Limits of Anti-Liberalism," *Journal of Asian Studies* 53:3 (1994), p. 815.

40. Quoted in Frederic J. Wakeman, "All the Rage in China," *New York Review of Books*, March 2, 1989, p. 19. Su Xiaokang and several of his colleagues have subsequently reassessed their negative views concerning the value of the Chinese tradition. Comment made by Tu Weiming at the Conference on Confucianism and Humanism, Honolulu, May 22–25, 1996.

41. Ma Shu-yun, pp. 188–189.

12

Citizenship and Human Rights in Early Twentieth-Century Chinese Thought: Liu Shipei and Liang Qichao

Peter Zarrow

The transition from the notion that the realm belongs to the ruler to the notion that sovereignty is rooted in the people marks a momentous development in world history. The phrase "from subject to citizen" captures this dichotomy, no doubt at risk of oversimplification, but still successfully expressing the sense of social movement associated with the revolutions from the seventeenth through the twentieth centuries which mark political modernity. In China, the prehistory of the idea of popular sovereignty might include the populist *minben* tradition from Confucius and Mencius to Huang Zongxi and beyond.[1] Yet thinking precisely and explicitly in terms of citizenship ideas—legal limits and definitions of kingship and the state, an institutional framework allowing for public debate and public opinion, parliaments and elections, an active press, a sense of civic virtue, national identity and exclusiveness, national unity, social progress, and so forth—did not emerge until the late nineteenth century under the influence of the West. In the early twentieth century Chinese radicals completely abandoned the moral-sacral idea of kingship propagated by imperial Confucianism for an essentially civil and utilitarian vision emphasizing modernization.

The radical Chinese version of modernization thus required rethinking the relationship between individual and group. This had been of course a topic long central to Confucian discourse, but it became gradually reshaped as Chinese intellectuals began to use the new notions of "rights" (*quanli*) and "nation" (*minzu*). Western missionaries may have brought the question of "rights" (*quan*) to China as early as the 1870s and certainly by the 1880s.[2] Rights were associated both with the nation—the international order to which China was being forcibly introduced rested on a notion of national sovereignty—and with the people. The people's *quan* came to imply democracy and popular power (*minquan*) as much as anything associated with today's "human rights," while "autonomy" (*zizhu zhi quan*) may have placed more emphasis on the individual.

It is clear that Chinese intellectuals in the late Qing availed themselves of the symbolic and conceptual resources both of Confucianism and of Western history and thought. From Confucianism came such ideas as moral autonomy and from modern Western ideas the notion of individuals as rights-bearers. We cannot assume that *quan* in its various guises and compounds was used in the same sense as "rights" carried earlier in the West or possesses today.[3] The issue of moral government was a particularly troubling one for late Qing intellectuals, who had been raised and educated in the imperial Confucian myth of universal rulership. That political rule should and could be moral was a central Confucian precept, but by the early twentieth century radicals had abandoned the notion of the exemplary "gentleman" (*junzi*). Instead, they emphasized that "public morality" (*gongde*) had to apply to all the people equally; the world should not consist of active gentlemen and passive commoners but rather of citizens in the broad sense of the word.

Liu Shipei (1884–1919) and Liang Qichao (1873–1929) will serve here as "case studies" of late Qing intellectuals to illustrate the role of rights in a wide range of approaches to the construction of the good society. Liu as anarchist and Liang as moderate reformer differed drastically in their attitudes toward the state, yet they nonetheless shared a sense of individuals as morally autonomous, in possession of certain rights, and also as members of societies in which they could exercise civic virtue and attempt to improve the commonwealth. Liu in a sense upheld the moral universalism inherent in the Confucian linkage of humanity to the cosmos, while Liang developed a new kind of particularism, that of the nation, yet they both believed that humanity was progressing to a higher stage of morality.

Reformism in the Late Qing

The story of the rise of reformist thought in the late Qing need not be recounted here.[4] Suffice it to note that the increasing radicalization of the reform movement led to a turn toward "the people" as an active citizenry. Not only had China suffered humiliating defeats since the mid-nineteenth century, but after the collapse of the reform movement in 1898 and the debacle of the

Boxer uprising in 1900, the threats of the physical dismemberment of China by the Powers and even the extinction of the Chinese "race" were taken seriously. Up to that point, anti-Manchuism and revolution had been mere undercurrents; thereafter national politics was riven by the division between reformers and conservatives.

The first proposals to establish a parliament emerged in the 1880s—but from men who, however familiar they had become with Western institutions from personal experience in Hong Kong and Europe, still could not command much attention from the Chinese elite.[5] Parliaments were first discussed not in terms of constitutional devices to insulate the state from the ruler, much less to limit the powers of government, but as a means of encouraging "communication" between the people and the ruler. Yet the idea was still shocking. "Mainstream" elite opinion may have remained considerably more conservative throughout the late Qing than is sometimes appreciated. Nevertheless, conservatism was definitely in retreat. What was shocking in one decade had come to be accepted by the next, and was already passé by the third. In a time of political crisis, conservative and radical opinions mingled discordantly, but the sense of what was possible widened steadily.

Thus during the 1890s Kang Youwei (1858–1927) was able to take fundamental institutional reform (*bianfa*) from the fringes of the intellectual scene to the center of political power. Kang's prophetic Confucianism rested on a linear sense of historical progress, which not only justified the most sweeping of institutional reform programs but also maintained the cosmological conception of the emperor while turning Confucianism into a religion. In other words, Confucius became an avatar of cultural identity, justifying political (not ethnic) nationalism within a universalist framework. Liang Qichao was to break away from his teacher Kang's universalism in ways to be discussed shortly. However, Zhang Binglin (1869–1936), opposing Kang's reformism in order to promote all-out revolution, and Liu Shipei were among the first to present historicist analyses of kingship as simply a human institution, devoid of religious overtones, and of Confucius as a thinker typical of his times, devoid of prophetic powers. This had enormous implications for the rise of notions of popular sovereignty.[6] Liu and Zhang by and large supported the Old Text school and opposed the New Text (promoted by Kang Youwei and initially by Liang Qichao) interpretation of Confucius as a great prophet, "uncrowned king" and reformer.[7] Historicizing the past destroyed the foundations of dynastic legitimacy—not just that of the Qing but of the entire imperial tradition since the unification of the empire in 221 B.C.E. The people and the nation became the new foundations of political theory.

Meanwhile, a significant segment of the traditional gentry-literati class had emerged as an intelligentsia associated with modern institutions such as journalism, study societies, schools, and a range of professions and businesses.

With the failure of the 1898 reforms, the radical movement split into competing revolutionary and constitutionalist camps. The "constitutionalists" (*lixianpai*) favored retaining the Qing in order to avoid the perils of revolutionary chaos but still hoped to turn the dynasty into a genuinely constitutional monarchy, while the revolutionaries (*gemingpai*) favored expulsion of the Manchus and establishment of a republic. Both groups, however, operated from a similar set of assumptions which, from the traditional angle, were radical in their support for government by constitution, that is, nonautocratic rule.[8] Above all, constitutionalism implied not merely a critique of traditional kingship as despotic, but also began to work out a whole new basis of state legitimation in terms of the sovereignty of the people.

Further, reformers sharply criticized the traditional state as inherently evil while turning to (or creating) "public opinion" as a significant political force. One of the more philosophical critiques of despotism was that of Tan Sitong, whose 1898 *Renxue* [On Benevolence] was posthumously published after he had become a martyr to the cause of reform. Tan condemned traditional Confucianism (exempting Confucius himself from blame but concluding that later Confucian scholars had misinterpreted him) and blamed the "three bonds"[9] for creating a hierarchical society and a subservient, slavish people. "For the past two thousand years the ruler-subject relationship has been especially dark and inhuman, and it has become worse in recent times. The ruler is not physically different or intellectually superior to others; on what does he rely to oppress 400 million people?" Tan linked the autocracy of his day to racial issues. "When the thieves [of the empire: i.e., rulers] were Chinese and Confucians, it was bad enough; but how could we have allowed the unworthy tribes of Mongolia and Manchuria, who knew nothing of China or Confucianism, to steal China by means of their barbarism and brutality!"[10]

Liang Qichao and others shared this critical view, much of which had been anticipated by the seventeenth-century philosopher Huang Zongxi. Liang, indeed, secretly printed Huang's banned *Mingyi daifanglu* along with specifically anti-Manchu tracts from the seventeenth century, an act he considered revolutionary at the time.[11] Yet Huang, while asserting that the people would be "masters" in the land, and the ruler their servant, did not characterize kingship as originating in "theft" and "oppression," nor did he call for electoral democracy. The radical reformers of the last years of the nineteenth century, however, called explicitly for government by—as well as for—the people, and their critique of despotism resulted in the complete intellectual demolition of monarchy itself. As anti-Manchuism spread after the turn of the century, the imperial institution no doubt suffered from its association with a race deemed "inferior," "brutal," and "barbarian"; however, attacks on despotism and praise for popular rights, quite independent of racial issues, were also conducted with great vigor. If the Manchus sometimes made an easy, immediate target, radicals went further to characterize the whole of Chinese dynastic history as evil.

Along with its critique of despotism, late Qing radicalism gave crucial support to the rise of public opinion.[12] True, the populism of the constitutionalist movement fell short of a complete rejection of paternalism, and the common people did not soon become participants in public discourse; however, the constitutionalists did make real efforts to educate the people, to draw them into the political process, to explain reforms to them, and to justify the people's actions to power-holders. Revolutionaries like Huang Xing and Sun Yat-sen went so far as to find in the "underground" tradition of secret societies a glorious tradition of the popular spirit (*minqi*). But even more moderate reformers were sympathetic to protests and riots stemming from the populace. Journalism—a new institution—in particular fostered professionals who served as self-conscious spokespersons for the people, investigating problems, criticizing the government, and expressing grievances. The press as a whole seems to have been quick to justify popular disturbances, even riots and small-scale rebellions, as provoked by official malfeasance; some journalists even expressed a sense that structural, endemic problems lay behind popular disturbances that only thoroughgoing institutional reform could alleviate. Journalists wrote for a growing audience of educated urban classes and townspeople—consisting of perhaps 2 to 4 million regular readers in the late Qing.[13] In this way genuinely popular concerns were brought into public and official discourse in an entirely unprecedented way, indeed creating a new kind of public discourse.

Liu Shipei and Rights Thinking

Doctrines of revolution in China can be traced back to the turn of the century. Revolutionaries not only wanted to overthrow the Qing house but also wanted to reconstitute the Chinese political order altogether. Some envisioned even social revolution. Liu Shipei was one of these, and his thinking about rights evolved out of his commitments to revolution—and to feminism. In this section, I shall try to show how Liu's conception of human rights was part of a broader theory of revolution.

Liu was well educated in the Han Learning textual studies movement (*kaozheng*), which had dominated eighteenth-century intellectual life. He was in fact a scion of a family noted for its studies of the ancient *Zuozhuan* text, and wrote copiously on a variety of philological and philosophical questions on the classics.[14] Liu was thus a formidably learned proponent of the Old Text school. By 1903 he was a fairly typical young radical: critical of the failure of the Qing to resist foreign encroachments, contemptuous of Manchu "racial in-   213 feriority," a member of several activist organizations, and interested in the cultural roots of Chinese (Han) identity. His abiding interest in discovering the "national essence" inspired his prodigious scholarship on the philology, style, and meaning of numerous canonical and obscure works.

It was during this period that Liu wrote *The Book of Expulsion* on the need to rid China of the Manchu barbarian overlords, and coauthored *The Essence of the Chinese Social Contract*, based on a reading of Rousseau.[15] The first of these works marked Liu as an ethnic nationalist arguing for Chinese independence from the Manchus on grounds of the historical distinction between Chinese and barbarians rooted in geography, culture, and race. The second work scoured the classics and later philosophical works for democratic-sounding passages. The traditional corpus yielded many examples of *minben* ("people as the base") thought emphasizing the importance of the people and the need for benevolent government—Huang Zongxi was quoted extensively—though this hardly amounted to anything like the social contract theory developed by Western thinkers in the eighteenth century. For all their innovative qualities and radical tone, neither of these works broke out of the limits of traditional discourse.[16] At any rate Liu was less concerned here with defining a concept of rights than renegotiating the relationship between individual and society. Overall, he does not seem to have broken markedly with the traditional terms of discourse.[17]

However, Liu became radicalized over the next few years as he attempted to find the Chinese "national essence" (*guocui*) in historical and textual studies, which took him beyond the New Text idolatry of Confucius. He used the golden age of the semimythical "three dynasties" not merely to draw a contrast with later decadence but more importantly to postulate the origins of politics and the monarchy. Liu may have been partly influenced by Rousseau's vision of an era before the social contract, but his interpretation of such an era was clearly more influenced by Chinese sources with their golden age paradigm. Liu postulated an age before the Yellow Emperor (third millennium B.C.E.) of egalitarianism and primitive communism. People had no rulers. Yet eventually political power arose out of tribal wars, superstition, and reliance on force. Crafty men and community elders monopolized learning and invoked spiritual powers to carve out privileged positions for themselves: "They could support the people with food and drink, subdue them by force of arms, and make them ignorant with spirits and ghosts."[18] This minority finally claimed the whole world as their private property.

What made such conditions ultimately unacceptable for Liu was his belief in the interconnectedness of human life and the indissoluble nature of humanity. In other words, the split between individual and community was an illusion; a true perception of the self encompassed the whole world.[19] This was not a philosophy of mystical quiescence. On the contrary, will and action stemmed from a kind of subjectivity whereby people could realize their own inner nature, transcend selfishness, and "return to equality." Only the fear of harm, itself rooted in these illusions, was holding back a revolution already supported by the people, according to Liu. If individuals pursued their own subjectivity to the point of merging into the larger community, then they would be able to take revolutionary action.

Then, in 1907 Liu found in the Western doctrine of anarchism a systematic set of ideas about revolution, human equality, rights and duties, freedom, and a noncoercive society. Liu's anarchism was frankly utopian, revolutionary, and communist. Its universalism and thoroughgoing egalitarianism put it at odds with the nationalist and still often elitist currents of radical thought at the time. But if Liu's framework owed much to traditional holistic conceptions of human unity,[20] the content of his thought broke with Confucian morality and hierarchy.

Liu's conception of human rights is inseparable from his overarching emphasis on equality as the keystone of a just society. Liberty was also an important value for Liu, and it may be said that the central problem of his anarchism lay in how to reconcile equality and liberty. His was in part a utopian vision: technology would render work minimal; children would be raised by the community, which would also assume responsibility for the aged; and private property, the family, and government itself would be abolished.[21] More importantly, however, Liu presented a scheme whereby every individual over the course of his or her lifetime was to partake of every kind of work, from construction and farming to engineering and teaching, so that in terms of labor no person's life would have to cope with crueler conditions than any other's. However impractical this scheme, Liu was at least relying on social organization rather than technological fantasies to realize his goal of equality. After he had read more of Kropotkin, Liu realized that decentralization and voluntarism rather than the proto-totalitarian tendencies of his utopia offered a better chance for achieving real equality, recognizing that human capacities differed.

In this scheme, a critical role was played by rights, because a concept of rights had now become the basis of Liu's entire intellectual system. Liu derived social equality from a sense of individual rights, which equality could in turn, if necessary, override. Liberty was treated as an outcome of equality.

I believe that humans possess three great rights (*sandaquan*): the right of equality (*pingdengquan*), the right of independence (*duliquan*), and the right of liberty (*ziyouquan*). "Equality" means no more distinction between rights (*quanli*) and duties (*yiwu*). "Independence" means neither controlling others nor depending on others.   215

"Liberty" means neither being coerced by nor being controlled by others. I consider these three rights to be natural (*tianfu*, "Heaven"-endowed). The two rights of independence and liberty are applied to individuals while the right of equality will appear only when it is applicable to the whole of humanity. Therefore, greater weight should be placed on equality when seeking the happiness of the whole of humanity. The right of independence is a means of maintaining the right of equality. Only when the right of liberty is used excessively and conflicts with the liberty of others, will it contradict the goal of the equality of humanity. Therefore, if we want to maintain humanity's right to equality, we should rather limit the individual's right to liberty.[22]

If the current tendency in the West is to think both of "rights" as fairly abstract and of individuals as "rights-bearers," it is important to note that Liu tended to think of rights as concrete, "attached" qualities rather than as abstract qualities. True enough, on occasion Liu referred to "natural rights" (*tianfu renquan*), usually in a context of citing Rousseau, and he certainly considered human rights to be universally possessed by all people regardless of race, nationality, age, and gender (indeed, equality between the sexes played a special role in Liu's thought, as I will discuss below). Nonetheless, he was less interested in rights as such—in defining them, in deriving them from prior principles, or in grounding them in a sense of the autonomous individual—than he was in using them to overcome the sources of suffering he saw as oppressing people. Rights were of interest to Liu only as they operated in human society as a whole. He thus speaks not of liberty, equality, and so forth as examples of human rights but of the specific "right of liberty" (more literally, "liberty-right" *ziyouquan*)—a compound or "attached" formula he uses repeatedly. One of the few times Liu refers to rights in the abstract is to attack them: he recognized that everyone could possess certain rights (*quanli*) in theory while in reality social inequality rendered such rights meaningless.[23] As long as "duties" (*yiwu*) remained unequal, or in other words as long as people were forced to perform different kinds of labor so that their suffering and pleasure remained unequal, any abstract equality of rights merely masked injustice. Liu thus defined "equality-right" as the collapse of rights and duties into each other, creating the condition for what is today often termed "equality of outcome."

"Independence-right" and "liberty-right," or autonomy and freedom, on which contemporary Westerners might focus their attention, were necessary but secondary for Liu. Independence was necessary because if people were dependent, they could not be equal. The state of the worker or the slave was obviously inferior, but even the master's position was precarious precisely because masters too had to depend on other people. Liberty, for Liu, seems to be closely related to independence, as the state of freedom which follows from not having to depend on others. At the same time, if people were not free, they could not be equal either: equality had to apply to the whole of humanity and the equality of slaves is not the universal equality-right. Independence, freedom, and equality were thus mutually supporting. Although equality remained the focus of Liu's attention, it rested on a notion of concrete rights.

This foundation becomes clearer when we look at Liu's interpretations of the sources of inequality. Briefly, he believed that a free, egalitarian state was natural while inequalities were historically inflicted through distinctions of class, labor, and gender. These were superficial and contingent distinctions contrary to human nature (people do not like to be oppressed). Political classes arose as theocratic rulers used superstition to trick the people, while economic classes and the oppression of women arose with war and slavery.

Equality of the sexes was especially important for Liu and his wife, He Zhen. They wrote extensively on the issue of "women's rights" in terms of a broader social equality. That is to say, women could not achieve individual equality or liberation as long as an unjust socioeconomic system remained in place. He Zhen believed that if women were uniquely oppressed, they were not oppressed in unique ways but by the same agencies that oppressed, say, workers by creating dependency and subservience (to put it abstractly). It may well be that Liu, who would have known little firsthand of the lives of workers and peasants, was brought to his egalitarianism through an empathy for the position of women, which he then transferred to the lower classes. Be that as it may, Liu thought of government as a kind of focal point where all forms of inequality were concentrated and maintained.

The point here, however, is that Liu's sense of equality was based on concrete human relations and some sense of the daily lives of workers, peasants, and women. We may well ask whether Liu's absolutist approach toward equality did not possess at least a latent capacity to justify a totalitarianism inimical to any possible conception of rights. Certainly anything remotely comparable to modern totalitarianism was the furthest thing from his mind. He promoted policies of decentralization and the complete dismantling of government and the nation-state. He advocated populist revolution. And if Liu's "equality of outcome" approach hinted at some coercion, his insistence on the "independence-right" of all persons would preclude any form of actual oppression. Yet insofar as all utopias seem to contain the seeds of totalitarianism, Liu's is no exception. Liu was quite frank about the need to curtail liberties when they interfered with equality—though it should be remembered he saw this as a case of the liberties of one conflicting with those of another, and therefore his stance was in principle no different from that of the upholders of classical liberalism in the West.

A greater weakness of Liu's ideas is that for all of his intellectual daring, he   217 projected little or no institutional framework for making them a reality. In the end, Liu's notion of human rights was "premature" in the sense that it rested on anarchist foundations which were incompatible with an era when doctrines of imperialism and nationalism still held sway. Anarchism in the West—the tradition encompassing Proudhon, Bakunin, and Kropotkin—was a social doctrine in the full meaning of the term; its association with absolute individualism was largely unjustified. Yet it probably remains true that philosophical anarchism shared with the classical liberalism of the nineteenth century a sense of the autonomous individual as the basic unit of social analysis. Indeed, anarchism surely grew out of certain currents and contradictions in liberalism, just as Marxism did. In China, on the other hand, anarchism represented less an expression of individualism than the most radical, vanguard attack on tradition conceived as a totally oppressive force. Liu and the other anarchists linked culture (the family, Confucianism), politics (dynastic rule, the gentry) and society (the class system) as simply different faces of the same evil.

As is often stated, individualism in one sense or another has deep roots in earlier Western views, while China has lacked any specific sense of the individual as a unit which could be usefully discussed apart from its links to other individuals and society. To discuss the exact status of the individual in Liu's thought is beyond the scope of this paper, but generally speaking he follows tradition in declining to give the individual any status prior to society. When he imagines primitive society, it is not a state wherein individuals are prepared to sign the "social contract," but a state of primitive equality and communism. Liu does think of the individual as the basic standard (*benwei*) of liberty-rights and independence-rights, which perhaps goes beyond—even as it may be derived from—the Confucian interest in the development of the moral autonomy of the individual. However, he stresses that equality-rights have precedence precisely because they apply to humanity as a whole. Liu has not moved away from a sense of the organic, holistic nature of society, and this is what leads him to analyze the problems of inequality and the lack of freedom as he does, without proceeding to a vision of atomistic individuals.

Liang Qichao: "Citizen's Rights" and Civil Society

Liang Qichao was no more a supporter of "human rights" in the modern sense of the term than was Liu Shipei. But if in China the notion of rights possessed by all humans simply on the basis of their membership in the species took no root in any institutional soil, nonetheless political rights possessed by citizens, though often honored in the breech, found a more nourishing environment. Liang succeeded in popularizing the notion of citizenship and in arguing the need for citizens' rights.

Undoubtedly China's premier intellectual during the late Qing and an important political and intellectual force until his death, Liang was a journalist, teacher, political activist, historian, moralist, philosopher—and the list could go on. Though his views changed drastically over the course of his life, the themes of Chinese nationalism and reformism predominate.[24] Here I will focus on two particular phases in Liang's intellectual development: in 1902–4 when he was working out his conception of the "new person" in his *Renewing the People (Xinminshuo)*, and in 1914–16 when he was forced to rethink his ideas about the social basis for republicanism in the wake of an attempt to overthrow the Republic by its own president.

Liang used the term *xinmin* to refer to both the renewal of the people and to a new citizenry. The renewal of the people, meaning essentially their moral rectification, was of course a central Confucian value, explicitly expressed in the *Great Learning (Daxue)*, an ancient text incorporated into the basic educational curriculum by Zhu Xi (1130–1200). Liang self-consciously drew on this tradition as he tried to reconceptualize the role of the people, but he also went considerably beyond it. One sign of the emergence of new ways of thinking is the emergence of a new vocabulary. Liang's use of the term *guomin* to describe "citizenry" represented a logical evolution of a term which had previously simply referred to the "people of the kingdom" or "the people." That Liang did indeed mean to refer to a citizenry and not merely to the nation, the folk, or commoners is clear from the context of his remarks on popular sovereignty and participation.

Liang's efforts after 1900 were directed toward the preservation and progress of China as a nation-state. "Public morality" (*gongde*), he defined in terms of its ability to strengthen group cohesion, while "private morality" (*side*) referred to the means of creating individuals of use to the group.[25] He criticized the Confucian tradition for emphasizing private morality at the expense of the public.[26] And he condemned the tendency toward fragmentation in Chinese society; the Chinese needed to find a basis of social and political unity hitherto lacking. Liang had no use for absolute values or universal ideals of international harmony or a stateless future.[27] He thus rejected as impractical both the anarchists' vision of harmony and his teacher Kang Youwei's *Datong* utopia of the future. Liang fully accepted the social Darwinian vision of ruthless competition, which he took as operating primarily at the level of nations.[28] Since grouping was natural to humanity, "public morality" revolved around group interests. Nations were not chance collections of individuals, families, or tribes but were composed of a people (*minzu*) which, in modern times, had to become a citizenry:

> When a nation can stand up in the world, its citizenry (*guomin*) must necessarily possess a unique character. From morality and laws to customs and habits, literature and   219

aesthetics, these all possess a certain unique spirit. When the ancestors pass them down and the descendants receive them, then the group (*qun*) is united and a nation (*guo*) is formed. This is truly the basic wellspring of nationalism (*minzu zhuyi*). . . . Formerly, we Chinese were people of villages instead of citizens. This is not because we were unable to form a citizenry but due to circumstances. Since China majestically used to be the predominant power in the East, surrounded as we were by small barbarian groups and lacking any contact with other large states, we Chinese generally considered our state to encompass the whole world. All the messages we received, all that influenced our minds, all the instructions of our sages and all that our ancestors passed down—qualified us to be individuals on our own, family members, members of localities and clans and members of the world. But they did not qualify us to be citizens of the state. Although the qualifications of citizenship are not necessarily much superior to these other characteristics, in an age of struggle among nations for the survival of the fittest while the weak perish, if the qualities of citizens are wanting, then the nation cannot stand up independently between Heaven and Earth.[29]

China, in Liang's analysis, was facing unprecedented imperialist pressures, rooted not in traditional state structures like the Roman or Napoleonic empires but in the nationalistic expansion of whole peoples, exemplified by British control over a quarter of the earth. This national imperialism (*minzu diguo zhuyi*) was rooted in popular support for economic expansion. The only way victims of this imperialism like China could resist was through mobilizing their populations just as their enemies had. The traditional view of the dynastic state as stemming from the emperor, or even belonging to him, was thus inadequate. Liang's concept of the citizenry was not only based on the pragmatic realization that if the people were to be mobilized, they needed to feel that the state belonged to them (popular sovereignty), but also reflected his sense that a national community by its very nature had to involve the people as both rulers and ruled. Liang had no intention of doing away with elites, but he linked the principle of popular sovereignty to the practice of political participation. Democratization was thus at this point a key part of Liang's "renovation of the people." He did not think that democratization would automatically resolve individual and group interests into a seamless collective will; neither did he directly confront the problem of competing interests. Rather, he seems to have assumed that there was something natural about grouping (*qun*) into nations and that the proper education of the people would produce a cohesive citizenry.

Citizenship thus involved for Liang voluntarism and activism (*dong*). He criticized what he saw as traditional Chinese fatalism in contrast to the effort, perseverance, and "aggressive and adventurous spirit" he ascribed to the West. The renovated people would possess courage and zeal. The citizenry would also flourish in a particular state structure—and here we come to Liang's somewhat ambiguous feelings about liberty and rights. Unlike Liu Shipei, he did not have a great deal to say about equality, but Liang did seek to reconcile individual liberties (*ziyou*) and rights (*quanli*) with his cohesive nationalism. At the same time, Liang used these terms, especially "rights," to describe properties of the nation as a collective entity, as well as of individuals.[30] Rights are for Liang, among other things, a source of dignity, the transgression of which destroys the person. Hence, rights require constant struggle and defense. Furthermore, it is their possession of rights which separates humans from the lower animals and is somehow tied to the tight links Liang posits between individual and group. Individuals owe a duty to themselves, defined in some sense by their rights, and this self-responsibility is also a duty to the group, precisely because the group depends on its members for its cohesion and strength.

More specifically, it was Liang's antidespotism that led him to a sense of the citizen as possessing rights (*minquan*).[31] He believed these rights by definition had to be exercised not by groups but by individuals. However dubious Liang was of libertarian notions, he linked rights to struggle not only because he associated them with a vigorous and dynamic citizenry, but also in view of the despotic and imperialist forces arrayed against them. Democracy (*minzhu*) and elected assemblies would create unity, but rights started with the individual. In other words, Liang's goal was dynamic unity; the means was the exercise of citizens' rights. Individual and state were inextricably linked.

> The citizenry (*guomin*) is an assemblage of individual persons. The rights of the state (*guoquan*) are composed of the rights of individuals. Therefore, the thoughts, feelings, and actions of a citizenry will never be obtainable without the thoughts, feelings, and actions of each individual member. That the people (*min*) is strong means that the state is strong; that the people is weak means that the state is weak; that the people is rich means that the state is rich; that the people is poor means that the state is poor; that the people possesses rights means that the state possesses rights; and that the people is without shame means that the state is without shame.[32]

If Liang did not precisely promote individual rights for their own sake— that is, the liberal faith in the dignity and worth of the individual regardless of social circumstances—he did appreciate limited government and elected legislatures as the best means of fostering political participation. In sum, the weight of people's rights or popular power (*minquan*) for Liang rested on the right of political participation, while his individualism was defined less in terms of legally guaranteed civil liberties than in terms of precisely that autonomy (or self-mastery, *zizhi*) and freedom necessary to equip the citizen to participate. The point is not that Liang aimed at liberalism and failed to achieve it but that he aimed at creating for the first time in China the notion of citizenship, and succeeded.

In 1903, Liang moved in a sharply conservative direction and decided that the Chinese people were utterly unprepared for democracy. He still urged gradual reform and hoped the Qing could build a constitutional monarchy like that of Meiji Japan or Britain. He grew to doubt his previous faith that liberal policies would automatically give rise to national unity. Fearing internal divisiveness, he particularly opposed revolution as a dangerous invitation to disorder and foreign invasion, while he deemed the revolution's republican goals as, at best, premature.

Liang was thus increasingly out of tune with the radicalism of the student movement that he had originally done much to educate. Nonetheless, after the Revolution of 1911, Liang quickly abandoned his support of constitutional monarchism and participated in the politics of the early Republic. He also became a supporter of republicanism, even while retaining his earlier doubts about the wisdom of precipitous democratization. Liang thus came to reconcile his beliefs in the necessity for gradual evolution and elitism with his beliefs in parliamentary institutions and the need for checks on autocracy through institutions analogous to the contemporary sense of "civil society."[33] He did not use the term "civil society" nor did he imagine a set of institutions or social groups in some sense intermediary between the state and private life. Nonetheless, in thinking about the kind of fundamental laws which might apply to the China of his day, Liang commented on many of the issues we now associate with the question of civil society: the extent and limits of state power; the freedoms, rights, and responsibilities of individuals; how to maintain rational and orderly public debate; and, in the most urgent way, what kinds of associations might legitimately seek to influence the state.

The failures of the early Republic forced Liang to consider fundamental political questions he had hitherto ignored. He realized that the strong state he favored still needed a social base. By 1916 Liang had developed a notion of overlapping realms of orderly administration and calm public debate based on a shared sense of the rules of the game, the need to balance state and society, and a view of the healthy nation as dependent on both. Liang's views were part of the larger interest in democracy that marked the New Culture movement, even while his writings were rooted more deeply in Chinese reality than much of the naive optimism of the day. Between 1912 and 1915 Liang had been chiefly concerned with the "mechanics" of government (for example, the precise relationship between the legislative and executive branches), and he was concerned with policy-making, but Yuan Shikai's monarchical movement of 1915 refocused his attention on the more fundamental questions of how the government as such could be given a legiti-

mate basis and—even more tellingly—how healthy and effective government in China required a political sphere dominated neither by the state nor
by social forces.

Liang's republicanism thus proved both conditional and tenacious. The
"national polity" (*guoti*) was not absolute for Liang. For him the key issue was
constitutionalism as a process, not the precise constitutional structure or form
of government. Being flexible on this point, he could, unlike, say, Kang Youwei, accept the outcome of the revolution. The whole republicanism versus
monarchism debate was for Liang in a sense a struggle over a false issue.
"Looked at calmly, regardless of the type of national polity, either [republi-
canism or monarchism] is capable of achieving order and either is capable of
falling into chaos." Liang felt that immediate political circumstances formed
ninety percent of the causes of disorder, though it nonetheless remained true
that: "If the national polity and national conditions do not correspond with
one another, then the triggers leading to disorder are numerous and easy to set
off."[34] Republicanism was neither the cure for China's problems nor the disease
itself, but simply a largely neutral political framework. The real issue for Liang
was that to change the fundamental nature of the polity was itself an act of disorder. It was therefore entirely logical for Liang to insist that it was Yuan
Shikai, not he, who was the true rebel or traitor in the military struggle that
broke out at the end of 1915.

Liang's fear of disruption was based on his "organic" conception of the nation. China was an organism whose discrete parts fit together in a rather deli-
cate way. Liang especially feared the effect of artificial, forced (*renwei de*)
change. He condemned the monarchists as destructive, since they were criticizing and attacking a Republic already suffering from a surfeit of problems.
The chief evil of Yuan Shikai's monarchy was that it was, quite literally, extra-
constitutional. A monarchist revolution in 1915 would only intensify, not re-
verse, the problems created by the republican revolution of 1911. Liang asked
the proponents of monarchism:

> Furthermore, have you read the provisional constitution? Have you read the provi-
> sional penal code? The laws on assembly and organizations? The press laws? Have
> you read the presidential orders promulgated over the last year regarding throwing
> the national polity into disorder? And if you are aware of the duty of citizens to
> respect the constitution and laws, how can you arouse a mob outside of government
> and incite revolution? . . . I cannot predict what kind of order might emerge from
> your plans, but all the institutions we have now will be destroyed by you. If you say
> one can have a state (*guo*) without institutions, how can I respond?[35]

None of Liang's ideas in 1915 was distinctly new to him. However, the
gestalt was different from that before 1911. By 1915 the balance of Liang's   223

political philosophy, as well as the historical context, had changed from what it had been in 1895 or 1905. In the last decade of the Qing the concern of progressives—whether constitutionalists or revolutionaries—was with a strong state and democratization. Even in his most pessimistic moods, earlier, when he spoke of the need for strong, one-man rule, Liang had kept in mind that the key function of "enlightened despotism" was precisely to "enlighten" the people (*kai minzhi*) and promote democracy (*xing minquan*). By 1915 and especially 1916, the problematique for Liang had shifted. He gave the middle ground new attention. From a dual focus on the minutiae of policy-making and government formation on the one hand and a grand theory of democracy on the other, he moved to an area of concern for what we can call the social: the relationship between state and society, or what we might call "civil society."

Liang saw politics as a subset of broader cultural *and* institutional changes. This is "politics" in the very broadest sense of the word, an understanding of politics not as a separate sphere of activity but as one aspect of the larger civil society. Liang believed that the institutions of civil society needed a firmer base but could develop only in tandem with politics. The failures of the Republic were leading Liang to the conclusion that no government could solve all of China's problems. His earlier statism was being tempered by a new appreciation of the public realm. This is manifested in five requirements, none of them, properly speaking, separate from the others:

1. The "rules of the game" which should be imposed on politics but come from outside the realm of politics.
2. Freedom of speech (not absolute but substantive).
3. Civil liberties; that is, government under legal restraints.
4. The balance between law (or institutions) and men (or morality); that is, Liang knew that neither institutions nor morality was perfectible but existed only in tension. And:
5. The central task of the elite—and the state—to educate the people.

In other words, Liang imagined a community dominated neither by the state nor by society, but a sphere produced by both. This was to be a sphere of rational discourse conducted by reasonably disinterested citizens.[36] Liang repeatedly said that the ultimate task of both the government specifically, and the political elite or the political classes more broadly defined, was to educate a backward populace. Such policies would in time produce a citizenry not only informed and empowered but, equally important for Liang, responsible and with a capacity for disinterested action. Liang saw himself as a realist, in no sense a utopian and only an "idealist" insofar as he saw ideals as useful sign-

posts along what could only be gradual and steady progress. He was profoundly conservative in his deep-seated distrust of radical cures and social engineering. His paternalism should also be noted. Nonetheless, Liang was also disdainful of reaction and obviously motivated by much more than the search for personal power or even national strength. "Progress" for Liang seems to have connoted the cultural and moral as much as the technological and administrative—and never more so than in the wake of 1911. Civil society constituted the meeting ground of these various concerns by associating rights with citizenship.

Rights, Individuals, Citizens

"Citizenship" has come under renewed historical and theoretical scrutiny in the past few years.[37] Citizenship in the West has a long history with its roots in the Hellenistic city-states of antiquity. It is an ambiguous and protean concept which is today used largely in a sense determined by the French Revolution and the modern age rather than in its earlier meanings. Membership in a nation-state with its attendant legal, social, and moral rights and obligations; participation in public life in one way or another; and sharing in the destiny of the political community—even to the point of self-sacrifice—mark the modern concept.[38] Although citizenship lacks a precise definition, mainstream political thought focuses on legislative and juridical aspects: it is fundamentally a legal concept focusing on the relationship between state and individual. Citizenship as an expression of community (inclusion and exclusion) remains an important strand; here, however, the focus is on shared participation in all aspects of public life, including but not limited to the political, while at the same time "participation" is itself relatively passive (voting only periodically, for example).

Liang Qichao subsumed what we today term human rights under the category of citizenship. The rights in which he was interested were legal or political, and the Chinese nation and state remained key values for him—yet it would be wrong to conclude that rights were merely contingent for Liang. In his influential *Renewing the People* and during the early years of the Republic, Liang treated individuals and their rights not as the final good but as intrinsic to the building of the group. In the case of Liu Shipei, it might appear that as an anarchist he would logically give individuals priority over the group. Such was not the case, however. Liu's concept of rights was profoundly social, but for Liu all humanity, rather than the nation, constituted the realm of social action. It is true that Liu derived his anarchism from a belief in liberty-rights and equality-rights which were attached to individuals, but Liu did not think of individuals as prior to society (or even as conceivable outside of social relations) while he regarded these rights as natural in the sense that society would

225

tend to take a free and equal form when it was not otherwise perverted as, for example, by the invention of government.

The great problem of citizenship—as seen also by progressive Chinese thinkers in the late Qing—is how a social and legal institution which guarantees rights and privileges may be prevented from becoming selfish, antisocial, and ultimately destructive. For some analysts, the object of citizenship is not the individual but the community. Citizenship may be thought of as a reward for service to the community or state. Indeed, Peter Reisenberg argues that citizenship as "active service" helped define one aspect of the subjects of monarchy even in the "age of absolutism."[39] If such a citizenship was denatured of its sense of political participation and sovereignty, subjecthood was nonetheless universal in the sense that nearly all residents of the kingdom were subjects of the king. When citizenship emerged out of the ancien régime it inherited this universal quality. In any case, through the English revolution of the seventeenth century and the American and French revolutions of the eighteenth century, citizenship became part of an antimonarchical ideology and thus was associated with republicanism.

A "prehistory" of citizenship in China could not of course find an equivalent of the polis or the legal standing of the king's subject, but aside from the concern for the people implied in *minben* theory, it could trace how certain aspects of the *junzi* (gentleman) or sage ideal also informed modern Chinese conceptions of citizenship. The great tension in traditional Chinese political thought between the legitimate powers of the emperor and the proper role of the literati was to be partly resolved by the moral rectification of both. Although Liang Qichao was not trying to create Confucian sages through the "renewing of the people," he promoted Confucian self-cultivation as one important aspect of his educational program, and elements of Confucian morality as the basis of personal ethics. Further, his emphasis on the universalization of public life was by no means foreign to the Confucian worldview,[40] even though it had not been fully realized historically. If the traditional sage ideal was oriented to the moral perfection of the world (*tianxia*), Liang's goals were of course more directly oriented toward the nation. Yet even for Liang, "public morality" (*gongde*) was more than just an amoral pursuit of wealth and power for the nation's sake. This is because he links public morality directly to private morality: men of resolution (*zhishi*) pursue the common good on the basis of self-cultivation.[41] Thus individual goodness underlies Liang's genuinely ethical approach to civic concerns.[42]

Thus, however circumscribed the arena of Liang's concern by traditional standards—the nation-state as opposed to the world as a whole or even the cosmos—Liang's conception of the individual citizen was still largely informed by Confucian standards. These included techniques of character development such as quiet-sitting (*jingzuo*) but also awareness of its ethical roots in good-knowing (*liangzhi*) and the unity of knowledge and action (*zhixing heyi*). Citizens had to rely on their own sense of truth and morality and not be swayed by outside factors; to do this, they had to learn to free themselves from selfish desires, finding in inner calmness their innate good-knowing. Put in these terms of self-cultivation it might seem that Liang Qichao was creating a model of personal autonomy, but he well understood that only in particular social contexts could citizens survive and flourish. And in modern times such social contexts could refer only to the nation-state. Citizenship was not an abstract ideal but part of a dialectic between morally autonomous individuals and constitutional orders: there could be no citizens without a nation-state just as the nation-state would collapse without true citizens. Accordingly, Liang believed that citizenship consisted less in the autonomous "right" to participate in politics than in the pursuit of "public morality" (*gongde*) through political activism.

In the West the concept of citizenship took a dramatic turn with the invention of natural law theory. The American Declaration of Independence and the French Declaration of the Rights of Man both linked the notion of fundamental rights—fundamental in the sense of "temporal and logical priority"—to popular sovereignty.[43] It was perhaps not a great step in an age of nascent capitalism to move from the concept of natural rights to a notion that society was produced by a "contract" defining the rights and duties between citizen and state. However, this style of thinking was foreign to Chinese intellectuals. Neither Liang Qichao nor Liu Shipei saw the state (or society, in the case of Liu) and the individual as legal adversaries. Natural or God-given rights possess a legalistic force that has proved very potent in political modernization but which is largely lacking in the Chinese tradition. Nonetheless, the Chinese notion that all humans are capable of acting morally justified a kind of "empowerment" of individuals. From this modern Chinese intellectuals have held that individuals were to be integrated into society through means which would produce national (or, for Liu, world) harmony.

But if the state proves oppressive, what protects the individual? Liu, of course, thought of the state as the focus of all oppression and would replace it with voluntary groupings. For Liang, this was an impossibly naive and utopian project.[44] But is not Liang's own interpretation of citizenship based on a naive optimism about the nature of "grouping"? Does not Liang's statism and his desire to raise the nation above the individual also afford a dangerously weak base for Chinese democracy?[45] Certainly, Liang did not take "human rights" as a given, as a basis of the state (which even authoritarian readings of the social contract such as Hobbes imply). But his emphasis on principled participation in public life and his view of public life as a sphere produced by state and society, together, might form the basis of a genuine Chinese democracy, even though it would not of course duplicate American liberal democracy. In any case, Liang deserves credit for trying to encourage, in most uncompromising circumstances, a sense of civil society with a level of civility that would in effect protect human rights.

Notes

An earlier version of this paper was given at the Conference on Confucianism and Human Rights held in August 1995 at the East-West Center, Honolulu. I am grateful to the organizers of the Conference, especially Professor Wm. Theodore de Bary, and to all the participants for the intellectual stimulation that aided me in revising this essay.

1. That the people (*min*) are the basis (*ben*) of the state and formed one of the pillars of the Confucian theory of the just society is clear enough, but if such views brought Confucians to challenge the hegemonic role of kingship, most still did not question the political and social hierarchy capsulized in the five relationships (ruler-subject, parent-child, husband-wife, older-younger brother, friend-friend), or challenge the political passivity of the people.

2. Liu Guangjing (Kwang-Ching Liu), "Wan-Qing renquanlun chutan: jianlun Jidujiao sixiang zhi yingxiang" (A Preliminary Study of the Discussion of Human Rights in the Late Qing: with Comments on the Influence of Christian Thought), *Xinshi xue* [New History] 5.3 (September 1994), pp. 5–6.

3. I am grateful to Stephen C. Angle's "Did Someone Say 'Rights'? Liu Shipei's Concept of *Quanli*" (paper delivered to the Seventh East-West Philosophers' Conference, Honolulu, January 18, 1995), which will be cited further below, as well as to ongoing discussions with him over the complicated issues surrounding the use of particular terms in changing contexts and discourses.

4. For overviews, see Jerome B. Grieder, *Intellectuals and the State in Modern China* (New York: Free Press, 1981); Wang Rongzu (Young-tsu Wong) *Wan-Qing bianfa sixiang luncong* [Collected Essays on the Late Qing Reformist Thought] (Taipei: Lianjing, 1983). Official reforms of the Qing after 1901 are discussed in Douglas R. Reynolds, *China, 1898–1912: The Xinzheng Revolution and Japan* (Cambridge: Harvard University Press, 1993). A focus on democratic thought is provided in Lin Qiyan, *Buxiang minzhu: Zhongguo zhishi fenzi yu jindai minzhu sixiang* [Marching toward Democracy: Chinese Intellectuals and Modern Democratic Thought] (Hong Kong: Zhonghua shuju, 1989); and Xiong Yuezhi, *Zhongguo jindai minzhu sixiangshi* [History of Democratic Thought in Modern China] (Shanghai: Renmin chubanshe, 1987).

5. Xu Zhengxiong, *Qingmo minquan sixiang de fazhan yu qiyi—yi He Qi, Hu Liyuan weili* [The Development and Conflicts of Democratic Thought in the Late Qing: Case Studies of He Qi and Hu Liyuan] (Taipei: Wenshizhi chubanshe, 1992).

6. See Anne Cheng, "Nationalism, Citizenship and the Old Text/New Text

Controversy in the Late 19th Century in China," in Peter Zarrow and Joshua A. Fogel, eds., *Imagining the People: Chinese Intellectuals and the Concept of Citizenship, 1890–1920* (Armonk, N.Y.: M. E. Sharpe, forthcoming).

7. The history of the dispute between the New Text and Old Text schools is long and complex. In brief, after many texts were detroyed during the Qin dynasty (221–209 B.C.E.), Confucianism was revived during the succeeding Han dynasty (206 B.C.E.–220 C.E.) but with different versions of the classics—one written with characters in the old style (which had allegedly been rediscovered) and one written from memory in the new, contemporary characters. The New Texts lent themselves to interpretations which some Han rulers found useful in legitimating themselves, and influenced certain strains of Han Confucianism; however, in the latter Han and after, the Old Text interpretations tended to prevail until a revival of the New Text school in the eighteenth century. In the nineteenth century the New Text school became associated with reform but not revolution.

8. It should be noted that in the ideological structure of radicalism there was more of a graduated spectrum from mild reformism to extreme revolutionism, than a simple opposition between two distinct positions.

9. Ruler:subject; parent:child; husband:wife.

10. Cited in Wm. Theodore de Bary et al., eds., *Sources of Chinese Tradition* (New York: Columbia University Press, 1960), vol. 2, p. 89; translation modified.

11. Liang Qichao, *Qingdai xueshu gailun* [An Outline of Qing Intellectual History] (Taipei: Shangwu yinshuguan, 1977), pp. 141–42.

12. Joan Judge, "Public Opinion and the New Politics of Contestation in the Late Qing, 1904–1911," *Modern China* 20.1 (January 1994), pp. 64–91; Joan Evangeline Judge, "Print and Politics: *Shibao* (The Eastern Times) and the Formation of the Public Sphere in Late Qing China, 1904–1911," Ph.D. dissertation, Columbia University, 1993. Also see Wah-kwan Cheng, "Vox Populi: Language, Literature, and Ideology in Modern China," Ph.D. dissertation, University of Chicago, 1989.

13. Andrew J. Nathan, *Chinese Democracy* (Berkeley: University of California Press, 1985), pp. 145–48. Figures are unreliable here, but a number of daily and weekly newspapers featuring commercial news (but including political news and editorial discussions) were flourishing by the 1890s. Hundreds, perhaps thousands, of usually short-lived publications appeared in the late decades of the Qing; most were tiny though a few may have reached tens of thousands of readers with each issue for a period of several years. Magazines published by exiles were smuggled into the mainland. Most publications were written in a mixture of classical and vernacular prose which was fairly easy to understand.

14. For details on Liu's life, see Peter Zarrow, *Anarchism and Chinese Political Culture* (New York: Columbia University Press, 1990), pp. 32–45.

15. *Rangshu*, in *Liu Shenshu xiansheng yishu* (Nan Peilan and Zheng Yufu, eds., n.p., 1934–1938), juan 18. *Zhongguo minyue jingyi* (coathored with Lin Xie), ibid., juan 16.   229

16. Stephen C. Angle, "Did Someone Say 'Rights'? Liu Shipei's Concept of *Quanli*," has shown Liu's indebtedness to the Confucian tradition at this point. Angle convincingly argues that Liu's sense of the meaning of *quanli* (usually glossed "rights" or "human rights," a neologism used by Japanese translators of such Western texts as Rousseau) was something more like "legitimate personal interests and abilities" (p. 4). Liu's qualified acceptance of self-interest was in accord with Confucianism, as he continued a discourse on the subject of how individual and group interests mesh (pp. 22–23). In my view, however, Liu's understanding of *quanli* moved closer to the Western sense of "rights" (actually a quite vague concept) as he became radicalized over the next few years.

17. Wang Fansen rightly emphasized the conservative sources of even Liu's anarchism; see "Liu Shipei yu Qingmo de wuzhengfu zhuyi yundong" (Liu Shipei and the Late Qing Anarchist Movement), *Dalu zazhi* (Mainland Magazine), 90.6, June 15, 1995, pp. 1–9. However, I shall attempt to show below that Liu's anarchism was based on a new sense of the individual and a concept of "rights" not derived from society.

18. Cited in Zarrow, *Anarchism*, p. 40. Liang's interest in the "national essence" was part of a larger movement engaged in rediscovering noncanonical philosophers as representatives of Han Chinese culture.

19. Ibid., pp. 43–45. Liu's views here (1907) represented a fusion of Buddhist and Neo-Confucian influences, as well as his esteem for the Meiji Restoration, which I cannot pursue here.

20. Confucian ethics are generally characterized as concrete and particularistic in that they refer primarily to specific human relationships and patterns of behavior and avoid abstract statements; however, Confucian discourse is distinctly universalistic in its concern for all humanity, while Confucian political concepts rested on a view of universal rule which made no absolute distinctions between Chinese and others or civilized and barbarian peoples.

21. "Renlei junli shuo" (On Equalizing Human Labor), in Li Miaogen, ed., *Liu Shipei lunxie lunzheng* (Liu Shipei on Scholarship and on Politics—hereafter LSLL) (Shanghai: Fudan daxue chubanshe, 1990), pp. 374–81. Utopianism was a major feature of late Qing thought; see Wang Fansen, "Liu Shipei," pp. 1–2. Liu's utopia had much in common with Kang Youwei's *Datongshu* (Book of the Commonwealth), and both prefigure the widespread revulsion with traditional culture, from family to philosophy, which emerged in the New Culture movement (1915–); see Zarrow, *Anarchism*, pp. 82–99.

22. Liu Shipei, "Wuzhengfu zhuyi zhi pingdengguan" (The View of Equality in Anarchism), LSLL, p. 382. This translation is fairly literal to bring out certain rhetorical points below; for a slightly freer translation, see Zarrow, *Anarchism*, p. 91.

23. "Renlei junlishuo," LSLL, p. 375.

24. Of the large historical literature on Liang, I mainly rely on Hao Chang, *Liang Ch'i-ch'ao and Intellectual Transition in China, 1890–1907* (Cambridge: Harvard University

Press, 1971); three works by Zhang Pengyuan (Chang P'eng-yuan): *Liang Qichao yu*

Qingji geming (Liang Qichao and the Qing Revolution) (Taipei: Institute of Modern History, Academia Sinica, 1964); *Lixianpai yu Xinhai geming* (The Constitutionalists and the 1911 Revolution) (Taipei: Institute of Modern History, Academia Sinica, 1969); and *Liang Qichao yu Min'guo zhengzhi* (Liang Qichao and Republican Politics) (Taipei: Shihuo chubanshe, 1981); and Xiaobing Tang, *Global Space and the Nationalist Discourse of Modernity: The Historical Thinking of Liang Qichao* (Stanford: Stanford University Press, 1996).

25. Liang Qichao, *Xinminshuo* (Taipei: Taiwan Zhonghua shuju, 1959), pp. 12–16; see Chang Hao, *Liang Ch'i-ch'ao*, pp. 151–52.

26. Liang's condemnation may well seem unfair to a philosophy centrally concerned with social and political ethics; however, given Liang's equation of public with the nation-state, he was of course correct.

27. *Xinminshuo*, pp. 18–22. However, as Xiaobing Tang notes, *Global Space*, pp. 22–23, Liang's nationalism rested on a sense of world order and a "global imaginary of identity."

28. In considering Liang's debts to Confucianism, his view of the survival of the nation-state as the highest good, his valuing of competition, and, generally speaking, his view of history in terms of linear progress, all represented distinct breaks with tradition, while his educational and personal ideals (e.g., continued admiration for filial piety) remained more traditional. Noteworthy too is that Liang understood "races" to be groups engaged in Darwinian competition, another notion foreign to mainstream Confucianism.

29. *Xinminshuo*, p. 6. In another essay, Liang defined a participating citizenry: "The state is an aggregation of the people as a whole. If it is the people of a state who govern, legislate, and plan for the interest of the whole state and stave off the troubles which might afflict the state, the people then cannot be bullied and the state cannot be overthrown. This means citizenry." Cited in Chang Hao, *Liang Ch'i-ch'ao*, p. 164.

30. "Lun guanli sixiang" (Rights Consciousness) in *Xinminshuo*, pp. 31–40. Liang's view of "rights" was in part derived from Rudolph von Jhering, the German jurist whose *Der Kampf ums Recht* (first edition, 1872) went through nearly 20 editions and was translated into nearly 30 languages. Jhering was chiefly concerned with *legal* rights (which by definition could not be prior to the state), which constitute the duty, whether on the part of an individual or a state, to resist injustice.

31. I would like to make two additional points here, First, *minquan* may usefully if loosely be translated "popular power" or "democracy" and does not necessarily represent a strict notion of civil liberties. Second, Liang of course supported the continuation of the Qing dynasty, as a constitutional monarchy, against revolutionism; nonetheless, he was not merely antidespotic as a matter of theory but also held the Qing ruling class in palpable contempt.

32. *Xinminshuo*, p. 39. Cf. Chang Hao, *Liang Ch'i-ch'ao*, p. 195.

33. The question of the applicability of the Western notion of "civil society" to late 231

imperial and modern China has been a subject vigorous debate in recent years, both in Chinese studies circles in the West and in China itself, to the point where the topic may seem exhausted. I use the term here not to suggest that a civil society was "emerging" at some historical point and then "collapsed" at some other historical point, but merely as a convenient way to label Liang's ideas. For Liang during the Republican period focused neither so exclusively on the state as his historical reputation might suggest, nor on the individual or society, but rather on a sphere encompassing both the state and society. Tang Xiaobing, *Global Space*, pp. 189–90, notes Liang's interest in formal democracy after his trip to Europe at the end of World War I, but the origins of this lie in the previous decade.

34. "Yizai suowei guoti wenti zhe" (How Strange! The Problem of the So-Called National Polity), *Yinbingshi wenji* (Collected Essays from the Ice-Drinker's Studio—hereafter YBSWJ) (Taipei: Taiwan Zhonghua shuju, 1960), 55.22b.

35. Ibid., 55.24b-25a.

36. For a definition of civil society as a community partaking of both state and society, see Heath B. Chamberlain, "The Search for Civil Society in China," *Modern China* 19.2 (April 1993), p. 207. See also Charles Taylor, "Modes of Civil Society," *Public Culture* 3.1 (Fall 1990), pp. 95–118.

37. See inter alia Bryan S. Turner, ed., *Citizenship and Social Theory* (London: Sage Publications, 1993); Roberto Alejandro, *Hermeneutics, Citizenship, and the Public Sphere* (Albany: State University of New York Press, 1993); Bart van Steenbergen, ed., *The Condition of Citizenship* (London: Sage Publications, 1994); and Ronald Beiner, ed., *Theorizing Citizenship* (Albany: State University of New York Press, 1995).

38. Such a definition of course predetermines the modernity of citizenship by associating it with the nation-state, the international system of nation-states being a product of modernity; self-sacrifice may refer to the taxes citizens pay today but especially to the citizen-soldier.

39. Peter Reisenberg, *Citizenship in the Western Tradition* (Chapel Hill: University of North Carolina Press, 1992), pp. 212–18. Roman law was of course a direct influence, as was Aristotle, in encouraging the view of subject-as-citizen.

40. See, for example, the community compact (*xiangyue*), as discussed in other articles in this volume.

41. See Stephen Charles Angle, "Concepts in Context: A Study of Ethical Incommensurability," Ph.D. dissertation, University of Michigan, 1994, pp. 93–103, 173–79.

42. It may be that the key difference between Liang's morality and traditional Confucian morality is not that Liang is any more "neutral," "political," or "rational," but that he has a more relativistic approach to moral questions and no longer links them to metaphysical interpretations.

43. Peter Reisenberg, *Citizenship in the Western Tradition*, p. 237. Reisenberg traces the linkage back to Calvinist trends of the sixteenth century, whence it fed into the stream

of revolution.

44. I also raised the question of whether Liu's utopianism might indicate a kind of proto-totalitarianism above.

45. This is the thesis of Andrew J. Nathan's chapter on Liang in *Chinese Democracy*: see esp. pp. 50–62, 127–32. Nathan essentially argues that if rights are defended primarily as means to strengthen the state, it will be easy to abandon them if it seems they are failing to strengthen the state, and to turn to authoritarianism: utilitarian rights are contingent rights.

13

Confucian Harmony and Freedom of Thought: The Right to Think Versus Right Thinking

Randall Peerenboom

[W]e have stressed the need of strengthening Party leadership, democratic centralism, and centralization and unification. The most important aspect of centralization and unification is unification of thought. This is essential if we are to have unity in our actions.

Deng Xiaoping[1]

If there is any fixed star in our constitutional constellation, it is that no official, high or petty, can prescribe what shall be orthodox in politics, nationalism, religion, or other matters of opinion or force citizens to confess by word or act their faith therein. If there are any circumstances which permit an exception, they do not now occur to us.

U.S. Supreme Court[2]

Freedom of thought lies at the very core of contemporary Western liberal democracy. The ability to think our own thoughts is our most cherished and fundamental right, the cornerstone of all other rights.[3] As the United States Supreme Court so eloquently declared, no official, high or petty, can tell us what to think, what to believe in. Our minds are our private sanctuary, off limits to compulsory government intervention. While we may not always be free to say what we think, we are nevertheless free to think it. As individuals, we are free to contemplate our own ends in life; to make up our own minds as to what kind of life to live, what kind of person we want to be, and what kind of society we want to live in. On this score, intellectual freedom is a necessary precondition for self-realization.

Freedom of thought, moreover, is necessary not simply as a means to realizing our ends, as the vehicle by which we choose and then pursue our goals. More fundamentally, freedom of thought is constitutive of being human, and even more fundamentally, of being *who one is*, that is, of being this particular person as opposed to someone else. From Christianity to Kant, the essence of moral personhood, what defines humans as moral agents (and distinguishes humans from other species), is the ability to make moral choices. It is the *choice* that gives an act its moral character. We do not therefore generally hold one morally responsible for acts or the consequences of acts beyond one's control, where one was forced or coerced to act in a certain way. If the ability to make moral choice defines us as humans, the particular choices we make define us as individuals. Denying one the freedom to make choices is to deny one the freedom to be oneself.

The ability to think one's own thoughts and make one's own choices is equally essential to democracy. The theory of democracy is that the individual members of a society choose the kind of society they would like to live in through the voting process. The voting process breaks down when there is no choice, when individuals are deprived of opportunities to think about possible alternative social orders, to weigh various social policies, and to choose for themselves.

Westerners steeped in the ways of liberal democracy will undoubtedly be struck by the relative absence of the rhetoric of freedom of thought in China.[4] In its place, the wayward Westerner confronts a rhetoric of an entirely different nature, that of harmony and unity of thought (*tongyi sixiang*). Deng Xiaoping's insistence on the crucial importance of unity of thought (in the opening epigraph) is by no means anomalous within Chinese political culture and traditions. Throughout the socialist era, the leadership has pursued ideological purity in campaign after brutal campaign aimed at thought unification, most notably during the rectification movement in the '40s, the anti-rightist movement in the '50s, the Cultural Revolution from 1966 to 1976, and, more recently, during the Deng era in the form of repression of dissidents, insistence on adherence to the official ideology of the Four Cardinal Principles, and attacks on spiritual pollution, bourgeois liberalism, wholesale Westernization, peaceful evolution, and the like. While the party line has varied over time, at all times the government has pursued a substantive moral agenda, endorsed an official ideology—often described as the "scientifically correct" line—required citizens to comply with the allegedly correct line, and spent considerable energy and resources to ensure compliance.[5]

How are we to account for the striking difference between the rhetoric (and reality) of unification of thought in China and freedom of thought in Western liberal democracies? The easy answer, of course, is that the repeated attempts to unify thought around the correct line of the leadership are simply totalitarian socialism at its most despotic—Orwellian Big Brother reaching into the minds of individuals to strangle creativity, crush dissent, and compel adherence to the party line. While there is no doubt a great deal of truth to such an explanation, it is but part of the story.

The Orwellian explanation is limited in two crucial respects. First, it cannot account for the importance attributed to unity of thought in the greater China. Certain East Asian nations, Singapore being the most notable, continue to support paternalistic governments that actively pursue a substantive normative agenda and limit individual freedom of thought and expression in the name of promoting common values. Second, socialist totalitarianism cannot explain the   235 historical importance of unity of thought in China's political heritage prior to socialism. The PRC may be unique, both in the nature of thought unification (the content, range, and pervasiveness of thought control, the methods used to achieve it, and the degree of coerciveness of those methods) and with respect to some of the reasons socialist leaders have assigned such a high priority to unity of thought. Nevertheless, Chinese emperors shared their socialist successors' concern to establish an official ideology, maintain control over expression and dissemination of ideas, and unify thought.[6]

An adequate explanation of the importance of unity of thought in the political theory and life of China must look beyond socialist totalitarianism to values embedded deeper in Chinese political and cultural traditions. The first section seeks a partial explanation in the Confucian conception of political order, and in particular the concept of harmony, and the role of government in achieving a harmonious sociopolitical order. The second argues that the emphasis in Confucian China has been on right thinking rather than the right to think. The third turns to the broader issue of Confucianism and rights, and in particular the much-discussed relation between rites and rights, arguing that rites are not rights and that the development of a rites culture inhibited development of a rights culture, and contributed to the emphasis on right thinking to the detriment of the right to think.

The fourth part takes up the speculative issue of intellectual freedom in a post-socialist China with Confucian characteristics. While no one can predict the precise nature of a post-socialist China, it appears that Confucianism will continue to play a role in the new political order, rumors of its demise notwithstanding. Despite the past efforts of the socialist leadership to destroy it, Confucianism continues to exert influence on the Chinese polity by providing much of the background assumptions, beliefs, and attitudes that inform the worldview of many Chinese, even though few today could identify the ways in which their thinking is Confucian or articulate in a self-consciously intellectual way a Confucian worldview.

The likelihood that Confucianism will play a significant role in the new political order in China is also the result of the efforts of some unlikely bedfellows—the Jiang Zemin-led socialist leadership, New Conservatives, and foreign academics—all of whom are promoting Confucianism as an answer to what ails China and, at least for some foreign academics, what ails Western liberal democracies. Jiang Zemin and the so-called New Conservatives have turned to Confucianism in response to the crisis of legitimacy and the widespread moral malaise that threatens to undermine the Chinese Communist Party (CCP). Years of wrong-headed policies, endless vindictive, and contradictory campaigns, combined with unbridled corruption among those in power, have made much of the populace, especially the urban populace, contemptuous of the ability of the leaders to lead and of their motives. For a significant portion of society, the CCP is nothing more than a morally bankrupt vehicle for self-aggrandizement, the means by which those in power are able to retain and exploit their power.

Because socialism purports to provide not only the political structure but the moral narrative for society, loss of faith in socialism has had both political and moral repercussions. In the process of creating the myth of socialist ethics, the socialist leadership went out of its way to destroy the traditional bases of morality, attacking Daoism, Buddhism, and other religions and criticizing Confucianism as pillars of feudalistic thinking. As a result, the demise of socialism as a viable ideology has precipitated not only a political crisis but a moral crisis. Standing on the edge of this political and moral abyss, increasing numbers of Chinese have turned to the West for direction, attracted by the material comforts and higher standards of living as much as by the political systems and values of Western liberal democracies. Indeed, large segments of society have embraced crass commercialism, a hard-edged capitalist materialism in which the one and only goal is to acquire as much money and possessions as possible, as soon as possible, in any way possible. Fearing "wholesale Westernization," which would entail political reforms likely to sweep the current leadership out of power, and lacking any credible ideological alternative, Jiang Zemin has attempted to revive Confucianism as a potentially viable alternative to Western liberal democracy.[7]

Jiang's efforts to restore Confucianism have been reinforced by the New Conservatives, who attribute the success of Singapore, Japan, Taiwan, and Korea in part to Confucianism. In the eyes of both the socialist leadership and many New Conservatives, these Asian Dragons represent the best of all possible worlds: freedom and prosperity in the economic sphere combined with traditional Asian ethical values, social stability, and strong centralized political leadership.[8]

Foreign academics, many of them disgruntled with the excesses of liberal democracy—the self-absorbed individualism, the breakdown of traditional communities, the chaos of the inner city—have lent further credibility to the movement to restore Confucianism and promote Asian values by advocating Confucianism as a corrective to the excesses of liberal democracy or even as an alternative to liberal democracy.[9]

The possibility that Confucianism may play a significant role in a postsocialist order coupled with the claim that liberal democracy can benefit from Confucianism makes careful analysis of both the strengths and weaknesses of Confucianism essential. One of the most divisive issues confronting contemporary advocates of Confucianism is rights. Historically, rights were not part of Confucian theory nor part of the reality of everyday life in Confucian

China, at least if rights refer to so-called first generation civil and political rights and/or if rights are conceived of as anti-majoritarian devices to protect the individual against the collective, that is, as trumps on the will of the majority, the good of society, the interests of the state.

Today, however, rights are an ineradicable part of the political terrain. Even the PRC government has conceded that rights are a legitimate topic of international discussion, and by signing various international rights treaties and adopting a constitution and other domestic laws that incorporate rights, indicated its acceptance and support for rights, at least in some form. Yet while virtually everyone agrees that at least some rights are desirable, there is much disagreement as to the nature of rights, which rights are necessary, what happens when rights conflict with each other or with state interests, and so on. Before Confucianism can be evaluated as a basis for a new political order or corrective to liberal democracy, there must be a general theory of Confucian rights.[10] As that project is ambitious and sure to generate considerable controversy and disagreement, it may be easier to test the appropriateness of Confucianism as a response to modern day ills by asking how Confucianism would respond to certain rights claims, such as freedom of thought.

But before turning to the Confucian conception of harmony and its relation to freedom of thought, it bears noting in passing that my point is not that the preference for unity of thought in traditional China, socialist China, and other East Asian nations is solely attributable to or the inevitable result of Confucian ideas about the nature of political order, the need to achieve harmony, the importance of moral exemplars and right thinking, the emphasis on rites over rights, and so forth. Other factors and rationales have also played a role, perhaps a dominant role, at different times in different places, including: the overriding concern with social stability (particularly in a country as large and diverse as China); the belief that the masses are too backward to govern themselves and hence need firm direction from the central leadership; the belief that unity of thought is a social good in itself, providing a common ground and hence psychological comfort to the members of society who feel they are a part of a group rather than alienated individuals; and, particularly with reference to unification of thought in socialist China, the war mentality of leaders such as Mao and Deng, who came of age fighting a guerrilla war, where commitment to a shared ideology spelled the difference between defeat and victory.[11]

Just as Confucianism is not the only explanation for unity of thought in China, neither is it the necessary cause of totalitarian mind control. In theory and in practice, Confucianism has been capable of tolerating some degree of freedom of thought. At the same time, in theory and in practice, Confucianism has been equally capable of supporting limitations on freedom of thought in the name of unity, stability and harmony. My claim then is that to the extent

Confucian ideals and ideas support unity of thought, the influence of Confucianism may explain in part the emphasis on unity of thought in practice in traditional China, contemporary East Asian nations and perhaps to some extent even in the PRC. Whether the emphasis on unity of thought is desirable and if so the ways in which a government may properly pursue it are additional issues about which reasonable persons may disagree, though presumably few would support the extreme, coercive measures used to obtain unity of thought in the PRC today.

The Nature of Political Order:
Politics as the Art of Achieving Harmony

The preference for unity of thought in China is in part a reflection of deeply held beliefs about the nature of political order and the role of government in achieving political order, beliefs that are at odds with contemporary liberal democratic political theory. One of the central tenets of Western liberal democracy is "the fact of pluralism."[12] The fact of pluralism is actually both an empirical and a normative claim. The empirical claim is that society is made up of individuals that have different interests and different conceptions of what constitutes "the good" for themselves and for society as a whole. The normative claim is that individuals not only disagree about what constitutes the good for themselves and society but that they reasonably disagree. In this Hobbesian-Enlightenment inspired view, society consists of diverse individuals each pursuing his or her own interests and ends, which inevitably leads to conflict. However, because people have different values, there is no common normative standard to judge which interests and ends are correct. Since people cannot agree on a substantive basis for resolving conflict, they first agree to fair procedures for choosing social ends. Democracy is one procedural response: value disputes are settled and social ends chosen by voting. The judicial system is another response. Parties take their disputes to court, where in theory impartial judges, constrained by rules of evidence, determine the facts and then on the basis of precedents and/or publicly promulgated statutes, reach a decision. Again, the emphasis is on proper procedures. Disputants are guaranteed a fair trial, though not necessarily one that will result in the victory of good over evil, truth over falsehood, justice over injustice.

In contrast, most Chinese political theorists have never accepted the inevitability of pluralism. The dominant belief has been that all interests, including the interests of the state and the individual, are reconcilable. For Confucians (and Daoists), social, even cosmic, harmony was attainable as long as moral rulers were on the throne.[13] Because the natural order and the human order were part of one organic whole, aberrations in the natural order were consid-   239 ered a reflection on the ruler, who as the Son of Heaven formed a triad with heaven and earth. Turn-of-the-century reformers abandoned the naturalist metaphysics, but they maintained the belief that the interests of the government and the people could be harmoniously reconciled.[14] As a result, authors of China's first constitution "drafted a compact for cooperation between state and people, not for conflict."[15] Later constitutions reflected a similar faith: "Chinese constitutions assumed a harmony of interests between state and citizen. They did not encourage or even recognize the possibility of conflict between the two. For them the purpose of citizen participation was to mobilize the popular energies to serve the state. What served the state's interest served the citizen's."[16]

Today, the socialist leadership continues to ground its legitimacy on its ability to unite harmoniously the interests of the people and state.[17] Like the sagely ruler of Confucian lore, the current leadership unites the interests of the people by providing correct ideological guidance and then rallying the masses around the chosen normative agenda. The government's efforts to unify thought are in part then an attempt to realize the traditional political goal of reconciling diverse interests and achieving social harmony.

As a normative concept, harmony is noteworthy in several respects. Most importantly, harmony is a contextual concept at odds with the idea of a single, objective, universal normative order. The goal is to combine the diverse elements of the many members of a particular society at a particular time into a single cohesive whole. Harmony is a reflection of the beliefs, values, and traditions, of the historical and economic conditions, of a given society at a given time. As the economic conditions change and the values and beliefs of the member of a society evolve, so does the proper social order.

The political leadership—the ruler and his ministers in Confucian theory, the CCP in contemporary China—is responsible for ensuring that government ideology and policy fits the evolving context. Accordingly, the emphasis is on flexibility rather than dogma, on practice rather than theory.[18] As a result, rulership in China has not been conceived as the science of reconciling diverse interests by appeal to universal truths or rights claims but rather as the art of persuading, cajoling and manipulating others to put aside narrow and irreconcilable self-interest in the name of achieving a richer and more comprehensive social harmony.[19] One of China's leading political theorists, the exiled democracy advocate Yan Jiaqi, provides an apt description of the art of Chinese rulership:

> My view . . . is that ruling is a special kind of art, a dynamic art that moulds society. Artistic creation is a process of making choices among limitless possibilities in the pursuit of beauty. . . . To mould an organized society and project a stable social order configuration, rulers make use of social "software," including the institutions

of government, laws, regulations, administrative acts, public opinion, legal and illegal force, and the threat of violence. . . . [R]ulers depend on the exercise of certain
powers while relying on the force of tradition to maintain relatively stable relations
among the people.[20]

Yan assumes that the disparate elements of society can be molded into a
harmonious whole. However, to achieve such harmony requires a common
value structure.[21] The role of government and particularly the ruler is to establish the basis for such a common value structure by providing ideological guidance and moral leadership. To ensure that everyone falls into line, the ruler has
at his disposal a variety of tools from persuasion (favored by Confucians) to
more violent means (favored by Legalists).

The importance attributed to the ruler in establishing order by Yan is characteristic of Chinese political theory in general and Confucianism in particular. If harmony is to be achieved and diverse interests unified, there must be a
unifying agent. Someone must set the pitch for others, as at a string ensemble
concert of classical music where the other musicians tune their instruments to
the lead violin. In Confucian theory, the ruler was the lead violin, or to use
Confucius's own metaphor, the Pole Star around which the social constellation
turned.[22] Today, the Party and in particular the core leadership is responsible
for charting the correct course and inspiring others to follow. Just as the Son
of Heaven was essential to political order for Confucians, so today the Party
is regularly portrayed as essential to the political stability of China. As Mao
put it, a revolution must have a revolutionary party, without which, we are
constantly reminded, China would descend rapidly and ineluctably into chaos
and anarchy.[23] Moreover, the party must have a core because "without a core,
no leadership can be strong enough."[24]

The ruler's authority to lead is a function of his ability to serve the interests
of the people and obtain a harmonious social order. As such, his ability to lead
is predicated on a heightened capacity to perceive patterns in the diversity, to
discern possibilities for order where others see only endless chaos. Whereas
today the CCP claims legitimacy based on special insights into the interests of
the masses and how best to achieve them, in the past Daoist and Confucian
rulers claimed the Mandate of Heaven and staked their claim to rule on their
ability to know *dao*. Conventionally translated as the Way, *dao* refers to the patterns in the world, the ways in which things are related, and the possible ways
in which they might be related. The one who "knows *dao*" is the one who perceived these patterns and relations. To know the way requires that one overcome
the limited perspective of narrow self-interest to see oneself in relation to others. The more truly cultivated one is the more relations and possible relations
one sees. The one who is able most fully to comprehend how all the diverse ele-

ments that constitute the social and natural realms are related and to bring out of the many possible relations a coherent and aesthetically pleasing sense of order is the most morally accomplished, and the one most qualified to rule.[25]

In theory, a ruler's personal and moral cultivation allows him to see things others do not. He is able to see a way (*dao*) to bring harmony out of diversity, to turn disorder into order. As a result of such special normative insights, he is able to lead others toward a morally superior social order. He is able, in Yan Jiaqi's words, to mold society through the art of rulership.

But to be successful in molding society, a ruler must persuade others to his vision. Unification of thought is an important means to rally support around the vision of the center. Unity of thought is all the more important because of the ways in which social order and rationality itself are understood. Because social order is the contingent, context-specific realization of one person's normative insights, a Confucian ruler cannot simply demand that his subjects bow to the power of universal reason. Long before the current postmodern attack on universal rationality came into vogue in the West, Confucians gave up on the hope of appealing to pure reason, to a context-independent universal rationality.[26] For the vast majority of Chinese philosophers, rationality is itself contextual. The term most similar to "rationality" in the Chinese lexicon is *li*. Originally, *li* referred to the pattern or order inherent in things, such as the veins or striations within jade. Thus, as Roger Ames points out, "Rather than entailing the discovery of reasons that reveal some pattern of linear causality as a basis for understanding, *li* suggests an awareness of those constitutive relationships which condition each thing and which, through patterns of correlation, make its world meaningful and intelligible."[27]

Li/rationality then refers to what is reasonable in light of the particular circumstances, specifically, the particular relations between the parties concerned, rather than to some ahistorical universal rational order or rights. As a consequence, one must first understand the particular background beliefs, attitudes, interests and values of the parties to understand what is reasonable. What counts as reason in one context may not in another. If a person does not share the same background beliefs, attitudes and values, then one is unlikely to be persuaded by the reasons of others.[28] Given the diversity of interests, beliefs, and values of the many members of society, multiple rational or reasonable social orders are possible. One could combine the many interests, values and beliefs in a variety of ways. The task of the leadership is to determine the most harmonious and efficacious way.[29] But if a ruler is to persuade others as to his own, context-specific, perspectival vision of the proper social order, he must first establish sufficient common ground, a common normative lexicon, as it were. Efforts to unify thought are the result, as the ruler attempts to ensure

similar beliefs and values.

Because the normative vision of the ruler and the core leadership is so central to the achievement of a harmonious social order, and because vision is at bottom personal, politics in China has been and remains personality driven. From the mythical prehistorical rulers Yao and Shun to Mao and Deng, strong cult figures have ruled. Indeed, considerable energy is invested in fostering the cultlike status of Chinese rulers. In the past, rulers were the Son of Heaven, shrouded in mystery and unfathomable. Elegantly dressed in a manner forbidden to others, rulers conducted elaborate ceremonies, inspiring awe among the masses. A complex set of rituals mediated between the ruler and his subjects, ensuring deference.

The socialists have employed more modern methods to foster support for their rulers. Movies dramatize the Long March and Mao's early years as a revolutionary leader; bookstores contain Mao's political writings, poetry, and hagiographic accounts of his life; the leading national paper displays his calligraphy; pictures of Mao swimming the Yangtze verify his virility; study sessions devoted to his writings and speeches reinforce the message that Mao is a great man.

More recently, the collected works of Deng were announced with great fanfare; work units have been instructed to organize study sessions to explore the intricacies of "Deng thought"; ninety-foot statues have been produced in his honor; and the classic moral primer the *Sanzijing* (*Santzu-ching*) has even been rewritten to focus on the feats of Deng Xiaoping.[30]

Even more recently, now that Jiang Zemin has emerged as the core of the third generation leadership, the seeds of a Jiang cult are being sown. A recent poster, showing Jiang gazing respectfully upward at Deng, makes clear that Jiang is indeed the anointed one. The poster was based on a painting titled "Glad and at Ease," a not so subtle reference to Mao's statement to his handpicked successor Hua Guofeng: "With you in charge my heart is at ease."[31] To further beef up Jiang's credentials as the right person to lead China's reform movement in the next century, the press trumpeted a preface on investment allegedly written by Jiang.[32] The press has also dutifully reported Jiang's efforts to provide leadership on the cultural and ethical front by publicizing his hodgepodge platform to develop socialist ethics, consisting of attacks on wholesale Westernization and bourgeois liberalism, celebration of the importance of national culture and art, praise for the indigenous and illustrious tradition of Confucianism, and exhortation of the masses to emulate such modern day Lei Fengs as Kong Fansun.

Because the ruler plays such a central role in defining social order, he is held personally accountable for the state of society.[33] He is judged by how well he achieves harmony or at a minimum stability. Social chaos is a challenge to his moral authority to rule. Traditionally, a ruler who failed to secure   243 social order was said to have lost the Mandate of Heaven (*tian ming/tien-ming*). Today, the leader of the previous order is purged, sent into disgrace along with his supporters.

The personal nature of rulership provides an added incentive for unification of thought. Political change implies the rejection of a given ruler's personal vision of how society ought to be constituted and his ability to realize that vision. Because of the exalted status of the ruler, greater blame attaches to the ruler personally than in the West, where power is distributed among different branches of government. Perhaps more importantly, apart from the personal embarrassment, the rejected leader will experience a dramatic reversal in his personal fortunes. In the past, the price for losing the Mandate of Heaven was often one's life. Today, the price is loss of perks and house arrest, a fate experienced most recently by Zhao Ziyang. Sacrificed at the altar of Tiananmen and pushed off the political stage, Zhao remains to this day a shadowy figure in Chinese politics, his movements closely watched and his efforts to return to power blocked.[34]

In sum, the traditional view of politics as the art of achieving social harmony contributes to the importance of unification of thought in China. Harmony entails the uniting of diverse interests into a cohesive whole. To achieve social harmony, there must be common values, a common social, political, and ethical ground. Traditionally the ruler and his ministers, nowadays the core leadership of the Party, is charged with the task of engendering the common ground. Unification of thought is one means to achieve that end. The leadership attempts to inspire society to rally around its particular normative vision. It claims the right to impose this vision on others by virtue of special normative insight as to how to unite the diverse interests of the many members of society and reconcile the interests of the people and the state. Ideally, a harmonious social order will allow for individual self-realization. Individuals will be able to maintain a degree of autonomy and uniqueness. The goal is not oneness in the sense of identity of the parts.[35] Rather than all voices singing the same note, each distinct voice sings a different note that taken collectively comprise a chord. However, everyone must still sing from the same songbook. When the voices stray too far from the melody, threatening to degenerate into cacophony, the conductor must exert his will. Preferably, the conductor will be able to gently nudge the straying voices back into line. But if persuasion fails, more coercive means may be and have been employed.

Right Thinking and the Right to Think

Autonomous moral choice claims a lofty position in the hierarchy of Western liberal values. Because the ability to make moral choices distinguishes us from beasts and because we as individuals are defined by the choices we make, moral choice is considered constitutive of personhood. Thus, for a government to deny one the right to make choices, to deprive one of autonomy and moral agency, is to deprive one of one's humanity and one's right to be oneself. Conversely, respect for the moral capacity of every individual supports the egalitarianism of democratic liberalism, wherein the legitimate authority of the state is dependent on the consent of individual members of society. Individuals are presumed to know what they want and to be capable of making moral choices that reflect their sense of the good. The state is neutral with respect to the good. Citizens, through democratic elections, determine the goals for society. As a precondition of autonomous moral agency, freedom of choice is therefore both a public good, necessary for democracy, and a private good, necessary for self-realization and full-fledged personhood.

The absence of this psychology of moral choice, that is of the normative *theory* of choice as morally significant in and of itself, has been much discussed by Western commentators on Chinese philosophy.[36] Neither Confucians nor any other school of Chinese thought located the essence of humanity and morality in individual autonomous choice. Doing what was right has been considered more important than the capacity to choose. In this sense, most Chinese ethical thinking, Confucianism included, is decidedly elitist. What is right has been determined by moral elites—the Confucian sage, ruler and ministers, today the CCP. The moral elite have then attempted to realize their ethical vision through persuasion (moral exhortation and setting a good example, as with Confucians), or through coercion (punishments and rewards, as with the Legalists), or both (as with the CCP). The people have been expected to follow.

In their efforts to realize their vision of a harmonious society, rulers have relied on unification of thought and the pursuit of an official ideology as one means to establish common ground among the people. Yet the ruler's efforts to engender common ground and achieve harmony by unifying thought will be in vain unless people are willing to put aside narrow self-interest. Hence considerable attention has been paid to moral education in the hopes of instilling the proper other-regarding values in the many members of society. The basic Confucian position is that one must learn to be moral, to be human/humane, *ren/ren* (*jen/jen*), a human being who acts humanely in interpersonal relations.[37] Proper social order, a humane society, depends on proper interpersonal relations, on humans who are humane.

On this model, both morality and social order are the result of a process of enculturation. All humans are assumed to have the capacity to become full-fledged moral beings, humane persons.[38] But one must be trained, educated. One needs proper instruction and the proper environment. By following the example of one's moral superiors, one will steadily make progress. On the other hand, if one is left unattended, one will stray from the moral way (*dao*).[39] Again, the elites must take a leading role in providing moral norms and instruction. To achieve the good society, the ruler and his coterie of ministers or cadres must ensure that everyone knows what the good society is. This explains in part the emphasis on the rites (*li*) and the many paternalistic attempts by the government to provide moral education in the past, the importance attributed to moral exemplars by Confucians and socialists alike, and to some extent at least the endless propaganda campaigns today aimed at developing socialist ethics.

One aspect of the unity of thought program that strikes most Westerners as quixotic is the excessive attention paid to language and the correct formulation of government policy. When a minister asked Confucius what his first priority would be upon assuming control of a state, Confucius cryptically replied "rectification of names."[40] Similarly, Mao once proclaimed that "one single [correct] formulation and the whole nation will flourish; one single [incorrect] formulation and the whole nation will decline. What is referred to here is the transformation of the spiritual to material."[41]

The insights of Chad Hansen may shed some light on the rather bizarre importance attributed to language. Hansen has argued that most Chinese thinkers not only lack the Kantian moral psychology of choice but share a pragmatic theory of language rather than a realist or semantic theory of language. That is, on the whole Chinese philosophy of language emphasizes the performative aspect of language. The key concern is not with semantic truth, with the relation between language and objective reality and whether sentences match or correspond to reality. Rather the emphasis is on language as a conventional, social practice and on the role of language in influencing behavior and thereby creating and shaping reality. Accordingly, Chinese political and ethical thinking has focused on the appropriateness of social practices and the prescriptive role of language in establishing the proper social practices and ultimately sociopolitical order.

> [L]anguage is a social practice. Its basic function is guiding action. The smallest units of guiding discourse are *ming* [names]. We string *ming* together in progressively larger units. The salient compositional structure is a *dao* [guiding discourse]. The Chinese counterpart of interpretation is not an account of truth conditions. Rather, to *interpret* a *dao* is to *perform* it. The interpretation of a *dao* starts from interpretation of the *ming* that compose it. In learning a conventional name, you learn the socially shared way of making discriminations in guiding your action according to *dao*.[42]

The role of the political leader is to choose the correct set of names, the correct normative social guidance program (*dao*), and to model it for and disseminate it to others. The idea is that by rectifying names and modeling correct understanding of the names, one can train the members of society to follow the correct political and moral way. Doing what is right—complying with the prescribed behavior—is the goal, not moral choice. The model of mind is behavioristic: the prescriptive *dao*/correct line conditions one's experiences and responses. One divides the world a certain way, and when one confronts a particular situation, one responds accordingly based on the programmed *dao*/correct line.

Whatever the explanation for the importance attributed to language, the low value ascribed to autonomous moral choice by Confucians and socialists alike has meant that legitimacy in China has not been based on popular sovereignty derived from the consent of the people. Rather, governments have claimed legitimacy based on their ability to serve the (welfare) interests of the people—or what the rulers determine the people's interest to be. As a result, there has been no need for democratic elections. Even today, in the so-called democratic dictatorship of the people, the PRC leadership bases its claims to legitimacy on its ability to serve the interest of the people rather than on democratic elections.[43]

Confucianism and Rights: Why Rites Are Not Rights

Freedom of thought is a fundamental right in most countries, although not in the PRC.[44] While the PRC does not accept freedom of thought as a right, it does recognize other rights. Indeed, despite the controversy surrounding the topic of rights, rights remain widely accepted and central to contemporary political theory and life. Few in China would pledge allegiance to a theory or state that denies any legitimacy whatsoever to rights. Thus contemporary advocates of Confucianism must respond to the challenge of rights, and in particular to the charges that Confucianism not only failed to develop a theory of rights but that it is in some fundamental sense incompatible with rights.

One response has been to argue that Confucianism in fact did embrace rights, or at least the functional equivalents thereof. Advocates of this position scour the Confucian corpus from Confucius in the Warring States to turn-of-the-century Confucian reformers, selecting from the many thinkers associated with Confucianism over the course of this 2,000-year period certain ideas, concepts, or practices that resonate with certain features of contemporary rights theory and practice. Various claims are then made on the basis of these similarities, including that: (1) certain rights were part of Confucian theory, (2) certain rights were part of Confucian practice and life in Confucian China even if not part of Confucian theory, (3) even if there were no rights per se, there were functional equivalents, such as the *li* (rites), that served the same or similar functions as rights, and thus (a) Confucianism is compatible with rights and contains the basis or the seeds of an indigenous theory of rights, or (b) Confucianism is compatible with and can incorporate a theory of rights, even if that theory cannot be considered indigenous.

This approach is not without problems. One difficulty is that the notion of a "right" has grown over time to include a variety of conflicting elements. In addition to the traditional Enlightenment civil and political rights of the individual, there are now second generation rights (economic and welfare rights) and third generation rights (group and collective rights and the rights of developing nations). Thus, in claiming that Confucianism embraced certain rights or similar notions, one must take care to stipulate which rights one means. The presence of second generation type welfare concerns arguably implicit in such notions as the people as the basis (*minben*) and Heaven's Mandate (*tianming*)— whereby the ruler who failed to serve the interests of the people lost the Mandate of Heaven and the right to rule—need not and in fact did not entail first generation civil and political liberties, such as freedom of thought.

More fundamentally, ideas that when examined out of context may bear some similarity to some type of right may upon closer examination turn out to have served quite different ends within the Confucian context. For instance, some scholars have drawn a comparison between Confucian rites (*li*) and rights. But while rites and rights may be similar in some respects, upon closer examination they differ in significant ways and are intended to serve different functions.

The rites (*li*) are the culture-specific norms, the ever-changing values and mores of a particular society that give shape to the normative space in which we live by defining the rules and guidelines for interpersonal relations and providing the ethical foundations for social institutions. They are the moral fabric of society, and as such belong primarily to the domain of ethics and morality, not law. Indeed, one of the primary goals of the rites was to avoid the need to rely on law to achieve social order. As Confucius himself stated: "Lead them with edicts, keep them in line with punishments, and the common people will stay out of trouble but have no sense of shame. Lead them by virtue, keep them in line with the rites (*li*), and they will not only have a sense of shame but order themselves."[45] Confucius feared that a society governed by law would be a litigious one, with individuals spending considerable time and resources on figuring out the laws and how to manipulate them. Modern day Confucians claim not only that the litigiousness of Western states confirms Confucius's worst fears, but that the emphasis on law and individual rights rather than social values and mores has lead to excessive individualism and a breakdown in the sense of community. The rites, they suggest, are needed to restore the sense of community and provide for social solidarity.[46]

To the extent that the Confucian rites (*li*) embody social values and reflect a shared sense of the past, they may be useful in restoring a sense of community. Yet while the rites may be useful in some respects, they are not the same as rights and do not serve the same function as rights.

One of the defining features of rights for most people is that they are legally enforceable. Indeed, one of the criticisms aimed at the PRC is that the long laundry list of rights included in the constitution (from which freedom of thought is conspicuously absent) are not legally enforceable but merely programmatic, a wish list of hortatory ideals to be realized at some future date.[47]

Whereas rights are legally enforceable claims, rites are not. As the communally owned repository of shared meaning and value on which people can draw in times of conflict, rites, like rights, have a role to play in dispute resolution. Individuals may appeal to the rites to justify their position and their claim. Yet rites-based claims are moral claims, not legal claims. To be sure, the rites and the values embedded in the rites may and did influence the legal system in China, through the so-called Confucianization of the law. The rites have also been central to dispute resolution in a variety of extra-judicial forums, from the informal settings of family and neighborhoods to the somewhat more formal setting of guild associations. Nevertheless, the rites themselves were not legally enforceable rights, claims or entitlements.

The most important difference between rights and rites, however, is that the primary function of rights as originally conceived is to protect individuals and minorities against the majority, be it the community or the state. As James Madison so passionately and persuasively declared in supporting the U.S. Bill of Rights:

> The great object in view is to limit and qualify the powers of Government, by excepting out of the grant of power those cases in which the Government ought not to act, or to act only in a particular mode. They point these exceptions sometimes against the abuse of the Executive power, sometimes against the Legislative, and, in some cases, *against the community itself; or, in other words, against the majority in favor of the minority.*
>
> . . . [T]he great danger lies . . . in the abuse of the community. . . . The prescriptions in favor of liberty ought to be levelled against that quarter where the danger lies, namely, that which possesses the highest prerogative of power. But this is not found in either the Executive or Legislative departments of Government, but in the body of the people, operating by the majority against the minority.[48]

In a pluralistic, heterogeneous society, people will have different interests. As a result, conflict is inevitable. Rights are necessary to protect the individual and minority against the majority. Significantly, the anti-majoritarian function of rights has been endorsed by the U.S. Supreme Court, thus ensuring that at least some rights are taken seriously in practice:

> The very purpose of a Bill of Rights was to withdraw certain subjects from the vicissitudes of political controversy, to place them beyond the reach of majorities and officials and to establish legal principles to be applied by the courts. One's right to life, liberty, and property, to free speech, a free press, freedom of worship and assembly, and other fundamental rights may not be submitted to vote: they depend on the outcome of no elections.[49]

Rites simply do not serve the same anti-majoritarian role as rights. They were never intended to protect the individual and minorities against the majority, the community, the state. On the contrary. Confucius set his ethical sights on the lofty vision of a harmonious society. He and his followers assume that the interests of the individual can be reconciled with the interests of the majority and the state. The *li* are intended to provide the necessary common ground and shared values to make such a harmonious society possible. The task of the rulers has been to inspire in people the desire to achieve a humane society and to direct their energies toward the attainment of a harmonious social order in which the interests of the individual and of the community or state are reconciled. In such a society, rights are not needed. Indeed, focusing on rights and the conflict of the individual and the majority detracts from the task of inculcating the social values implicit in the rites that make possible a harmonious society in which individuals realize themselves in and through the community.

Unfortunately, we do not live in or *even believe in* the Confucian utopia where the interests of the individual and the community coincide. In the pluralistic society of today, the interests of the individual and the community and state collide as often as they coincide. When they do, rights prevent the community or state from running roughshod over the individual. In focusing on the ideal of harmony rather than the reality of conflict, Confucius failed to provide a basic minimum level of protection to individuals and minorities.

In both theory and practice Confucian rites were undeniably hierarchical. They served the interests of the elite and those in power, be it the ruler in the public sphere or men in the private sphere. In an ideal world, the privileged would deserve their privilege by virtue of moral self-cultivation. Those in the inferior position would defer to the moral excellence of their superiors, and in return the superiors would look after and serve the interests of those in the subordinate position. In the real world, the privileged have not always been so morally cultivated.

Rights, on the other hand, while they provide a minimum floor for society, are arguably incapable of generating a thick sense of community and deep bonds of social solidarity. Accordingly, both rights and rites are needed. In most instances, rites can complement rights, providing a moral dimension to interpersonal actions, suggesting additional possibilities above and beyond the legal relations defined by rights. In some instances, rites may even temper the harshness of rights by encouraging individuals to be judicious in their claims and to be considerate of others. After *Cohen*, we in the United States all have the right to use offensive language in public, but we may choose not to do so.[50] The rites may help remind us of our moral obligations, our duties, to others.[51] At the same time, while rites often complement rights, there is a tension between them, and when they conflict, rites must give way. If communal pressure in the form of rites is able to trump rights, then the right is a hollow one.[52]

The Confucian emphasis on rites rather than rights threatens freedom of thought. Rites alone did not and cannot guarantee freedom of thought. Rites support a hierarchy in which moral elites determine what is right and the people defer (or are forced to defer) to the judgment of the elites. To the extent that rites represent the moral consensus of the community, they exert pressure to conform one's thinking to others. The very purpose of the rites—to provide sufficient common ground to achieve harmony—is better served by unity rather than freedom of thought.

Perhaps most importantly, the emphasis on rites as a means to achieve social solidarity has contributed to the enduring appeal of the utopian myth of harmony, thereby blinding rulers and reformers alike to the realities of disharmony, and retarding the development of a strong theory of rights intended to protect the individual against the majority, community and state. To this day the anti-majoritarian function of rights remains all but ignored by Chinese rights advocates.

Rights in China have been and continue to be conceived of as interests.[53] In contrast, most Western rights advocates draw a distinction between rights and interests, arguing that rights are deontological in character whereas interests are consequentialist or utilitarian.[54] That is, rights are based not on utility or social consequences but on moral principles whose justification is derived independently of the good. Rights trump interest in the sense that rights impose limits on the interests of others, the good of society, and the will of the majority. The basic intuition supporting the distinction is that there are some things no person, no government, no society can justly impose on an individual, regardless of how much social good would be produced.

The difference in conception of rights has important practical consequences. Translating rights into the language of interests generally produces outcomes favoring state action and impinging upon individual protections. When one weighs the interest of a single individual against the interest of   251 many individuals, the community, the state, the many usually win.[55] The inclination to prefer the interests of the state or society over those of the individual is reinforced in China by a culture that has traditionally subordinated the interests of the individual to those of the group. By emphasizing the possibility of harmony and reconciliation of the interests of the individual and the group, Confucianism made the conception and acceptance of an anti-majoritarian theory of rights less likely.

Freedom of Thought in a Post-Socialist China with Confucian Characteristics

Confucianism is being hailed by Jiang Zemin and the New Conservatives as a cure to the political and moral crisis in China and by Western academics as a corrective to the excesses of Western liberal democracies. But we must resist the tendency to glamorize Confucianism, particularly by those disgruntled with late twentieth-century capitalism and liberal democracy. We need, as Deng says, to seek truth from facts. The fact of the matter is that Confucianism was elitist. The *li* were hierarchical and inegalitarian. There was no theory of anti-majoritarian rights to protect individuals or certain disempowered groups, including women, gays, and other minorities. Nor did Confucianism legally guarantee popular sovereignty, democratic elections, or such basic civil and political liberties as freedom of thought and speech.

Of course Confucianism can change and evolve in response to contemporary circumstances. Modern day Confucians may attempt to recast Confucianism to allow for greater equality for women and more protection for minorities. One may try to make Confucianism more egalitarian, less elitist, perhaps even allowing that the masses know better what is in their interest than aging paternalistic leaders sequestered in Zhongnanhai, and recognizing accordingly the legitimacy of popular sovereignty and the need to hold democratic elections. One may even attempt to incorporate a theory of anti-majoritarian rights that gives precedence to first generation civil and political rights over second and third generation rights. But at what point does Confucianism cease to be Confucianism?

There seems little point in remaking Confucius in the image of Locke, Rawls, or Dworkin. Confucianism is not liberal democracy. Moreover, advocates of "Asian values" are happy that it is not. If we are to take Confucianism seriously, we must respect the ways in which Confucianism differs from liberal democracy. In the process of adapting Confucianism to fit contemporary realities, we must take care not to throw the baby out with the bath water. We must make sure we conserve the essential and valuable aspects of Confucianism, recognizing of course that reasonable people may disagree about what is essential and valuable, and also recognizing that each choice comes with certain costs, and that there is no perfect political system.

One can get a sense of what a post-socialist Confucian China might be like by reflecting on the experiences and realities of other Asian countries, particularly Taiwan and Singapore, even allowing that these countries differ in significant ways from China. While a post-socialist China will most likely eventually become democratic, there could very well be an authoritarian transition period combining free-market or at least reformist economic policies with tight controls over social and political matters. Indeed, it is somewhat worrisome that Confucianism is being so highly touted by today's socialist leadership. Not only has the CCP criticized Confucianism in the past, it has repeatedly deprived and continues to deprive countless individuals of their most basic human rights, including the right to think freely. By emphasizing the more conservative, authoritarian aspects of Confucianism, the CCP may discredit Confucianism as a viable alternative in the eyes of the populace and thwart the development of a contemporary version of Confucianism able to respond to today's challenges.

Assuming Confucianism is able to escape guilt by association with the CCP, it must face up to the issue of individual rights. While rights will most likely be part of a post-socialist Confucian China, they will differ in theory and practice from rights in Western liberal democracies. The extreme deontological position that an individual possesses an inviolability that even the good of society as a whole cannot override is out of step with the Confucian emphasis on harmony and stability.[56] Rights will most probably continue to be understood as a kind of interest rather than as trumps over interests, and thus less likely to serve to the same degree the anti-majoritarian function of rights in Western liberal democracies. In practice, even a revamped and updated Confucianism will tend to support and uphold restrictions on political and civil liberties, limit or deny rights in the name of rites, and suppress or at least curtail freedom of thought and speech in the name of community solidarity, social harmony and stability.

Of course a post-socialist Confucian China need not and presumably would not be nearly as politically restrictive or repressive as the PRC. The PRC is notable for the range of thought restricted, the pervasiveness of the efforts to unify thought, and the degree of coercion used to achieve such unification. In contrast, countries such as Singapore and Taiwan, while more restrictive of thought and speech perhaps than the United States or other Western liberal democracies, are nevertheless by and large tolerant and open societies. In the end, every society must determine for itself the proper relation between individual rights and the interests of society. If the citizens of a post-socialist China prefer Asian or Confucian values to liberal democratic values, so be it. 253

Notes

I would like to thank Wm. Theodore de Bary, R. Randle Edwards, and Louis Henkin for their kind invitation to attend the Confucianism and Human Rights Conference held in Honolulu, Hawaii in August 1995. In preparing this article, which is based on a paper presented at the conference—"Voices in Muted Harmony: Unification of Thought in China" (hereafter "Voices in Muted Harmony")—I owe a debt of gratitude to all of the attendees at the conference for their thought-provoking papers and stimulating comments.

1. Deng Xiaoping, *Selected Works of Deng Xiaoping* (Beijing: Foreign Language Press, 1992), vol. 1, p. 286; hereafter, *Selected Works.*

2. *West Virginia State Board of Education v. Barnette,* 319 US 624 (1943).

3. Freedom of thought is often linked with speech as a fundamental first amendment right. Speaking of "the freedom of thought, and speech," Justice Cardozo stated, "Of that freedom one may say that it is the matrix, the indispensable condition, of nearly every other form of [freedom]." *Palko v. Connecticut,* 302 US 319 (1937).

4. Even where there is mention of freedom of thought and speech, it is freedom within limits. From time to time the government, confronting a listless population and intractable socioeconomic problems, will loosen the reins on freedom of thought in an attempt to stimulate creative solutions. However, such freedom is temporary, subject to government whim (as those who dared speak out in response to Mao's call for criticism in the '50s, and were then persecuted as rightists, found out), and limited in scope (for instance, Deng's calls for freedom of speech and to let the proverbial hundred flowers bloom did not extend to criticism of the four cardinal principles). See, e.g., Deng, *Selected Works,* vol. 2, p. 238; vol. 3, p. 57.

5. I discuss in more detail the importance of the rhetoric of unity of thought in socialist theory and practice and the means to achieve thought unification in "Voices in Muted Harmony." For personalized accounts of the effect of thought unification policies on the every day lives of individuals, see Jung Chang, *Wild Swans* (London: Harper Collins, 1993); Nien Cheng, *Life and Death in Shanghai* (New York: Penguin, 1986); for a psychological account, see Robert J. Lifton, *Thought Reform and the Psychology of Totalism: A Study of Brainwashing in China* (New York: Norton, 1961).

6. Presocialist Chinese leaders sought to achieve unity of thought in a variety of ways, including censorship (from the infamous burning of the books by Qinshihuangdi to prohibitions on unauthorized publication of certain kinds of works to prepublication requirements), promulgation of official "histories" by each new dynasty, moral indoctrination (sponsoring of community lectures and dissemination of moral primers), and perhaps most importantly the imperial examination system, which indoctrinated the elite in Confucian values, including the duty to obey the ruler. See William Alford, *To Steal a Book Is an Elegant Offense* (Stanford: Stanford University Press,

1995); Ku Chieh-gang, "A Study of the Literary Persecution During the Ming Dynasty" (trans. L. Carrington Goodrich), 3 *Harvard Journal of Asiatic Studies* 254 (1938); L. Carrington Goodrich, *The Literary Inquisition of Ch'ien-lung* (1935; rev. ed. New York: Paragon, 1966).

7. Willy Wo-lap Lam, "Jiang's Crusade," *South China Morning Post* ("SCMP"), May 3, 1995, p. 19 (revival of Confucianism by Jiang in attempt to develop socialist spiritual civilization).

8. "Curb Moral Decline," *China Daily*, May 22, 1995, p. 4 (claiming that blind imitation of the West will result in loss of social order and praising Confucian values such as harmony, cordialness, the golden mean where one does not treat others as one would not want to be treated, and limitations on individualism and the blind pursuit of profits).

9. That liberal democracy may benefit from Confucianism was a recurrent theme at the Confucianism and Human Rights Conference. Henry Rosemont was the primary spokesperson for the more extreme position that Confucianism may represent a viable alternative to rights-centered liberal democracy. See his "Why Take Rights Seriously? A Confucian Critique," in Leroy Rouner, ed., *Human Rights and the World's Religions* (South Bend: University of Notre Dame, 1988), pp. 167–82; *A Chinese Mirror: Moral Reflections on Political Economy and Society* (La Salle: Open Court, 1991). See also Tu Wei-ming, Milan Hejtmanek, and Alan Wachman, eds., *The Confucian World Observed: A Contemporary Discussion of Confucian Humanism in East Asia* (Honolulu: East-West Center, 1992).

10. I have begun to sketch out such a theory in "What's Wrong with Chinese Rights? Toward a Theory of Rights with Chinese Characteristics," 6 *Harvard Human Rights Journal* 29 (1993). Two points bear noting. First, I offer merely a sketch of a theory. Many points need to be worked out. For instance, the extent to which Confucianism is compatible with a strong deontic theory of right is debatable, as is how the situational-ethics, relational character of Confucianism will be manifest in actual practice, and whether Confucianism can draw a normatively attractive balance between first generation rights (civil and political) and second (economic and welfare rights) and third generation rights (collective rights and development rights of less-developed countries). Second, the theory presented is merely *a* theory. The long history of Confucianism and the many different thinkers and theories that fall under the Confucian umbrella will no doubt give rise to a whole range of Confucian-based rights theories, as scholars pick and choose from the corpus ideas and practices that support their particular vision of a good society. That said, at some point, one must ask the question: when does Confucianism cease being Confucianism? If the term is infinitely elastic, capable of generating Rawlsian theory of liberal democracy or a Dworkinian theory of rights, then it loses its explanatory power and becomes simply an appeal to ancient sagely authority as a justification for one's own contemporary beliefs. Thus, just as one task facing the contemporary Confucian is to develop a Confucian theory of rights, another is to identify certain core features of Confucianism that make Confucianism Confucianism, even if such features are to be understood along the lines of Wittgensteinian family resemblances rather than essences.

11. For a more thorough discussion of these alternative explanations, see "Voices in Muted Harmony."

12. See, e.g., John Rawls, "The Idea of the Overlapping Consensus," 7 *Oxford Journal of Legal Studies* 1 (1987).

13. Confucius, *Analects* 15:5.

14. Andrew Nathan, *Chinese Democracy* (Berkeley: University of California Press, 1985), p. ix.

15. Andrew Nathan, "Political Rights in Chinese Constitutions," in R. Randle Edwards, Louis Henkin, and Andrew Nathan, *Human Rights in Contemporary China* (New York: Columbia University Press, 1986), p. 86.

16. Ibid., p. 23.

17. For example: "In the final analysis, under the socialist system there is unity of personal interests and collective interests, of the interests of the part and the whole, and of the immediate and long-term interests. We must adjust the relations between these various types of interests in accordance with the principle of taking them all into proper consideration." Deng, *Selected Works*, vol. 2, p. 183.

18. Roger Ames and David Hall, developing insights of Herbert Fingarette, are largely responsible for reversing the appraisal of Confucius as inherently conservative, a mere apologist for Zhou culture awash in nostalgia for the good old days that in reality were never so good. While some scholars have taken issue with the degree of flexibility and openness ascribed to Confucius by Hall and Ames, Hall and Ames's general point that philosophically Confucius evinces a pragmatic concern for situational-ethics and a distaste for universal principles and absolutist moral claims seems (to me at least) to be correct as both a textual matter and as a matter of intellectual history. After all, one of the chief complaints of the Legalists was that Confucianism afforded too much discretion to those in power and that publicly promulgated laws and a rigidly enforced system of clearly articulated rewards and punishments were necessary to rein in such discretion. See Hall and Ames, *Thinking Through Confucius* (Albany: SUNY Press, 1989). The emphasis on practice in socialist theory is evident from Mao's stubborn insistence that the truth of Marxism must be integrated with the characteristics of the nation and given a definite national form before it can be useful; it must not be applied subjectively as a mere formula. Mao Tse-tung, *Selected Works* (Beijing: Foreign Language Press, 1965), vol. 3, pp. 153–55. Less philosophical, Deng has captured the same idea in his pragmatic assertion that what matters is not the color of the cat but whether it catches mice.

19. I discuss the inspirational aspects of Confucianism at greater length in "Confucian Justice: Achieving a Humane Society," 30 *International Philosophical Quarterly* 17–32 (1990). See also A. S. Cua, *Ethical Argumentation: A Study of Hsun Tzu's Moral Epistemology* (Honolulu: University of Hawaii Press, 1985), p. 124 (drawing a distinction between aspirational ideal norms and the inspirational ideal themes of Confucianism).

20. Yan Jiaqi, *Toward a Democratic China* (Honolulu: University of Hawaii Press,

1992), pp. 98–99

21. Ibid., p. 70.

22. Confucius, *Analects* 2:1.

23. Mao, *Selected Works*, vol. 4, p. 284; see also vol. 3, p. 118; Deng, *Selected Works*, vol. 2, pp. 178, 252, 339; vol. 3, p. 196.

24. Deng, *Selected Works*, vol. 3, p. 300. Mao, of course, was the core of the first generation leadership, Deng of the second, and now Jiang Zemin of the third.

25. This image of the moral influence of the ruler growing and spreading out in increasingly larger concentric circles or waves as the ruler grows as a moral being is most succinctly stated in the *Daxue* (Great Learning).

26. In the classical period, the Mohists tinkered with the idea of a universal logic and ethical code. The school died out shortly thereafter, in part, one suspects, because it is so thoroughly at odds with the notion of context-sensitivity central to Confucianism, Daoism, and the Yijing.

27. Roger Ames, "Chinese Rationality: An Oxymoron?," 9 *Journal of Indian Council of Philosophical Research* 104–5 (1992).

28. One of the problems with U.S. rights policy toward China is that it tends to rely on the rhetoric of universal rights. Time and again China answers with a situational-ethics critique calling for a more contextualized approach to human rights that respects the differences in the historical, political, and cultural traditions and economic conditions of China and the West. Consider China's official statement on human rights:

> "China is in favor of strengthening international cooperation in the realm of human rights on the basis of mutual understanding and seeking a common ground while reserving differences. However, no country in its effort to realize and protect human rights can take a route that is divorced from its history and its economic, political and cultural realities. . . . It is also noted in the resolutions of the 46th conference on human rights that no single mode of development is applicable to all cultures and peoples. It is neither proper nor feasible for any country to judge other countries by the yardstick of its own mode or to impose its own mode on others. . . . Consideration should be given to the differing views of human rights held by countries with different political, economic and social systems, as well as different historical, religious and cultural backgrounds. International human rights activities should be carried on in the spirit of seeking common ground while reserving differences, mutual respect, and the promotion of understanding and cooperation."

"Human Rights in China," *Beijing Review* 34, November 4–10, 1991, p. 8.

29. See, e.g., Deng, *Selected Works*, vol. 2, p. 183 (noting that role of government is to take into consideration diverse interests of the individual members of society as well as interests of the collective and unite them).

30. See, e.g., "Programme Drafted for Study of Deng Theory," *China Daily*, May 26,

1995, p. 1; Daniel Kwan, "Campaign Lifts Profile of Party," SCMP, June 30, 1995; "Deng Sharpens Moral Edge," SCMP, March 30, 1995, p. 9.

31. "Bid to Boost Chosen Heir," SCMP, March 23, 1995, p. 10.

32. "Jiang Writes Preface on Investment," China Daily, May 22, 1995, p. 1.

33. Wm. Theodore de Bary has noted that Chinese political theory historically did not place the blame for social and political disorder on the people. Rather, the rulers were supposed to look out for the interests of the people. If something went wrong, the ruler was to blame: "the entire burden falls on the self-cultivation and self-transformation of the noble man"; de Bary, The Trouble with Confucianism (Cambridge: Harvard University Press, 1991), p. 22. There is in China no tradition of the people assuming political responsibility for their own fate in the sense that they should be involved in important daily decisions of governing; de Bary, ibid., pp. 21–23.

34. See, e.g., Dede Nickerson, "Disgraced Zhao Attends Funeral," SCMP, July 8, 1995 at 10.

35. Confucius, Analects, 13:23; see also Hall and Ames, Thinking Through Confucius, pp. 165–67.

36. Herbert Fingarette, Confucius: The Secular is Sacred (New York: Harper and Row, 1972) (arguing against the tendency to cast ren in the subjective psychological vocabulary of choice and will); Henry Rosemont, "Against Relativism," in Interpreting Across Boundaries (1988) (noting absence of vocabulary of moral choice in classical Confucianism); Hall and Ames, Thinking Through Confucius, pp. 265–66 (arguing that while there are ethical choices, they are "aesthetic" choices made in light of the particular circumstances and contrasting such choices with the nature and role of choice in Kantian ethical theory, which takes ethical choice to be rational and universalizable); Chad Hansen, A Daoist Theory of Thought (Cambridge: Oxford University Press, 1992) (absence of theory of choice as essence of morality in classical Chinese philosophy).

37. The classic definition of the virtue of moral excellence (ren) is human person (ren zhe ren ye). That is, excellence in interpersonal relations is to be a person. See Zhong Yong (Doctrine of the Mean); Mencius, 7b16.

38. See, e.g., Analects 17:2.

39. See, e.g., Xun Zi, ch. 1, "On Learning" (individuals need moral guidance, emphasis on following example of moral exemplars, habituation and training); Analects 12:17, 13:1 (importance of leaders setting moral examples); Mencius 6a8, 7a40, 7b21 (importance of environment, ethical guidance and habituation).

40. Confucius, Analects 13:3.

41. Cited in Michael Schoenhals, Doing Things with Words (Berkeley, Institute of East Asian Studies, 1992), p. 3.

42. Chad Hansen, A Daoist Theory of Chinese Thought, pp. 3–4.

43. Nathan, Democracy in China, p. 228.

44. Freedom of thought is also protected in major international rights documents.

Article 18 of the Universal Declaration of Human Rights provides: "Everyone has the right of freedom of thought, conscience, and religion; this right includes freedom to change religion or belief, and freedom, either alone or in community with others and in public or private, to manifest his religion or belief in teaching, practice, worship and observance." G.A. Res. 217, UN Doc. a/810, at 71 (1948). See also Article 18 of the International Covenant on Civil and Political Rights, G.A. Res. 2200A, 21 UN GAOR Supp. (No. 16) at 55, UN Doc. a/6316 1966; Article 12 of the American Convention on Human Rights, Nov. 22, 1969, O.A.S. Doc. OEA/Ser. L/V/II.65, Doc. 6 (1985); Article 9 of the European Convention for the Protection of Human Rights and Fundamental Freedoms, 213 U.N.T.S. 222.

45. *Analects* 2:3. Confucius himself contrasted rites (*li*) with punishments or penal law—*xing*. Later Confucians juxtaposed *li* with *fa*, the impartial standards or laws of the Legalists and others, such as the Huang-Lao school.

46. Western advocates of Confucianism often argue that greater emphasis on the *li* may be of particular value to Western liberal democracies. Yet the PRC may be even more lacking in common network of communal values than most Western states. For all the talk about *li*, Confucianism never succeeded in producing a civil society. In the Confucian system, ethical obligations extended outward in concentric circles: self, family, state, nation. As one moved outward, one's duties became increasingly attenuated. In practice, Confucianism has led to excessive emphasis on one's family at the expense of others in the community. Today, years of misguided movements, in particular the Culture Revolution, have left the moral fabric of society in tatters. Traditional belief systems have been destroyed, socialism discredited. To fill the moral vacuum, many have turned to getting rich, as China attempts to make the radical socioeconomic transition from a socialist economy to a market economy. The lack of ethical restraints combined with a lack of political will and resources to control the market by enacting and enforcing regulations has led to the Wild Wild East, a marketplace corrupted by bribes and overflowing with fake products, many of which are harmful to the health of the consumer and all too often have caused death.

47. See, e.g., the essays in R. Randle Edwards, Louis Henkin, and Andrew Nathan, *Human Rights in Contemporary China*.

48. James Madison, Speech before the House of Representatives, June 8, 1789 (emphasis added).

49. See *West Virginia State Board of Education v. Barnette*, 319 US 624 (1943).

50. In *Cohen v. California*, 403 US 15 (1971), the U.S. Supreme Court held that an individual's right to free speech extends to wearing a jacket with "Fuck the Draft" on it, even though others may find such language offensive.

51. Contemporary communitarians who argue that Western liberal democracies need to pay more attention to social values and the duties owed to the community by the individual rather than simply emphasize rights might find the concept of rites useful.

52. As Ronald Dworkin notes: "The existence of rights against the Government would be jeopardized if the Government were able to defeat such a right by appealing 259

to the right of a democratic majority to work its will. A right against the Government must be a right to do something even when the majority thinks it would be wrong to do it, and even when the majority would be worse off for having it done. If we now say that society has a right to do whatever is in the general benefit . . . then we have annihilated [individual] rights." Dworkin, *Taking Rights Seriously* (Cambridge: Harvard University Press, 1977), p. 194.

53. See Peerenboom, "Rights, Interests, and the Interests in Rights," 31 *Stanford Journal of International Law* 359 (1995).

54. See, e.g., J. Roland Pennock, "Rights, Natural Rights, and Human Rights—A General View," in 23 *Nomos* 1, 5 (Pennock and John Chapman, ed., 1981) ("Rights are one thing; interests are another; and when they collide rights are trumps").

55. See Clark, "Guidelines for the Free Exercise Clause," 83 *Harvard Law Review* 327, 330–31 (1969) ("The purpose of almost any law can be traced back to one or another of the fundamental concerns of government: public health and safety, public peace and order, defense, revenue. To measure an individual interest directly against one of these rarefied values inevitably makes the individual interest appear less significant"); Roscoe Pound, "A Survey of Social Interests," 57 *Harvard Law Review* 1, 2 (1943) ("When it comes to weighing and valuing claims or demands with respect to other claims or demands, we must be careful to compare them on the same plane . . . [or else] we may decide the question in advance in our very way of putting it").

56. John Rawls, *A Theory of Justice* (Cambridge: University of Harvard Press, 1971), p. 3.

14

Confucian Influence on Intellectuals in the People's Republic of China

Merle Goldman

As the Judeo-Christian tradition influences Western societies, even though most Westerners do not know exactly what it is, Confucianism continues to influence Chinese society, even though most Chinese, including intellectuals, have not read the Confucian texts. Indeed, they have accepted the May Fourth Movement's and the Chinese Communist Party's repudiation of Confucianism as part of the "feudal" past. The regimes of Deng Xiaoping and especially Jiang Zemin, however, no longer categorically reject Confucianism as the Mao regime had done. Although Confucianism is still regarded as one of the "feudal" traditions which must be rectified, Jiang and his associates single out for approval certain aspects of Confucianism that enhance their authoritarian rule, pragmatic economic approach, and increasing nationalism.

Even under Mao's revolutionary rule, elements of Confucianism continued, albeit diffusely, to influence the ideas and actions of China's intellectuals. Most of the politically engaged intellectuals of the Mao period (1949–1976) had not studied Confucianism nor did they know much about pre-Communist Chinese history. Yet, they related to the party-state and political leadership very much in the manner of their literati predecessors. And they expressed their views and concerns in a style reminiscent of their Confucian forebears. It was not so much what they said, but what they did and the values they stressed that resonated with their ancestors. Their behavior may thus have been influenced by an unconscious or preconscious use of literati precedents.

Like the literati, they believed that intellectuals had a responsibility to participate in government either as officials or as advisers to high officials. They also saw themselves as acting as the moral conscience of the government as well as of society. In the manner of their predecessors, they sought to remind the leaders of the ideals from which they had strayed. Since Confucianism ideologically, though not legally, encouraged criticism of government misdeeds, they believed it was their duty to speak out against the abuse of official power and unfair treatment of the population. Also like the literati, the intellectuals in the People's Republic, regarded themselves as the intermediaries between the rulers and the ruled, informing the leadership of the effect of their policies on society and urging reforms if the effect was deleterious and evoked resistance. Similarly like the literati, they thought of themselves as an elite, charged with guiding the people and even the leaders toward a more humane, more just society.

It is not surprising, therefore, that China's modern intellectuals emphasized freedom of the press and expression in their definition of democracy, because these freedoms made it possible for them to fulfill their responsibility as intellectuals. An American social theorist, Craig Calhoun, who took a poll of the participants in the 1989 Tiananmen Square demonstration, found that the overwhelming majority defined democracy not so much as electoral politics, which would be the case in the West, but as freedom of speech. To them, having one's views heard was more important than having a regular system of elections.[1] Their use of petitions and articles in the party press and the Democracy Wall activists' use of wall posters and unofficial journals to advise and criticize resembled the literati's use of memorials offering advice and criticism to higher officials or the emperor.

Because these "freedoms," as in traditional times, were not guaranteed by law or an independent judiciary, if the leader or official disagreed with the criticisms or the advice and felt threatened, he retaliated with varying degrees of harshness. Nevertheless, none of China's emperors, including the despotic First Emperor of the Qin dynasty (221–202 B.C.E.), who was said to have burned Confucian books and buried scholars alive, unleashed a persecution as violent and as massive as the intensifying campaigns that Mao launched against intellectuals from the mid 1950s until his death in 1976. Although the campaigns affected virtually all intellectuals, their specific targets were politically engaged intellectuals who had remonstrated with the leadership to live up to its ideals.

In the early days of the Mao regime, most intellectuals gave their unquestioning support to the government, as many of their literati predecessors had given their support to new dynasties. They sought to help the party-state that they believed would finally make China a "rich and powerful" nation once again. A number of them, especially the literary intellectuals, who had helped bring the Communist Party to power in 1949, took on the role of intermediaries. In 1954, the left-wing writer Hu Feng and his disciples presented a long report to the party leadership, very much like a memorial to the emperor, in which they pointed out that China's intellectual life was languishing because it was increasingly controlled by a group of dogmatic officials, who had distorted the leadership's "good" policies. Considering Hu's advice a challenge to his and the party's authority, Mao in 1955 launched the first nationwide campaign in which not only a small number of literary intellectuals, but scores of independent thinkers in all areas of endeavor were attacked.

After the silencing of intellectuals that ensued, Mao was still in need of their services in China's modernization, so in 1956 he sought to revive their support by promising to "let a hundred flowers bloom; a hundred schools contend," a saying of the Confucian era. Mao's Hundred Flowers policy also encouraged intellectuals to criticize officials for repressive and bureaucratic behavior, the very policy which Hu Feng had advocated and for which he had been imprisoned. In response to Mao's encouragement, many intellectuals pointed out the abuses of officials in their *danwei*, places of work. The most sensational critiques were made by two young writers, Wang Meng and Liu Binyan, both rising members of the China Youth League, who published short stories about young, idealistic intellectuals in conflict with incompetent, corrupt officials— a typical Confucian conflict. But as the intellectuals' criticisms increased and extended to higher echelons of government and even to the party itself in spring 1957, the party in June 1957 launched the anti-rightist campaign in which it is estimated that from five hundred thousand to one million intellectuals were labeled rightists and purged from their positions.

Despite the persecution of some of China's most famous intellectuals and the anti-intellectual bias of the subsequent Great Leap Forward, which sought to rely on the masses rather than on intellectuals to modernize China, the intellectuals still remained loyal to the party. In part their loyalty can be attributed to intimidation and the fear that they and their families might suffer the same fate as the rightists if they did not proclaim their allegiance to Mao and the party. Their loyalty can also be attributed to the Confucian belief that as intellectuals they had the responsibility to partake in government, advise the leaders and rectify their policies. In the early 1960s, when intellectuals were called on to help repair the economic disasters caused by the Great Leap Forward, those who had not been labeled rightists welcomed the opportunity.

A few intellectuals came to the fore at this time and behaved more explicitly in the manner of their literati ancestors than the critics in the Hundred Flowers. The most prominent were the historian and a vice mayor of Beijing, Wu Han, and the former editor of the party's premier newspaper, *People's Daily*, Deng Tuo. These two scholar-officials in their fifties may have been more consciously motivated by their Confucian predecessors than the younger writers, 263

Wang Meng and Liu Binyan, who received most of their education under party auspices. Wu Han was educated in the pre-Communist period and had immersed himself in the study of Chinese history. He took as his model the upright Confucian official, Hai Rui, who was willing to risk death for his principles. When Hai Rui remonstrated with an abusive Ming emperor, he brought with him his own coffin. Deng Tuo, though a believer in Marxism-Leninism, still wrote in the classical language and quoted from ancient texts and stories.

Both men in the aftermath of the Great Leap Forward used the allegoric, indirect language of the literati to convey their criticisms of Mao's policies. Also, like their predecessors, they used historical analogies to make criticisms of the present. As in the Hundred Flowers, Mao saw these criticisms and those of his party colleagues as efforts to undermine his authority and launched the Cultural Revolution against his intellectual and party critics. Deng Tuo committed suicide, the first intellectual to lose his life in the Cultural Revolution; Wu Han died in prison. Both acted like martyred literati before them. It is estimated that one hundred million people were persecuted in the Cultural Revolution and several million people lost their lives, a major portion of them intellectuals.

Confucian Influences in the Deng Xiaoping Era

Despite the terrible persecution they had suffered under the Mao regime, when Deng came to power in December 1978, most intellectuals once again gave their full-hearted support to the new government as the intellectuals had done in 1949 and the literati before them. They believed that finally China had a leader who would introduce the humane and just government toward whose establishment they had devoted their lives. Their support can be explained by the fact that Deng and his disciple, Hu Yaobang, had rehabilitated virtually all the intellectuals purged in the Mao period, returned them to their former or higher positions, and relaxed Mao's tight controls over intellectual life. But it also can be attributed to the Confucian expectation that they would finally be able to advise and participate in an enlightened government. As in traditional times, intellectuals were given enhanced status and held in high esteem. They were also allowed a degree of freedom in their academic and creative activities. The political scientist Tang Tsou has called these spaces "zones of indifference," similar to those that existed in traditional times, in which intellectuals could pursue their interests as long as they did not challenge the political structure or political leadership.[2]

One of the zones to which the Deng regime was indifferent was the study of Confucianism. In addition to appreciating the authoritarian and pragmatic aspects of Confucianism, this regime has also stressed the Confucian concern

for education, harmonious social relations, and stability as part of the effort to repair the damage of the Cultural Revolution. Consequently, a small number of intellectuals (but some of them quite prominent) began studying Confucian texts in a search for ways to deal with the present and to answer questions about the nature of Chinese civilization and why it had such difficulty modernizing. Institutes, study societies, and journals were established devoted to the study of Confucianism; traditional operas were performed with upright Confucian literati as the heroes. Nevertheless, for the majority of intellectuals, Confucianism remained an inchoate influence that affected what they did rather than what they thought.

Those highly placed intellectuals in the party-government, journalism, and think-tanks, who became advisers to Deng and Hu Yaobang, were primarily humanist intellectuals. Like the literati, they were well-versed in ideology, in this case Marxism-Leninism. Their main concern early in the Deng era was to revise Marxism-Leninism, so that it could become the foundation for political as well as economic reforms. Also like their literati predecessors, they sought to use ideological arguments and moral persuasion to rectify the abuses of the past and bring about an enlightened government. Even though the ex-Red Guard activists in the Democracy Wall movement of late 1978-early 1979, who would have been intellectuals if not for the fact that the Cultural Revolution deprived them of an education, advocated reforms similar to those of Hu's advisers, these advisers did not join with them. The establishment intellectuals observed, but did not participate in the Democracy Wall debates, journals, and wall posters. They did not want to do anything to jeopardize the opportunity they had finally gained to advise the leadership.

Like their Confucian predecessors, their major energies early on in the Deng era were devoted to ideological issues. From January until March 1979, they dominated the theory conference convened by Hu Yaobang to lay the ideological basis for the reforms. At the same time, they were involved in another ideological discussion in the party media. The focus of this discourse was on the Western concept of alienation, which a number of Hu's intellectual network attributed to the repression of the Mao years; they urged an emphasis on humanism as a way of alleviating this alienation. Although they associated humanism with the revisions of Marxism-Leninism going on in Eastern Europe, their proposing humanism as an answer to China's problems was a Confucian rather than a Marxist solution. In fall 1983, Deng launched a campaign against those most closely involved in the discussion of alienation and humanism, calling such concepts "spiritual pollution." Although campaigns against dissident intellectuals continued in the Deng era, they had none of the fanaticism, mass mobilization, and violence of the Mao period. Nevertheless, they were a less draconian version of the Mao campaigns and once more politically engaged intellectuals were targeted for specific attack.

265

By the mid 1980s, therefore, the humanistic intellectuals, advising Hu, began to reevaluate their previous behavior and question whether their stress on ideology, their alliance with the leadership, and their role as intermediaries may have been their undoing. When their protector, Hu Yaobang, was purged in January 1987 and their new patron, Zhao Ziyang, became an advocate of neo-authoritarianism, the bonds between them and the party government that had remained intact even in the terrible Mao years had become frayed beyond repair. Like the ex-Red Guard activists of the Democracy Wall movement, they began for the first time to try to establish associations and publish journals outside party control. Of course, by the late 1980s, more autonomy was possible as China moved to a market economy and became intertwined with the outside world. Nevertheless, their increasing independence had more to do with a change in their view of their relationship with the state than with the economic changes.

Typical of this transformation was the ideological evolution of Hu Jiwei, a member of Hu Yaobang's intellectual network, who had remained loyal to Mao until the Cultural Revolution, when he was purged from his position at *People's Daily*. He was rehabilitated in the late 1970s and returned as editor in chief of *People's Daily*. It was under his auspices that *People's Daily* printed the discussion of alienation and humanism. Initially, his main interest was in such ideological issues and in promoting a tolerance of a variety of views. He became a major voice calling for freedom of the press. After he was purged as editor of *People's Daily* in the 1983 campaign against spiritual pollution, he became an advocate of the rule of law, declaring that freedom of the press was impossible unless it was accompanied by a code of laws to protect those who expressed differing views. Moreover, he supported the establishment of nonofficial media, which could present alternatives to the official views. Hu Yaobang then put him in charge of drawing up a journalism law to protect journalists. By the late 1980s, Hu Jiwei called for an independent judiciary and urged more independence for the hitherto rubber-stamp legislature, the National People's Congress, as an institution that could also help protect differing views.

Hu Jiwei's move toward a more Western view of democracy stemmed from increasing knowledge about freedom of the press and the rule of law in other countries as well as from his own experience in China. But being able in the Deng area to look beyond Marxism-Leninism for answers to China's problems also gave him more access to the Confucian past. His greater appreciation of Western institutions did not prevent and perhaps may have given him more appreciation for certain aspects of Confucianism, which he also looked upon as another source of inspiration for China's reforms. In addition, by the late 1980s the intellectuals as well as the leadership were impressed by the accelerating economic dynamism of their ethnic and Confucian neighbors in East Asia. But unlike their leaders, some of the intellectuals were also impressed by the movement of these countries toward democracy. They began to question whether Confucianism was the hindrance to democracy and modernization that their leaders and May Fourth forebears had claimed. Debate, pro and con, on such issues became so heated that it was termed "cultural fever."

This debate moved beyond intellectual circles in spring 1988, when "River Elegy" (*He shang*), a television series on this subject, reached an audience of millions. The producers, a group of ex-Red Guards, showed through vivid cinematography that China's tradition had hindered its modernization. One episode—a critique of the intellectuals' alliance with the government—particularly evoked great debate in the intellectual community. The producers of "River Elegy" argued that because of their economic and ideological dependence on the political leadership, the intellectuals had remained weak and ineffectual. Unless they were genuinely independent, ideologically as well as economically, they insisted that intellectuals could not exert influence on the leadership or society. Other ex-Red Guards, most prominently, the literary "enfant terrible," Liu Xiaobo, elaborated on this critique of the intellectuals. His articles specifically singled out the writer Liu Binyan as well as by implication the well-known intellectuals close to Hu Yaobang and Zhao Ziyang as examples of powerless intellectuals.

The independent think-tanks, journals, and study groups of ex-Red Guards that emerged in the mid-1980s indeed did exert wider influence at least on the younger generation than their older, more established elders. Because of their past activities, these ex-Red Guards were unable to get positions in the party-government, though many of them aspired to such positions. Thrust out on their own, they built their own institutions, which began to lay the foundations for a civil society. The most famous of these was the Social and Economic Research Institute, the first nonofficial social science think-tank in Beijing, headed by ex-Red Guard Chen Ziming and Wang Juntao, activists in the April 5, 1976, and Democracy Wall movements.[3] Becoming economically self-sufficient with the move to the market, they established their own publishing company, polling organization, and newspaper, *Jingjixue Zhoubao* (Economic Weekly). These institutions expressed a broad range of views on political and cultural issues. Establishment intellectuals sought to publish in their publications and participate in their seminars, which also included members of the burgeoning entrepreneurial class. Yet, while their independent actions were radical in a Chinese context, Chen's and Wang's political views were relatively moderate. Like their literati forebears, they sought reform within the prevailing political system.

They had become so influential with students in the Beijing area that at the height of the 1989 Tiananmen demonstration, Zhao Ziyang had sought their assistance in getting the students to leave the square. Another indication of their influence was that members of Hu's intellectual network, who during the Democracy Wall movement had kept their distance, by the late 1980s sought to join their activities. This was not only because they could fund their projects, but more important, these establishment intellectuals had come to question their alliance with the government. They had learned from bitter experience in the Deng period that not only could their political patrons be purged as happened to Hu Yaobang or change their mind as was the case with Deng Xiaoping, but their patrons whether Hu or Zhao Ziyang were also not strong enough or committed enough to respond to their proposals and protect them from retribution.

Another assumption that they reconsidered at this time was their belief that, like the literati, they could speak on behalf of the people or at least for the benefit of the people and the party would respond. By the late 1980s, they reluctantly acknowledged that their paternalistic presumption of "speaking for the people" had fallen on deaf ears. Moreover, their efforts to inform the leadership of its shortcomings and their calls for rectification had provoked retaliation, leading to their own persecution and sometimes a retreat from the reforms currently underway. Gradually they shifted their emphasis from ideological revision and moral persuasion to stressing the need to establish democratic institutions through which the people could speak for themselves. Yet, they still retained the Confucian belief that it was necessary to guide the people in making their choice at the ballot box. Certainly institution-building can also be found in Confucianism, as pointed out by Wm. Theodore de Bary,[4] but the stress on the rule of law and electoral politics was new in Communist China.

The Confucian Legacy

The Confucian view of the intellectual as a member of the political establishment and in alliance with the leadership gradually began to wane in the late 1980s and especially after the June 4, 1989, crackdown. Because of increasing market opportunities for their talents and expertise and China's expanding interaction with the outside world, intellectuals became less dependent on the state for their livelihood and prestige. Moreover, because of continuing repression, even under the supposed reform leadership of Deng Xiaoping, politically engaged intellectuals sought to have a more independent relationship with the government. Their intellectual networks, journals, and study groups in the 1980s had become increasingly independent channels that influenced society directly rather than indirectly through their association with political leaders. Although in the 1990s the Jiang Zemin leadership has repressed direct political dissent, remonstrance was revived in a 1995 petition addressed to the leadership. The authors, a group of politically engaged intellectuals, again felt it was their responsibility to protest against the imprisonment of political dissenters and to urge greater tolerance of differing views.

The ex-Red Guard political activists, who may be more representative of the politically engaged intellectuals of the future than their establishment elders, appear more in the tradition of the East European intellectual dissidents than in the literati tradition. Like their East European counterparts before 1989, they seek to produce political change by working from the bottom up and building coalitions with other classes, such as the workers and emerging middle class. Nevertheless, they too retain elements of Confucianism. Chen Ziming and Wang Juntao, who after the June Fourth crackdown were accused of being the "black hands" behind the 1989 Tiananmen demonstration, speak in the language and in the spirit of their literati forebears. After being sentenced to thirteen years in prison, Chen composed an eloquent 40,000-word essay, summarizing his arguments used in the courtroom. Paraphrasing Confucius, he wrote: "He who wins the people's hearts wins all under heaven. But he who wishes to win the people's hearts must first win the hearts of the scholar."[5] Similarly, Wang Juntao, also sentenced to thirteen years in prison, wrote in a letter thanking his lawyer that "I feel sad to see that so many leaders and sponsors of the movement, when facing the consequences, dare not shoulder their responsibility. . . . Yet, what I am most concerned about is the loss of spirit and morality of our nation . . . what I value is whether a human spirit has nobility—a noble and pure soul."[6]

Their literati predecessors would have had no trouble understanding these declarations of two members of the Cultural Revolution generation, totally educated in the People's Republic. The further removed from the Confucian era, the less conscious are China's intellectuals of Confucian teachings and actions. Yet, the words, cadences, and even some of the values of that era still inspire their later-day descendants.

Notes

1. Craig Calhoun, *Neither Gods nor Emperors: Students and the Struggle for Democracy in China* (Berkeley: University of California Press, 1995), p. 258.

2. Tang Tsou, *The Cultural Revolution and Post-Mao Reforms* (Chicago: University of Chicago Press, 1986), pp. 3–66.

3. Merle Goldman, *Sowing the Seeds of Democracy in China* (Cambridge: Harvard University Press, 1994), pp. 338–54.

4. Wm. Theodore de Bary, *The Liberal Tradition in China* (Hong Kong: Chinese University Press, 1983).

5. George Black and Robin Munro, *Black Hands of Beijing* (New York: Wiley, 1993), p. 313. This book gives full biographies of Chen Ziming, Wang Juntao, and their associates.

6. Ibid., p. 314.

15

Confucianism Contested: Human Rights and the Chinese Tradition in Contemporary Chinese Political Discourse

Jeremy T. Paltiel

Almost twenty years after the end of the Cultural Revolution, despite the marked decline of revolutionary rhetoric and ideology, Chinese intellectuals continue to a great extent to hold quite antitraditional views. This paper explores this antitraditionalism in the context of juxtaposing contemporary views concerning Confucianism and human rights. Despite the forceful reiteration of the regime's opposition to "bourgeois liberalization" and positive references to authoritarian practices of China's neighbors in the Sino-Confucian cultural belt from Japan to Singapore, many Chinese intellectuals appear to draw inspiration from different versions of Enlightenment liberalism and to compare this form of Western thought invidiously with the products of the Chinese intellectual tradition, in particular, Confucianism. While Chinese intellectuals are no less preoccupied with China's identity and position in world history than they were previous generations, by and large they seem to reject Professor Tu Weiming's efforts to revive Confucianism with new meaning for the contemporary age. "Chinese culture" is contested and political rather than static or immutable. As Barrett McCormick and David Kelly argue, culture is "an open-ended repertoire of symbolic forms and practices."[1] Discussion of "Chinese culture" today cannot ignore the fact that some notion of "Western culture" is never outside the frame of reference. In 1995, there is not, nor can there be, a pristine Chinese culture "uncontaminated" by Western values, concepts and theories.[2]

Confucian Chinese values and Western liberal values are not mutually exclusive, but they are different. To view cultures in dichotomous terms exaggerates these differences and destroys points of tangency. Intercultural encounters can recognize common attributes of humanity. These attributes need not form the same categorical list, nor be easily reconciled with the rights and values enumerated in the International Bill of Rights of the United Nations. Therefore, common values of humanity need not be coterminous with human *rights*. The theory of "human rights" may be looked upon as a practical legal tool to limit the power of modern states, distinguishing between "human rights" and those humane values which human rights discourse serves to protect. The traditional Chinese culture cherishes many of the same values as those in the post-enlightenment West, but does not express these in rights language. Furthermore, the significance of rights discourse in the Western tradition appears in the context of a legal discourse which privileges legal texts and constrains the exercise of authority by strict reference to these. China does not share the same traditional reverence for legality, nor it has been argued, does the Chinese tradition approach "sacred texts" in quite the same way.[3] It is important not to identify "difference" with rejection or absence. The extent to which Chinese discourse adapts or adopts rights discourse today has much less to do with primordial factors in the Chinese tradition, than with the circumstances which have forced Chinese to turn their attention to Western modes of political discourse.

Tradition, Modernity, and Human Rights: Contested Authority

Belying every effort to submerge or repress controversy, authority, and legitimacy are strongly contested in contemporary China. Underlining most objections to individual rights there is a concern for the fragility of the state. To a great extent, the Chinese tradition is today even more remote than Western liberal discourse, and aspects of Marxist discourse continue to legitimate this trend.

The Chinese regime is at great pains to assert its authority domestically, and claim its sovereignty internationally. Both these claims were combined in the show of force at Tiananmen. Unanimous belief in "modernization" and progress, means on the one hand, that official spokespersons for the Chinese government insist on the significance of the "right to development" as a basic human right proclaimed by the General Assembly of the United Nations in 1979 and 1986.[4] This position tends to relativize the importance of individual rights, and also to view rights as programmatic and evolutionary rather than as absolute claims.[5]

In the post-Cultural Revolution period Chinese intellectuals have increasingly distinguished their own fate from that of the Chinese state, and are   271 increasingly vocal about the authority that individuals must claim *against* the state. This informs intellectual views of Confucianism as well as of the current regime.

The Contemporary Period

The humiliation inflicted on dynastic China rendered traditional China obsolete and, at least in some respects, bankrupt. The *ti* and *yong* ("substance" and "utility") formula[6] response to the challenge of the West during the Self-Strengthening Movement of the 1860s[7] emerged as a way of insulating "Chinese values" from the reluctant necessity to adopt Western technology. Since the 1860s, the effort to reconcile the absorption of foreign teaching with the reassertion of Chinese value has taken different forms, most recently in Deng Xiaoping's formula of "socialism with Chinese characteristics." The logic of "substance" and "utility" was rationalized in the 1860s as in the 1990s, as a problem of means and ends, but the distinction ultimately gets consumed in an irresolvable debate over identity. How far can the Chinese identity be redefined in the pursuit of national power?

Following the humiliation inflicted in the nineteenth century, Chinese intellectuals (and Chinese broadly) have come to near unanimity on the idea of progress or evolution. In this context, some intellectuals see their own tradition as genetically defective and grant some sort of "competitive advantage" to the modern West.[8] There may be disagreement about the exact location and nature of this genetic defect but there is little disagreement as to its presence. For these Chinese intellectuals, therefore, any search for value in the Chinese tradition has become an exercise akin to sifting through the ashes in search of the few objects of value left behind by the great conflagration that consumed dynastic China. The effort to come to terms with national humiliation left a hiatus in the Chinese culture, whereby the tradition lost any aura of "sanctity" that once clung to it.[9] Consumed by the project of grasping the key to progress and modernization, such intellectuals turn their attention outward, toward the shining towers and gleaming machinery of the West rather than expend their effort to pour moribund ashes through a sieve to discover the rough nuggets left behind. Those intellectuals that do, construct their "sieve" according to "Western" principles.

In a process which Joseph R. Levenson called the search for equivalence,[10] between China and the West, Chinese intellectuals have attempted to find ways of incorporating in their own views of China the things that they valued in the West, and at times to look back at the Chinese tradition for answers to the problems which they see as arising from the development of the West.

The collapse of the traditional dynastic system in 1911 ended the role of orthodox Confucianism as a ruling ideology. In the aftermath, traditional culture was blamed for allowing China to fall behind the West. Contemporary China continues to be shaped by the iconoclastic tradition born during this period. It is therefore inappropriate to identify the contemporary Chinese approach to human rights with "the Chinese tradition." The cultural revaluations and self-reflection of such Chinese intellectuals has raised a new problem concerning the way in which rights discourse fits into contemporary political debates rather than the degree of fit between rights discourse and the Chinese tradition.

In the context of professing allegiance to the ideal of progress and acknowledging the advance of the West, Chinese disagree over the traditional values they might wish to reaffirm. The quest for "national salvation" has involved several generations in a shopping spree of imported ideas as well as Western technology. Alongside support for "Mr. Science" and "Mr. Democracy" the resounding slogan of the May Fourth Movement (1919), was "Down with Confucius & Co." Some have viewed the hiatus of the Chinese tradition as a historical process analogous to the European Renaissance. Chou Tse-tsung, the foremost historian of the May Fourth Movement, disagrees. Instead, he insists that it marks a true hiatus—a reevaluation of the Chinese tradition and a turn toward the West.[11] The central problematique which arose at this time was how to revive China as a symbol of pride while systematically rejecting its moribund traditions. This debate forms part of the problem of history and value.[12] The intellectual history of modern China is a narrative of contested authority and contested legitimacy. Different ideological trends, some militantly iconoclastic, others resolutely conservative and even neo-traditional have claimed the allegiance of intellectuals in this century. For a while, Communist ideology, particularly in its Leninist form, seemingly provided an answer. China could join the vanguard of history, overtaking the "moribund" capitalist West even as it rejected its own tradition. To draw a direct line of continuity between the contested iconoclasm of the May Fourth era, when the forces of tradition were still relatively robust, and the anti-traditionalism among contemporary intellectuals is an over-simplification of historical trends. Contemporary intellectuals have not experienced Confucian orthodoxy within their own lifetimes (instead being all-too familiar with dogmatism of the Mao Zedong variety) while the intellectuals of the May Fourth Movement reacted against a vital tradition which had shaped their own education. Nevertheless, encouraged by the revolutionary ethos fostered by Chinese communism, a deep-seated anti-traditional orthodoxy has taken root which traces its origins to the May Fourth Movement. Dedication to ideas of progress and evolution has reinforced antitraditionalism even in the face of deep disillusionment with Marxist discourse.

Scholars both inside and outside China disagree vigorously over the extent and depth of Confucianism in the contemporary Chinese political culture. Only in the process of trying to establish some value in the maintenance of a distinctive Chinese identity, pressured by the overwhelming weight of invidious comparison, do Chinese scholars turn toward the treasury of cultural tradition. To be full participants in the modernization project and not mere objects of modern utility, Chinese must find ways to reaffirm their own identity. At the same time, to explain China's apparent failure to realize greatness in the contemporary period, it is important to critique it. Scholars therefore approach the traditional culture from two directions, as tropes of debate and engagement. The Chinese tradition is almost always an object to be evaluated and used rather than as a continuous fountainhead of value.[13]

Unanimous acceptance of evolution and progress, and constant international comparison and attention to relative international position has not yielded a unified worldview, except when in the throes of enforced ideological conformity. The ideal of progress may be adopted from two different and potentially conflicting value premises. One view is cosmopolitan, and sees progress as participation and involvement in a universal project which distributes value according to the relative contribution to this universal goal. A different approach to progress is utilitarian and particularistic. Here progress is a means or a tool to reestablish the innate glory and greatness of China. This begs the question of why China has to be great and glorious. The answer to that almost inevitably triggers a reflexive homage to the Chinese tradition. The result is the concoction of formulae which link current ideas of progress with China's unique past, such as "Socialism with Chinese Characteristics." Scholars of the former type may be called modernists of a cosmopolitan universalist persuasion and scholars of the latter type may be termed nativist and utilitarian modernists. The place of human rights in the mix of universal values (which join China to the mainstream of world-historical development) depends on the kind of political claim one wishes to advance and the target audience against whom that claim is to be asserted.

Liberal ideas have been one ideological weapon with which to attack the failures of the Chinese state. However, the liberal impetus in the Chinese revolution was undermined by the need to create a new state which would be capable of protecting the Chinese culture and society from foreign invasion and occupation as well as internal turmoil. In the first half of the twentieth century there was widespread acceptance of the notion that the central political problem was not to limit the power of the Chinese state, but to increase it.[14]

Mao Zedong and Tradition

China's political leaders have been active participants in debates concerning culture. Mao Zedong, whose judgments on the traditional culture were the official orthodoxy for more than a quarter century, viewed the traditional culture in starkly invidious terms:

> There is in China an imperialist culture which is a reflection of imperialist rule, or partial rule, in the political and economic field. . . . China also has a semi-feudal culture which reflects her semi-feudal politics and economy, and whose exponents include all those who advocate the worship of Confucius, the study of the Confucian canon, the old ethical code and the old ideas in opposition to the new culture and new ideas. Imperialist culture and semi-feudal culture are devoted brothers and have formed a reactionary cultural alliance against China's new culture. This kind of reactionary culture serves the imperialists and the feudal class and must be swept away. Unless it is swept away, no new culture of any kind can be built up. There is no construction without destruction, no flowing without damming and no motion without rest; the two are locked in a life and death struggle.[15]

And yet, the same article reveals unresolved tensions and a deep ambivalence, as the following quotations show:

> To nourish her own culture China needs to assimilate a great deal of foreign progressive culture, not only from present-day socialist and new democratic cultures but also from the earlier cultures of other nations. For example, the culture of the various capitalist countries in the Age of Enlightenment. However we should not gulp any of this foreign material down uncritically, but treat it as we do our food— [first chew it, then digest it to absorb its nutrients].[16]
>
> A splendid old culture was created during the long period of Chinese feudal society. To study the development of this culture, to reject its feudal dross and assimilate its democratic essence is a necessary condition for developing our new national culture and increasing our self-confidence but we should not swallow anything and everything uncritically.[17]

The ambivalence revealed here, was reflected in Mao's own life—he sent Red Guards rampaging against China's cultural monuments, but was himself absorbed in reading dynastic history and classical poetry.[18] The violent dichotomies—progressive/reactionary; nationalist/imperialist; socialist/capitalist, etc.—employed by Mao exemplify the revolutionary impulse in the modern Chinese political culture. The modern Chinese political culture is revolutionary insofar as it has attempted to incorporate the achievements of the modern West. It is "restorationist" insofar as it seeks to recover the prestige and world-historical significance of the Chinese civilization in former times. In contemporary discussion of the Chinese culture there is much confusion   275 concerning what constitutes the "dross" and what the "essence" of the Chinese civilization. Nationalism is Janus-faced: it presents a revolutionary face to those who would renew the Chinese state, but it can present a traditionalist face to those who would challenge the legitimacy of Chinese culture from the outside.

All approaches to human rights were conditioned by the sharp juxtapositions of revolutionary rhetoric throughout the period of Mao's rule and beyond.[19] The Chinese approach to Marxism emphasized class-struggle and determined class status by behavior and heredity rather than objective criteria of a person's relationship to property or the means of production. Not only did Maoist ideology specifically deny any universal human character or nature which could form the basis of "human rights," but the boundary between classes became so elastic as to render any rights attributable to "the people" equally meaningless. The term "human rights" almost never appeared without the modifier "bourgeois" and hence, to claim such rights was an automatic ideological error if not an outright crime. As late as 1982 (the same year the current Chinese constitution was promulgated), a standard dictionary of the social sciences defined "human rights" as "a class concept" raised by the bourgeoisie in the Enlightenment "against feudalism."[20] The standard approach to human rights was one which was conditioned by ideological discourse rooted in Marxism. Confucianism, was all-but embalmed and placed in the museum prior to the Cultural Revolution.[21] Prior to the end of the 1980's, 'culture' was never raised as a significant reason to reject human rights standards of the West.

The mobilizational regime created by Mao Zedong and the Chinese Communists, subordinated the individual to the group in a manner never seen before in Chinese history. It would be as wrong to view the Maoism of the Cultural Revolution (1966–1976) as the quintessence of Chinese culture as it would be to look upon Fascism and Nazism as the exemplars of the West. During the radical totalitarian iconoclasm of the Cultural Revolution there was direct, officially sanctioned, anti-traditionalism. This culminated in the vandalism of "smash the four olds" (old habits, old thinking, old culture, old tradition) at the outset of the Cultural Revolution. Later on, in 1973–75, another campaign directly targeted Confucianism (the anti-Confucius anti-Lin Biao campaign). During these periods positive expressions toward Confucianism or traditional culture became serious crimes which were severely and harshly punished, not excluding the threat of death. While this enforced conformity did not reflect the views of large numbers of intellectuals, it was nevertheless an offshoot of a strong segment of iconoclastic political opinion concerning the relationship of traditional thought to the modern state. However, the fact that the Cultural Revolution period of Chinese history in many respects represents an aberration both from Chinese culture and from Western liberalism has since become the basis for some intellectuals to propose a radical rupture with the Chinese tradition (with which they identify the Cultural Revolution) and by contrast, for others to propose a partial return to the more pristine Chinese culture.[22]

Cultural Self-Reflection in the Post-Mao Period

The reaction to the frightening and tragic extremism of the Cultural Revolution opened up a space for the reassessment of traditional thought, which might now be judged relatively benign in comparison with the excesses of the immediate past.[23] Confucianism regained some respect as a martyred object of persecution in the Cultural Revolution.

> It is unfortunate that very often in the press some articles lacking maturity and profundity completely negate traditional philosophy. They only emphasize negative aspects, such as its closedness (*fengbi*), muddledness (*mohu*), undifferentiated (*wuduan*) and intuitive (*zhiguan*) nature without any excellent characteristics, or saying that Chinese modes of thought were stopped at the primitive level of not distinguishing between chaos and objectivity; or that Chinese traditional thought would not recognize the objective world hence preventing the progress of science and therefore urging a clean break from that way of thought. Traditional thought is blamed for the lack of independence of Chinese intellectuals and their descent into tools of the autocracy. In general Chinese traditional culture and philosophy are regarded as obstacles to modernization, which must be completely repudiated. The new slogans "open up a complete battle against traditional culture" "extirpate traditional culture to the last man" "deny it all successors." Some people think that the only way out is wholesale Westernization, and that modernization is equal to Westernization . . . these sentiments are not only extreme and unreasonable, but also harmful to the confidence and self respect of the Chinese nation.[24]

However, the overwhelming desire to turn toward the mainstream of world history, to return to the project of "modernization" and back out of the cul-de-sac of radical ideology also opened up a new set of invidious comparisons between the developed West and "backward" China during the period of the "open door." It was as if to turn one's back in search of things of value left from the past might distract China from the great project of catching up and overtaking the developed West.

> Some people argue that modernization is not the same as Westernization, which in a certain sense is reasonable, but this way of speaking also has its shortcomings, since it might easily be used to exaggerate the specificities of our own cultural tradition, which will obstruct the progress of our national modernization. In fact, modernization means to study the advanced things of the West.[25]

In certain respects the contrasting views about the origins and implications of the Cultural Revolution underline the contemporary Chinese debate over human rights and liberalism.[26] Throughout the 1980s there was a broad-ranging movement of cultural reflection, known as *wenhua fansi*.[27]

Perhaps the best example of this is the TV series *River Elegy* (*He Shang*) which aired in China in the year prior to Tiananmen and which so angered the authorities as to force its author into exile. The program draws an explicit contrast between the silted-up flow of the Yellow River, representing Chinese traditional culture, and the deep blue sea, representing modernity, openness, and the West. The Yellow River culture is explicitly tied to authoritarianism and backwardness, illustrated by the person of Mao Zedong in the guise of Emperor. The program's message is that China must dredge up its culture in order to reach the sea. Chinese dissidents reach outside of China, and implicitly continue the iconoclastic revolutionary culture to tap sources of authority to critique the Chinese state.[28] The Tiananmen demonstrators directly traced themselves to the iconoclastic traditions of the May Fourth movement and its slogans of "democracy and science" in the campaign against the contemporary policies of the Chinese state.

It should therefore come as no surprise that those who see themselves in conflict with the Chinese state adopt international standards. The example of liberal thinkers who have become dissidents, such as Yan Jiaqi and Fang Lizhi is well known.[29] Fang Lizhi in particular was explicitly accused of "wholesale Westernization" for his advocacy of universal standards of democracy and freedom of speech.[30]

The vast majority of dissident critics are for the very same reason highly critical of the traditional culture and tend to tar the regime and the traditional culture with the same brush.[31] The "progressive" orientation of dissidents tends to look at China's lagging position with respect to individual rights as an example and consequence of Chinese "backwardness." Dissidents such as the long-term human rights activist Ren Wanding was arrested after the "Democracy Wall" period of 1978–79. He, like others, tends to blame the absence of rights on the "Chinese tradition."

> [T]he long-term goal of China's democratic movement is a peaceful transformation of the monistic political and social structure of the Communist Party, replacing it with a pluralistic socio-political structure, a pluralist structure of democracy, a pluralist culture and a pluralist ethnic structure. . . . The monistic socio-political structure of China is an outcome of protracted feudalism and backward productivity. It will inevitably disappear in the wake of economic development, an increasing production, and an open society.[32]

278   Not only do dissident liberal intellectuals tend to an antitraditional stance, so

too do supporters of "Neo-authoritarianism" who oppose them. The latter adopt authoritarianism as a pragmatic utilitarian tool for the rapid transformation of Chinese society, loosely basing their arguments on the experience of the "Four Dragons" of South Korea, Taiwan, Singapore and Hong Kong as well as the ideas of the American political scientist Samuel Huntington.[33]

Those who uphold "neo-authoritarianism," such as the social scientist He Xin, do not favor it on value grounds, and do not base their arguments on the Chinese traditional culture. Instead, they see authoritarianism as a means to development. As He Xin argues, if China were to pursue the political system recommended by the United States, "China would only become a 'soft state' fragmented and lacking in national cohesion." Such a state, he argues, "would lose its last opportunity and hope to catch up to the developed countries."[34]

Barrett McCormick and David Kelly have argued that the decline of Marxism in China has weakened opposition to liberalism, and has increased the likelihood that both state elites and antistate elites will adopt liberal discourse as a means of furthering their interests.[35] A recent trend toward nationalism and xenophobia among younger artists and intellectuals may be seen both as a form of artistic rebellion against the invidious implication of "progress" (which places the West in a superior position) and as a form of cultural boasting about East Asian (and Chinese) economic success. It does not appear to portend a serious revival of Chinese traditional learning.[36] Even the foremost exponent of "neo-Confucianism" outside China, the Harvard Professor Tu Weiming himself concedes that his project to pursue a "third wave" of Confucianism involves grafting the Western liberal sense of "the dignity, independence and autonomy of the person into [the Confucian] concept of selfhood as a center of relationships and as a broadening process of self-realization."[37]

"Modernization" and Human Rights

Following the death of Mao Zedong, Deng Xiaoping consciously promoted a policy of international comparison in an effort to speed up China's modernization. The repudiation of the Cultural Revolution and the open door have stimulated broad-based value changes. In the first place, the effort to repudiate the Cultural Revolution and the "Gang of Four" reawakened interest in the liberal elements of the Marxist tradition and, in particular, "socialist legality" and "socialist democracy."[38] In the second place there were the marketizing elements of economic reform, legitimated profits, private property, and individual interests. Legal reform increasingly looked to Western jurisprudence and legislation to accommodate political and economic change.

The near-unanimous acceptance of the idea of progress means that in particular disciplines which are of utilitarian or applied practical value to the pro-   279 cesses involved in progress—economic growth, technological innovation, industrialization, etc.—there is unquestioning acceptance of Western models and at least rhetorical rejection of traditional influence. There is widespread acceptance by Chinese historians of thought that Chinese culture failed to generate the scientific and industrial revolutions and this is seen also as a fundamental shortcoming of the Chinese tradition.[39] In technical and scientific fields the Chinese philosophical tradition may even be repressed into the subconscious and receive no conscious or explicit recognition. A somewhat uncritical acceptance that the radical excesses of the revolutionary period, and the Cultural Revolution in particular, can somehow be attributed to the deficiencies of the Chinese tradition seems to pervade much contemporary social thought. In some ways the Chinese tradition is a convenient whipping boy for current political and social ills which it would become risky to blame on Communist ideology or the leadership of the Communist Party. Confucianism, which is not collectivistic in the way that Marxism-Leninism is, becomes the mulberry tree which is pointed to while criticizing the scholar tree (*zhi sang ma huai*).

Here is an example of this tendency to view the tradition in contrast to the West and in somewhat invidious terms:

> The humanist spirit of Chinese traditional political culture is completely different from the humanism of the contemporary West. Traditional Chinese humanist thought took the recognition of basic human nature as its starting point, ancient thinkers used morality as their standard, to distinguish qualities, that is, whether human nature was good or bad. However, regardless of whether human nature was seen as good or bad, the point of return was always about how to establish the control of the group and society over the individual. Therefore the traditional theory of human nature always emphasized obligations rather than the value of the individual. The value of the individual could only be realized in a social setting.[40]

The substance of this analysis is not so different from common comparisons of Chinese and Western thought such as those of Hall and Ames.[41] Noteworthy, however, is the invidious and negative tone of the discussion. For the contemporary Chinese, particularly contemporary Chinese intellectuals who lived through the Cultural Revolution, the moral independence of the Confucian scholar is not enough. The desire for political autonomy turns such intellectuals in an antitraditional and anti-Confucian direction.

> Because the Chinese tradition exemplified by Confucianism restricted the desire of people to seek the truth, this resulted in the inability of natural science to develop for a long time, and caused social development to lack a theoretical basis; in resolving the relationship between the individual and the collectivity it did not pay attention to the individual and the value of the self; in formulating personality it empha-

sized a modal personality of "superficial moral power," without stressing the stratum of human needs, and for this reason right up to the modern era China never achieved a renaissance equivalent to that of Italy, or an intellectual current equivalent to the humanism of France during the period of the bourgeois revolution. All this was determined by the inner specificities of the humanistic spirit of the traditional Chinese culture. The incompleteness of modern opposition to feudalism by the bourgeoisie has a profound ideological-cultural basis, which is because of the absence or incapacity of an important ideological weapon.[42]

There is an acute consciousness of "difference" which may be used either in a radical direction to build up "obstacles" to China's "modernization" which must be removed, or else, in a conservative direction, to construct "national characteristics" *guoqing*, which *limit* the applicability of "Western" principles to China.[43]

> The distinctions between Chinese and Western cultures are sharply defined over attitudes toward what is a human being and what are human rights. This distinction does not seem to some as outstanding as [differences in social system or status as a developing country] and some do not think it crucial to the discussion of human rights. Precisely the opposite is true. . . . In contrast to the Western tradition which considers the humanity of human beings entirely in the concept of human freedom, the Chinese tradition views what makes people human totally in terms of their relationships. Although freedom and "humanization" are not necessarily mutually exclusive in essence, they obviously emphasize quite contrasting things. For this reason the two types of culture and philosophical anthropologies have deeply influenced history down to this very day.[44]

The Chinese State and Human Rights

Given that China had suffered the coercive impact of Western institutions, it is understandable why Chinese in official positions would be reluctant to embrace the values of the erstwhile imperial powers. Instead of universal values, international human rights are scrutinized and accepted or rejected as a set of political claims. Reluctance to accept international (read foreign) human rights standards is asserted as a defense of Chinese state sovereignty.

In the aftermath of Tiananmen, with China's growing participation in the international arena and in particular United Nations diplomacy, the Beijing authorities belatedly recognized in 1989 that they required a domestic body of specialists in human rights law to answer China's foreign critics. This is a significant change. The post-Tiananmen world coincided with the collapse of the old Soviet bloc and the 1993 UN Conference on Human Rights in Vienna. This context invited the first effective Chinese recognition that rights exist. Accordingly China issued its first White Paper on human rights. The Chinese   281 authorities once again stressed the importance of national independence as the first principle. "Without national independence, there would be no guarantee for the people's lives."[45]

In the context of sharp exchanges over human rights, Chinese observers argued: "some Western personages raise their own human rights notions to be the common standard based on considerations of political privilege and cultural self-centeredness, and moreover use this to judge and to make demands on peoples and states with different cultural traditions and different actual circumstances who have chosen different social systems and different developmental paths."[46]

The post-Tiananmen period witnessed concerted efforts to draw distinctions between Chinese human rights standards and Western demands.[47] These distinctions may be drawn either from ideological considerations, or, as has been more evident in the 1990s by reference to "cultural specificity." Nevertheless, by the early 1990s Chinese observers were ready to concede:

> The recognition of human rights, respect for human rights, and the protection of human rights has already become a common faith of humankind. Nevertheless, based on differences in political economic or cultural background, there are major differences existing between different human rights concepts; however, after the second World War, the contemporary world has at least achieved this kind of cultural ambiance: public professions of behavior which do not recognize, do not respect and do not protect human rights no longer have any market.[48]

Joining other Asian states, the Chinese government claims a purported tradition that "rights" pertain to states and society, and stand prior to the individual.[49] However, the language of difference also continues to be ideological, as the following example shows:

> Internationally, capitalist countries are always using "human rights" spokespersons as part of their design for "peaceful evolution." They always use "human rights" spokespersons to attack the principles and standpoint of Marxism and socialism on questions of human rights, slander socialist countries for suppressing, disregarding and showing contempt for human rights, and raise their voices to proclaim that through "human rights offensives" they will force socialist countries to enter into human rights dialogue with "the free world." They take on the identity of the international police and saviours of "the protection of human rights" to foment, instigate, and support a tiny number of liberalizing elements in the socialist countries to take part in anti-communist and anti-socialist activities, to the extent of ignoring the most basic principles of international law to interfere in the internal affairs of socialist states. This time the anti-Chinese and anti-communist "human rights" clamor raised by the Western states led by the United States over the just actions of our country to pacify a violent riot is just a typical example.[50]

Liberal Economics and the New Legalism

Given the rise of a market ideology and the impact of the open door,[51] there is a natural affinity growing between the development of the Chinese economy and the legal and ideological concepts of the liberal West.[52] The old dichotomy of "bourgeois" and "proletarian" or "socialist" and "capitalist" has broken down.[53] The booming Chinese economy under conditions of market reform has, through a convoluted form of Marxist logic, justified liberal ideas on material grounds: since markets promote productive power, the logic of markets must be pursued wholeheartedly—otherwise "modernization" would be obstructed. "Market economies are in a certain sense economies under the rule of law."

> In the past when people discussed democracy, and mentioned freedom, it was as though just to speak of freedom is to engage in "bourgeois liberalization." However, contemporary market economies are not laissez faire economies, but are free under the macroeconomic regulation of government. Market economies are free economies, and to "open up and enliven" [the economy] necessarily implies autonomous management, free competition, autonomous assumption of risk accountability for profit and loss, autonomous development, automatic regulation. . . . For this reason, simultaneously with the legalization of democracy, we must promote the legalization of freedom.[54]

The individualistic logic of market economics has made inroads in legal thought and philosophy. As one author states,

> From the evolution of modern and contemporary ethical thought, the problem of protecting the ethics of the market economy is even more important, more fundamental than the moral demands of the market economy. Because, only after protecting the ethical basis of an economic system, only after providing a rationale for the support of an economic system and providing ideals acceptable to the vast majority of the members of that society can people follow the moral demands raised by that system.[55]

Not surprisingly, therefore, legal scholars can find points of contact between rights thinking and the progressive elements of Marxism, as can be seen in the following:

> To regard human rights as those rights which a person should enjoy solely on his/her natural belonging and social essence, and to deny that human rights are a gratuitous grant from any sort of external agency, provide the most powerful ideological weapon of any oppressed people, any oppressed nation, and all weaker members of society, in order to struggle for gain and protect human rights. Interests lie at the basis of rights. The relationship between the rights and duties of people is essentially a relationship of interest.[56]

283

There has been a sea change in intellectual life generally. An ongoing debate on the value basis of the law, and in particular the rule of law couched in the language of *benwei* ("standard" or benchmark) illustrates how far the discourse has changed.[57] The debate straddles the watershed of June 1989. Articles begin in the months prior to the Tiananmen demonstrations and continue up to June 1992. The debate was joined in at least three law journals including two published in Beijing. The important premises of the arguments that rights form the basis of law appear below:

1. We require a common understanding, and could we not say this for people living in the contemporary period: an ideal legal system, or at least one worthy of respect, should cause people to equally enjoy various basic rights and be equally bound by obligations. It [the legal system] should justly protect all rightful interests. If we could come to a common understanding on this basic value, then a discussion over "the standards of rights" (*quanli benwei*) is possible because both sides would have common value objectives, both sides would be limited to discussion of means (modalities) and technical questions.
2. Conceptual boundaries. The standard of rights arises from this underlying belief: only by making each and every person equally enjoy sacred and inviolate basic rights (human rights) then, and only then, could a just society be built; binding obligations will become necessary if and only if these are required to guarantee and realize these equal rights. In relation to rights, obligations are a means.
3. Rights are the legal guarantee that the people may freely arrange their activities and exercise their interests.
4. The basic place of rights is the demonstration of multiple interests [in society].[58]

The influence of Marxist materialism ("existence determines consciousness") is pervasive even when the conclusions drawn from the current stage of material existence (the "commodity economy") do not exactly fulfil Marxist predictions.

> At present some people are discussing the conflict between the traditional Chinese culture and modernization. Some people advocate the complete negation of the traditional culture and wholesale Westernization; some people advocate the revival of traditional culture and want to promote the "third period" of Confucianism. Some want to use Western culture as a reference model to recreate and transform the traditional culture etc. These people forget the ways in which culture depends on the existing economic base and the analysis that this requires, and therefore their analysis stops at the level of superficial phenomena. Culture is a reflection of material conditions.[59]

Ironically, "traditional values" are more apt to be seen as "obstacles" to modernization and "restrictions" on people's thinking. Ideas, therefore can hold back material changes, but, it seems, may never accelerate them.

Take for example the problematic of *yi* (rightness) vs. *li* (interest or profit) in traditional thought. In the initial period of the ongoing process of reform and opening up, this was obviously expressed in the form of a restriction on people's thinking, so there was a passing fad of criticizing the old mode of thought which emphasizes rightness over profit. With the deepening of the commodity economy and the emergence of unprecedented social problems, people gradually began to take notice of the ways in which the cultural essence (*wenhua jinghua*), the traditional approach to right and profit, could resolve aspects of ethics and material interest.[60]

In another article in the debate over "the standard of rights" as the basis of law, the author justifies his position by reference to the work of John Rawls. He sums up the position in the following language:

> Put simply, the standard of rights has two major components: equal rights as the basic principle of social justice and the legislative principle that obligations (duties) are subordinate to rights. This is not just a certain recognition of the relationship of rights to duties, but is first and foremost an ideal concept of social justice.[61]

Even among those authors who uphold the Marxist view of law and who disagree vehemently with the notion that "rights are the standard of law" one finds a positive evaluation of the place of rights in contemporary law and the principle of democratic accountability:

> The author holds that the crux of whether contemporary China will fully realize the value objective of social order [the author's position on the question of the impetus behind law] depends on whether the state can legislate the following aspects of the allocation of rights and duties. First, by the allocation of rights and duties ensure that state power is firmly in the hands of the people (that is 99.95% of the citizens) and that the people are endowed with broad and effective powers to participate in decision making and to avoid the situation in some socialist states where mistakes by some leaders have led to nationwide chaos. Second, to carry through the principle of the unity of rights and duties so as to build a structure whereby citizens' rights check state power and to guarantee citizens' rights in order that state corruption may be stopped. Third, to adjust rights and duties in step with the requirements of social and economic development, in order to ensure that rights are consistent with the social value contributed by different classes and interest groups, and to the greatest extent possible to alleviate social discontent, to stimulate the enthusiasm of the whole citizenry and to strengthen social solidarity and legal authority.[62]

Naturally the point of view expressed above was opposed by those with a more traditional—that is both Marxist and Confucian—position, arguing that "obligations are central to law."

The formulation that "obligations are central to law" indicates, that insofar as law is 285 a means to organize social order, it achieves the realization of goals mainly through categories of obligation. That is to say, that after the value objective of a law has been specified, or in a class society, the will of the ruling class has been clarified, the legislature takes this as its priority and directs its attention to the duties to be specified in law as well as the negative consequences if the duties thus specified are flouted, so that it is carefully crafted to enable the law to be effective.[63]

The reference to *class will* is instructive here, yet an early participant, who does not agree that rights are primary in law, curtly dismisses the relevance of Marxist discourse.

We believe that "the will of the ruling class" is far from able to delimit the basic qualities of law, and rather that to understand the law from the perspective of the self-regulation of society is much more in accordance with objective reality.[64]

The former author, however, bases his discussion of duty on a very different conception of society than do the proponents of rights:

The formulation that obligations are central is based on an uncomplicated understanding that society is made up of persons capable of willful action (without consideration of any binding conditions). Society has spontaneous tendencies both to order and to disorder and the main goal of self-organization is social stability and development. . . . Human society is a mechanism with tendencies both toward conscious control and against control. The main role of law is to stabilize a certain order in order to have society display a certain order and stability.[65]

This debate arises in the context of changes in the Chinese political economy. As the initiator of the debate argues:

With the reforms and opening up, along with which have come the development and construction of democratic politics and a commodity economy, a situation of pluralized interests has begun to appear. Independent individual and group economic interests as well as independent political interests have become the dominant subjects of the commodity economy and democratic politics. Our legal system is faced with an inevitable choice between a system based on obligations and one based on rights. Otherwise our laws will not be able to effectively protect various legitimate interests and there will be no basis for the development of democratic politics and a commodity economy.[66]

The sentiments reflected in the above quotations are, I believe, generally representative of the trained legal community. Over the past years, the legal profession has arrived at a position which recognizes the universality of human rights and moreover, the applicability of international conventions. While national sovereignty is still perceived as the premise of any human rights regime, it is now recognized that "sovereignty is not higher than rights."[67]

Rights discourse has penetrated Chinese society among urban intellectuals, but not simply as an ideological construct. Among articulate members of Chinese society, the awareness and responsiveness to rights discourse belies assertions that Chinese culture is hermetically sealed off. Granted, this paper has focussed mainly on the views of educated elites and intellectuals, and for reasons of methodology and subject matter has not made a systematic evaluation of public opinion.[68] Common people, those outside positions of power, will tend to employ the language that is most effective in pressing their claims— language capable of gaining recognition because it is made available by those in power. Rights language is a peculiarly instrumental form of language. Intellectuals and other articulate elites have a broader lexicon available, as well as wider audience—an international one—to appeal to.

We should be cognizant of the trends that have expanded the language of rights. The rule of law is no longer just seen as a counterpart or juxtaposition to "rule by men," it is seen as involving the exercise of rights by an engaged citizenry. Chinese intellectuals are aware that these ideas lack precedents in their own tradition, but take comfort in the notion that there was also a "revolutionary" break with the past in the Western Renaissance and Enlightenment. For this reason many feel comfortable in embracing liberal ideals without any sense of "betraying" their national tradition. This does not, of course, exempt them from the charge of "wholesale Westernization." However, in a world system which is no longer sharply divided into opposed camps, and a society no longer organized according to the principle of "class struggle" this epithet lacks the force it once had. Having embraced "modernization" along Western lines, the Chinese state is vulnerable to rights claims that are couched in the language of economic progress. By contrast, the revolutionary break with Confucian orthodoxy deprives Confucian discourse of any equivalent instrumental purpose.

Chinese intellectuals are understandably reluctant to concede the separate greatness of China out of fear that this will be used by the Chinese state as a means of censoring their own endeavors. Instead, they are easily seduced by liberal values of the West today as a means of having a standard before which they might hold their own government accountable and thereby buttress their own authoritative position. Having once been coopted into the official system of power in the name of patriotic service and having suffered grievously for it during the Cultural Revolution, intellectuals look for ways of reinforcing their personal and intellectual autonomy from the state.

Of course not all intellectuals take liberal positions. There are those who are explicitly "antiliberal," including the partisans of neo-authoritarianism. Some do this for opportunistic motives, other do so because they feel threatened by the embrace of Western ideology and Western intellectual fashions. Some are sim-   287 ply not equipped, either because they lack contemporary academic training or the linguistic skills to participate in this venture, others may have made too great an intellectual investment in Marxist-Leninist ideology to extricate themselves from it. For those with the aforementioned linguistic handicaps but equipped with the appropriate skills for literary and classical Chinese, cultural studies, and traditional philosophy can become a bastion from which to sally forth and criticize Westernizers. These hybrid Marxo-traditionalists are not a fashionable group nor an influential one, but they are useful spokespersons for a regime which occasionally feels threatened by foreign criticisms of human rights policies.

The cautious embrace by the regime of the neo-authoritarian "Confucianism" of Lee Kwan Yu is widely seen as a transparent shield for Beijing's own brand of post-Leninist authoritarianism. The most typical comments by intellectuals are that the "third wave" of Confucianism is an "overseas" phenomenon. This is a sign that it is not viewed favorably domestically. Forty-five years of history have taught intellectuals to avoid becoming too closely identified with the current line. Instead, by emphasizing modernization they can at the same time use another aspect of the regimes rhetoric for their own purposes. They can "borrow" the regime's fascination with the success of market capitalism to make small moves in the direction of liberal individualism. If in so doing they lose touch with China's own Confucian heritage, they are only continuing the iconoclastic tradition of the May Fourth Movement.

The value standards employed by Chinese intellectuals today respond to the incomplete context of personal intellectual autonomy in which they live. They can make use of the social project offered by the regime—"modernization" to expand the claims of personal autonomy. This also leads them in an antitraditional direction. There is an implicit recognition that the social context which inspires Professor Tu Wei-ming and the "third wave" of Confucianism overseas is not the same as that operative on the Chinese mainland. "Antifeudalism" and "modernization" are means to achieve the potential of liberalism and cosmopolitanism. Chinese intellectuals "need" modernity and the West to establish their autonomy in the Chinese state system. There is an inner need to escape from particularism, and wriggle out of too close an identification with the state and the regime. Confucianism is the patriarch, whose achievements are acknowledged and grudgingly admired, whose influence cannot be denied, but whose suffocating grasp is something to keep at bay. Intellectuals may acknowledge the contributions of Confucianism, and may even note, as Zhang Dainian does, the particular relevance of the Confucian and Daoist approach to nature in the age of ecology.[69] However, insofar as there is a growing consciousness of "rights" these rights are seen as following

from a particular kind of economic development (in the "materialist" version of the new liberalism), or else plainly regarded as the product of the Western enlightenment from which China must increasingly learn. Those who proclaim a lingering importance for Confucianism generally do so from conservative positions which favor a moral discourse to counter the effects of commodification and the market economy.[70]

For the most part, the kind of discourse which speaks the language of national identity does not find widespread adherence in the professional classes who are pushing the expansion of legality and rights language. Still, whenever the stature of the Chinese state in the world at large is placed in question, nativist particularism can become a badge of legitimacy. Fortunately or unfortunately, those intellectual currents which speak directly to the value of the individual are attractive today, and the indirectness of the Confucian approach to the human personality is found wanting.[71] So long as Chinese intellectuals and Chinese generally have yet to acquire the legal guarantees and the political power consistent with their ideals of the human personality, they will continue to search for Western models. This effort is reinforced, but not superseded, by a desire to achieve authority domestically and legitimacy internationally. Only when the contest for authority and legitimacy has yielded to a search for meaning will greater effort possibly be put into restoring Confucianism as a living tradition from which to draw universal values.

Notes

1. Barrett L. McCormick and David Kelly, "The Limits of Antiliberalism," *Journal of Asian Studies*, vol. 53, no. 3 (August 1994), p. 804.

2. "We live in an era in which a critique of the West has become not only possible, but mandatory. Where does this critique leave those ethnic peoples whose entry into culture is precisely because of the history of Western imperialism, already "Westernized"? . . . The task facing us is not the advocacy of a return to pure ethnic origins. Rather it is to articulate the specific ways in which ethnicity, as a site both of an inevitable cultural predicament and of possible formation of collective identities-in-resistance, functions." Rey Chow, *Woman in Chinese Modernity: The Politics of Reading Between East and West* (Minneapolis: University of Minnesota Press, 1991), p. xi.

3. See Janet E. Ainsworth, "Interpreting Sacred Texts: Preliminary Reflections on Constitutional Discourse in China," *Hastings Law Journal*, no. 43 (1992), pp. 273–80.

4. See, for example, Don Yunhu and Liu Wuping, *Shijie Renquan Yuefa*, pp. 182, 209–10. See also "Human Rights in China" ("The White Paper"), pp. 43–45.

5. In what is in effect an extended response to the Chinese White Paper, Ann Kent has written a wide-ranging evaluation of Chinese human rights in thought and practice. See Ann Kent, *Between Freedom and Subsistence: China and Human Rights* (Hong Kong: Oxford University Press, 1993).

6. The formula comes from the Chinese reformer Zhang Zhidong, who advocated "Chinese learning as the substance (or essence—*ti*) and Western learning for use (or utility—*yong*). For a fuller discussion of the formula see Min Tu-ki, "Chinese 'Principle' and Western 'Utility': A Reassessment," in Philip A. Kuhn and Timothy Brook, eds., *National Polity and Local Power* (Cambridge: Harvard Yenching Institute, 1989), pp. 52–88.

7. For a full discussion of this period, see Mary C. Wright, *The Last Stand of Chinese Conservatism: The T'ung-chih Restoration, 1862–1974* (Palo Alto: Stanford University Press, 1966).

8. For a recent example of such negative views about Chinese tradition, see the open letter sent by 45 leading scientists and academics and written by Xu Lianying and Lin Mu. In an accompanying letter, which focussed on the UN designation of 1995 as the Year of Tolerance, the authors write "China's traditional culture . . . is accustomed to enforcing a unified way of thinking. The lack of a spirit of tolerance is the major obstacle in achieving China's modernization." See "Chinese Scholars Demand Freedoms," *The Globe and Mail*, May 17, 1995, p. A7.

9. This is the thesis of Joseph Levenson's seminal work, *Confucian China and Its Modern Fate* (Berkeley: University of California Press, 1968).

10. See Joseph R. Levenson, *Liang Ch'i-ch'ao and the Mind of Modern China* (Berkeley: University of California Press, 1967), pp. 1–8.

11. "The assumption that the study of China's cultural heritage by modern methods resembled a feature of the European Renaissance is not even half true. The early critical study of Chinese antiquity and the classics was really an attack upon them aimed at replacing the old by new findings. 'Down with Confucius and Sons' was the spirit of the times. The main current in the May Fourth Movement was never the restoration of the ancient spirit. If there was any restoration, it was a rediscovery of the real nature of antiquity as a result of the New learning from the West. The new learning of the modern world constituted a driving force of the movement, while the study of the heritage was only one of the fruits of this new learning. . . . Chinese antiquity and classics differed in essence from those of ancient Greece. Science and democracy were not features of ancient China." Chou Tse-tsung, *The May Fourth Movement: Intellectual Revolution in Modern China* (Stanford: Stanford University Press, 1967), p. 340.

12. J. R. Levenson, " 'History' and 'Value': the Tensions of Intellectual Choice in Modern China," in Arthur F. Wright, ed., *Studies in Chinese Thought* (Chicago: University of Chicago Press, 1953), pp. 146–94. For a further discussion of Levenson's views on the problem of history and value, see the foreword by Frederick E. Wakeman to Joseph R. Levenson, *Revolution and Cosmopolitanism: The Western Stage and the Chinese Stage* (Berkeley: University of California Press, 1971), pp. ix–xxix.

13. For an example of the effort to affirm the achievements of Chinese humanism in the context of reaffirming human rights, see Xia Yong, "Human Rights and Chinese Traditions," *Chinese Social Sciences Yearbook, 1994* (Beijing, 1994), pp. 268–80. The author suggests a complementarity of traditions which acknowledges the absence of rights dis-

course in the Chinese tradition but reaffirms support for the values protected by human rights within Chinese humanism.

14. "It is hardly surprising that the Chinese bourgeoisie and part of the May Fourth intelligentsia arrived at the conclusion that it was necessary to restore government authority, and that despite the fact that it meant giving up the autonomy they had acquired thanks to the economic expansion and the decline of the bureaucratic apparatus over the preceding years, they worked toward that end." Tu Weiming, "Intellectual Effervescence in China," *Daedalus*, vol. 121, no. 2 (Spring 1992), p. 279.

15. Mao Tse-tung, "On New Democracy," *Selected Works* (Peking: Foreign Language Press, 1965), vol. 2, p. 369.

16. Mao Tse-tung, "New Democracy," *Selected Works*, vol. 2, p. 380.

17. Ibid., p. 381.

18. Some flavor of Mao's private reading can be gleaned from photographs of his study—all of which feature traditional volumes placed in horizontal pigeonholes rather than modern hardcover books placed spine upright. A devastating portrait of Mao's private life confirms his preference for classical reading. See Li Zhisui, *The Private Life of Chairman Mao* (New York: Random House, 1994).

19. For example, even though the Chinese Communists and the PRC have always proclaimed the principle of popular sovereignty, "the people" too, is a dichotomous concept. The "people" is defined in relation to those termed as "the enemy." See Mao Tse-tung, "On the People's Democratic Dictatorship," *Selected Works*, vol. 4.

20. "Human rights: generally refers to rights of the person and democratic rights, a class concept which has its historical developmental process. Initially, the bourgeoisie raised 'human rights' in opposition to feudal privilege and clericalism . . . the fundamental purpose and core of the bourgeois slogan of human rights is the protection and development of the bourgeois ownership system. The proletariat does not enjoy human rights in general, but in some circumstances may insist on the protection of fundamental human rights. For the proletariat to achieve its own human rights, and truly gain emancipation it must first destroy the system of private property and establish public property. For this reason the proletariat never makes human rights its basic program but instead subsumes its own task and slogan in the destruction of the system of private property." *Jianming Shehuikexue Cidian* [A Concise Dictionary of the Social Sciences] (Shanghai: Shanghai Cidian Chubanshe, 1982), pp. 16–17.

21. See Joseph R. Levenson, "The Problem of Historical Significance," *Confucian China and Its Modern Fate*, vol. 3 (Berkeley: University of California Press, 1968), p. 114.

22. "The national effort of introspection, painful though it is, is actually one of the most helpful indicators that we have for the prospect of democratic political reform in China. As many Chinese tell me, if it were not for the cultural revolution, China's chances for democracy would not be as good as today they are. In a sense, precisely because they are so pessimistic about China, I am relatively optimistic." Andrew J. Nathan, *China's Crisis* (New York: Columbia University Press, 1990), p. 125.

23. One article concerning the development of the study of Confucius and Confucianism in the post-Mao period (referred to as the "period following the smashing of the Gang of Four") lamented the fact that "politics had swallowed up academic discussion." Interest had overtaken the pursuit of truth. "Once the only standard of true and false was that which was articulated by leaders, then the masses had no right to judge what was right and wrong, without the standard of right and wrong contributed by the masses, the leaders' standard of right and wrong lost its value, and there was no standard of truth. Since everyone had no sense of right and wrong, academic discussion was just chaos." Long Bu "Ping Sannian lai de Kongzi pingjia" [An Evaluation of Evaluations of Confucius over the Past Three Years], *Renmin Ribao*, January 29, 1980.

24. Mou Zhongjian "Zhongguo chuantong zhexue de pingjia ji qi lishi mingyun" [The Evaluation of Traditional Chinese Philosophy and Its Fate], *Hongqi*, no. 2, 1987, pp. 10–16 (*Zhexue Yanjiu*, no. 9, 1986).

25. Bao Zunxin "Ming Qing zhi ji de shehui sichao he wenyi fuxing" [Intellectual Trends in the Ming-Qing Transition and the Renaissance], Zhongguo Wenhua Shu Yuan *Zhongwai Wenhua Bijiao Yanjiu di er ji* (Beijing: Sanlian, 1988), p. 299.

26. For a fascinating debate concerning the origins of the Cultural Revolution according to whether it was seen as "anarchic" or a manifestation of "traditional despotism," see "Liang dai zhishifenzi duihualu"; Zhang Zuoyi, "He laoshimen tantan xin"; Ran Jie, "Women bu pa jianku, zhi pa pinyong," *Zhongguo Qingnian Bao*, October 9, 1986; Gao Jie "Guannian gengxin—linagdai zhishifenzi de jichu," *Zhongguo Qingnian Bao*, October 29, 1986.

27. See Leo Ou-fan Lee, "The Crisis of Culture," *China Briefing 1990* (Boulder: Westview Press, 1990), pp. 83–105; for a more critical view of this movement from the perspective of the idiosyncratic dissident critic Liu Xiaobo, see Geremie Barmé, "Confession, Redemption, and Death: Liu Xiaobo and the Protest Movement of 1989," in George Hicks, ed., *The Broken Mirror: China After Tiananmen* (Harlow, Essex UK: Longman, 1990), pp. 52–99.

28. Andrew Nathan has exposed the fallacious argument of *River Elegy*, "its assumption that Chinese civilization today is still traditional civilization. This ignores the very facts that make *River Elegy* and works like it possible—the historic experience of Maoism, the ability of Chinese to draw lessons from that experience, and the force of the new attitudes that *River Elegy* and works like it embody." *China's Crisis*, p. 125.

29. Both Yan and Fang, political scientist and astrophysicist respectively, began as members of the intellectual establishment. Yan Jiaqi is the former director of the Political Science Institute of the Chinese Academy of Social Sciences (CASS); Fang Lizhi was President of the China University of Science and Technology in Hefei until January 1987. For a compendium of Yan's liberal ideas, see David Bachman and Dali L. Yang, eds., *Yan Jiaqi and China's Struggle for Democracy* (Armonk, N.Y.: M. E. Sharpe, 1991); for Fang's ideas, see "On Patriotism and Global Citizenship," xxi–xxv; Perry Link, "The
Thought and Spirit of Fang Lizhi," in Hicks, *The Broken Mirror*, pp. 100–114.

30. Deng Xiaoping alludes to his authorship of this epithet in "Paichu ganrao, jiandingde shixing kaifang zhengce" [Overcome the Trouble, Resolutely Carry Out the Policy of Reform and Opening Up], *Shiyi*, p. 1193.

31. Despite this, Peter Moody believes they still betray the elitism of the traditional literati rather than modern democrats; see Peter R. Moody, Jr., "The Political Culture of Chinese Students and Intellectuals: A Historical Examination," *Asian Survey*, vol. 28, no. 11 (November 1988), pp. 1140–60.

32. Ren Wanding, "On the Historical Tasks and Goal of the Fighting People's Democratic Movement," in James Tong, ed., *Death at the Gate of Heavenly Peace: The Democracy Movement in Beijing, April-June 1989. Chinese Law and Government*, vol. 23, no. 1 (Spring 1990), p. 38.

33. For a discussion of "neo-authoritarianism," see Barry Sautman, "Sirens of the Strongman: Neo-Authoritarianism in Recent Chinese Political Theory," *The China Quarterly*, no. 129 (March 1992), pp. 79–102.

34. "Guanyu Zhongguo de Minzhu yü Weilai" [On China's Democracy and Future], *Beijing Ribao*, June 22, 1990.

35. McCormick and Kelly, "The Limits of Anti-Liberalism in China."

36. This xenophobic movement expresses a kind of antinomian iconoclasm in direct reaction to the trite clichés of modernization and progress. This opposition to the sloganeering of modernization enables this movement to be at once nativist and anti-official. It expresses cultural ambivalence of identity within the framework of modernization but has a tenuous connection to China's intellectual legacy (resonating rather more strongly with the anti-official traditions of popular culture than with the moral idealism of Confucianism). Furthermore, efforts to adapt Buddhist and Daoist themes to create a Chinese form of "Magical Realism" present an instrumental response to cosmopolitan competition, rather than a reinterpretation of tradition. See Geremie R. Barmé, "To Screw Foreigners is Patriotic: China's Avant-garde Nationalists," *The China Journal*, no. 34 (July 1995), pp. 209–34.

37. Tu Weiming, "Intellectual Effervescence in China," *Daedalus*, vol. 127, no. 2 (Spring 1992), p. 288.

38. The opening salvo in this came in a long article on "Democracy and the Rule of Law" by a "Special Commentator," published in the *People's Daily* [*Renmin Ribao*], July 13, 1978. The article reads in part, "Our socialist society, was born out of a semi-feudal semi-colonial Old China with no democratic tradition. Feudal ideas, feudal ethics, and feudal habits are quite deep, and seep into the corners of social life. The old society has been destroyed, but the old ideology cannot be destroyed all at once. We can clearly see the feudal specter hovering over the 'Gang of Four.' Therefore to clean out the poisonous influence of the Gang of Four also means to clean out the poisonous influence of feudal autocracy."

39. See, for example, Jin Guantao, Liu Qingfeng, *Xingcheng yu weiji: Lun Zhongguo Shehui Chaowending Jieguo* [The Cycle of Growth and Decline: On the Ultrastable Struc-

ture of Chinese Society] (2d rev. ed.; Hong Kong: Chinese University Press, 1992), p. 260. See also the influential intellectual historian Zhang Dainian, who states flatly "Confucianism and Daoism fail to investigate nature," "The Impact of the Thought of the School of Confucianism and the School of Daoism," *Chinese Studies in Philosophy*, vol. 24, no. 4 (Summer 1993), p. 84.

40. Zhu Riyao, Cao Deben, and Sun Xiaochun, *Zhongguo chuantong zhengzhiwenhua de xiandai sikao* [A Modern Consideration of the Traditional Chinese Political Culture] (Changchun: Jilin Daxue chubanshe, 1990), p. 28.

41. David L. Hall and Roger T. Ames, *Thinking through Confucius*. Albany: SUNY Press, 1987.

42. Zhang Huibin, "Zhongguo Chuantong Wenhua Renwen Jingshen de tedian" [The Special Character of the Humanistic Spirit of the Traditional Chinese Culture] *Xuexi yu Tansuo*, no. 52 (October 1987), pp. 57–65, esp. p. 62.

43. For a broad-ranging survey of the political contestation in contemporary Chinese historiography, see Jonathan Unger, ed., *Using the Past to Serve the Present: Historiography and Politics in Contemporary China*. Armonk, N.Y.: M. E. Sharpe, 1993.

44. Yang She, "Renquan lilun yanjiu: renquanguan he Zhongxi wenhua chuantong chayi" [Studies on Human Rights: Views on Human Rights and Differences Between Chinese and Western Culture], *Beijing Daxue Xuebao* (Zhexue Shejuikexue ban), no. 3, 1992, pp. 41–42.

45. Information Office of the State Council, "Human Rights in China" (White Paper on Human Rights), *Beijing Review*, November 4–10, 1991, p. 9.

46. Ibid.

47. See Chih-yu Shih, "Contending Theories of 'Human Rights with Chinese Characteristics,'" *Issues and Studies*, vol. 29, no. 11 (November 1993), pp. 42–63.

48. Xu Weidong, Shen Zhengwu, and Zheng Chengliang, "Lun Renquan de Yishixingtai biaojun yu Falü biaojun" [On Ideological and Legal Standards of Human Rights], *Zhongguo Faxue*, no. 1 (1992), p. 3.

49. This was the position enunciated by the Chinese delegation to the Bangkok Conference of February 1993: "In the long process of history, the hard-working, brave and intelligent Asian people have created the splendid cultural tradition of respecting the rights of the state, society, family and individuals. This particular culture had played an important role in promoting the stability of the state and promoting the steady development of economy and society." See Sidney Jones, "Culture Clash: Asian Activists Counter Their Government's Restrictive View of Human Rights," *China Rights Forum*, Summer 1993, p. 9.

50. "Makesizhuyi Renquanguan" [The Marxist View of Human Rights], in Dong Yunhu and Liu Wuping, eds., *Shijie renquan Yuefa Zonglan* [A Compendium of World Human Rights Documents] (Chengdu: Sichuan Renmin Chubanshe, 1991), p. 3.

51. The former editor of the *People's Daily* and a prominent "liberal" forced out of the

Chinese Communist Party argues that "Basing ourselves on the knowledge that the traditional notions are now changing, as well as on an analysis of the current situation, we can put forward the following recognition—the development of the market will become the basis and the motive force for Chinese democracy." He distinguishes the traditional system where political power was based on the direct control of one person by another, to a system where more and more people are able to pursue their own values and realize their own interests. See Hu Jiwei, "Shichang Jingji: Shixian Zhongguo Minzhu de Jichu he Dongli" [The Market Economy: The Basis and Motive Force of Chinese Democracy], *Ming Bao Yuekan* (June 1994), pp. 83–87.

52. For further discussion of this problem, see the author's *Self and Authority in Contemporary China: The End of Ideology?* East Asian Institute, Columbia University (April 1993).

53. During his "southern tour" of February 1992, Deng Xiaoping in effect called for a moratorium on the employment of these dichotomous concepts with his call to end debate over whether phenomena are called "socialist" or "capitalist" (*xingze; xingshe*). See Deng Xiaoping, *Wenxuan* III.

54. Guo Daohui, "Shichang Jingji yu faxue lilun, fazhi guannian de biange" [The Market Economy and Change in Jurisprudential Theory and Ideas about the Rule of Law], *Xinhua Wenzhai*, no. 5, 1994, p. 17.

55. Zhao Xiuyi, "Shichang jingji, jinjixue yu lunlixue: [Market Economies, Economics and Ethics], *Xinhua Wenzhai*, no. 5, 1994, p. 30.

56. Li Buyun, "Shehuizhuyi Renquan de Jiben Lilun yu Shijian" [The Basic Theory and Practice of Socialist Human Rights], *Faxue Yanjiu*, no. 4 (1992), p. 3.

57. Historians may remember the assault by intellectuals close to the KMT on "Chinese Culture as *benwei*," another version of the conservative defenders of the school of "national essence." To regard *rights* as *benwei* is an ironic reversal of such traditionalism.

58. Zheng Chengliang, "Quanli Benwei Shuo" [Talking of the Basic Position of Rights], *Zhengzhi yu Falu* [Political Science and Law], no. 4 (1989), pp. 2–5.

59. Gong Pixian, Li Yisheng, "Shangpin Jingji yu zhengzhi wenhua guannian" [The Commodity Economy and the Notion of Political Culture], *Zhengzhixue Yanjiu*, no. 1 (1987), pp. 11–16.

60. Wang Jian, "Wenhua jicheng de duowei shenshih" [The Interwoven Fabric of Cultural Inheritance], *Xuexi yu Tansuo*, no. 1 (1992), pp. 16–21, esp. p. 19.

61. Bei Yue, " 'Yiwu Zhongxin' yu 'quanlibenwei' bianxi" [Debating and Analyzing the Centrality of Obligations and the Basic Place of Rights], *Zhongwai Faxue* [Peking University Law Journal], no. 3 (1992), pp. 17–23.

62. Xie Pengchen, "Quanli Yiwu Silun" [Four Doctrines about Rights and Duties], *Faxue Yanjiu*, no. 3 (1992), pp. 1–7

63. Zhang Hengshan, "On Obligations as the Center of Law," *Zhongguo Faxue*, no. 5 (1990), pp. 29—35.

64. Zhang Hengshan, "Faxue Bujieshou 'quanli benwei' " [Jurisprudence Will Not Accept the Standard of Rights], *Zhengshi yu Falu*, 4 (1989), pp. 6–9

65. Zhang Hengshan, p. 31.

66. Cheng supra

67. "With respect [to the relationship of human rights and sovereignty] there are three points of view: human rights are higher than sovereignty; sovereignty is higher than human rights; human rights and sovereignty are closely linked, in line with one another. With respect to any particular country, without sovereignty, there can be no human rights, and sovereignty is a precondition for human rights; however, in some countries, having sovereignty does not necessarily imply that human rights are present there. Therefore to surmise that sovereignty is higher than human rights would not be favorable to the self-conscious and diligent improvement of the human rights situation in some countries according to international conventions, social morality and public opinion. Therefore the majority of scholars believe that the third point of view is relatively scientific." "Zhonguo Faxue hui Faxue ji chulilun yanjiuhui" [The Chinese Legal Association Conference on Fundamental Jurisprudential Theory], *Zhonguo Faxue*, no. 4 (1992), pp. 113–4.

68. Some preliminary efforts in that direction were made by Andrew Nathan and Tianjian Shi, "Cultural Requisites for Democracy in China: Findings from a Survey," *Daedalus*, vol. 122, no. 2 (Spring 1993), pp. 95–3. The findings do indeed demonstrate some significant differences between educated and less educated Chinese. Surprisingly, on a comparative basis, less educated Chinese showed relatively high expectations of equal treatment from government officials, despite the fact they also showed low awareness of the impact of government in their lives. By contrast the better educated, particularly those with tertiary education, were much more skeptical.

69. Zhang Dainian, "Zhongguo zhexue guanyu ren yu ziran de xueshuo" [Chinese Philosophy on Man and Nature] in Tang Yijie, ed., *Zhongguo Wenhua yu Zhongguo Zhexue*. Beijing: Sanlian, 1987, pp. 43–.

70. See, for example, Luo Guojie "Shemme shi Zhonghua Minzu youliang chuantong" [What Is the Excellent Tradition of the Chinese Nation], *Xinhua Wenzhai*, no. 5 (1994), pp. 30–31.

71. See, for example, the invidious comparison made by the philosopher Zhang Sheying of Enlightenment thinkers such as Kant, Fichte, Schelling, and Hegel on the importance of human subjectivity and even the Ming thinkers such as Wang Yangming. "When the Song, Yuan and Ming-Qing philosophers talked of the linkage between heaven and Man, this however does not amount to a confirmation of human subjectivity," "Cong Zhutixing Yuanzi kan ZhongXi Zhexue de chayi" [A Look at the Discrepancy between Western and Chinese Philosophy from the Principle of Subjectivity] in Tang Yijie, ed., *Zhongguo Wenhua yu Zhongguo Zhexue* (Beijing: Sanlian, 1987), p. 58.

Epilogue: Human Rights as a Confucian Moral Discourse

Tu Weiming

Human rights discourse may be conceived as the contemporary embodiment of the Enlightenment spirit. While it does not directly address the question of human survival, it specifies the minimum requirements and basic conditions for human flourishing. It is a powerful, if not the most persuasive, universal moral discourse in the international arena. It may very well be the most effective, if not the only, "instrument" by which the states' ordinary standards of behavior can be judged by the international community without infringing upon the prerogatives of sovereignty.

The universality of human rights broadly conceived in the 1948 Declaration is a source of inspiration for the human community. The moral and legal imperative that any civilized state treat its citizens in accordance with the political rights guaranteed by its own constitution is still a compelling argument. The desirability of democracy as providing to this day the most effective framework in which human rights are safeguarded is obvious. However, the human rights movement as a dynamic process rather than a static structure requires that the human rights discourse be dialogical, communicative and, hopefully, mutually beneficial.

Seen from a comparative cultural and trans-generational perspective, the inclusive agenda of the United Nations Declaration of Human Rights reflects the pragmatic idealism and optimistic aspirations of the postwar world mentality at its most generous and future-oriented moment. It may not be far-fetched to characterize it as a manifestation of the American spirit in its most broad-minded internationalist incarnation. All three generations of human rights as an evolving moral discourse are accounted for: (1) political rights, (2) economic, social, and cultural rights, and (3) group rights. The comprehensiveness of the agenda, which may have resulted from negotiation and compromise, suggests that, under the American leadership, the international community was willing to subscribe to a moral vision not only for a human survival but also for human flourishing. Implicit in such a document is the idea of a good society, the value of a humane form of life for all members of the human community, and the ethic of responsibility of all "civilized" governments to work toward a common goal of universal peace. The foundation of the Universal Declaration of Human Rights has been broadened and strengthened by governments, nongovernmental organizations, and conscientious citizens throughout the world for almost half a century since 1948 when Professor Wu Teh Yao, an original drafter of the United Nations Universal Declaration of Human Rights in 1948, took part in an unprecedented effort to inscribe, not only on paper but on human conscience, the bold vision of a new world order rooted in respect for human dignity as the central value for political action. With this background understanding in mind, although the situation in the 1990s presents new challenges unanticipated and perhaps unimaginable more than forty years ago, it also affirms the prescient goodwill of the original drafters of this unprecedented historical document.

The Vienna Declaration and program of action resulting from the World Conference on Human Rights in June 1993 directs our attention to women, children, minorities, disabled persons, and indigenous peoples, groups not included in the original conceptions of human rights. The three key regional meetings in Tunis, San José, and Bangkok were an integral part of the preparatory process for the Vienna Conference in which several human rights declarations outlining particular concerns and perspectives of the African, Latin American and the Caribbean, and Asia-Pacific regions were produced.[1] The recognition of interdependence between democracy, development, and human rights led to the cooperation of international organizations and national agencies in broadening the concept of human rights to include the right to development.[2] While some human rights advocates view this confluence of social and economic concerns as undermining the effectiveness of some national and intentional instruments focusing on well-defined political rights, these convergent concerns have already engendered new mechanisms for the promotion of human rights.

The Social Summit in Copenhagen in January 1995, which focused on the critical issues confronting the global community (poverty, unemployment, and social disintegration), is indicative of a new awareness that human rights ought

to be broadly defined to include economic, social, and cultural dimensions of the human experience. The idea of human dignity features prominently in the documents in preparation for the Summit. Indeed, the participants of the Seminar on the Ethical and Spiritual Dimensions of Social Development organized by the preparatory committee strongly endorsed the view that human rights, which have more to do with ethics, law, and politics and can be verified and measured, constitute preferred means of putting into practice the concept of human dignity. They also underscored the inseparability of human rights as a political agenda and human dignity as an ethical-religious concern.[3]

This renewed awareness of the ecumenical character of the original United Nations Declaration serves as a critique of the claim that since human rights are understood in a variety of ways according to culture, history, stage of economic development, and concrete political situation, they cannot be universally appreciated as values and aspirations for the global community. Indeed, this accords with the underlying assumptions of Confucian "core values": the perception of the person as a center of relationships rather than simply as an isolated individual, the idea of society as a community of trust rather than merely a system of adversarial relationships, and the belief that human beings are duty-bound to respect their family, society, and nation. These values are not only compatible with the implementation of human rights; they can, in fact, enhance the universal appeal of human rights. The potential contribution of in-depth discussion on Asian values to a sophisticated cultural appreciation of the human rights discourse is great.

Actually there is virtual consensus that since respect for rights and the exercise of responsibility toward others are evidence of human dignity, rights and responsibility are inseparable in all domains of human flourishing: self-cultivation, regulation of family, order in society, governance of state, peace throughout the world, and harmony with nature. In any concrete situation of human encounter, rights and responsibility ought to be mutually informing at all levels of human-relatedness from the family to the global community.[4] The Asian, specifically Confucian, values discussion that emerged in the regional meeting in Bangkok in 1993 provides us with an opportunity to develop a truly ecumenical agenda allowing the human rights discourse to become a continuously evolving and edifying conversation.[5] The danger of using Confucian values as a cover for authoritarian practices notwithstanding, the authentic possibility of dialogue, communication, and mutually beneficial exchange must be fully explored. The perceived Confucian preference for duty, harmony, consensus, network, ritual, trust, and sympathy need not be a threat to rights-consciousness at all.

The critique of acquisitive individualism, vicious competitiveness, pernicious relativism, and excessive litigiousness help us to understand that Enlightenment values do not necessarily cohere into an integrated guide for action.   299

The conflict between liberty and equality and the lack of concern for community have significantly undermined the persuasive power of human rights based exclusively on the self-interest of isolated individuals. Confucian values as richly textured ideas of human flourishing can serve as a source of inspiration for representing human rights as the common language of humanity. The challenge is how to fruitfully introduce a Confucian perspective on the evolving human rights discourse without diffusing the focused energy of the national and international instruments that have been promoting political rights with telling effectiveness in some selected areas of the world. The difficulty, however, is that the concretely demonstrable successes of the narrowly focused political rights persuasion are not easily sustainable. A confrontational strategy, if not politically arrogant and culturally insensitive, is predicated on and handicapped by, an outmoded faith in instrumental rationality. It is doubtful that it can continue to work well as a liberalizing and democratizing force in the global community.

In the long-term, a better strategy is to cultivate a communal critical self-awareness that instruments for promoting human rights, while universally connected, are firmly grounded in indigenous cultural conditions as well. Through intercultural dialogue, face-to-face communication, and mutually beneficial exchange, a truly ecumenical conceptualization of human rights can overcome the narrowly defined instrumental rationality, intellectual naiveté, and self-imposed parochialism characteristic of the current state of affairs in North America. The time is ripe for a comparative civilizational discourse on human rights to serve not only as a moral basis for the new discourse on world order but as a spiritual joint venture for human coexistence and mutual flourishing.

A key to the success of this spiritual joint venture is to recognize the apparent absence of the idea of community, let alone the global community, in the Enlightenment project. Fraternity (one of the three cardinal virtues of the French Revolution—liberty, equality, and fraternity), the functional equivalent of community, has received scant attention in modern Western economic, political, and social thought. Surely, "community" features prominently in "Kant's (and Adam Smith's) strong commitment to a cosmopolitan political ideal."[6] This may have been the continuation of the Greek idea of polis and more specifically the Stoic tradition, "a tradition in which we also find an image of concentric circles of human attachments, extending outward to the community of humankind."[7] Yet, it is undeniable that in modern Western political philosophy the tension is so exclusively focused on the relationship between the individual and the state that all other forms of human-relatedness, including the basic dyadic relationships of the family, are relegated to the background. It seems that contemporary political theoreticians in the West, either by choice or by default, have abdicated their responsibility to consider family as a critical issue in adjudicating the relationship between the individual and the state, allowing the sociologists and anthropologists to worry about the political implications of the family. The situation in the United States has begun to change mainly as a result of the recent attention on "family virtues" in national political debates.

Family, which plays so crucial a role in political order, is not absent in the major classics in Western political thought. Aristotle's *Politics*, Locke's *Second Treatise*, Rousseau's *Social Contract*, Kant's *Rechslehre*, and Hegel's *Philosophy of Right* all provide thought-provoking accounts of the family.[8] Furthermore, "the leading contemporary philosopher, John Rawls, explores the role of the family as a fundamental unit of moral education."[9] Yet, as Professor Joshua Cohen of the Massachusetts Institute of Technology notes, the main thrust of the political theories from Aristotle to Hegel is to make a clear distinction between the affective and ethical bonds operative in the family on the one hand and politics on the other. By sharply contrasting political obligations from filial piety, they perceive a major rupture between familial and political relation.[10] Understandably, they do not see the relevance of ethical behavior in the privacy of the family to the moral obligations of the public domain. It seems curious that the family is absent in the definition that man is a political animal.

The unintended negative consequences of this inattention to the relevance of family to politics are grave. The incongruity between what we do as responsible and responsive members of the family and as a rights-bearing and self-interested political animals is a case in point. This incongruity may have contributed to the development of a public persona informed by values that are clearly antithetical to moral self-cultivation. As a result, our willingness to tolerate preposterous inequality, greedy self-interest, and aggressive egoism have greatly poisoned the good well of progress, reason and individualism.

The need to express a universal ethic for the formation of a global village and to articulate a possible link between the fragmented world we experience in our ordinary daily existence and the imagined community for the human species as a whole is deeply felt by an increasing number of concerned intellectuals. This requires at the minimum the replacement of the principle of self-interest, no matter how broadly defined, with the Confucian golden rule: "Do not do to others what we would not want others to do to us."[11] Since the new golden rule is stated in the negative, it will have to be augmented by a positive principle:

> In order to establish ourselves, we must help others to establish themselves; in order to enlarge ourselves, we must help others to enlarge themselves.[12]

An inclusive sense of community based on the communal critical self-consciousness of the reflective minds is an ethico-religious goal as well as a philosophical ideal. The centrality of the family as politically significant and self-cultivation as a public good rather than a private concern must be recognized.

We can actually envision the Confucian perception of human self-development, based upon the dignity of the person, in terms of a series of concentric circles: self, family, community, society, nation, world, and cosmos. We begin with a quest for true personal identity, an open and creatively transforming selfhood which, paradoxically, must be predicated on our ability to overcome selfishness and egoism. We cherish family cohesiveness. In order to do that, we have to go beyond nepotism. We embrace communal solidarity, but we have to go beyond parochialism to fully realize its true value. We can be enriched by social integration, provided that we overcome ethnocentrism and chauvinistic culturalism. We are committed to national unity, but we ought to transcend aggressive nationalism so that we can be genuinely patriotic. We are inspired by human flourishing, but we must endeavor not to be confined by anthropocentrism—the full meaning of humanity is anthropocosmic rather than anthropocentric. On the occasion of the international symposium on Islamic-Confucian dialogue organized by the University of Malaya (March 1995), the Deputy Prime Minister of Malaysia, Anwar Ibrahim, quoted a statement from Huston Smith's *The World's Religions*, which captures the Confucian spirit of self-transcendence:

> In shifting the center of one's emphatic concern from oneself to one's family one transcends selfishness. The move from family to community transcends nepotism. The move from community to nation transcends parochialism and the move to all humanity counters chauvinistic nationalism.[13]

We can even add: the move toward the unity of Heaven and humanity (*tianrenheyi*) transcends secular humanism, a blatant form of anthropocentrism characteristic of the intellectual ethos of the modern West. Indeed, it is in the anthropocosmic spirit that we find communication between self and community, harmony between human species and nature, and mutuality between humanity and Heaven. This integrated comprehensive vision of learning to be human can very well serve as the core of Confucian humanist concerns.

Confucians do not require an ideal speech situation. Nor are they ready to defend a new "communicative rationality"[14] based upon abstract principles. They do ask fundamental questions. Should we understand the self as an isolated individual or as a center of relationships? Should we approach our society as a community based upon trust or simply the result of contractual arrangements of conflicting forces? As we begin to appreciate our embeddedness in our linguistic universe, not to mention our historicity, we cannot escape a de facto parochialism, no matter how open-minded we intend to be and how liberated we think we are, we must respect alternative intelligence and radical otherness.

East Asian intellectuals are earnestly engaged in probing the Confucian tradition(s) as a spiritual resource for economic development, nation-building, social stability, and cultural identity. While they cherish the hope that their appreciation of their own cultural values will provide ethical moorings as they try to locate their niche in the turbulent currents of the modern world, they remain active participants in the Enlightenment project. The revived Confucian values are no longer fundamentalist representation of nativistic ideas; they are, by and large, transvaluated traditional values compatible and commensurate with the main thrust of modern ideology defined in terms of Enlightenment ideas. The critical issue, then, is not traditional Confucian values versus modern Western values, but how East Asian intellectuals can be enriched and empowered by their own cultural roots in their critical response to an already partially domesticated Enlightenment heritage. The full development of human rights requires their ability to creatively transform the Enlightenment mentality into a thoroughly digested cultural tradition of their own; this, in turn, is predicated on their capacity to creatively mobilize indigenous social capital and cultural assets for the task. They must be willing to confront difficult and threatening challenges, identify complex real options, and make painful practicable decisions.

The conflicts between liberty and equality, economic efficiency and social justice, development and stability, self-interest and the public good, not to mention rights and duty, are harsh realities in practical living. The enhancement of liberty, economic efficiency, development, self-interest, and rights is highly desirable, but to pursue these values exclusively at the expense of equality, social justice, stability, the public good, and duty is ill-advised. As the supposed exemplification of modernity—North America and Western Europe—continue to show ignorance of the cultures of the rest of the world and insouciance about the peoples who do not speak their languages, East Asia cannot but choose its own way. It is in this sense that a Confucian perspective on human rights is worth exploring.

Confucian humanism offers "an account of the reasons for supporting basic human rights that does not depend on a liberal conception of persons, and that operates from within an ethical outlook dominated by notions of persons as embedded in social relations and subject to the obligations associated with those relationships: therefore an account that responds to the concern about sectarianism."[15] The liberal ideas of the persons as fundamentally choosers of their aims and of rights as ways to acknowledge the human capacity to formulate and revise their aims affirm individuals to have worth or dignity in abstraction from social setting. Thus John Rawls defines individuals as "self-authenticating sources of valid claims." These individualistic claims are "regarded as having weight of their own apart from being derived from duties and obligations owed to society."[16] On the contrary, the Confucian position asserts:

> The notions of persons standing in social relationships and of duties associated with positions in those relationships remain fundamental in that rights are presented as flowing from the demands of these duties, and an account of the worth of human beings is tied to their fulfilling of social responsibilities.[17]

While the Confucian position seems to subscribe to a view that Rawls rejects in his political doctrine, it gets to the basic rights incorporated into the Universal Declaration without presupposing the ideas of the person commonly associated with liberalism.

Furthermore, as bearers of obligations, we can demand proper treatment as conditions for fulfilling the obligations we are assumed to have. Similarly, if our human worth is predicated on our ability to fulfill responsibilities, we can demand of others—as a condition of acknowledging that worth—that they assure the conditions required for fulfilling their responsibilities. If we become more powerful and influential, we are more obligated, responsible, and duty-bound to assure the well-being of others. As a corollary, we can demand that those in power fulfill their responsibility of caring for the good of society. The basic human rights can, therefore, flow from political leadership. Rights understood in this way are not derived from "ascribed roles in a social hierarchy justified by religious or aristocratic values." Nor, strictly speaking, are they derived from "duties and obligations owed to society."[18] It is in the dignity and worth of the self as a center of relationships that the justification for rights is located.

The Confucian perspective can respond to the criticism about the sectarianism of human rights views by stating that "such views can provide a common language, a framework of political argument that can be shared across religious, moral, philosophical traditions."[19] However, while we can envision the relevance and significance of human rights from a variety of ethical outlooks, we do not endorse the view that human rights discourse is theory neutral. The pluralism of moral-political positions makes it unlikely that cross-cultural conversation or dialogue of civilization will generate consensus or convergence on a single philosophical anthropology. However, although reasonable people will disagree on philosophies and worldviews, they cannot afford to endorse relativism just because "pluralism is a basic fact of international life." Surely, "Human rights are not the special property of any single outlook,"[20] but probing the deeper issues of philosophical anthropology is required not only by the desire to develop a global ethic but also by the necessity of a shared commitment to the dignity of the person.

Guided by pragmatic idealism and optimistic aspiration, the original drafters of the Universal Declaration, intent on consensus formation, deliberately avoided references to any specific cultural heritage, spiritual tradition, philosophical position, or ethical system. The thinness, if not vacuity, of its theoretical under-pinnings may give the impression that its universality is predicated on an inat-tention to context, historicity, and value commitment. The belief in the mini-malist quest for the lowest common denominator is a reflection of the instru-mental rationality of the Enlightenment mentality. While such an approach makes good political sense in terms of legality, it fails to inspire the noble senti-ments of the soul which, in a highly contentious pluralistic world, are necessary for human flourishing. The Confucians believe that a sense of rootedness is not at all incompatible with a global ethic intended for the human community. They further believe that the confluence of the local stories of self-realization, indi-vidually and communally, gives rich texture to human self-understanding. This suggests that an ecumenical exploration of the good life for our species at this critical juncture is an urgent task for the human rights discourse.

Paradoxically, the Confucian personality ideals—the authentic person (*jun-zi*), the worthy (*xianren*), or the sage (*shengren*)—can be realized more fully in the liberal-democratic society than either in the traditional imperial dictator-ship or a modern authoritarian regime. East Asian Confucian ethics must cre-atively transform itself in the light of Enlightenment values before it can serve as an effective critique of the modern West.[21] Yet, those of us who are blessed with political rights in the first world must recognize that, in a comparative cultural perspective, our style of life, corrupted by excessive individualism, pernicious competitiveness, and vicious litigiousness, is not only endangering the well-being of others but is also detrimental to our own wholesomeness. Our willingness to learn from significantly different conceptualizations of the rights discourse and to respond openly and responsibly to criticisms of defi-ciency in our own human rights records must serve as a precondition for our determination to share our experience with the rest of the world and to make sure that human rights violations are clearly noted and properly corrected by the instruments at our disposal. An inquiry on global ethic, with this attitude in mind, is relevant to and crucial for human rights discourse on the interna-tional scene toward the next century.

Acknowledgments

I am indebted to the Management Committee of the Wu Teh Yao Memorial Fund, Directors of the National University of Singapore Centre for the Arts, and the Singapore Hainan Hwee Kuan for inviting me to give the Inaugural Wu Teh Yao Memorial Lecture in March 1995. Portions of the current state-ment are based on an edited transcription of my oral presentation. I am also grateful to the China Forum, organized by the MIT International Science and Technology Initiative, for sponsoring a lecture on "A Confucian Perspective on

Human Rights," April 29, 1996. Professor Joshua Cohen's written comments are most instructive for reformulating my thoughts. I wish also to acknowledge my gratitude to participants of the 1995 Conference on Confucianism and Human Rights. Their active involvement helped to make the Conference a truly open and open-ended dialogue. The Triglar Group, organized by Jacques and Barbara Baudot, has been a source of inspiration for my continuing education in human rights discourse.

Notes

1. Boutros Boutros-Ghali, "Human Rights: The Common Language of Humanity," statement made in Vienna at the opening of the World Conference on Human Rights, June 14, 1993. *World Conference on Human Rights: The Vienna Declaration and Programme of Action, June 1993* (New York: UN Department of Public Information, 1993), p. 3.

2. See "The Human Rights to Development," in *United Nations World Summit for Social Development* (New York: American Association for the International Commission of Jurists, 1995), pp. 11–14.

3. *Ethical and Spiritual Dimensions of Social Progress* (New York: United Nations Publication, 1955), pp. 25–34.

4. Based on the Confucian insight originally presented in the *Great Learning*, see Daniel K. Gardner, *Chu Hsi and the Ta-hsüeh: Neo-Confucian Reflection on the Confucian Canon* (Cambridge: Council on East Asian Studies, Harvard University, 1986).

5. In addition to the famous Bangkok Governmental Declaration endorsed all the Asian governments at the April 1993 Asian regional preparatory meeting for the Vienna World Conference on Human Rights, there is also the statement of Asian NGO's (nongovernmental organizations) issued March 27, 1993. For an informative account of the vital issues involved, see Yash Ghai, "Human Rights and Governance: The Asian Debate," Occasional Paper No. 4 (The Asia Foundation: Center for Asian Pacific Affairs, 1994). For a thought-provoking account of a new vision on human rights from an Islamic perspective, see Chandra Muzaffar, *Human Rights and the New World Order* (Penang: Just World Trust, 1993).

6. Joshua Cohen, "Comments on Tu Weiming, 'A Confucian Perspective of Human Rights,'" at the China Forum sponsored by the MIT International Science and Technology Initiative, April 29, 1996, manuscript, p. 4.

7. Ibid, pp. 4–5.

8. Ibid., p. 5.

9. Ibid.

10. Ibid.

11. *Analects*, 5:11, 12:2.

12. Ibid., 6:28.

13. Quoted in the address by Anwar Ibrahim at the opening of the international

seminar on Islam and Confucianism: A Civilizational Dialogue, sponsored by University of Malaya, March 13, 1995. It should be noted that Huston Smith's particular reference to the Confucian Project, bases it on my discussion on the meaning of self-transcendence in Confucian humanism. If we follow my "anthropocosmic" argument through, we need to transcend "anthropocentrism" as well. See Huston Smith, *The World's Religions* (San Francisco: Harper San Francisco, 1991), pp. 182, 193, 195 (notes 28 and 29).

14. Jürgen Habermas, *The Theory of Communicative Action*, trans. Thomas McCarthy (Boston: Beacon Press, 1984), vol. 1.

15. Joshua Cohen, Comments, p. 8.

16. Ibid., p. 9.

17. Ibid., p. 8.

18. Ibid. In this sense, I am modifying Professor Cohen's use of Rawls's distinction to explain the force of the Confucian argument.

19. Ibid., p. 9.

20. Ibid., pp. 9–10.

21. This idea was first presented in Chinese at the conclusion of the international conference celebrating the 2,545th anniversary of Confucius's birth and the formation of the International Association of Confucian Studies, sponsored by the Confucius Foundation, Beijing, October 5, 1994.

Epilogue: Confucianism, Human Rights, and "Cultural Relativism"

Louis Henkin

Deliberations about Confucianism and constitutionalism, taking place during the final years of the twentieth century, echo other contemporary discussions and debates. For example, at the World Conference on Human Rights held in Vienna in 1993, some Asian delegations seemed to challenge the universality of human rights: they insisted that human rights have to be understood and applied in the context of particular cultures and their particular values, and that Asian values differ from Western values in relevant respects.[1] At the same time, other Asian voices—governmental as well as nongovernmental—rejected arguments for "Asian human rights" and insisted on the universality of human rights. (Even those who insisted on "Asian values" did not reject the idea of *human* rights, i.e., rights of all human beings, expressing reservation only as to the elaboration of the idea and the definition of its content in United Nations instruments as construed by "Western" states.) In the end, moreover, since, by their own ideology, international human rights are not absolute and may bow to public interest, essentially the Asian delegations were questioning the particular balance which human rights instruments and the International Human Rights movement have struck between the human rights of the individual and the interests of the community.

The essays in this volume discuss Confucianism and human rights, not Asian values and human rights. "Asian values" have not been defined, and may well include more than, or other than, Confucianism. But the debates at Vienna suggest the desirability of exploring—by way of "epilogue" to the discussions reproduced in this volume—the relevance of Confucianism to the international law and politics of human rights in Asia.

What has Confucian thought in common with the human rights idea, and where might the two diverge? In particular, does Confucianism today resist the human rights idea, its ideology, and its elaboration in national and international instruments? Or, might a society committed to Confucianism today also need the human rights idea, its norms and institutions, its forms and remedies?

The Idea of Human Rights

According to the idea of human rights, every human being in political society has legitimate claims upon his or her political society to certain rights *as of right*. Society must respect and ensure these rights. Society must be organized so that rights are realized in fact—that officials and public institutions respect them, ensure that they are respected by others, and provide remedies if rights are violated.

Human rights are rooted in a conception of human dignity; indeed, for the human rights movement, human dignity implies human rights. Human dignity determines and defines rights; human dignity requires that human rights be recognized and realized. Human rights are defined, particularized, in the Universal Declaration of Human Rights, proclaimed by the General Assembly of the United Nations in 1948; those rights, and means for realizing them, are developed in the two international covenants deriving from the Declaration.

The Universal Declaration (and the Covenants) recognize civil, political, economic, and social rights. They include: a right to equality in rights for all without discrimination, as well as the right to equality before the law; the right to life, liberty, security, and personhood; to physical integrity, including freedom from torture or inhuman and degrading treatment or punishment; freedom from slavery; freedom from interference with one's autonomy and liberty, from arbitrary arrest, detention, or exile; freedom from incarceration or other punishment without fair trial, and due process of law; freedom of movement and residence; freedom of conscience, thought, and religion, of expression, of association; rights to family and privacy, and rights of men and women to equality in marriage; rights of self-government, including the right to vote and seek public office. Society must provide remedies for violations of these rights. The individual also has economic and social rights required for his/her dignity and development—rights to property, education, work, and leisure, housing, health care, social security. (Economic and social rights, it was later recognized, may have to be achieved progressively and to the extent of available resources.)

The individual also has duties and responsibilities to society. Individual rights bow to public needs and interests, but they do not bow readily or lightly. (At   309 bottom, the dignity of each individual member of society is itself an important public interest.) And the requirements of human dignity impose limits on the limitations on rights that may be imposed in the public interest.

Human Rights and Confucian Values

The values reflected in the commitment to human dignity, in the idea of human rights, and in the particular rights set forth in the Universal Declaration, do not appear to be foreign to the values of Confucianism as presented in this volume. Confucian teachings, we have learned, encouraged civility, and inspired humane concern and mutual respect. The enlightened emperor, and loyal, incorruptible officials committed to Confucian values, practiced virtue and behaved justly, and set examples of justice and virtue for the people. The laws which Confucian leaders promulgated and administered reflected fairness, reasonableness, and human concern.

Confucian values differ markedly from those of human rights in their origin, in their articulation, in how they are to be realized. Confucian values were born in an earlier age, an age of princes and kings. Values derived from the ordinations of Heaven. They were conceived in, and for, rural, pre-urban, agrarian, preindustrial society; for an economy that was essentially domestic and a society for which international intercourse was still primitive and secondary. Human rights were born in, and for, the modern age, when it was moving to the Industrial Revolution, to parliamentarianism, toward "one world." Human rights values may be inherent, natural,[2] but they come effectively from the will of the people and are endorsed by the people who ordain and establish the national constitution.[3] At the end of the twentieth century, human rights assume societies of millions or hundreds of millions, societies that are urban, industrial (or in the process of development), linked to a global economy and a global network of communication.

Confucianism and human rights differ in how their values are to be realized. Confucianism addressed the actor—the ruler, the scholar, the sage, the official; human rights focus on the "rights holder," on the object of action, on the "victim." Confucianism sought to achieve the good society by molding the character of the elite, by enhancing their moral stature through education and by the practice of rites. Human rights are not concerned with the character of those in authority but with how they behave, with their actions or inactions; human rights lay down not principles of morality but norms of behavior, of law, establishing institutions to monitor them and to remedy their failures.

Confucianism and human rights differ in their relation to political institutions. For Confucianism, the ruler and his officials determined the implications of these values, and how they were "played out" in actuality depended on the wisdom, good will, integrity, competence of ruler and officials, on the benefits, privileges, and remedies they saw fit to provide. Confucianism encouraged self-governance but did not include any commitment to representative democracy. Human rights begin with the individual, and the individual begins with his/her rights. They have grown in the age of the "Liberal state," of social contract, of democracy, of universal suffrage. In the human rights ideology, the individual depends, largely, on self-governance through his/her elected representatives, on law, on articulated norms administered by an honest, competent officialdom, enforceable by an independent judiciary.

Confucian values were articulated in general terms; human rights have been defined specifically. Confucian values were articulated by scholar-officials under the aegis of rulers and they saw less need to define and particularize: it was left to the magistrate to exercise discretion in light of circumstances. Perhaps it went without saying, or with little saying, that any investigation or trial should be fair, that those in authority should not torture or degrade.[4] Thought and expression did not have to be regulated by law; they were self-regulated by commitment to moral values and mutual respect. Human rights have been identified by contemporary thinkers but have been recognized and promulgated by political bodies, mostly by governments. At the end of the eighteenth century, in America and France, recent history led to bills of specific rights; in the twentieth century, recent history in Europe after Hitler, after the Holocaust, led to the recognition of the idea of rights as universal, as in the United Nations Charter, then to the decision to define and particularize them, as in the Universal Declaration of Human Rights.

Some of the values reflected in particular rights might not have been congenial to Confucianism in the past; some may not be acceptable to Confucian thought today. For example, in the human rights ideology, family is an individual right and the individual has a right to the protection of his/her family against "arbitrary interference" (Universal Declaration, Article 12); for Confucianism, the family was primary and paramount (not merely an individual's right), and Confucianism might not recognize any priority as between the individual and the family. For another example, the Universal Declaration recognizes the right to freedom of conscience and religion (Article 18), and forbids discrimination in rights on the basis of race, gender, or religion (Article 2); Confucianism apparently did not recognize or face those issues directly. While affirming human moral equality, it accepted certain social inequalities.

There may be deeper differences. Human rights are individual rights, dedicated to individual dignity. Confucianism might have found the focus on the individual, even on individual dignity, uncongenial. For Confucianism, the individual found dignity not in self-expression but in fulfilling the will of Heaven; not in individualism but in membership in family, clan, community; 311

not in equality but in mutual respect within an hierarchial order; less in law and legal remedies administered by judges, than in the morality and compassion of rulers and officials.

Confucianism did not seem to accept—as a principle—stated limitations on public policy or public interest out of concern for individual dignity; it relied on the wisdom and morality of rulers. Under the human rights idea, the individual has duties as well as rights; and the individual, often reluctantly, sacrifices his/her inherent autonomy, liberty, rights, to the public interest. But the human rights idea limits limitations on rights to defined categories of public good (national security, public order, public health or morals, or the protection of the rights of others, "in a democratic society"). Even in time of public emergency that threatens the life of the nation, society may take measures derogating from rights only to the extent strictly required by the exigencies of the situation, and even these are limited by certain rights.[5]

Confucianism and Human Rights Today—and Tomorrow

One might compare Confucianism and human rights in the abstract, as an intellectual exercise. It might be interesting also, more interesting, to consider Confucianism as a living ideology, for living human beings in contemporary society at the end of the twentieth century. As such, one might apply the values of Confucianism to a society that is inescapably part of a global network—politically, economically, and for communication and transportation; in an age where emperors who ruled by a Mandate of Heaven have given way to popular sovereignty and representative government; when the moral intuition of our times has replaced religious imperialism with religious tolerance (if not accommodation); chauvinism and xenophobia with "live-and-let-live"; "master-race" and ethnic superiority with racial equality and nondiscrimination; and—in large measure—unquestioned patriarchy with the equality of women.

How do Confucianism and human rights cohabit today? Confucianism sought to achieve the good society by the development of moral character, notably in the leaders of society, and through them all members of society. The human rights movement also recognizes that respect for human rights is enhanced if the moral character of human beings, and particularly of those in authority, is developed; indeed, respect for human beings cannot be achieved—realized—without commitment by officials and by citizens to values kin to those of Confucianism. But, for the human rights movement, one cannot rely on character alone; it is necessary to articulate norms and establish institutions, both to bolster moral character and to protect against

failures of moral character. Some Confucians recognized that not all human beings, not all leaders, have the necessary moral character, and they were willing to support norms and institutions, even while they pursued self-reflection, teaching, rites, to maintain and improve moral character. Especially in urban and urbanizing societies, depersonalized, with family ties gradually giving way to individual independence, the welfare of individual human beings, as well as societal order, harmony, may depend on legal norms, articulated in detail, on independent institutions and remedies.

At the end of the twentieth century, the human rights ideology insists, human dignity cannot tolerate racial or religious discrimination. Human dignity, if not the inexorable demands of political, social, and economic development, can no longer tolerate the subordination of half, the female half, of the human race. Are these not also the imperatives of Confucian values today?

The human rights idea is not monolithic, imperialist. It does not demand uniformity, conformity. It allows—indeed it insists on—large autonomy for individuals as well as for societies. The ideology it insists on is a minimum, the minimum required for individual human dignity. Are these not also the imperatives of Confucian values today?

The human rights idea is not alien to Confucian values today. With the imperial tradition vanished, and with it the quest for benign, wise, humane monarchy, societies committed to Confucian values need not find democratic theory and representative government uncongenial. In complex societies, in which complex government is essential, Confucians need not resist devolution of values, of ideas and ideals, into norms. In large, impersonal, societies, Confucianism might well recognize the erosion of clan and family bonds. Confucianism might insist, and the human rights movement might recognize and grant, that the realization of values requires wise, benign, honest government; Confucianism today might grant that, in the twenty-first century, societies cannot depend on the wisdom and good will of leaders alone, but require normative prescriptions and independent institutions; that laws deriving from representative bodies are not necessarily less worthy than those promulgated by wise officials; that Confucian "rites" should and do support the values that human rights claim. Ancient China depended on both laws and rites, but on moral authority more than on law enforcement; on nongovernmental bodies more than on official bodies. Confucians today might well agree that rites and rights, moral authority and legal authority, should be mutually supportive.

There is no intrinsic inherent tension between Confucianism and human rights. The "Asian values" of Confucianism need not reject any of the prescriptions of the Universal Declaration; not the conversion of official moral duties into rights for the beneficiaries; not equality in rights, not equal protection of the laws, not individual autonomy and liberty, not economic and social rights, not acceptance of the individual and his/her rights as fundamental val- 313 ues often trumping interests of others, even of majorities, even of the community. "Asian values"—"Confucian values"—are universal values too.

Notes

1. These delegations also declared that states, individually or through U.N. organs, may not monitor or criticize the condition of human rights within another sovereign state. That, however, is a question of international law and politics, and not of concern here. Presumably, Confucianism addresses the "good society" internally, not the limits of a state's sovereignty in relation to other states. Asian states have not refrained from criticizing what they deemed to be violations of human rights in other countries, e.g., apartheid in South Africa.

2. Men and women "are endowed by their Creator with certain unalienable rights." American Declaration of Independence.

3. Compare the Preamble to the U.S. Constitution.

4. Compare the specific injunctions in the Universal Declaration of Human Rights, articles 5, 9–11, and in the International Covenant on Civil and Political Rights, articles 6–17.

5. International Covenant on Civil and Political Rights, Article 4.

Index

Revolutionary morality, xiv